FASHION AND INTELLECTUAL PROPERTY

Fashion is a multi-billion-dollar global business, which is not surprising because of our basic need to wear clothes and shoes. The fashion system thrives on ephemerality, novelty, seduction and hedonism. There are countless books on intellectual property law, numerous books on fashion theory and a few books on fashion law but hardly any on fashion *and* intellectual property. This book assembles a constellation of some of the best-known intellectual property scholars around the world to present their analysis of how different aspects of intellectual property laws interact with and regulate the fashion industry.

It presents a meticulously curated collection of how intellectual property laws interact with contemporary fashion and culture studies in protecting fashion creations that range from clothing and footwear to textiles. It covers key features of intellectual property rights regimes in the United States, United Kingdom, Europe, Australia and Asia that include copyright, trademarks, patents and geographical indications. This title is also available as open access on Cambridge Core.

DAVID TAN is the Co-Director of the Centre for Technology, Robotics, Artificial Intelligence & the Law and head (Intellectual Property) at the EW Barker Centre for Law & Business at the Faculty of Law, National University of Singapore. He has published over 100 articles, comments, book chapters and op-eds.

JEANNE C FROMER is the Walter J Derenberg Professor of Intellectual Property Law and Co-Director of the Engelberg Center on Innovation Law & Policy at New York University School of Law. She publishes broadly about all areas of intellectual property and has co-written a widely adopted open-source textbook on copyright law.

DEV S GANGJEE is presently Director of the Oxford IP Research Centre, with research interests in trademarks and brands, geographical indications (GIs), copyright and the protection of data. He wishes he had spent a little less time researching GIs and a little more time enjoying them.

FASHION AND INTELLECTUAL PROPERTY

Edited by

DAVID TAN

National University of Singapore

JEANNE C FROMER

New York University

DEV S GANGJEE

University of Oxford

CAMBRIDGE
UNIVERSITY PRESS

CAMBRIDGE
UNIVERSITY PRESS

Shaftesbury Road, Cambridge CB2 8EA, United Kingdom

One Liberty Plaza, 20th Floor, New York, NY 10006, USA

477 Williamstown Road, Port Melbourne, VIC 3207, Australia

314–321, 3rd Floor, Plot 3, Splendor Forum, Jasola District Centre, New Delhi – 110025, India

103 Penang Road, #05–06/07, Visioncrest Commercial, Singapore 238467

Cambridge University Press is part of Cambridge University Press & Assessment, a department of the University of Cambridge.

We share the University's mission to contribute to society through the pursuit of education, learning and research at the highest international levels of excellence.

www.cambridge.org
Information on this title: www.cambridge.org/9781009519601

DOI: 10.1017/9781009519618

First published 2025

Cover image: *Hermes #01, acrylic on canvas.* Andre Tan.

A catalogue record for this publication is available from the British Library

A Cataloging-in-Publication data record for this book is available from the Library of Congress

ISBN 978-1-009-51960-1 Hardback

FASHION AND INTELLECTUAL PROPERTY

In this concise and immensely readable volume, the editors have (in addition to contributing three wonderful, and very different, chapters of their own) assembled a first-rate collection of authors. Fashion provides a superb vehicle for analysis of the full range of intellectual property regimes, and contributors here touch on them all. The result is a 360-degree examination of how intellectual property law protects fashion and how IP's treatment of fashion shines a light on many challenges confronting intellectual property law.

Graeme B. Dinwoodie, University Distinguished Professor, Global Professor of Intellectual Property Law, IIT Chicago-Kent College of Law

This book brings together the latest research findings from many world-renowned intellectual property scholars. It covers cutting-edge topics at the intersection of fashion and intellectual property, such as postmodern interpretations of intellectual property, the use of IP to regulate signs of social distinction, the nuanced meanings of functionality in fashion design, the distinctiveness of non-traditional trademarks, challenges in intellectual property faced by fashion upcycling, and the interplay between identity politics and fashion intellectual property. This collection offers a valuable opportunity to reassess the foundational theories and policy objectives of existing intellectual property systems and gain numerous profound insights. Its relevance extends far beyond the fashion industry, making it essential reading for all intellectual property professionals.

Guobin Cui, Professor of Law, Director of the Center for Intellectual Property, Tsinghua University School of Law

This book makes an exceptional contribution to the study of fashion and intellectual property. It offers a comprehensive examination of cutting-edge legal issues while also delving into various perspectives in culture, politics, and economics. It is an essential read for anyone seeking a deeper understanding of the intricate relationship between fashion and intellectual property.

Haochen Sun, Professor of Law, University of Hong Kong Faculty of Law

This is a terrific collection of papers exploring a wide range of legal issues relating to fashion. It's an A-list group of contributors, and the topics are timely and important, especially in the global context. A must read for anyone interested in the area.

Mark P. McKenna, Professor and Faculty Co-Director of the UCLA Institute for Technology, Law & Policy, UCLA School of Law

This is an essential volume for anyone interested in fashion law and a must-read for those pushing the boundaries of law and fashion.

Jeannie Suk Gersen, John H. Watson, Jr. Professor of Law, Harvard Law School

Anyone interested in fashion or intellectual property law will benefit from considering the use of trademark law to reinstate scarcity and hierarchy in a high-tech post-scarcity world; the legal implications of fashion's function of making bodies look better; the potential environmental sustainability benefits of stronger protection for geographic indications of origin; the similar potential for upcycling to contribute to sustainability if not choked off by trademark law; and other topics in this wide-ranging collection of essays at the intersection of fashion and law.

Rebecca Tushnet, Frank Stanton Professor of the First Amendment, Harvard Law School

From brands and designs to copyright, patents and geographical indications, passing through upcycling and cultural appropriation. Fashion IP law could not be better presented and explained to us. David Tan, Jeanne C. Fromer and Dev S. Gangjee have put together a stellar line up of academics with a clear, critical and environmentally-focused perspective of Fashion IP.

Enrico Bonadio, Reader in Intellectual Property Law, The City Law School, City, University of London; editor of *The Cambridge Handbook of Copyright in Street Art and Graffiti* (2019)

The editors have done a wonderful job assembling a group of leading intellectual property scholars from the USA, Europe, Australia, Hong Kong and Singapore for this impressive and timely collection. Collectively, the eleven essays explore the complex, evolving, and largely under-theorised relationship between domestic intellectual property laws and the creation, protection and reuse of fashion, and the cultural impact of this relationship. Each chapter is meticulously researched, engagingly written, and illuminating.

Michael Handler, Professor, School of Private and Commercial Law, Faculty of Law & Justice, University of New South Wales

This book includes a fascinating, diverse range of theoretical, doctrinal and political insights into how fashion and IP laws interact. Leading scholars provoke us to consider what role fashion plays in society, how fashion exposes tensions in designs, trade mark and copyright doctrines, and to what extent IP laws facilitate upcycling or enable cultural appropriation.

Tanya Aplin, Professor of Intellectual Property Law, Dickson Poon School of Law, King's College London

Not just for fashionistas! Like a delicately woven fabric, this book offers a complex pattern of legal, economic and sociological aspects of fashion law, vividly detailed and rich in background information, presented by a panel of eminent scholars. A real page-turner!

Annette Kur, Professor and Affiliated Research Fellow, Department of Intellectual Property and Competition Law, Max Planck Institute for Innovation and Competition

CONTENTS

FIGURES

TABLES

CONTRIBUTORS

BARTON BEEBE is the John M Desmarais Professor of Intellectual Property Law at New York University School of Law. He has been the Anne Urowsky Visiting Professor of Law at Yale Law School, a visiting Professor of Law at Stanford Law School and a visiting research fellow at Merton College, Oxford. He is the author of *Trademark Law: An Open-Source Casebook*, which is a free online trademark casebook now in use in over eighty law schools around the world. Beebe received his JD from Yale Law School, his PhD in English Literature from Princeton University and his BA from the University of Chicago.

CHRISTOPHER BUCCAFUSCO is the Edward & Ellen Schwarzman Distinguished Professor at Duke University Law School in Durham, North Carolina. His research covers a wide range of topics and methods related to creativity, innovation and intellectual property law. He uses novel social science experiments to explore the nature of innovation markets, and he writes about evolving issues in copyright, patent and trademark law, including music copyright litigation, pharmaceutical patents and IP rights for industrial design. Prior to joining Duke Law, Christopher taught at Cardozo Law School and Chicago-Kent College of Law. At Chicago-Kent, he won the Student Bar Association's professor of the year award in his first year of teaching, and he later won a university-wide award for excellence in teaching.

ROBERT BURRELL is Professor of Intellectual Property & Information Technology Law at the University of Oxford and Professor of Law at Melbourne Law School. Robert's previous academic positions include posts at the Australian National University and King's College London. He has held visiting positions at the University of Cambridge, the Benjamin N. Cardozo School of Law in New York and the National University of Singapore. Robert teaches and researches across all areas of intellectual property law. He is the author (with Allison Coleman) of *Copyright*

Exceptions: The Digital Impact and (with Michael Handler) of *Australian Trade Mark Law*. Outside of academia, Robert has spent many years working as a consultant to boutique Australian firms and, in particular, has substantial experience in litigation before the Australian Trade Marks Office.

IRENE CALBOLI is Regents Professor of Law at Texas A&M University School of Law. She also holds several honourary and visiting appointments, including at the University of Geneva, the University of Bologna, Sciences Po Paris, Bocconi University, Melbourne University and Stanford University. In 2022, she was a Fulbright-Hanken Distinguished Chair in Business and Economics in Finland and, in 2018, a Fulbright specialist at the Royal University of Law and Economics in Cambodia. Irene is a member of the editorial board of the *Oxford Journal of Intellectual Property Law and Practice*, the *Queen Mary Journal of Intellectual Property* and the *WIPO-WTO Colloquium Papers*. She is also an elected member of the American Law Institute and the European Law Institute and serves on the board of the Comparative Law and European Law Sections of the Association of American Law Schools, the International Law Association, the European Policy for Intellectual Property Law Association and the International Trademark Association.

ROGER ALLAN FORD is a Professor of Law at the University of New Hampshire, faculty fellow at the Franklin Pierce Center for Intellectual Property and affiliated fellow at the Yale Information Society Project. He teaches and writes about intellectual property, privacy and other ways the law regulates information. He previously taught at the University of Chicago, George Mason University and the Massachusetts Institute of Technology; was a fellow at the NYU Information Law Institute; practised IP litigation at Covington & Burling LLP; and served as a law clerk to Chief Judge Frank H Easterbrook of the United States Court of Appeals for the Seventh Circuit. Roger received a bachelor of science in chemistry from MIT and a law degree, with honours, from the University of Chicago, where he was an editor of the *Law Review*. He is admitted to practise law in Massachusetts and the District of Columbia.

JEANNE C FROMER is Walter J Derenberg Professor of Intellectual Property Law at New York University School of Law and Co-Director of the Engelberg Center on Innovation Law & Policy. She has testified before Congress and been cited by the US Supreme Court on trademark law. Fromer was awarded the American Law Institute's inaugural Young

Scholars Medal for her scholarship in intellectual property and served as a law clerk to Justice David Souter of the US Supreme Court. Jeanne received her JD magna cum laude from Harvard Law School, serving as articles editor of the *Harvard Law Review* and editor of the *Harvard Journal of Law and Technology*. She earned her BA summa cum laude in computer science from Barnard College, Columbia University. Jeanne received her SM in electrical engineering and computer science from the Massachusetts Institute of Technology and worked at AT&T Bell Laboratories in the area of artificial intelligence.

DEV S GANGJEE is Professor of Intellectual Property Law at the Oxford Law Faculty. Dev's research focuses on intellectual property (IP), with a special emphasis on branding and trademarks, geographical indications (GIs) and copyright law. Thematic research interests include the history and political economy of IP, collective innovation, the significance of registration for intangibles and, more recently, rights in data. He has acted in an advisory or expert capacity on GIs for national governments, law firms, international organisations and the European Commission.

VICKI HUANG is Associate Professor of IP Law at Deakin Law School and is a co-author of one of Australia's leading intellectual property textbooks: S Ricketson, M Richardson, M Davison and V Huang, *Intellectual Property: Cases, Material and Commentary*, 6th ed (LexisNexis, 2019). Her research work focusses on empirical methods and IP law, particularly the intersection of IP with gender and race. Vicki has taught numerous law units including IP, property, marketing, fashion and cyber law. She is the University's Teacher of the Year (2022) and recipient of the Law School's Teaching Excellence Award (2022). Vicki is dual-qualified as an Australian lawyer and a US attorney. She graduated from the Melbourne Law School with a PhD and first-class honours in the LLB. She also completed an LLM at Columbia University Law School as Burton Memorial Fellow with honours.

EMILY HUDSON is Professor of Law at the Oxford Faculty of Law and Tutorial Fellow at The Queen's College. She has previously held posts at King's College London, the University of Queensland and the University of Melbourne. Emily's research spans many areas, including intellectual property, personal property, trusts and law as it relates to cultural institutions and the creative industries. She is author of the monograph, *Drafting Copyright Exceptions: From the Law in Books to the Law in Action* (Cambridge University Press, 2020).

JYH-AN LEE is Professor and the Executive Director of the Centre for Legal Innovation and Digital Society (CLINDS) at the Chinese University of Hong Kong Faculty of Law. He has been the legal lead of the Creative Commons Hong Kong Chapter since October 2018. Since 2016, he has held a panelist position for the Asian Domain Name Dispute Resolution Centre (ADNDRC). Professor Lee has been featured on *ABC News, BBC News, Bloomberg News, Financial Times, Fortune* and *South China Morning Post* as an expert on intellectual property and internet law. His works have been cited by the US Court of Appeals for the Fifth Circuit, the UK High Court of Justice, the US International Trade Commission and the European Union (in a WTO dispute-settlement case).

SUSANNA H S LEONG is a professor at the National University of Singapore (NUS) and holds several leadership roles there. She is Vice-Provost for Masters' Programmes and Lifelong Education, dean of the School of Continuing and Lifelong Education and president advisor overseeing development of the NUS Chongqing Research Institute. Susanna was previously a vice-dean at the NUS Business School and helped oversee its MBA programmmes. She joined NUS in 1991 and rose to a full professorship in 2016. She received several teaching awards, including the Outstanding Educator Award. Susanna is a legal scholar specialising in intellectual property and technology-related laws. She has published in international and local journals and authored works such as *Intellectual Property Law of Singapore*. Her contributions have been cited by Singapore's Court of Appeal and the High Court. She also serves in organisations like WIPO and IPOS. Susana received the Singapore Public Administration Medal (Silver) in 2022 for her contributions.

JINGWEN LIU is a PhD candidate at the Chinese University of Hong Kong Faculty of Law and a legal journalist at JURIST. She has been listed as a WIPO ADR Young Member since 2023. Her research interests include intellectual property law, competition policy, data governance and comparative legal study. Her publications appear in various academic journals such as the *Columbia Journal of Law & the Arts, American Business Law Journal, European Intellectual Property Review* and *Journal of Intellectual Property Law & Practice*. Prior to commencing her PhD study, she was a practising lawyer in the People's Republic of China specialising in trademark and brand protection. She also held a visiting position at Singapore Management University Yong Pung How School of Law in 2021.

KAL RAUSTIALA is the Promise Distinguished Professor of Comparative and International Law at UCLA. His scholarship encompasses international law and intellectual property. He is the author, with Christopher Sprigman, of 'The Piracy Paradox: Innovation and Intellectual Property in Fashion Design' in the *Virginia Law Review* (2006) as well as many other articles on copyright, trademark and luxury goods. Their book *The Knockoff Economy: How Imitation Sparks Innovation* (Oxford University Press, 2012) has been translated into Japanese, Korean and both simplified and traditional Chinese.

MARTIN SENFTLEBEN is Professor of Intellectual Property Law and Director of the Institute for Information Law (IViR) at the Amsterdam Law School. His activities focus on the reconciliation of private intellectual property rights with competing public interests of a social, cultural or economic nature. His current research topics include institutionalised algorithmic copyright enforcement in the EU, the interplay between robot creativity and human literary and artistic productions, the preservation of the public domain of cultural expressions, and the impact of targeted advertising on supply and demand in market economies. Senftleben is a member of the Copyright Advisory Committee of the Dutch State. He has provided advice to WIPO in several trademark and copyright projects. He is the President of the European Copyright Society (ECS), President of the Trademark Law Institute (TLI), and a member of the Executive Committee of the Association Littéraire et Artistique Internationale (ALAI) and the International Association for the Advancement of Teaching and Research in Intellectual Property Law (ATRIP). His numerous publications include *Copyright, Limitations and the Three-Step Test* (Kluwer Law International 2004), *European Trade Mark Law – A Commentary* (with Annette Kur, Oxford University Press 2017) and *The Copyright/Trademark Interface* (Kluwer Law International 2020).

CHRISTOPHER JON SPRIGMAN is the Murray and Kathleen Bring Professor of Law at NYU School of Law and Co-Director of NYU's Engelberg Center on Innovation Law and Policy. He teaches intellectual property law, antitrust law, torts and comparative constitutional law. His research focuses on how legal rules affect innovation and the deployment of new technologies. He is the author, with Kal Raustiala, of 'The Piracy Paradox: Innovation and Intellectual Property in Fashion Design' in the *Virginia Law Review* (2006) as well as many other articles on copyright, trademark and luxury goods. Their book *The Knockoff Economy: How*

Imitation Sparks Innovation (Oxford University Press, 2012) has been translated into Japanese, Korean and both simplified and traditional Chinese.

DAVID TAN is Co-Director of the Centre for Technology, Robotics, Artificial Intelligence & the Law and Head (Intellectual Property) of the EW Barker Centre for Law & Business at NUS Law, He holds PhD, LLB (First Class Honours) and BCom degrees from the University of Melbourne and an LLM from Harvard. He was also the valedictorian at Trinity College Melbourne. At NUS Law, David pioneered courses in Entertainment Law, Fashion Law, Freedom of Speech and Privacy & Data Protection Law; he has also taught as a visitor at Melbourne Law School, Tsinghua, Tokyo (Todai) and University of Hong Kong. His areas of research cover personality rights, copyright, trademarks, freedom of expression and tort law. He has published over 100 articles, comments and book chapters since joining NUS Law in 2008. David is also a fine art and fashion photographer and has had a number of solo exhibitions since 2000, including collaborations with Versace and Cartier (davidtanphoto.com).

EDITORS' PREFACE

Miuccia Prada said in an interview: 'The job is to do something interesting with ideas . . . and if it is copied I couldn't care less.'[1] Gabrielle 'Coco' Chanel was reported to have declared that imitation was the highest form of flattery.[2] It would seem that there is little that is completely new or original in the world of fashion. Over a decade ago, at the awards ceremony of the Council of Fashion Designers of America, author Fran Lebowitz quipped that 'homage is French for stealing'.[3] In music, we call it sampling. In other cultural circles, it is known as appropriation. Many fashion brands today, however, do not simply sit back and enjoy the copying or referencing of their creations by another designer. They are more likely to assert their intellectual property rights that span the spectrum of trademarks, copyright, patents, registered designs and geographical indications in order to protect their brand investments and businesses.

This book is long overdue. There are countless books on intellectual property law, numerous books on fashion theory and a few books on fashion law but hardly any on fashion *and* intellectual property. This book assembles a constellation of some of the best-known intellectual property scholars around the world to present their analysis of how different aspects of intellectual property laws interact with and regulate the fashion industry. Some of the chapters also feature an interdisciplinary analysis of

[1] Andrew O'Hagan, 'Power of One | Miuccia Prada's Circle of Influence', *The New York Times Style Magazine* (May 27, 2013) <https://www.nytimes.com/2013/05/27/t-magazine/power-of-one-miuccia-pradas-circle-of-influence.html>.

[2] Fridolin Fischer, 'Design Law in the European Fashion Sector', *WIPO Magazine* (February 2008) (citing Paul Morand, *L'allure de Chanel* [Hermann, 1996]) <https://www.wipo.int/wipo_magazine/en/2008/01/article_0006.html>.

[3] Guy Trebay, 'Ideas & Trends: Fashion Replay; Imitation Is the Mother of Invention', *The New York Times* (July 7, 2002) <https://www.nytimes.com/2002/07/07/weekinreview/ideas-trends-fashion-replay-imitation-is-the-mother-of-invention.html>.

fashion and intellectual property, drawing from key classical and contemporary writings in cultural studies.

Trends in the Fashion Industry

Fashion is a multi-billion-dollar global business, which is not surprising because of our basic need to wear clothes and shoes. The fashion system thrives on ephemerality, novelty, seduction and hedonism. In 2019, McKinsey reported that research showed that the average person today buys 60% more items of clothing than they did 15 years ago. In a survey done in Britain, one in seven consider it a fashion faux pas to be photographed in an outfit twice.[4]

For the fashion industry around the world, 2020 was the year in which everything changed. At the start of 2020, the luxury fashion industry was enjoying a boom and then the pandemic hit. When COVID-19 ravaged the world in 2020, the fashion industry suffered its worst year on record with almost 75% of listed companies losing money. According to the McKinsey Global Fashion Index analysis, fashion companies posted approximately a 90% decline in economic profit in 2020, after a 4% rise in 2019.[5] In *The State of Fashion 2021* report, it was observed that 'the pandemic will accelerate trends that were in motion prior to the crisis, as shopping shifts to digital and consumers continue to champion fairness and social justice'.[6] With diminished demand for fashion, the trendsetters at the apex of the fashion industry have been rethinking their business models. A full recovery of global fashion sales to pre-pandemic levels was expected to come around the third quarter of 2022 at the earliest.[7] However, things are not that rosy. Eighty-four per cent of industry leaders said they expect market conditions to decline or stay the same in 2023, with the global slowdown, rising inflation, geopolitical instability and supply chain disruptions brought about by the war in Ukraine and further outbreaks of the new COVID-19 variants[8] and, more recently, the Israel-Hamas war. In *The State of Fashion 2024* report released at the end of November 2023, 'uncertainty' was the word most

[4] The Business of Fashion and McKinsey & Company, *The State of Fashion 2019* (2018) 39.
[5] The Business of Fashion and McKinsey & Company, *The State of Fashion 2021* (2020) 10.
[6] Ibid, 11.
[7] The Business of Fashion and McKinsey & Company, *The State of Fashion 2021* (2020) 25.
[8] The Business of Fashion and McKinsey & Company, *The State of Fashion 2023* (2022) 12.

often mentioned by executives surveyed;[9] the top-line year-on-year growth is expected to be lacklustre as consumers restrain spending after a post-pandemic shopping surge.[10] That being said, the LVMH group nonetheless outperformed Nike in terms of economic profit.[11] Last but not least, sustainability is a buzzword in the fashion industry as new regulations in the European Union and the United States will require brands and manufacturers to reduce greenhouse gas emissions and waste; fast fashion houses such as Shein and Temu have already come under scrutiny.[12] According to McKinsey, of the fashion executives survey, '12 percent cite sustainability as a principal opportunity for 2024, placing it at the top of the C-suite agenda'.[13] By 2025, it appears that the non-luxury sector will be driving the increase in economic profit. In *The State of Fashion 2025* report, fashion executives shared that they will be shifting their focus to 'finding ways to differentiate, whether through new designs, customer experiences or finding new customer niches.'[14]

Just a few years ago, fashion leaders were anticipating a continuation of the post-COVID chic casualisation trend that took hold during the pandemic with casualwear, followed by sportswear and sneakers, being the highest-ranking categories in terms of where executives see the greatest growth potential.[15] According to *The State of Fashion 2021* report, this form of casualisation is a trend that 'is likely to emerge as a dominant force across many fashion categories in 2021' as more flexible work-from-home arrangements are entrenched around the world.[16] This has evolved into the 'gorpcore' trend at the time of writing – functional, outdoors-inspired fashion – which luxury fashion players such as Dior, Prada and Burberry have established as part of their permanent collections.[17]

9 The Business of Fashion and McKinsey & Company, *The State of Fashion 2024* (2023) 10.
10 Ibid, 14.
11 Ibid, 112.
12 Ibid, 11.
13 Ibid, 17.
14 The Business of Fashion and McKinsey & Company, *The State of Fashion 2025* (2024) 13.
15 The Business of Fashion and McKinsey & Company, *The State of Fashion 2023* (2022) 16.
16 The Business of Fashion and McKinsey & Company, *The State of Fashion 2021* (n 5) 27. See also Patricia Marx, 'The Slob-Chic Style of the Coronavirus Pandemic', *The New Yorker* (July 13, 2020) <https://www.newyorker.com/magazine/2020/07/20/the-slob-chic-style-of-the-coronavirus-pandemic>.
17 The Business of Fashion and McKinsey & Company, *The State of Fashion 2024* (2023) 52–55.

At the same time, gender-fluid fashion is 'gaining traction amid changing consumer attitudes towards gender identity and expression ... [with] the blurring of lines between menswear and womenswear'.[18] Resale revenue is also expected to grow to US$47 billion by 2025, from US$15 billion in 2022[19] – 11 times faster than apparel retail overall – and these upcycling and resale businesses are likely to attract the attention of luxury brands such as Chanel and Rolex, which will want to enforce their intellectual rights.[20]

Last but not least, fashion brands are making forays to explore the nascent opportunities associated with technologies like the metaverse and non-fungible tokens (NFTs). Brands are expected to embrace creative campaigns, new media channels and the metaverse,[21] as NFTs are strategically deployed to build communities and stronger affinity for the brand.[22] The metaverse conjures up possibilities of a space without limits where our physical selves move seamlessly into virtual worlds as digital avatars in altered realities to play, work, learn, create, shop, socialise and trade. Even though things are looking less rosy at the time of writing as the metaverse is looking more and more like a collage of virtual games and social networking sites that lack interconnectedness and interoperability, fashion brands are nonetheless making inroads into this new digital environment. In particular, luxury fashion brands such as Louis Vuitton, Gucci, Balenciaga, Dolce & Gabbana and Burberry, as well as sporting apparel titan Nike, are actively exploiting the metaverse with a proliferation of online collaborations, digital experiences and NFT sales.

Scope of This Book

This book is divided into four parts. The Part I comprises two chapters that adopt different theoretical perspectives in an attempt to understand

[18] The Business of Fashion and McKinsey & Company, *The State of Fashion 2023* (2022) 18. See also ibid, 55–58.

[19] Ibid, 44.

[20] E.g., *Chanel, Inc. v. Shiver and Duke, LLC, et al., 1:21-cv-01277 (SDNY)*; *Copad SA v Christian Dior Couture SA*, Case C-59/08, ECLI:EU:C:2009:260 (ECJ, April 23, 2009). See also 'Chanel Settles Trademark Suit against Resaler; Site Crepslocker Over its Use of Chanel Name, Logo' (The Fashion Law, July 7, 2021) <https://www.thefashionlaw.com/chanel-settles-trademark-suit-against-crepslocker-over-resale-offerings/>.

[21] The Business of Fashion and McKinsey & Company, *The State of Fashion 2023* (2022) 19.

[22] Ibid, 101, 103–106.

the meaning of fashion, its role in contemporary society and how intellectual property laws may respond to this phenomenon. The Part II has five chapters that address how the kaleidoscope of established intellectual property doctrines – more specifically the laws relating to trademarks, copyright, patents and design rights – are and can be applied to fashion. Part III presents two chapters that interrogate two successful business models that skirt on the fringes of intellectual property infringement: fashion upcycling and *shanzhai* fashion. Part IV concludes with two chapters that evaluate emerging issues regarding the protection of traditional knowledge, culture, heritage and craftsmanship.

Part I

In 'Fashion, Post-postmodernism and Intellectual Property', David Tan discusses how fashion – the way we dress – is often an important reflection of the zeitgeist or the spirit of a given point and place in time. He contends that the fashion phenomena of recent years, such as self-disruption, upcycling and phygital experiences, can be studied as characteristics of a post-postmodern condition where a new cultural paradigm has emerged. The term *post-postmodern* has appeared in an increasing number of scholarly works that address a new cultural milieu – one that faces shifting global political centres and geopolitical boundaries, threats of climate change and an endangered ecosystem, destabilisation from armed conflicts and pandemics, obsessions with autonomous individuality, accelerating advances in artificial intelligence and the pervasiveness of information and communications technology in our daily lives. This chapter explores how such theories may be relevant to understanding contemporary fashion trends and their implications for intellectual property laws.

Barton Beebe, in 'Intellectual Property Law and the Dream of Post-scarcity Society', explains that luxury fashion seeks to aestheticize scarcity and transform its possession into a sign of social distinction. Intellectual property law plays a crucial role in this process. In this chapter, he considers the social function that intellectual property law may continue to play in a purportedly 'post-scarcity' society of the future, asserting that though intellectual property law has long played a technologically progressive role in modern societies, its social function in such societies has been and will continue to be largely reactionary. Even in an otherwise post-scarcity society, intellectual property law will be used, as it is already being used, to preserve 'social scarcity' and regulate signs of social distinction.

Part II

In 'Fashion's Function in Intellectual Property Law', Christopher Buccafusco and Jeanne C Fromer make the point that clothing designs can be beautiful, but they are also functional. Indeed, fashion's dual nature sits uneasily in intellectual property law, and its treatment by copyright, trademark and design patent laws has often been perplexing. Much of this difficulty arises from an unclear understanding of the nature of functionality in fashion design. This chapter argues that aspects of garment designs are functional not only when they affect the physical or technological performance of a garment but also when they affect the perception of the wearer's body. Generally, clothes are not designed or chosen simply to look good. They are also characteristically designed or chosen to look good on. This approach clarifies the appropriate treatment of fashion design in intellectual property, and it exposes the conceptual limitations of the US Supreme Court's copyright decision in *Star Athletica, L.L.C. v. Varsity Brands, Inc.*

Vicki Huang, in her chapter 'Shape Trademarks Are in Fashion: A Study of Footwear and Sneakers in Australia', confronts one of the most significant sartorial transformations in recent history – the evolution of the sneaker from sports equipment to high-end fashion. Expanding demand and competition in the sneaker market (primarily driven by renewed interest in fashion by men) has meant designers are seeking more ways to protect the overall appearance of their shoe designs. This chapter demonstrates that empirically, the sneaker revolution has increased demand for Australian 3D shape trademarks as an adjunct to, or replacement for, registered design rights. It presents this trend as a cautionary tale for those who might call for a sui generis design right for fashion. Ultimately, the failed demand for Australian design rights appears to stem from failing to consider aspects of culture, commerce and the matrix of related rights, particularly trademark rights.

In 'Non-traditional Trademarks, Distinctiveness and the Fashion Industry', Susanna Leong and Irene Calboli analyse the use of non-traditional trademarks (NTTMs) in the fashion industry. With reference to selected cases in the United States, the European Union and Singapore, the authors study the arguments for and against the protection of these signs as trademarks, as well as the appropriate test for the evaluation of distinctiveness. Although some fashion designers and enterprises have celebrated victories in court, it has been widely noted that the registration and protection of these NTTMs can be problematic and potentially detrimental to innovation in the fashion industry. The authors also critically examine the different tests of 'association' and 'reliance' as discussed in recent court decisions on acquired distinctiveness of NTTMs and conclude with a recommendation that the 'reliance' test is the preferred test.

Roger Allan Ford in 'Utility Patents and the Fashion Industry' reviews the fashion industry's uses of utility patents. The chapter first provides an overview of the fashion industry's patenting activities, looking at how many patents are granted for fashion-related inventions and how large apparel companies obtain those patents. It then examines companies' use of patents, looking at how patent litigation in the fashion industry compares to other industries. Finally, it turns to the uneasy tension in fashion between function and aesthetics, examining the specific technologies and inventions being claimed in fashion patents to see what can be inferred about the relationship between fashion and intellectual property.

Working from the premises that fashion designers ought to enjoy some form of intellectual property protection over their creations and that they benefit from such protection, Robert Burrell and Emily Hudson in 'Barriers to Enforcing Design Rights over Fashion in the United Kingdom' explore the problems that fashion designers are likely to face when seeking to enforce their rights in the United Kingdom. Like other commentators, they conclude that design laws in the United Kingdom are in need of reform. They also demonstrate that Brexit has made the problems faced by designers worse, without necessarily creating the policy space for meaningful national reform. The consequence is that designers are likely to rely even more heavily on the copyright system, but this merely shifts the tensions of Brexit from the legislative and political realms to the judicial realm.

Part III

Fashion upcycling offers unprecedented opportunities for the sustainable reuse of clothing: using second-hand garments as raw materials for new creations, upcyclers can transform used pieces of clothing into new fashion products that may become even more sought-after than the source material. Martin Senftleben, in his chapter 'Fashion Upcycling and Trademark Infringement: A Circular Economy/Freedom of the Arts Approach', tackles how upcycling may trigger allegations of consumer confusion and unfair freeriding when fashion elements bearing third-party brand insignia become components of the upcycled product.

Considering the overarching policy objective to ensure a circular economy, the use of trademark-protected fashion elements for upcycling purpose can be qualified as a particularly important form of artistic expression. The chapter concludes that the referential use defence in the European Union can be invoked successfully to rebut infringement arguments – regardless of whether these arguments are based on confusion, blurring, tarnishment or unfair freeriding.

Since the 2000s, Chinese factories have been notorious for imitating and copying luxury fashion designs, a phenomenon known as *shanzhai*. In their chapter '*Shanzhai* Fashion and Intellectual Property in China', Jyh-An Lee and Jingwen Liu explain that within the fashion industry, two primary categories of *shanzhai* practices exist: the imitation or copying of a brand's name or trademarks, referred to as 'counterfeits', and the imitation or copying of a brand's designs, referred to as 'knockoffs'. While brand owners can easily enforce their legal rights against the trademark-infringing counterfeits, knockoffs remain a significant concern for international brand owners, since these design features are frequently denied trademark protection. The authors contend that recent judicial practices suggest that fashion designs and design features in China can be protected under the Anti-Unfair Competition Law. Moreover, Chinese courts are increasingly open to the registration of signature design patterns NTTMs, including three-dimensional trademarks and colour trademarks. This chapter provides a comprehensive exploration of China's evolving approach to these issues and provides a detailed comparison of copyright, trademark, design patent and unfair competition protections against fashion copycats.

Part IV

Dev S Gangjee, in 'Threads That Last: Geographical Indications for Textiles', investigates the potential use of geographical indications (GIs) for both increased visibility and as an effective legal regime to protect a hard-earned reputation for traditional crafts and textiles. He argues that supporting traditional textiles through this form of IP has additional synergies with the shift towards more sustainable production and consumption in the global fashion industry. By utilising natural fibres, organic dyes, artisanal modes of production and fabrics intended to be worn multiple times, GIs can be positioned as the polar opposite of fast fashion; as 'threads that last'. However, the methods for legally 'locking in' sustainability commitments are still being developed, while there are countervailing economic pressures to 'backslide' on sustainable modes of production.

In 'Culture and Cosmopolitanism in the Global Fashion Industry', Kal Raustiala and Christopher Jon Sprigman posit that the global fashion industry is increasingly subject to accusations of cultural appropriation. Their chapter analyses why the fashion industry's practices – in particular, its mashup-magpie mode of creativity and its rapid innovation cycle – make it a frequent target of these claims. They explain the challenges to legal protection for cultural designs, explore and critique the normative case for property claims in traditional cultural designs and offer a qualified defence of the industry's practice of re-interpreting those designs. The authors suggest that many designs seen as originating in a particular culture have roots that extend outward to other cultures; this network of cultural interchange often undermines any particular ownership claim. And while appropriation can signal disrespect for source cultures and be objectionable for that reason, appropriation is not disrespectful per se, as there are strong normative arguments supporting many instances of appropriation.

We would like to express our appreciation for the generous funding extended to this book project by the EW Barker Centre for Law & Business at the Faculty of Law, National University of Singapore (NUS Law), which enabled chapter authors to meet in Singapore for a roundtable discussion in 2023, as well as the efforts of lead student editor Muzainy Shahiefisally and student editor Ciara Oleary at NUS Law. We would also like to record our thanks to the artist Andre Tan who allowed us to use his extraordinary artwork for the cover of this book.

We hope you will enjoy this meticulously curated collection of essays and, even as fashions change and new styles emerge, we trust that they will remain a fashionable read in the years to come.

ABBREVIATIONS

ACIP	Australian Council for Intellectual Property
ATMO	Australian Trade Marks Office
AUCL	Anti-Unfair Competition Law
CDPA	Copyright, Designs and Patents Act 1988 (UK)
CFR	European Union Charter of Fundamental Rights
CIP	crafts and industrial products
CJEU	Court of Justice of the European Union
CNIPA	China National Intellectual Property Administration
CPC	Cooperative Patent Classification
DMCA	Digital Millennium Copyright Act
EUGC	European Union General Court
EUIPO	European Union Intellectual Property Office
EUTMDR	European Union Trade Mark Delegated Regulation
EUTMIR	European Union Trade Mark Implementing Regulation
EUTMR	European Union Trade Mark Regulation
GI	geographical indication
IP	intellectual property
ISD	Information Society Directive
LV	Louis Vuitton
MMORPG	multiplayer online role-playing game
MSME	micro, small and medium enterprise
NFT	non-fungible token
NGO	non-governmental organisation
NTTM	non-traditional trade mark
OHIM	Office of Harmonization in the Internal Market
oriGIn	Organization for an International Geographical Indications Network
PSCP	parody, satire, caricature and pastiche
RCD	registered community design
RMB	Renminbi
SPC	Supreme People's Court
SUD	supplementary unregistered design right
TMD	Trade Mark Directive

TRAB	Trademark Review and Adjudication Board
TRIPS	Trade-Related Aspects of Intellectual Property Rights
UCD	unregistered community design right
UKIPO	United Kingdom Intellectual Property Office
UNEP	United Nations Environment Programme
UNESCO	United Nations Educational, Scientific and Cultural Organization
USPTO	United States Patent and Trademark Office
VCA	Van Cleef & Arpels
WCT	WIPO Copyright Treaty
WIPO	World Intellectual Property Organization
WOAC	works of artistic craftsmanship
WTO	World Trade Organization
XR	extended reality
YSL	Yves Saint Laurent

PART I

Theoretical Frameworks

1

Fashion, Post-postmodernism and Intellectual Property

DAVID TAN

ABSTRACT

Fashion – the way we dress – is often an important reflection of the zeitgeist or the spirit of a given point and place in time. The fashion phenomena of recent years, such as self-disruption, upcycling and phygital experiences, can be studied as characteristics of a post-postmodern condition where a new cultural paradigm has emerged. The term *post-postmodern* has appeared in an increasing number of scholarly works that address a new cultural milieu – one that faces shifting global political centres and geopolitical boundaries, threats of climate change and an endangered ecosystem, destabilisation from armed conflicts and pandemics, obsessions with autonomous individuality, accelerating advances in artificial intelligence and the pervasiveness of information and communications technology in our daily lives. This chapter explores how such theories may be relevant to understanding contemporary fashion trends and their implications for intellectual property laws.

1.1 Introduction

Fashion is a reflection of the zeitgeist by virtue of who wears what, when, where, why and how. The way we dress, and the way in which we are expected to dress in a panoply of work environments and specific occasions, is a manifestation of the condition of modernity. In the decades after the Second Industrial Revolution when capitalism was widely embraced, mass production and mass consumption allowed for certain fashion codes to be universalised, such as the power suits in corporate offices from New York to Japan, uniforms for workers in factories as statements of discipline and unity and the evolution of denim jeans as a sexy and hip symbol of youth rebellion. One could argue that conformity was a product of modernity.[1] Fashion also became a visual language to signify one's social standing.[2] Fashion may be perceived as a way of life in an industrial society where 'the body serves as a means of the presenting the power of capitalism and its social hierarchy'.[3]

The postmodern challenge to modernity in fashion is difficult to pin down with an exact definition and has been said to be a cultural ethos that is characterised by 'a new recognition and valuing of diversity, multiculturalism, marginalized people and viewpoints' and a consequential denial of values and thinking that are typical of 'white, male-dominated, Western culture in the modernist period'.[4] It encompasses subversion, inversion, disruption, idiosyncrasy, appropriation and deconstruction. It rejects the canons of beauty and refinement, seeking instead to embrace shock, provocation and transgression. It came in waves and from the ground up: from the hippies and punks to the goth and cosplay subcultures. In the world of high fashion, the artistic oeuvres of designers such as Yohji Yamamoto, Rei Kawakubo, Jean-Paul Gaultier and Alexander 'Lee' McQueen have often been referred to as being postmodern. In the 2020s, scholars are now discussing post-postmodernism. As Gilles Lipovetsky comments, 'the label "postmodern" is starting to look old; it has exhausted its capabilities to express the world now coming into being'.[5] The term *post-postmodern* has appeared in an increasing number of scholarly works that address a new cultural milieu – one that faces shifting global political centres and geopolitical boundaries, threats of climate change and an endangered ecosystem, destabilisation from armed conflicts and pandemics, obsessions with autonomous individuality, accelerating advances in artificial intelligence and the pervasiveness of information and communications technology in our daily lives.

[1] See generally Christopher Breward and Caroline Evans (eds), *Fashion and Modernity* (Berg, 2005). Modernity has also been said to be 'simultaneously a state, a cultural condition and an intellectual framework defined by the ideas of Enlightenment and the realities of industrial capitalism'. See Alla Eizenberg, 'With No Twist: The Metamodern Sartorial Statement of Vetements' in Jose Blanco F. and Andrew Reilly (eds), *Fashion, Dress and Post-Postmodernism* (Bloomsbury, 2021) 51, 53 (hereafter Eizenberg, 'With No Twist').

[2] Eizenberg, 'With No Twist' at 54.

[3] Žarko Paić, 'Fashion Theory: Orientations, Directions, Disciplines' in Žarko Paić (ed), *Fashion Theory and the Visual Semiotics of the Body* (Cambridge Scholars, 2022) 1, 11.

[4] Marcia A Morgado, 'Fashion Phenomena and the Post-postmodern Condition: Inquiry and Speculation' in Jose Blanco F and Andrew Reilly (eds), *Fashion, Dress and Post-Postmodernism* (Bloomsbury, 2021) 9, 10 (hereafter Morgado, 'Fashion Phenomena').

[5] Gilles Lipovetsky, *Hypermodern Times* (Polity, 2005) 30.

In *The State of Fashion 2019* report jointly released by The Business of Fashion and McKinsey & Company, it was observed that: 'The ones who will succeed will have to come to terms with the fact that in the new paradigm that is taking shape around them, some of the old rules simply don't work . . .. They need to . . . have the courage to "self-disrupt" their own identity and the sources of their old success in order to realize these changes and win new generations of customers.'[6] In the following year, *The State of Fashion 2020* report cited sustainability, digitisation and innovation as the three top opportunities for the fashion industry in the face of an economic slowdown.[7] The luxury heritage fashion house Gucci, and followed later by Louis Vuitton and Balenciaga, are doing precisely that since 2015: employing irreverent designers to revamp their brands, inventing a new vernacular in fashion vocabulary that introduces terms like 'counterfeit chic', 'logo hacking', 'geek chic', 'gender fluidity' and 'downmarket irony' and capturing the attention and pockets of the social media–obsessed millennial generation with Instagram-worthy designs. Even Donatella Versace herself has resorted to reproducing the Ford Motor Company's logo as a recurring motif on shirts and sportswear for the iconic Versace brand in the Fall–Winter 2019 runway collection unveiled in Milan.[8] In the most recent *The State of Fashion 2025* report, fashion executives said that their priorities in 2025 will be dedicated to 'finding ways to differentiate, whether through new designs, customer experiences or finding new customer niches'.[9]

Fashion does not refer simply to clothes but to clothes in relation to identity, society and politics. Essentially, dressed bodies become texts, creating 'spaces of uniformity and conformity as well as spaces of conflict . . . in which vestimentary signs and individual and social identity dialogue and translate each other'.[10] In the twenty-first century, fashion has evolved from its well-established formats into new interwoven digital

[6] The Business of Fashion and McKinsey & Company, *The State of Fashion 2019* (2018) 11 (hereafter The Business of Fashion and McKinsey & Company, *The State of Fashion 2019*).

[7] The Business of Fashion and McKinsey & Company, *The State of Fashion 2020* (2019) 14.

[8] Luke Leitch, 'Fall 2019: Menswear', *Vogue* (January 13, 2019)<https://www.vogue.com/fashion-shows/fall-2019-menswear/versace>. Leitch commented: 'The logo-heavy interaction with Ford was a little strange, especially in the context of an Italian thoroughbred asserting its aristocracy, but deals are deals.'

[9] The Business of Fashion and McKinsey & Company, *The State of Fashion 2025* (2024) 13.

[10] Chiara Battisti and Leif Dahlberg, 'Focus: Law, Fashion and Identities' (2006) 10(1) *Pólemos* 1, 4.

cross-media multiplatform genres[11] that today include the immersive environment of the metaverse and non-fungible tokens (NFTs). Intellectual property (IP) laws have only recently begun to contemplate how *fashion studies* as a field can bring valuable interdisciplinary insights to the legal domain of copyright and trademarks.[12] In the field of fashion studies, scholars are looking increasingly to media and communication studies for theoretical concepts and methodologies so as to more fully comprehend 'a domain characterized by finely attuned signs and semiotic distinction'.[13] Viewed in this way, fashion and IP laws will be inextricably interwoven with the constitutional doctrines of freedom of speech as fashion becomes integral as a form of expression. In the last couple of decades, entrepreneurs and artists such as Haute Diggity Dog, Nadia Plesner, MSCHF and Mason Rothschild have argued that their parodic or artistic appropriations of the symbols of Louis Vuitton, Nike and Hermes constitute protected speech.[14]

Section 1.2 surveys the key trends in the fashion industry in the last few years and highlights the new fashion vocabulary that will be influential in the years ahead. Section 1.3 explains how post-postmodern theories find a parallel in contemporary fashion phenomena. It also postulates that one may usefully adopt a semiotics approach to IP rights, particularly when dealing with fashion which is infused with symbolic meaning as a means to express one's feelings, political views and experiences. Section 1.4 considers how trademark and copyright laws may be enforced in light of these fashion trends and discusses some of the challenges ahead. Section 1.5 concludes that one would have to carefully evaluate the zeitgeist and make important – and correct – policy choices when

[11] Synne Skjulstad, 'Vetements, Memes, and Connectivity: Fashion Media in the Era of Instagram' (2020) 24(2) *Fashion Theory* 181, 184 (hereafter Skjulstad, 'Vetements, Memes, and Connectivity').

[12] David Tan, 'Logo Hacking, Downmarket Irony, and Counterfeit Chic: A Study of Contemporary Fashion Trends and Their Implications for Trademark Laws' in Haochen Sun and Barton Beebe (eds), *Charting Limitations on Trademark Rights* (Oxford University Press, 2023) 52, 53.

[13] Ibid, at 186.

[14] Eg, *Louis Vuitton Malletier, SA v Haute Diggity* Dog *LLC*, 507 F 3d 252 (4th Cir. 2007); *Plesner v Louis Vuitton Malletier, SA*, No.KG ZA 11-294 (Court of the Hague, July 21, 2011); *Hermès International v Rothschild*, 2022 WL 1564597 (SDNY, May 2022). See also David Tan, 'The Semiotics of Alpha Brands: Encoding/Decoding/Recoding/Transcoding of Louis Vuitton and Implications for Trademark Laws' (2013) 32 *Cardozo Arts & Entertainment Law Journal* 221.

enforcing IP laws and balancing how the freedom of expression features in the manifestations of the post-postmodern condition.

1.2 A New Fashion Vocabulary

At the start of 2020, the luxury fashion industry was enjoying a boom as consumers were increasingly buying experiences over things, and then the pandemic hit. Online innovation occurred in a matter of months as brands focused on generating revenue from the only channel available in many markets: e-commerce.[15] Lauren Sherman, writing in *The State of Fashion 2021*, thinks that while brands like Hermes, Louis Vuitton and Bottega Veneta had seen an improvement in sales in the third quarter of the 2020 fiscal year, it is 'unlikely consumers will continue to prioritise "things" longer-term after the pandemic'.[16] But there are contrary views. When the COVID-19 pandemic forced the world into quarantines and lockdowns, bankrupted fashion brands and retailers (such as John Varvatos, Neiman Marcus, Brooks Brothers, J.C. Penney)[17] and face masks became de rigueur in many countries, some alpha brands – in particular, Hermes – remained 'virus proof'.[18] The global casualisation of the wardrobe will also unleash pent-up demand for investment pieces in the high-end sector of the luxury fashion market. On a more mundane level, the worldwide proliferation of face masks as quintessential daily fashionwear has also sparked a flurry of trademark registrations[19] and, eventually, trademark disputes and counterfeit claims.[20]

15 The Business of Fashion and McKinsey & Company, *The State of Fashion 2021* (2020) 37–42.

16 Lauren Sherman, 'Covid-19 and the New Era of Luxury' in The Business of Fashion and McKinsey & Company, *The State of Fashion 2021*, ibid at 33.

17 The Fashion Law, 'Retail Woes: A Running List of Fashion and Retail Bankruptcies', *The Fashion Law* (April 5, 2021) <https://www.thefashionlaw.com/retail-woes-a-bankruptcy-timeline/>.

18 The Fashion Law, 'Luxury in the Age of COVID: Hermes Is "Resilient", Ferrari is "Extraordinarily Stable"', *The Fashion Law* (August 24, 2020) <https://www.thefashionlaw.com/luxury-in-the-age-of-covid-hermes-is-resilient-ferrari-is-extraordinarily-stable/>.

19 Ellie Sanders, 'As Face Masks, Shields Become a Fashion Category of Their Own, Brands Are Rushing to File Trademark Applications', *The Fashion Law* (December 1, 2020) <https://www.thefashionlaw.com/as-face-masks-shields-become-a-fashion-category-of-their-own-brands-are-rushing-to-file-trademark-applications/>.

20 Harry Archer, 'Sorry These Gucci Face Masks Aren't Real', *Editorialist* (October 20, 2020) <https://editorialist.com/news/gucci-face-masks/>; Danny Parisi, 'The Rise of the Fake Designer Mask', *Glossy* (July 21, 2020) <https://www.glossy.co/fashion/the-rise-of-the-fake-designer-mask/>; The Fashion Law, 'Counterfeit Fashion-Manufacturers Are

Self-disruption, the top-ranked 2019 trend that fashion executives predict will shape the fashion industry in the immediate future,[21] has continued in the ensuing years post–COVID-19 pandemic. This is unsurprising since heritage brands like Gucci and Balenciaga have been enjoying soaring profits by paradoxically selling merchandise bearing misspellings of their famous marks evocative of counterfeit goods (eg, GUCCY) and ill-fitting ugly clothes.[22] The collections unveiled online during the pandemic between June 2020 and January 2021 show no abatement of these design trends. Luxury brands have greater latitude to deviate from their dominant brand aesthetic and doing so may have a positive impact in 'refreshing' a brand's tired aesthetic in a novel way that increases consumer interest and memorability.[23] Unfortunately, consumers do get tired of repetition, and perhaps the death knell for counterfeit chic and geek chic has been sounded. With the passing of Virgil Abloh at the end of 2021,[24] and the sudden departure of Alessandro Michele from Gucci in November 2022,[25] it would seem that another wave of fresh creativity is in the brewing. As Nicole Phelps writing for *Vogue* comments: 'But in fashion even the brightest stars don't shine forever . . .. Gucci's sales eventually started to dip, and in the wake of the pandemic parent company Kering's shares fell amidst the brand's slow-down. A recent WWD report quoted an anonymous source

Pivoting to Make Counterfeit Masks', *The Fashion Law* (March 31, 2020) <https://www.thefashionlaw.com/counterfeit-fashion-makers-pivot-to-making-counterfeit-masks/>.

[21] The Business of Fashion and McKinsey & Company, *The State of Fashion 2019*, above n 6, 17.

[22] Dhani Mau, 'Millennials Bought a Lot of Gucci in 2018', *Fashionista* (February 12, 2019) <https://fashionista.com/2019/02/gucci-kering-revenue-profits-fy-2018>; Dhani Mau, 'Balenciaga Is about to Hit a Major Revenue Milestone', *Fashionista* (April 24, 2019) <https://fashionista.com/2019/04/balenciaga-sales-growth-1-billion-euros>. See also Andrea Cheng, 'Why Everyone Is into Ugly Fashion: An Explainer', *Fashionista* (November 14, 2017) <https://fashionista.com/2017/06/ugly-fashion-mainstream-trend>; 'Does Gucci's £1,800 Shell Suit Signal the Return of the 1980s' Worst Look?', *The Guardian* (June 25, 2019) <https://www.theguardian.com/fashion/shortcuts/2019/jun/25/gucci-1800-pound-shell-suit-return-1980s-worst-look?>.

[23] Christin Seifert, Tianyu Cui and Veena Chattaraman, 'Can Brands Deviate from Their Brand Aesthetic? Brand Luxury Status as a Moderator' (2019) 23(2) *Journal of Fashion Marketing & Management* 176.

[24] Vanessa Friedman, 'Virgil Abloh, Path-Blazing Designer, Is Dead at 41', *The New York Times* (November 28, 2021) <https://www.nytimes.com/2021/11/28/style/virgil-abloh-dead.html>.

[25] Nicole Phelps, 'Alessandro Michele Is Exiting Gucci after an Extraordinary Seven-Year Run', *Vogue* (November 23, 2022) <https://www.vogue.cosm/article/gucci-announces-alessandro-michele-exit>.

claiming Michele 'was asked to initiate a strong design shift.' If that is so, it appears Michele resisted it.'[26] It was reported that over 80 per cent of shoppers plan to spend the same or less on clothing, footwear and accessories in 2025,[27] and that it is non-luxury fashion sector that will drive the entirety of the increase in economic profit for the first time since 2010 (excluding the COVID-19 years).[28] This only means the luxury fashion sector will have to continually find ways to remain attractive and desirable to a wide range of consumer segments from the Gen-Z and Millennials to the silver generation.[29]

What seems to be more certain is a gravitation of these trendsetting fashion brands towards new logos, NFTs, the metaverse, social and environmental causes, streetwear and celebrity collaborations to engender a cooler image amongst a younger demographic. While such creative and business manoeuvres had led to revenue growth, some of these developments also present specific challenges to the established doctrines of IP laws, in particular trademark and copyright laws. The rest of this section will highlight in detail some of the key trends.

1.2.1 Hacking/ Downmarket Irony/ Counterfeit Chic

The fashion brand Vetements (meaning 'clothing' in French) is organised as a creative collective by seven designers who initially remained anonymous, but subsequently Georgian creative director Demna Gvasalia became the most profiled designer and was synonymous with the brand. As one of the most popular contemporary fashion hackers in the last decade, Vetements have proven themselves to be the experts at creating 'viral' garments, items that have the irony and popularity of internet memes, with as much life online as off.[30] The brand's earlier phenomenal success is intimately tied to its deep understanding of contemporary digital media culture and its adroit social media practices. Gvasalia had arguably brought anti-fashion back to fashion in its

26 Ibid.

27 The Business of Fashion and McKinsey & Company, *The State of Fashion 2025* (2024) 64.

28 Ibid, at 8.

29 Ibid, at 49–56.

30 Emma Hope Allwood, 'The Fashion Meme: How Clothes Went Viral', *Dazed* (March 30, 2016) <https://www.dazeddigital.com/fashion/article/30561/1/the-fashion-meme-vetements-vetememes-viral-clothes-dhl> (hereafter Allwood, 'The Fashion Meme').

Spring–Summer 2016 runway collection when Vetements paraded a DHL T-shirt with a price tag of £185.[31] According to trends analyst Aleksandra Szymanska of the Future Laboratory: 'They are hacking the fashion system … and they're credible [enough] to make these statements of capitalist kitsch.'[32] Szymanska also believes that unlike the logomania phenomenon in the 2000s, when a luxury brand's logo – Louis Vuitton's LV or Chanel's double-C – was an ostentatious symbol of the wealth of the wearer, fashion brands today use non-fashion logos that plug into the cool vibe of the millennial generation. Synne Skjulstad observes that it is 'achieved by way of a distinctive blend of unexpected moves, humor, irony, and contradictory intellectual anti-conceptualism, one which permeates both [Vetements'] collections and public profile'.[33] The Vetements aesthetic is characterised by a 'calculated disruption and assault on the status quo' and essentially 'taking the products that each individual label is known for or does best (T-shirts for Hanes, heels for Manolo Blahnik) and reworking it à la Vetements, which often amounts to a sort of creative defacement',[34] and then charging customers a high price for these. Although not all the brands initially gave their permission, for many of the globally recognised companies that Gvasalia approached, the opportunity to be part of the Vetements aesthetic – and consequently garnering widespread attention on social media – was simply irresistible. Vetements sought to romanticise the ordinary and the mundane and to bring visibility to peoples, communities and places often not considered to be inspiring through elevation of the garments by their display in the context of expensive high fashion and in the status of fetishised commodities.[35] The phrase 'to Vetementize' was thus born.[36]

These 'hackings' or reworkings of popular yet often inexpensive products sold by renowned streetwear brands such as Hanes T-shirts, Champion hoodies and Levi's denim jeans, and the ubiquitous bright yellow DHL logo T-shirts, have also been referred to as the 'downmarket

[31] Lauren Cochrane, 'Scam or Subversion? How a DHL T-shirt Became This Year's Must-Have', *The Guardian* (April 20, 2016) <https://www.theguardian.com/fashion/2016/apr/19/dhl-t-shirt-vetements-fashion-paris-catwalk>.

[32] Ibid.

[33] Skjulstad, 'Vetements, Memes, and Connectivity', above n 10, 189.

[34] Ibid.

[35] Eizenberg, 'With No Twist', above n 1, 61–63.

[36] Skjulstad, 'Vetements, Memes, and Connectivity', above n 10, 189.

irony': the trend for luxury fashion brands to create designs that have the look of bootleg creations found at cheap market stalls.[37] The recent aesthetic objectives for brands like Gucci and Balenciaga appear to be to make their logos look as cheap and as ugly as possible on their clothing and then charge a high price for these products.

By creating 'fashion memes',[38] Vetements, and later Balenciaga, under the creative direction of Demna Gvasalia, aim to situate the brands in the centre of discursive activity in the community, as audiences and consumers are invited to actively participate in commentary, debate, parody, satire and pastiche. *Dazed Digital*'s head of fashion, Emma Hope Allwood, commented, 'while once being transformed into meme was a mark of derision, now it's a signifier of cultural relevance, to be encouraged rather than feared'.[39] This trend stands in stark contrast to a design or a trademark traditionally conceived of as an original and not to be tampered with – one that exists in a reverential rights-based system that frowns against copying and imitation.

As the creative director for Balenciaga (and previously Vetements), Demna Gvasalia's present cult status within the fashion industry can be polarizing. His appeal to an increasingly affluent younger generation obsessed with social media and a quest to appear 'authentic' is legendary, but others who desire elegantly tailored clothes will naturally find his antics to be repellent and view his fame as transitory. Nonetheless, during the COVID-19 pandemic years, Gvasalia has courted controversy with his

[37] Lauren Cochrane, 'It's a Rip-off: Now Bootleg Logos Are a Fashion Must-have', *The Guardian* (December 30, 2017) <https://www.theguardian.com/fashion/2017/dec/30/bootleg-logos-designers-copyright-fashion>. In October 2006, fashion designer Marc Jacobs shocked the world of high fashion by sending models down the runway for Louis Vuitton carrying cheap-looking checked tote bags reminiscent of the ugly plaid nylon canvas ones that are ubiquitous in Chinatown and carried by rural workers in the People's Republic of China. Perceived then to be a marketing gimmick, established fashion brands nonetheless adhered to more traditional aesthetics, albeit with sporadic deviations, until designers Alessandro Michele and Demna Gvasalia shattered the mould in 2015 when they were appointed creative directors of the heritage luxury houses of Gucci and Balenciaga. See Maria MacKinney-Valentin, *Fashioning Identity: Status Ambivalence in Contemporary Fashion* (Bloomsbury Academic, 2017) 54–56.

[38] Skjulstad, 'Vetements, Memes, and Connectivity', above n 10, 188 ('fashion designed for prospective and collaborative mediation and design practices' and is thus 'a product or a garment designed like an Internet meme, for being *copied, changed, modified, shared, spread, and commented*'). On internet memes, see, eg, Limor Shifman, 'The Cultural Logic of Photo-Based Meme Genres' (2014) 13(3) *Journal of Visual Culture* 340.

[39] Allwood, 'The Fashion Meme', above n 26.

runway shows[40] and advertising campaigns for Balenciaga,[41] and he is continuing in the tradition of fashion hackers like Martin Margiela and Rei Kawakubo for Comme des Garçons (who will deconstruct clothes from the way they are traditionally worn and reconstruct them into a new shape or volume) and logo hackers like Moschino (who will appropriate famous logos and subvert them in a playful manner). Hacking in the fashion world is neither sinister nor destructive. Although it is often done to prove a point, share information and subvert prevailing codes to create something new, clever and elegant,[42] it has so far been lucrative for the fashion brands and especially for Gucci and Vetements.

'Logo hacking' was taken perhaps to the extreme by Gucci under the creative direction of Alessandro Michele who possibly started the trend of 'self-hacking' amongst the luxury fashion brands. When graffiti artist Trevor Andrew, aka GucciGhost, who in late 2013 and 2014 scrawled the label's signatures all over Brooklyn and Manhattan, Gucci did not respond with a copyright-infringement suit or a cease-and-desist order. Instead, Michele extended an invitation to Andrew to make clothes together, and the collaboration was presented in the Fall–Winter 2016 collection.[43] Logo hacking was taken to the next level when in the Gucci Cruise 2018 collection, perhaps spawning the 'counterfeit chic' trend, Michele unveiled the 'GUCCY' motif, which created a frenzy on social media, that was a deliberate mocking of poorly made Gucci knock-offs (Figure 1.1). Indeed, Gucci has reclaimed 'GUCCY' from the counterfeiters and have turned it into an asset for the brand as it continues to develop clothing, bags and accessories with the 'GUCCY' motif alongside its official 'GUCCI' logo. In a surprising postmodern turn, Gucci has articulated its own countercultural statement by parodying its own bootlegs by selling, amongst other merchandise, a sweater that resembles a bad counterfeit, with Gucci replaced by 'GUCCY', for £950.[44] It seems

[40] Vanessa Friedman, 'Balenciaga Goes Where Fashion Hasn't Dared Go Before', *New York Times* (March 7, 2022) <https://www.nytimes.com/2022/03/07/style/balenciaga-ukraine-valentino.html>.

[41] Elizabeth Paton, Vanessa Friedman and Jessica Testa, 'When Fashion and QAnon Collide', *New York Times* (November 28, 2022) <https://www.nytimes.com/2022/11/28/style/balenciaga-campaign-controversy.html>.

[42] Clara Yong, 'What Fashion Hacking Is And How It's Redefining the Industry', *Fashion Magazine* (May 3, 2017) <https://fashionmagazine.com/fashion/fashion-hacking/>.

[43] Frank Bruni, 'Alessandro Michele, Fashion's Modern Mastermind', *The New York Times Style Magazine* (October 15, 2018) <https://www.nytimes.com/2018/10/15/t-magazine/alessandro-michele-gucci-interview.html>.

[44] Ibid.

Figure 1.1 Official 'GUCCY' merchandise by Gucci.

that this decision to sell a line of 'GUCCY' products, a logo that parodied the luxury industry's problem with counterfeits and *shanzhai* products, was perceived to be witty by Chinese consumers who made up 30% of Gucci's worldwide sales of US$7.2 billion in 2017.[45] It was a gambit that paid off handsomely. Scottish artist/art director Hey Reilly commented that 'the best or most powerful fashion labels can play with their icons because the message is still about them. It appears that the message and meaning of brands and logos can still operate even when disturbed: they continue to transmit powerful statements of status and identity, even when presented in bastardized form'.[46] The semiotic sign of 'GUCCI' when subverted by its very brand owner to become 'GUCCY' is communicating a message that the luxury symbol is cool, hip, irreverent and, most importantly, relevant to the millennial generation. At the Gucci Fall–Winter 2020 men's fashion show, the brand continues its

[45] Susanna Nicoletti, 'The New Logo-Restyling Mania: A Risk or an Opportunity in China?', *Jing Daily* (January 8, 2019) <https://jingdaily.com/logo-restyling-mania/>; Faith Cooper, 'Gucci Strikes Red: China's Love Affair with Gucci', *Fashion History Timeline* (March 8, 2019) <https://fashionhistory.fitnyc.edu/gucci-strikes-red/>.

[46] Katie Baron, 'Why Brandalism Has Become a Luxury Brand's New Best Friend', *Forbes* (June 4, 2018) <https://www.forbes.com/sites/katiebaron/2018/06/04/why-brandalism-has-become-a-luxury-brands-new-best-friend/#2a88c81949cf> accessed 30 November 2020 (hereafter Baron, 'Brandalism').

Figure 1.2 Official 'FAKE NOT' Gucci bag.
© Prestige

successful 'playful commentary on the idea of imitation', this time presenting the fake Gucci logo with the bicolour stripe that was first seen in the 1980s, with the ugly words 'FAKE' and 'NOT' in bright yellow prominently plastered on either side of the bags (Figure 1.2).[47]

Fashion journalist Sarah Mower writing for *Vogue* called this form of brandalism – a portmanteau of brand and vandalism – 'conscious self-parody'.[48] It was commented that:

> While it arguably looks somewhat like a spelling mistake, the primitive spelling of the name [GUCCY] is an ironic jab at the momentous presence of knock-offs that are sold in droves – both from physical retailers and online – around the world. This particular spelling of the name was incredibly popular with counterfeit retailers in the 1980s.[49]

On November 15, 2021, Gucci and Balenciaga engaged in a creative contamination of each other's logos in The Hacker Project – a lucrative series of clothing, bags and accessories that feature both fashion houses

[47] 'Gucci's New Fake/Not Collection Drew Inspiration from the Unlikeliest of Place – Imitation Knockoffs – and Features a New Signature Print and Motif', *South China Morning Post* (September 21, 2020) <https://www.scmp.com/magazines/style/luxury/article/3102149/style-edit-guccis-new-fake/not-collection-drew-inspiration>.

[48] Sarah Mower, 'Gucci: Resort 2018', *Vogue* (May 30, 2017) <https://www.vogue.com/fashion-shows/resort-2018/gucci>.

[49] Emma Portelli Bonnici, 'Putting the "Y" in Gucci', *Times of Malta* (November 24, 2018), <https://timesofmalta.com/articles/view/putting-the-y-in-gucci.695003>.

Figure 1.3 The Hacker Project by Gucci.
© Condé Nast. All rights reserved. Credit: David Tan. © Gucci

playing with each other's house codes. Emphasising that this was not officially a collaboration, press notes read: 'Exploring ideas of authenticity and appropriation, Gucci and Balenciaga motifs merge to create new interpretations of signature pieces'[50] (Figure 1.3). Other fashion commentators noted: 'In many ways, Balenciaga's portion of The Hacker Project appears like counterfeits one would find on the black market or even random goods stalls in open-air bazaars. And that's one of the main reasons why this isn't a collaboration.'[51] This is quite unlike the official Fendi and Versace collaboration in May 2022, billed as 'Fendace'.[52]

This 'counterfeit chic' movement does not remain exclusively within the domain of luxury fashion brands to re-appropriate *shanzhai* and counterfeit practices for themselves by designing and selling what appears to be cheap and poor copies for the usual designer premium prices. In 2018, Diesel created a pop-up store on Canal Street in SoHo New York that sold official 'DEISEL' clothing, with Renzo Rosso, the founder of Diesel, commenting that a brand can create its own fakes and

[50] Erica Kagan, 'Gucci x Balenciaga "Hacker Project": Not Just Another Collaboration', *Sotheby's* (December 3, 2021) <https://www.sothebys.com/en/articles/gucci-x-balenciaga-hacker-project-not-just-another-collaboration>.

[51] Azri Jasman, 'Creative Chaos: Gucci and Balenciaga's The Hacker Project', *Esquire Singapore* (November 15, 2022) <https://www.esquiresg.com/features/hacker-project-gucci-balenciaga-collection-alessandro-michele-demna-gvasalia/>.

[52] Henrik Lischke, 'Fendace Is Here: Get a First Glimpse of 2022's Most Anticipated Designer Drop', *Vogue* (May 12, 2022) <https://www.vogue.com/article/fendace>.

Figure 1.4 The Hacker Project by Balenciaga.
© Sotheby's
© Balenciaga

embrace its own imitation.[53] This 'self-hacking' trend, while popular with customers willing to pay top dollars for fake-looking authentic products, is likely to result in problems for enforcement of intellectual property rights in the future. Some questions have already been raised:

> Will high fashion's whirlwind upside-down, inside-out, love/hate relationship with bootlegging create consumer confusion and what are the long-term repercussions? . . . Will Gucci to 'Guccy' lessen the stigma and condition shoppers to view counterfeit goods as socially acceptable?[54]

1.2.2 NFTs, the Metaverse, Social Media and the Phygital

Fashion is also making big strides in the immersive environment of the metaverse and the minting of NFTs.[55] Often spoken (and frequently

[53] Matthew Schneier, 'To Knock Out Knockoffs, Knock Off Knockoffs', *The New York* Times (February 11, 2018) <https://www.nytimes.com/2018/02/11/fashion/diesel-deisel-new-york-fashion-week-pop-up.html>.

[54] J'Net Nguyen, 'Fake Gucci to Real Guccy: Fashion's Identity Crisis or Alter Ego?', *The Right Brain Studio* (February, 8, 2018) <https://www.therightbrainstudio.com/fake-gucci-real-guccy-fashions-identity-crisis-alter-ego/>.

[55] Isabelle Sinclair, 'NFTs and Luxury Fashion: A Conscious Coupling', *L'Officiel USA* (November 21, 2022) <https://www.lofficielusa.com/fashion/nfts-luxury-fashion-collab

erroneously) in conjunction with the metaverse, NFTs are digital assets that have been verified using blockchain technology, and they can exist *independently* of the metaverse of games and social networking platforms or integrated into these digital worlds. By the end of 2022, most of the luxury fashion brands have jumped on the bandwagon of the metaverse (eg, 'Gucci Vault Land' is an experimental space where users will go on a journey through the fashion brand's history through games and NFTs; Burberry has a capsule phygital collection with Minecraft; Polo Ralph Lauren collaborated with Fortnite where players can win items from the digital collection) and have minted non-fungible tokens, a number of which have been sold at astronomical prices (eg, Dolce & Gabbana setting a US$6 million record for fashion NFTs; Balmain partnering MINTNFT to premiere 'The Balmain Thread' on the eco-friendly XRP Ledger at Paris Fashion Week, becoming the first global fashion house to create a NFT-based membership program).[56]

The metaverse is a new name for an existing idea, and it is a befuddling concept. It is fundamentally the combination of aspects of social media, gaming, augmented and virtual reality, and the internet that forms an immersive and interconnected digital world. In this virtual space, people from across the world may socialise, work, play, learn, shop and innovate. Despite doubts whether the version of the metaverse peddled by Mark Zuckerberg will ever happen, investment bank Morgan Stanley nevertheless has predicted that digital fashion could boost industry sales by US$50 billion by 2030.[57] There is much money to be made in the metaverse, but many legal issues are unresolved. The frequency with

orations-gucci-louis-vuitton>; Rachel Breia, '15 Fashion Brands Leveraging the Metaverse', *Sensorium* (October 6, 2022) <https://sensoriumxr.com/articles/fashion-brands-in-the-metaverse>; Oscar Holland, 'Luxury Fashion Houses Are Funneling Millions into the Metaverse. But to What End?', *CNN* (September 8, 2022) <https://edition.cnn.com/style/article/fashion-metaverse-millions-september-issues/index.html> (hereafter Holland, 'Luxury Fashion Houses').

56 Bernard Marr, 'Gucci Enters the Metaverse', *Forbes* (November 30, 2022) <https://www.forbes.com/sites/bernardmarr/2022/11/30/gucci-enters-the-metaverse/?sh=4039d8141d66>; Azrin Tan, 'The Latest from the Fashion Metaverse: Rimowa Launches NFTs, Burberry's Capsule Collection on Minecraft and More', *Vogue* (November 8, 2022) <https://vogue.sg/updates-from-fashion-metaverse/>; Dana Thomas, 'Dolce & Gabbana Just Set a $6 Million Record for Fashion NFTs', *New York Times* (October 4, 2021) <https://www.nytimes.com/2021/10/04/style/dolce-gabbana-nft.html>; Madeleine Schulz, 'Balmain Launches Web3 Hub at Paris Fashion Week', *Vogue Business* (September 27, 2022) <https://www.voguebusiness.com/technology/balmain-launches-web3-hub-at-paris-fashion-week>.

57 Holland, 'Luxury Fashion Houses', above n 51.

which brands' trademarks were being used on the virtual goods in the Second Life ecosystem without their authorisation led to metaverse-related lawsuits. Due to swift settlements or the defendants' failure to turn up in court, these lawsuits provided little insight into how courts would treat trademarks – and claims of trademark infringement – in the metaverse.

On January 1, 2023, the 12th edition of the Nice Classification entered into force and it had been updated to more explicitly refer to uses in what we would call the metaverse, as well as NFTs. When minting and selling NFTs that comprise its own trademarks or when using its marks in an online game, a company should register its mark in the appropriate class. These are the four most relevant classes:

- Class 9: includes 'downloadable virtual goods/digital files authenticated by non-fungible tokens [NFTs]'
- Class 35: includes 'retail store services featuring virtual goods'
- Class 41: includes 'virtual entertainment services, namely, providing online, non-downloadable virtual footwear, clothing, bags, sports equipment, art, toys and accessories for use in virtual environments; providing online virtual guided tours'
- Class 42: includes 'mining of crypto assets/cryptomining'.

Although there exists much ambiguity as to cohesive and viable business strategies regarding the metaverse and NFTs, well-known global brands are definitely registering their trademarks in these classes and commencing a spectrum of extended reality (XR) activities and issuing of NFTs. Generally, fashion brands have rushed to register a panoply of trademarks in these classes seeking to cover their bases for their future endeavours in this realm, even if they do not know exactly what those ventures will look like.[58] In particular, luxury fashion brands such as Louis Vuitton, Gucci, Balenciaga, Dolce & Gabbana and Burberry, as well

[58] The Fashion Law, 'Trademark Offices Provide Guidance As Metaverse, NFT-Focused Applications Grow', *The Fashion Law* (September 7, 2022) <https://www.thefashionlaw.com/the-euipo-has-provided-guidance-on-metaverse-nft-focused-trademarks/>; The Fashion Law, 'What Is Really Driving Companies' Metaverse-Focused Trademark Filings', *The Fashion Law* (November 30, 2022) <https://www.thefashionlaw.com/what-is-really-driving-companies-metaverse-focused-trademark-filings/>; Julie Zerbo, 'Birkins in the Metaverse? A Look at Hermes' Web3-Focused Trademark Applications', *The Fashion Law* (September 7, 2022) <https://www.thefashionlaw.com/birkins-in-the-metaverse-a-look-at-hermes-web3-focused-trademark-applications/>.

as sporting apparel titan Nike, are actively exploiting the metaverse with a proliferation of online collaborations, digital experiences and NFT sales.[59] Over the past year, watch brands like Hublot, Bulgari and Panerai have also embraced the possibilities of NFTs as a way to release works by notable artists inspired by the companies' watch designs, to serve as a mark of authentication and ownership and to enhance customer experiences.[60] Jewellery brands are similarly hopping onto the bandwagon.[61]

On May 17, 2021, Gucci teamed up with Roblox, one of the most renowned gaming platforms, to exhibit Gucci handbags, hats and sunglasses on avatars, in the Gucci Garden space.[62] It ran for two weeks, allowing enthusiasts and gamers to buy collectibles and several rare Gucci accessories, and more than 20 million players visited the Garden. It followed up with a permanent space on Roblox called Gucci Town, where players can compete in games to earn GG gems, discover and create art pieces and purchase from a boutique of limited-edition virtual items from Gucci for their avatars.[63] In June 2021, Gucci offered up its first NFT, a film inspired by its *Aria* Fall–Winter 2021 fashion runway collection, for auction at Christie's. The sale, titled *Proof of Sovereignty: A Curated NFT Sale by Lady PheOnix*, is an NFT-specific auction that features a single work from Gucci, and it realised US$25,000.[64] It later collaborated with Superplastic to launch a three-part SUPERGUCCI NFT collection. The first drop in February 2022 featured 10 unique

[59] See David Tan, 'Trademarks in the Metaverse: Everything Everywhere All at Once' (2023) 25 *Media & Arts Law Review* 285.

[60] Jessica Bumpus, 'Expanding the Watch World's Metaverse with a Gaming Twist', *The New York Times* (June 14, 2022) <https://www.nytimes.com/2022/06/14/fashion/watches-nfts-nimany.html>.

[61] Jessica Bumpus, 'Jewelry Decorates the Metaverse', *The New York Times* (March 24, 2022) <https://www.nytimes.com/2022/03/24/fashion/jewelry-nft-jevels.html>.

[62] 'The Gucci Garden Experience Lands on Roblox', *Roblox* (May 17, 2021) <https://blog.roblox.com/2021/05/gucci-garden-experience/>; Maghan McDowell, 'Inside Gucci and Roblox's New Virtual World', *Vogue Business* (May 17, 2021) <https://www.voguebusiness.com/technology/inside-gucci-and-robloxs-new-virtual-world>.

[63] Andrew Webster, 'Gucci Built a Persistent Town Inside of Roblox', *The Verge* (May 27, 2022) <https://www.theverge.com/2022/5/27/23143404/gucci-town-roblox>.

[64] Angelica Villa, 'Gucci Sells NFT Inspired by Latest Collection at Christie's', *ArtNews* (June 2, 2021) <https://www.artnews.com/art-news/market/gucci-nft-auction-christies-1234594632/>; Online Auction 20669 – Proof of Sovereignty: A Curated NFT Sale by Lady PheOnix, *Christie's* (June 3, 2021) <https://onlineonly.christies.com/s/proof-sovereignty-curated-nft-sale-lady-pheonix/gucci-est-1921-6/121268>.

NFTs each accompanied by a handmade Italian ceramic sculpture designed by both Gucci and Superplastic.[65]

To celebrate the 200th birth anniversary of the founder of Louis Vuitton, the brand launched a mobile game known as Louis the Game in August 2021. The phone app follows the protagonist, Vivienne, through a number of different worlds, where she needs to collect 200 candles to commemorate the birthday of Louis Vuitton. One is able to customise the Vivienne character with different Louis Vuitton monogram prints and colourways. There are 30 embedded NFTs in the game; each NFT is a collectible that can only be found through playing the game and cannot be sold. The latest version in April 2022 has two additional locations and 10 new NFTs featuring Vivienne in different looks. Players who successfully collect a certain number of free NFTs in the game will stand a chance to qualify for an NFT raffle; eventual winners will be able to use these NFTs across multiple platforms like a PFP (profile NFTs that can be used on Twitter etc) that owners can wear like a badge of honour.[66]

Balenciaga's adroit commitment to exploiting business opportunities in the metaverse has been a case study at Insead.[67] In December 2021, the brand announced that the company is creating a department dedicated to the virtual world, in order to explore its marketing and commercial opportunities. Balenciaga was the first fashion house to partner with Epic Games, which is behind Fortnite, a famous multiplayer online role-playing game (MMORPG) that is increasingly attracting more players due to its VR concerts. The unique items from its vast collection are to be sold as avatars' skins and accessories. The new gear will be available both in Fortnite's usual in-game storefront and in the Balenciaga-themed 'Strange Times' Creative hub, which includes a virtual Balenciaga store. It created a digital avatar, known as Doggo, wholly dressed in a Balenciaga outfit. Users can also submit avatar photos, which are often included in billboards in the Fortnite's town square. That animated Doggo billboard that will appear in-game and in actual cities

[65] Jake Silbert, 'Superplastic X Gucci = SuperGucci NFTs', *High Snobiety* (January 17, 2022) <https://www.highsnobiety.com/p/gucci-superplastic-supergucci-nft-collab/>.

[66] Isa Muhammad, 'Louis Vuitton's NFT Game Amasses More Than Two Million Downloads', *Beyond Games* (April 29, 2022) <https://www.beyondgames.biz/22051/louis-vuittons-nft-game-amasses-more-than-2-million-downloads/>.

[67] InTheCase, 'Balenciaga in the Metaverse: When Luxury Meets Gaming', *Insead Digital* (June 7, 2022) <https://digital.insead.edu/post/in-the-case-balenciaga-in-the-metaverse-when-luxury-meets-gaming/>.

such as Tokyo, London, Seoul and New York City.[68] Adam Sussman, president of Epic Games, said: '*Fortnite* is fashion .... The entire experience of *Fortnite* is centred around self expression, player agency, and the ability to live out a fantasy of portraying characters and outfits that people want to wear.'[69]

In October 2021, Nike was the first apparel brand to file a number of new intent-to-use applications for its most famous trademarks in the United States for use on various virtual goods/services that foreshadowed Nike's since-confirmed intentions to make big strides into the metaverse. Since then, it has launched 'Nikeland' in partnership with Roblox, launched NFTs created in conjunction with RTFKT Studios[70] and sued online resale marketplace StockX for, inter alia, infringing its trademarks by selling NFTs tied to physical sneakers.[71] Nike acquired RTKFT, which was established in 2020 and has already posted an impressive performance, teaming up with crypto artist Fewocious in 2021 to sell 600 pairs of shoes as NFTs, amassing a total of US$3.1 million in less than seven minutes.

Last but not least, even before the COVID-19 pandemic struck, social media was integral to the promotion of fashion brands and the celebrity persona in the last half decade. It has now become a key driving force for revenues. It has been observed that brands with celebrity endorsements typically see a 4% increase in sales, but millennial shopping habits have demonstrated a shift in the efficacy of celebrity endorsements through traditional media such as print and broadcast. Younger consumers are inclining toward 'authenticity' – or at least, perceived authenticity – as represented by paparazzi photos and social media posts.[72] Additionally, brands have also shifted their marketing efforts to digital influencers,

[68] Jay Peters, 'Epic's High-Fashion Collaboration with Balenciaga in Fortnite Includes a Hoodie for a Walking Dog', *The Verge* (September 20, 2021) <https://www.theverge.com/2021/9/20/22679754/fortnite-balenciaga-collaboration-epic-games-unreal-engine>.

[69] Ibid.

[70] Bernard Marr, 'The Amazing Ways Nike Is Using the Metaverse, Web3 And NFTs', *Forbes* (June 1, 2022) <https://www.forbes.com/sites/bernardmarr/2022/06/01/the-amazing-ways-nike-is-using-the-metaverse-web3-and-nfts/?sh=6c001b56e94f>.

[71] *Nike, Inc v StockX LLC*, Case 1:22-CV-00983 (SDNY, complaint filed February 3, 2022). See also The Fashion Law, 'Nike Adds Counterfeiting, False Advertising Claims to Case Against StockX', *The Fashion Law* (May 31, 2022) <https://www.thefashionlaw.com/nike-adds-counterfeiting-false-advertising-claims-to-case-against-stockx/>.

[72] The Fashion Law, 'Are the Most Valuable Brand Endorsements Free?', *The Fashion Law* (September 4, 2019) <https://www.thefashionlaw.com/are-the-most-valuable-brand-endorsements-free/>.

which are generally viewed as more authentic alternatives to their traditional celebrity counterparts in the film, music and sporting industries. Since 2018, more and more designers sought to display their collections in 'Instagram-ready' spaces, designed for instantaneous diffusion over social media and livestreaming. As many live fashion shows in Paris and Milan have been replaced with highly creative digital shows and arthouse mini-movies in the latter half of 2020,[73] fashion is no longer defined solely as a semiotic system of production and consumption but also a whole system of media representation governed by forms of digital performance.[74] The term 'phygital' – a portmanteau of physical and digital – was born.[75] Today, phygital fashion refers to the fusion of physical and digital elements in the fashion industry, such as using virtual or augmented reality technology in fashion shows and retail experiences, integrating wearable technology into clothing and accessories and blurring of lines between online and offline fashion consumption.[76]

In summary, it would appear that brands will likely be able to rely on existing trademark rights (in physical products and retail services) in order to bring enforcement actions, and may not need to file new applications for virtual goods. The unauthorised minting and sale of NFTs associated with trademarks that have been the subject of high-profile lawsuits will set important legal precedents, such as Hermes suing artist Mason Rothschild for the sale of the MetaBirkins NFTs[77] and Nike

[73] Steff Yotka, 'Fashion Shows Are Dead, Long Live Fashion Shows!', *Vogue* (December 16, 2020), <https://www.vogue.com/article/future-of-fashion-shows-2020-2021>; Nicole Phelps, '"Faced With Restrictions, These Are the Designers Who Took Us Somewhere New" – Vogue Editors Weigh in on the Most Innovative Presentations of Spring 2021', *Vogue* (October 14, 2020) <https://www.vogue.com/article/good-morning-vogue-the-editors-eye-part-one>.

[74] Silvano Mendes, 'The Instagrammability of the Runway: Architecture, Seriography, and the Spatial Turn in Fashion Communications' (2019) 25(3) *Fashion Theory* 311.

[75] Thalia Barrera, 'Phygital Fashion: The Perfect Blend of Tradition and Innovation', *TechFashionista* (January 7, 2023) <https://thetechfashionista.com/phygital-fashion/>.

[76] Eg, Nitin Kumar, 'Fashion Brands and the Phygital Business', *Newsweek* (April 14, 2023) <https://www.newsweek.com/fashion-brands-phygital-business-model-1794281>; Amanda Chai, 'Year of Phygital Fashion, from the Runway to Retail Design', *The Straits Times* (December 17, 2022) <https://www.straitstimes.com/life/style/year-of-phygital-fashion-from-the-runway-to-retail-design>. Vogue has dedicated an online page to a catalogue of phygital fashion stories. *Vogue Business* <https://www.voguebusiness.com/tag/phygital>.

[77] Mason Rothschild launched his furry colourful digital renditions of a Hermes Birkin at Art Basel in Miami – 100 digital collectibles created on the Ethereum blockchain – and then sold them on the OpenSea NFT marketplace. After a nine-day jury trial, a New York district court found Rothschild liable for trademark infringement and dilution as well as

claiming that online reselling platform StockX had infringed its marks by displaying and selling its Vault NFTs that are each tied to a specific pair of Nike sneakers.[78]

1.2.3 Sustainability and Upcycling

Last but not least, 'eco-design', 'sustainable fashion' and 'upcycling' are just some of the many words in vogue today in a post-pandemic world. The LVMH group, which owns brands such as Louis Vuitton, Dior and Givenchy, for the first time, released the *2020 Social and Environmental Sustainability Report*, which outlined the fashion conglomerate's commitment to responsible growth amidst the backdrop of the global pandemic.[79] The upcycling trend – which is a creative reuse of old or unwanted materials to make new products – has witnessed artists like the MSCHF group in the United States creating mashups of Hermes Birkin bags and Birkenstock footwear; these *Birkinstocks* involve cutting up authentic Birkin bags and they are sold for between US$34,000 to US$76,000.[80] At a parochial level, Chanel is taking Shiver + Duke to court for using buttons bearing the interlocking CC mark from the French brand's garments and refashioning them into jewellery.[81]

The COVID-19 pandemic has given impetus to the boom in online shopping and, consequently, a proliferation of resale websites that would repurpose or refashion luxury goods in myriad ways. The luxury resale market is growing rapidly, reaching a total worth of US$25 billion in 2018, and it was expected to grow to US$36 billion in 2021. With the

cybersquatting. An injunction was issued against the artist prohibiting the sale of the NFTs and orders issued for disgorgement of profits and transfer of domain name to Hermes. See *Hermès International v Mason Rothschild*, Case 1:22-cv-00384 (SDNY, complaint filed January 14, 2022); *Hermès International v Rothschild*, 2022 WL 1564597 (SDNY, May 18, 2022); *Hermès International v Rothschild*, Case 1:22-cv-00384-JSR (Opinion and Order) (SDNY, June 23, 2023).

78 *Nike, Inc v StockX LLC*, Case 1:22-CV-00983 (SDNY, complaint filed February 3, 2022).

79 LVMH, *2020 Social and Environmental Sustainability Report* (2021).

80 The Fashion Law, 'MSCHF Drops the "Most Exclusive Sandals Ever Made", They're Called Birkinstocks', *The Fashion Law* (February 8, 2021) <https://www.thefashionlaw.com/mschf-drops-the-most-exclusive-sandals-ever-made-theyre-called-birkinstocks/>.

81 The Fashion Law, 'Chanel Is Suing an Accessories Company over Jewelry Made from Authentic Logo-Bearing Buttons', *The Fashion Law* (February 15, 2021) <https://www.thefashionlaw.com/chanel-is-suing-shriver-duke-over-jewelry-made-from-authentic-logo-bearing-buttons/>. See also *Chanel, Inc v Shiver and Duke, LLC, et al, 1:21-cv-01277* (SDNY, complaint filed February 12, 2021).

exception of *Hamilton International Ltd v Vortic LLC*,[82] where the US Second Circuit Court of Appeals found that defendant Vortic LLC did not run afoul of trademark law by selling restored and modified watches consisting of original Hamilton parts and bearing Hamilton's branding (as Vortic's use of the Hamilton trademark is not likely to confuse consumers), most of the upcycling cases have not provided much guidance by way of substantive decisions from the courts.[83]

Fashion brands like Louis Vuitton and Chanel have actively pursued litigation against resellers such as The RealReal and What Goes Around Comes Around, but success has been limited especially where the goods are genuine and had not been altered.[84] On February 2, 2021, Louis Vuitton sued upcycler Sandra Ling Designs, Inc for selling apparel and accessories made from 'material obtained from purportedly authentic pre-owned, disassembled, and deconstructed Louis Vuitton items' and 'purportedly authentic pre-owned Louis Vuitton items that have been fundamentally altered by the addition of decorations such as tassels, stones, or beading' – all of which continue to bear Louis Vuitton's trademarks.[85] Sandra Ling Designs counterclaimed and sought a declaration from the court that its sales of the 'upcycled' goods amounts to 'fair use of LV's trademarks, and does not constitute an infringement of LV's trademarks', arguing that Louis Vuitton, 'through misrepresentation and improper use of its trademarks, sought to prevent [SLD] from making and selling upcycled goods comprising material salvaged from used and discarded but genuine and authentic LV products'. Unfortunately, the dispute was settled in October 2022.[86] MAD Paris, however, has established itself as the upcycler par excellence, customising highly covetable

[82] *Hamilton International Ltd v Vortic LLC*, 13 F 4th 264 (2d Cir. 2021).

[83] The Fashion Law, 'Louis Vuitton, Sandra Ling Wind Down Trademark Suit Amid Rise in Upcycling Cases', *The Fashion Law* (November 7, 2022) <https://www.thefashionlaw.com/louis-vuitton-sandra-ling-settle-trademark-suit-amid-rise-in-upcycling-cases/>.

[84] Jordan Phelan, 'Infringement or Identification? Nominative Fair Use and the Resale of Luxury Goods' (2022) 97 *Fordham Law Review* 757.

[85] *Louis Vuitton Malletier, SAS, v Sandra Ling Designs, Inc, et al, Case 4:21-cv-00352* (SD Tex, February 2, 2021).

[86] The Fashion Law, 'Louis Vuitton, Sandra Ling Wind Down Trademark Suit amid Rise in Upcycling Cases', *The Fashion Law* (November 7, 2022) <https://www.thefashionlaw.com/louis-vuitton-sandra-ling-settle-trademark-suit-amid-rise-in-upcycling-cases/>. See also The Fashion Law, 'Chanel Settles Upcycling Suit over Jewelry Made from Logo-Bearing Buttons', *The Fashion Law* (November 18, 2022) <https://www.thefashionlaw.com/chanel-settles-upcycling-suit-over-jewelry-made-from-logo-bearing-buttons/>; The Fashion Law, 'Rolex, La Californienne Get Court's Approval on Settlement Over "Counterfeit" Modified Watches', *The Fashion Law* (June 1, 2020) <https://www

iconic luxury watches such as the Rolex Daytona and Audemars Piguet Royal Oak, affixing its own logo on the dial of the watches alongside the original logos and selling them at a premium over the original watches. For instance, MAD's black matte finish version of the Rolex Datejust 41 was going for US$34,500 while a regular Rolex model in yellow gold and steel with diamond hour markers was selling for a significantly lower US$14,450.[87] MAD Paris displays the following disclaimer prominently on its website: 'Watches displayed are second hand watches, personalised upon order, independently and with great care by craftsmen. Unless stated, MAD is not official distributor nor partners from those watches brands. Original warranties are not valid anymore, only is the one MAD offers.'[88] Nonetheless, in 2024, Chanel won its trademark infringement lawsuit in New York against a luxury online reseller What Goes Around Comes Around (WGACA) with a unanimous jury ruling in favour of Chanel and awarding $4 million in statutory damages; in February 2025, Chanel succeeded in securing a permanent injunction that restrains WGACA's use of its marks. Similarly, in 2024, Rolex succeeded in the US Fifth Circuit Court of Appeals, in obtaining an injunction against BeckerTime for using non-genuine bezels and non-genuine dials on Rolex-branded watches.[89]

While these upcycling cases do not implicate freedom of expression concerns, MSCHF, the Brooklyn collective known as 'the Banksys of consumer culture'[90] that launched the controversial Satan Shoes (where MSCHF injected the soles of 666 pairs of Nike shoes with red ink and a single drop of human blood)[91] and Birkinstocks (Birkenstock-like footwear with an official Birkenstock cork-and-rubber sole but with a leather

.thefashionlaw.com/rolex-la-californienne-get-courts-approval-on-settlement-over-counterfeit-modified-watches/>.

87 Alex Rose, 'MAD Paris & Rolex Is a Match Made in Custom Heaven', *Highsnobiety* (August 2022) <https://www.highsnobiety.com/p/mad-paris-rolex/>; Martin Lerma, 'MAD Paris Reimagined the Rolex Datejust with a Matte Black Finish', *Robb Report* (August 8, 2020) <https://robbreport.com/style/watch-collector/mad-paris-rolex-datejust-black-blue-palette-2942001/>.

88 MAD Paris <https://www.mad-paris.com/>.

89 *Rolex Watch USA, Inc v BeckerTime LLC*, 96 F 4th 715 (5th Cir. 2024).

90 Vanessa Friedman, '$76,000 Birkinstocks Made from Actual Birkin Bags?', *The New York Times* (February 8, 2021) <https://www.nytimes.com/2021/02/08/style/MSCHF-birkenstocks-birkin-bags-hermes.html> (hereafter Friedman, 'Birkinstocks').

91 *Nike, Inc v MSCHF Product Studio, Inc*, Case 1:21-cv-01679 (EDNY, March 29, 2021). See also The Fashion Law, 'Nike, MSCHF Settle 2-Week-Old Lawsuit Over Allegedly Infringing "Satan Shoes"', *The Fashion Law* (April 8, 2021) <https://www.thefashionlaw.com/nike-mschf-settle-2-week-old-lawsuit-over-allegedly-infringing-satan-shoes/>.

upper made from purposefully chopped-up Hermès Birkin bags)[92] may just be able to avail itself of a free speech defence. Daniel Greenberg, a founding team member at MSCHF, said that the MSCHF team bought four Hermes Birkin bags on resale sites for a total of US$122,500 and then disassembled the purses to use them as the material for the slip-on shoes.[93] Regrettably, the Nike lawsuit has been settled whilst the Birkinstocks are sold out without nary a squeak from either Hermes or Birkenstock.

Moving ahead, one would have to distinguish between potentially permissible expressive artistic upcycling (such as MSCHF's *Birkinstocks*) and perhaps impermissible commercial recycling (Shiver + Duke's costume jewellery using buttons bearing the Chanel CC mark). Such uses present new issues in trademark law regarding trademark exhaustion, infringement and dilution, which Martin Senftleben will discuss in depth in Chapter 8, and therefore will not be addressed further in this chapter.

1.3 Fashion, Post-postmodernism and IP Law

1.3.1 Post-postmodern Theories Can Provide an Analytical Framework

Writings that approach contemporary culture as representing a postmodern period are generally based on the notion that major changes in social practices, artistic expressions and economic developments have transformed the values, ideals and behaviours associated with the historical period identified with modernism. Postmodernity represents the period where social structures and grand ideologies have lost their authority, 'giving rise to the expression of individual desires, self-fulfilment and self-esteem'.[94] More recent writings of an emerging and new cultural paradigm – the post-postmodern condition – can be grouped into five main categories: altermodernism, perfomatism, automodernity, digimodernism and hypermodernity.[95] While fashion is

[92] Birkinstock <https://birkinstock.shoes/>. See also Friedman, 'Birkinstocks', above n 85.

[93] Celia Fernandez, 'A Company Is Selling Birkenstock-inspired Sandals Made from Birkin Bags for up to $76,000', *Insider* (February 11, 2021) <https://www.insider.com/birkinstock-shoes-birkenstock-hermes-birkin-bag-sandals-reactions-2021-2>.

[94] Sébastien Charles, 'Paradoxical Individualism: An Introduction to the Thought of Gilles Lipovetsky' in Gilles Lipovetsky (ed), *Hypermodern Times* (Polity, 2005) 8–9.

[95] See Morgado, 'Fashion Phenomena', above n 4, 9–11. Morgado contends that the term 'post-postmodernism' is one of at least a dozen labels that address a new cultural milieu but adopts culture scholar Alan Kirby's taxonomy of the five as 'the foremost theories of

rarely addressed in these key works on post-postmodernism, Marcia Morgado has usefully extrapolated from these writings to suggest how contemporary fashion phenomena might be interpreted as expressing the post-postmodern characteristics identified in each theoretical framework.[96] However, Morgado's examples do not include developments in the last couple of years such as NFTs and the metaverse, and this chapter will supplement these omissions.

Altermodernism is the name French curator and art critic Nicolas Bourriaud coined in describing artistic expression that resists the pressure of globalisation, commodification and standardisation and instead seeks to engage in spontaneous heterogeneous invention, productive compromise and collaboration among disparate factions.[97] In the context of contemporary fashion, two trends are exemplars of altermodernism. First, the commitment to sustainability and environmentally sensitive practices and, in particular, the reuse and recycling of fashion apparel. In his earlier work, *Relational Aesthetics*, which influenced his articulation of altermodernism, Bourriaud writes about how relational art invites the audience to participate in the creative process and to co-create meaning. Upcycling can be viewed as paradigmatic of altermodernism, especially where artistic craftsmanship is involved, such as when an individual repurposes a luxury brand product (eg, cuts up an old Louis Vuitton monogram bag or a vintage printed Versace dress) and combines it with new material. Second, the mass customisation practices in the fashion industry, where shoppers may participate in the design of personal items by selecting from a predetermined set of style elements and colours (eg, shoe colours at New Balance, T-shirts at Uniqlo or tote bags at Longchamp), cohere with Bourriaud's thesis that relational artworks come about as shared activities, rather than result from an individual's, artist's or brand's effort.[98]

Performatism, according to Raoul Eshelman, functions by artificially framing readers or viewers in such a way that they have no choice but to accept the external givens of a work and identify with the characters within it; its aesthetic elements include theistic plotlines and manipulated

the post-postmodern'. See Alan Kirby, 'Successor States to an Empire in Free Fall', *Times Higher Education* (May 27, 2020) <https://www.timeshighereducation.com/features/successor-states-to-an-empire-in-free-fall/411731.article>.

96 Morgado, 'Fashion Phenomena', above n 4.

97 Nicolas Bourriaud, *The Radicant* (trans James Gussen and Lili Porten) (MIT Press, 2009); Nicolas Bourriaud, *Relational Aesthetics* (trans Simon Pleasance and Fronza Woods) (Les Presses du réel, 2002). See also Morgado, 'Fashion Phenomena', above n 4, 12–15.

98 Morgado, 'Fashion Phenomena', above n 4, 15.

interpretations.[99] It is often used to study representations in film and art, which includes the blurring of distinctions between art and fashion, and the erasure of cultural categories such as gender and sexual orientation. However, in relation to the fashion phenomena, one can use Eshelman's analytic frame to study how brands make use of performative works that revolve around the narrative theme of perfecting the self. Paula von Wachenfeldt postulates 'performative luxury' to be a ritual exercise of the wealthy. Examining the mediation of luxury brands and the high-flying lifestyles of the Rich Kids of Instagram (#rkoi), von Wachenfeldt claims that when prominent brands are displayed as part of the user's digital storytelling, 'that the represented world of luxurious living on Instagram and in the subsequent TV show distorts the expected or lived experience of luxury as something distinctive and unique, and turns it into a kitsch object'.[100] Morgado refers to the short film, *Electric Holiday*, that was a 2012 Christmas collaboration between Barneys New York and the Walt Disney Company in which Disney cartoon characters were reimagined as glamorous fashion models (such as Minnie Mouse wearing Lanvin) and high-profile fashion industry celebrities were depicted as cartoon characters.[101] For Paris Fashion Week in the fall of 2021, luxury fashion house Balenciaga helmed by Demna Gvasalia unveiled a Simpsons video with the cartoon characters modelling clothes by the fashion brand for its Spring–Summer 2022 collection.[102] By tapping into the semiotic connotations of the Simpsons, which consumers around the world would be familiar with, Gvasalia played with irony and humour to advance the Balenciaga brand narrative that he had reinvented since taking over the reins at the venerable fashion house.

Automodernity, according to Robert Samuels, is seen to be the result of an unexpected collusion of two opposing social forces of digital technology and human autonomy.[103] In 2008, Samuels argued that the

[99] Raoul Eshelman, *Performatism, or End of Postmodernism* (The Davies Group, 2008); Morgado, 'Fashion Phenomena', above n 4, 18–19.

[100] Paula von Wachenfeldt, 'The Mediation of Luxury Brands in Digital Storytelling' (2019) 25 *Fashion Theory* 99, 103.

[101] Morgado, 'Fashion Phenomena', above n 4, 20; Adam Tschorn, 'Barneys New York Plugs into Disney for "Electric Holiday"', *Los Angeles Times* (August 29, 2012) <https://www.latimes.com/fashion/la-xpm-2012-aug-29-la-ar-barneys-disney-20120829-story.html>.

[102] Alice Newbold, 'The Simpsons Make A PFW Cameo For Balenciaga', *Vogue UK* (October 2, 2021) <https://www.vogue.co.uk/news/article/the-simpsons-balenciaga>.

[103] Robert Samuels, 'Auto-Modernity after Postmodernism: Autonomy and Automation in Culture, Technology and Education' in Tara McPherson (ed), *Digital Youth, Innovation, and the Unexpected* (n.p., 2008) 219, 228.

interaction between digital youth, digital technologies and contemporary media has resulted in a radical restructuring of these forces, where youths in particular are experiencing technological automation as a vehicle of empowerment through which they express their independence. Today, his thesis rings with greater resonance as many individuals and consumers around the world are becoming comfortable with different aspects of the emerging metaverse and the minting and selling of NFTs. In the world of fashion, one is witnessing examples of automodernity in textiles, garments and accessories that integrate contemporary technology with wearable items (eg, smartwatches, fabrics printed with photochromic ink, yoga pants with built-in sensors to correct the users' posture by vibrating as they move through yoga poses) or fashion designs that have a futuristic appearance.

Digimodernism is a term used by Alan Kirby to signal the exhaustion of postmodernism and its gradual replacement with new cultural and artistic forms predicated on the widespread adoption of digital technologies.[104] He approaches the impact of technology on society and culture differently from Samuels, viewing digimodernism to have the traits of evanescence, haphazardness, fluidity, boundlessness and multiple authorship. In particular, he thought social media platforms such as Facebook and Twitter, and other web-based platforms like Wikipedia and video games, or those that enable user-generated content such as blogs, to be highly facilitative of the democratisation of authorship. The proliferation of social media influencers and bloggers in the fashion world today is a testament to the post-postmodern expressions of digimodernism. Axel Bruns sees a paradigm shift in the nature of production in the digital age, coining the term 'produser', arguing that

> within the communities which engage in the collaborative creation and extension of information and knowledge ... the role of 'consumer' and even that of 'end user' have long disappeared, and the distinctions between producers and users of content have faded into comparative insignificance.[105]

[104] Alan Kirby, *Digimodernism: How New Technologies Dismantle the Postmodern and Reconfigure Our Culture* (Continuum, 2009); Morgado, 'Fashion Phenomena', above n 4, 26–29.

[105] Axel Bruns, *Blogs, Wikipedia, Second Life, and Beyond: From Production to Produsage* (Peter Lang, 2008) 2. See also David Tan, 'De(Re)Constructing Narratives in Intellectual Property Law: Transformative Play, Culture Jamming, and Poststructural Disruptions' (2020) 32 *Law & Literature* 75, 86.

Using Alternate Reality Games as an illustration, Booth concludes that fans' treatment of copyrighted works on new media 'transgress the line between production and consumption, and more importantly, alter our interpretation of that boundary'.[106] Kirby's observations over a decade ago may be extrapolated to the 2020s where consumers are increasingly au fait with myriad activities in the so-called metaverse – where they may purchase Balenciaga hoodies in the game Fortnite or explore the Gucci Garden Space on Roblox – or purchase NFTs featuring Burberry Blankos Block Party characters. Kirby's description of multiple authorship in digimodernism can also be seen in the 'novel collaborations across previously antithetical industry sectors – between upscale designer brands and downmarket retailers and between upscale and downmarket retailers'.[107] However, this fashion phenomena is viewed differently through the lens of hypermodernity.

Hypermodernity may be a more familiar term. In *Hypermodern Times*, Gilles Lipovetsky argues that commercial practices and the media have generated a post-postmodern 'mania for consumption' and the key features of a hypermodern culture are 'galloping commercialization' and the excessiveness of everything.[108] In a society of hyperconsumption, there is an erosion of the old institutions of class and 'the appearance of a volatile, fragmentary and deregulated consumer'.[109] Lipovetsky in his earlier work, *The Empire of Fashion*, has commented that fashion has come to be the defining feature of contemporary social life, where its qualities – such as superficiality, artificiality, transience and frivolity – have become organising principles of modern collective life.[110] He notes that fashion 'is no longer an aesthetic embellishment, a decorative accessory to collective life; it is the key to the entire edifice'.[111] Hypermodernity as a post-postmodern condition is perhaps the most relevant theory to the interdisciplinary study of fashion and intellectual property rights. The excessive consumption of fashion-related items speaks to the hedonistic impulse that Lipovetsky considers to be endemic of the contemporary ethos, and

[106] Bruns, ibid at 180.
[107] Morgado, 'Fashion Phenomena', above n 4, 29.
[108] Gilles Lipovetsky, *Hypermodern Times* (Polity, 2005) 31–37.
[109] Ibid at 83.
[110] Gilles Lipovetsky, *The Empire of Fashion: Dressing Modern Democracy* (trans Catherine Porter) (Princeton University Press, 1994) 6.
[111] Ibid.

fashion has also facilitated the bourgeois market economy and consumption of ephemera, thereby bringing about the advancement of individual autonomy.[112] According to Morgado, excess, overabundance, frivolity and irrationality characterise the plethora of available products and much of the consumption behaviour in the marketplace, including apparel and accessories for animal pets.[113] The allure of Veblen brands in the hypermodern consumption of fashion is particularly prominent in how high fashion luxury brands have entered into multi-collaborations with so-called high street retailers and even household appliances (eg, Balmain x H&M, Versace x H&M, Dolce & Gabbana x Smeg), engaged in creative partnerships with one another (eg, Gucci x Balenciaga 'The Hacker Project', Fendi x Versace 'Fendace') and the perplexing *shanzhai* phenomenon in China (with deliberate misspellings of well-known fashion brands such as 'CUCCI' and 'BANEBERRY').[114]

The constraints of this chapter unfortunately do not permit a lengthier evaluation of the five theories. However, it suffices to say that each theory offers an important perspective on contemporary trends in fashion, and the most relevant for IP laws being performativity in luxury brand narratives, multiple authorship, hyperconsumption and the rapid advancement of technologies in relation to the metaverse and NFTs. But these theoretical frameworks do not take us far enough in terms of informing IP doctrine and judicial decision-making. Because fashion is symbolic in so many ways, semiotics – the study of signs – as a methodological tool in an interdisciplinary endeavour will prove useful to courts in understanding these fashion phenomena and ensuring that IP laws strike the appropriate balance between protecting the rights owners and ensuring that other consumers, artists and entrepreneurs have the adequate breathing space to thrive.

[112] Eun Jung Kang, 'Fashion, Subjectivity and Time: From Deleuze's Transcendental Empiricism to Lipovetsky's Hypermodernity' in Jose Blanco F and Andrew Reilly (eds), *Fashion, Dress and Post-Postmodernism* (Bloomsbury, 2021) 39, 44.

[113] Morgado, 'Fashion Phenomena', above n 4, 16–17.

[114] See, eg, Lawrence Page, 'Goodbye, Shanzhai: Intellectual Property Rights and the End of Copycat China' (2019) 45 *University of Western Australia Law Review* 185; Barton Beebe, 'Shanzhai, Sumptuary Law, and Intellectual Property in Law in Contemporary China' (2014) 47 *UC Davis Law Review* 849; Haochen Sun, 'Can Louis Vuitton Dance with HiPhone? Rethinking the Idea of Social Justice in Intellectual Property Law' (2012) 15 *University of Pennsylvania Journal of Law and Social Change* 389. For an analysis of *shanzhai* in this book, see Chapter 9.

1.3.2 Semiotics as a Methodological Tool

Semiotics is fundamentally the study of signs.[115] Semiotics seeks to understand the operation of a given system or process by observing the function of signification, expression, representation and communication.[116] Umberto Eco describes semiotics as a social science discipline that studies 'everything that can be taken as a sign'.[117] A sign is simply a thing that stands for something else. Although it has its origins in the study of language, semiotic analysis is a trans-linguistic activity[118] that can be applied to the inquiry of '[a system] of structural codes ... that engages with culture, consumption, and communication in the marketplace'.[119] A trademark is as symbolic as it is functional: it does much more than designate source or origin of goods. Judicial and scholarly treatments of trademark law are increasingly making reference to the semiotic nature of trademarks. In particular, the application of semiotics to assist the development of IP laws relating to logos, images and literary works has received significant scholarly attention.[120] In his critique of consumption, Jean Baudrillard contends that the consumer 'no longer relates to a particular object in its specific utility, but to a set of objects in its total signification'.[121] Thus, increasingly, when consumers buy goods, they buy into the significations of these commodities in the construction of their self-identities. For example, Barton Beebe, in his seminal works on a semiotic account of trademark doctrine,[122] has persuasively demonstrated that 'semiotic concepts can be applied to clarify and ameliorate

[115] Eg, John Deely, *Introducing Semiotic: Its History and Doctrine* (ed Thomas A Sebeok) (Indiana University Press, 1982) 133; see also Eg, Ferdinand de Saussure, *Course in General Linguistics* (trans Wade Baskin) (Columbia University Press, [1959] 2011) 113–114.

[116] Michael Pulos, 'A Semiotic Solution to the Propertization Problem of Trademark' (2006) 53 *UCLA Law Review* 833, 844.

[117] Umberto Eco, *The Theory of Semiotics* (Indiana University Press, 1979) 7.

[118] Roland Barthes, *Elements of Semiology* (trans Annette Lavers and Colin Smith) (Hill and Wang, [1964] 2000) 11.

[119] Laura R Oswald, *Marketing Semiotics: Signs, Strategies, and Brand Values* (Oxford University Press, 2012) 47.

[120] Eg, David Tan, 'Intellectual Property and Semiotics: The Signs of the Times' in Irene Calboli and Maria Lillà Montagnani (eds), *Handbook on Intellectual Property Law Research: Lenses, Methods, and Approaches* (Oxford University Press, 2020) 372.

[121] Jean Baudrillard, *The Consumer Society: Myths and Structures* (trans Chris Turner) (Polity, [1970] 1998) [trans of: *La Société de Consummation*] 27.

[122] See, eg, Barton Beebe, 'The Semiotic Account of Trademark Doctrine and Trademark Culture', in Graeme B Dinwoodie and Mark D Janis (eds), *Trademark Law and Theory: A Handbook of Contemporary Research* (Edward Elgar, 2008) 42 (hereafter Beebe,

fundamental areas of trademark doctrine and policy'.[123] I have also investigated the influence of semiotics on the laws relating to works of copyright,[124] famous marks[125] and the commercial appropriation of the celebrity personality in the right of publicity.[126] In her analysis of semiotic disobedience, Sonia Katyal explains that a reader might choose to adopt the preferred reading of a particular 'text' but also might 'resist and modify the code to reflect his or her "own positions, experiences, and interests"'.[127] While some antibranding projects adopt an oppositional framework to a certain brand, the more complex commentaries such as Gvasalia's, however, adopt Stuart Hall's tactic of negotiation, perhaps 'seeking to both decode and recode particular images in ways that subtly reveal the need for consumers to actively 'talk back' to the hidden codes'.[128] However, with Demna Gvasalia's departure from Vetements in September 2019,[129] it remains to be seen if Vetements will continue to exert its disproportionate influence in the fashion world, but it seems certain that Gvasalia's individual stardom – especially with his continuation of the Vetements aesthetic at the couture house of Balenciaga in Paris – will be a force to be reckoned with.

It has been said that famous marks or well-known brands like Louis Vuitton, Apple and Nike are *alpha brands* that carry significant 'semiotic freight', and they possess particular configurations of meanings and can 'offer peculiarly powerful affirmations of belonging, recognition, and

'Semiotic Account'); Barton Beebe, 'The Semiotic Analysis of Trademark Law' (2004) 51 *UCLA Law Review* 621 (hereafter Beebe, 'Semiotic Analysis').

123 Beebe, 'Semiotic Account', ibid, 42.

124 David Tan, 'The Lost Language of the First Amendment in Copyright Fair Use: A Semiotic Perspective of the "Transformative Use" Doctrine Twenty-Five Years On' (2016) 26 *Fordham Intellectual Property, Media & Entertainment Law Journal* 311 (hereafter Tan, 'The Lost Language').

125 David Tan, 'The Semiotics of Alpha Brands: Encoding/Decoding/Recoding/Transcoding of Louis Vuitton and Implications for Trademark Laws' (2013) 32 *Cardozo Arts & Entertainment Law Journal* 221 (hereafter Tan, 'Semiotics of Alpha Brands').

126 Eg, David Tan, *The Commercial Appropriation of Fame: A Cultural Analysis of the Right of Publicity and Passing Off* (Cambridge University Press, 2007); David Tan, 'Political Recoding of the Contemporary Celebrity and the First Amendment' (2011) 2 *Harvard Journal of Sports & Entertainment Law* 1.

127 Sonia Katyal, 'Stealth Marketing and Antibranding: The Love That Dare Not Speak Its Name' (2010) 58 *Buffalo Law Review* 796, 806.

128 Ibid.

129 Miles Socha, 'Exclusive: Demna Gvasalia Exits Vetements', WWD (September 16, 2019) <https://wwd.com/fashion-news/designer-luxury/demna-gvasalia-exits-vetements-exclusive-1203283590/>.

meaning in the midst of the lives of their [consumers]'.[130] For famous fashion marks, the brand signifier/signified relationship would have become universally codified for the consuming public; these consumers will automatically and consistently think of the coded brand meanings and values (the signified) when they are exposed to the signifiers such as the logo. Thus, the brand logo or trademark becomes a sign for a predetermined set of cultural codes and consumer experiences associated with the brand. When Gucci introduces the subverted sign 'GUCCY' alongside the ubiquitous well-loved 'GUCCI' or when it juxtaposes the 'GG' logo with 'BALENCIAGA' in The Hacker Project collection, it is drawing on the consuming public's familiarity with the affective encoded meanings associated with Gucci and advancing a new cultural narrative that resonates better with the millennial generation evident by the increased sales. The signs are also protected by copyright law – for example, the Hermes logo, which comprises a Duc carriage attached to a horse, is also an artistic work. Like trademarks, these copyrighted works function in a similar manner as semiotic signs with connotative values,[131] and unauthorized uses are likely to be subject to a fair use analysis that evaluates the extent to which the new work 'adds something new, with a further purpose or different character, altering the first with new expression, meaning, or message'.[132]

The US Supreme Court in the twin decisions of *Matal v Tam*[133] and *Iancu v Brunetti*[134] emphatically recognised that trademarks 'have an expressive component in addition to a commercial one'.[135] In *Matal v*

[130] Tan, 'Semiotics of Alpha Brands', above n 121, 224.

[131] This semiotic aspect of copyrighted works has been discussed at length in a number of my writings and will not be revisited here. See David Tan, 'Intellectual Property and Semiotics: The Signs of the Times' in Irene Calboli and Maria Lillà Montagnani (eds), *Handbook on Intellectual Property Research: Lenses, Methods, and Approaches* (Oxford University Press, 2020) 372; David Tan, 'Semiotics and the Spectacle of Transformation in Copyright Law' (2017) 30(4) *International Journal for the Semiotics of Law* 593; David Tan, 'Taking the Mickey out of Disney: A Cultural Approach to the Transformative Use Doctrine in Copyright Law' in Rochelle Cooper Dreyfuss and Elizabeth Ng Siew Kuan (eds), *Framing Intellectual Property Law in the 21st Century: Integrating Incentives, Trade, Development, Culture and Human Rights* (Cambridge University Press, 2018) 171; Tan, 'The Lost Language', above n 120.

[132] *Campbell v Acuff-Rose Music Inc*, 510 US 569, 579 (1994); *Google LLC v Oracle America, Inc*, 141 S Ct 1183, 1202 (2021).

[133] *Matal v Tam*, 137 S Ct 1744 (2017) (*Matal*).

[134] *Iancu v Brunetti*, 139 S Ct 2294 (2019) (*Iancu*).

[135] *Iancu*, 139 S Ct 2294, 2305 (2019).

Tam, in a separate judgment by Justice Kennedy, with whom Justices Ginsburg, Sotomayor and Kagan joined, it was noted that

> In the realm of trademarks, the metaphorical marketplace of ideas becomes a tangible, powerful reality .... These marks make up the expression of everyday life, as with the names of entertainment groups, broadcast networks, *designer clothing*, newspapers, automobiles, candy bars, toys, and so on.[136]

This view of the *expressive* cultural symbolism of trademarks was affirmed in *Iancu v Brunetti* where a majority of the Supreme Court in 2019 found that the Lanham Act's prohibitions on registration – one applying to marks that consist of or comprise immoral or scandalous matter[137] – was viewpoint-based and hence unconstitutional.[138]

Although *Iancu* was concerned with how the public may use the communicative function of trademarks to convey ideas and *Matal* dealt with how the government may not censor speech by denying registration of particular categories of marks, what is important here is the unequivocal declaration by the US Supreme Court that trademarks can have an *expressive purpose* that triggers First Amendment protection, in addition to their traditional source-designating function. In 2023, despite declining to apply the *Rogers* artistic relevance test in *Jack Daniel's Properties Inc v VIP Products LLC*, the Supreme Court nonetheless acknowledged that trademarks may be used 'not to designate a work's source, but solely to perform some other expressive function'.[139] Even the public act of

[136] *Matal*, 137 S Ct 1744, 1768 (2017) (emphasis added). The First Circuit has also pointed out that 'famous trademarks offer a particularly powerful means of conjuring up the image of their owners, and thus become an important, perhaps at times indispensable, part of the public vocabulary. Rules restricting the use of well-known trademarks may therefore restrict the communication of ideas'. *LL Bean, Inc v Drake Publishers, Inc*, 811 F 2d 26, 30 (1st Cir. 1987) (*LL Bean*).

[137] Lanham Act 1946, 15 USC §1052(a) (US).

[138] *Iancu*, 139 S Ct 2294, 2299 (2019). Justice Sotomayor's disagreement was not based on whether trademarks also have a symbolic expressive function, but rather that 'prohibiting the registration of obscene, profane, or vulgar marks qualifies as reasonable, viewpoint-neutral, content-based regulation' and that 'scandalous' in §1052(a) 'can reasonably be read to bar the registration of only those marks that are obscene, vulgar, or profane'. Ibid, at 2317-8. This decision has attracted some criticism within and outside the US for its 'absolutist view of the First Amendment'. Rochelle Cooper Dreyfuss and Susy Frankel, 'Trade Marks and Cultural Identity' in Graeme W Austin, Andrew F Christie, Andrew T Kenyon and Megan Richardson (eds), *Across Intellectual Property: Essays in Honour of Sam Ricketson* (Cambridge University Press, 2020) 227, 237.

[139] *Jack Daniel's Properties Inc v VIP Products LLC*, 143 S Ct 1578, 599 US ___ (2023) (Slip Opinion, June 8, 2023) 11.

'consuming' a brand can in itself be a form of commentary on or critique of the coded social meanings in that brand thus rendering it an 'expressive' act.

For copyright-protected works, they may be imbibed with similar semiotic connotations. In his oft-cited work on the semiotic analyses of consumer cultures, *Mythologies*, Roland Barthes explains that 'any semiology postulates a relation between two terms, a signifier and a signified'[140] and that a sign 'is the associative total of the first two terms'.[141] A well-known literary or artistic work does much more than simply educate, inform or entertain, it also functions as a *signifier* of a set of *signified* meanings. The representative fictional characters from these works may function as signifiers of both individualised and a shared set of meanings. A 'myth' is thereby created when meaning within a semiological system is transformed into form as represented by a sign;[142] each sign becomes naturally associated with a set of meanings or 'historical intention',[143] which is ultimately consumed. Like famous trademarks, the copyrighted character signifier/signified relationship would have become universally codified for the audience; the audience will automatically and consistently think of the coded meanings and values (the signified) when they are exposed to the character signifiers. In other words, the fictional character becomes a sign for a predetermined set of cultural codes and audience experiences associated with the work or the author of the work.[144] Referring to Barthes' work on modern myths, Stuart Hall has discussed the politics of signification[145] and how ideological discourses of a particular society are classified and framed through semiotic signs.[146] As Barthesian myths, cartoon characters such as Mickey Mouse, Snow White and Sleeping Beauty, well-known superhero characters such as

[140] Roland Barthes, *Mythologies* (trans Annette Lavers) (Jonathan Cape, [1957] 1972) 111.

[141] Ibid.

[142] Ibid, at 131.

[143] Ibid, at 142.

[144] See generally David Tan, 'The Semiotics of Alpha Brands: Encoding/Decoding/Recoding/Transcoding of Louis Vuitton and Implications for Trademark Laws' (2013) 32 *Cardozo Arts & Entertainment Law Journal* 221, 227.

[145] Stuart Hall, 'The Rediscovery of "Ideology": Return of the Repressed in Media Studies' in Michael Gurevitch, Tony Bennett, James Curran and Janet Woollacott (eds), *Culture, Society and the Media* (Methuen, 1982) 56, 70–74.

[146] Ibid, at 74. See also David Tan, 'Harry Potter and the Transformation Wand: Fair Use, Canonicity and Fan Activity' in Dan Hunter, Ramon Lobato, Megan Richardson and Julian Thomas (eds), *Amateur Media: Social, Cultural and Legal Perspectives* (Routledge, 2012) 94.

Superman, Captain America and Wonder Woman, as well as fictional characters from popular television series like Star Trek, can contain subject positions and models for identification that are heavily coded ideologically.[147] Therefore, when Barneys New York featured Disney cartoon characters in its 2012 *Electric Holiday* film, and when Balenciaga tapped into the cultural connotations of The Simpsons for its Spring–Summer 2022 collection, the fashion brands were drawing on the public's familiarity with these signs in order to advance their brand narratives.[148]

1.4 Intellectual Property Rights Enforcement – Some Challenges Ahead

Due to the constraints of this short chapter, I shall only be able to highlight how the enforcement of copyright and trademark rights by fashion brands are likely to clash with the freedom of speech/expression in a post-postmodern context.

1.4.1 Copyright

Parodies abound in the world of fashion. We all love a good laugh. But we often loathe others having a laugh at our expense. Parody enjoys an exalted protected status in intellectual property jurisprudence, and courts generally are concerned that the enforcement of intellectual property rights does not have a chilling effect on free speech.[149] Besides parody, other forms of expression, ranging from political speech to pastiche, invariably receive varying degrees of protection under constitutional freedom of speech or freedom of expression guarantees in different jurisdictions around the world. In countries that do not have an open-ended fair use provision, the fluidity of 'parody' to morph into 'satire', 'caricature', 'pastiche' or other related genres may result in an infringing

[147] See generally David Tan, 'The Transformative Potential of Countercultural Recoding in Copyright Law: A Study of Superheroes and Fair Use' in Irene Calboli and Srividhya Ragavan (eds), *Diversity in Intellectual Property: Identities, Interests and Intersections* (Cambridge University Press, 2015) 403.

[148] See also David Tan, 'De(Re)constructing Narratives in Intellectual Property Law: Transformative Play, Culture Jamming, and Poststructural Disruptions' (2020) 32 *Law and Literature* 75.

[149] Eg, *Campbell v Acuff-Rose Music Inc*, 510 US 569 (1994); *Deckmyn v Vandersteen*, Case C-201/13, ECLI:EU:C:2014:2132 (CJEU, September 3, 2014).

work losing its requisite sting to enable it to fall within the protection of the categorical fair dealing exception of criticism or review of the original work.[150] The various copyright law reform reports from Australia,[151] the UK[152] and Hong Kong[153] over the last decade have all either advocated the enactment of an open-ended fair use provision like in the US or a categorical fair dealing exception broad enough to cover parody and its related genres of humour.

In the US, the Supreme Court has commented of the impact of the First Amendment on copyright law, pronouncing that 'copyright law contains built-in First Amendment accommodations' found in the idea-expression dichotomy and fair use doctrines that had been codified.[154] Justice Ginsburg, delivering the opinion of the Court in *Golan v Holder*, emphasised the 'speech-protective purposes and safeguards embraced by copyright law'[155] and assured that the public may freely use the author's expression 'in certain circumstances'.[156] In the EU, the CJEU has declared parody to be an autonomous concept in European law and should be interpreted uniformly throughout the European Union.[157] In the UK, section 30A(1) to the Copyright, Designs and Patents Act 1988 states: 'Fair dealing with a work for the purposes of caricature, parody or pastiche does not infringe copyright in the work.'[158] In 2022, Hong Kong finally inserted a provision into its Copyright Ordinance that declared: 'Fair dealing with a work for the purpose of parody, satire, caricature or pastiche does not infringe any copyright in the work.'[159]

150 See Copyright, Designs and Patents Act 1988 s 30 (UK); Copyright Act 1968 (Cth), s 41 (Australia); Copyright Act (Cap 63), s 36 (Singapore); Copyright Ordinance (Cap 528), s 39(1) (Hong Kong).

151 Australian Law Reform Commission, *Copyright and the Digital Economy: Final Report*, ALRC Report 122 (2013).

152 Ian Hargreaves, *Digital Opportunity: A Review of Intellectual Property and Growth* (2011) (Hargreaves Report).

153 Legislative Council Panel on Commerce and Industry, *Treatment of Parody under the Copyright Regime* (2014).

154 *Eldred v Ashcroft*, 537 US 186, 219 (2003). See also *Golan v Holder*, 132 S Ct 873, 890 (2012) (*Golan*); *Harper & Row, Publishers, Inc v Nation Enterprises*, 471 US 539, 560 (1985).

155 *Golan*, 132 S Ct 873, 890 (2012) (internal citations omitted).

156 Ibid (citing *Eldred*, 537 US at 219).

157 *Deckmyn v Vandersteen*, Case C-201/13, ECLI:EU:C:2014:2132 (CJEU, September 3, 2014) at [15].

158 Copyright, Designs and Patents Act 1988, s 30A(1) (UK).

159 Copyright Ordinance (Cap 528), section 39A(1) (Hong Kong).

In many cultures, humour has traditionally been given significant leeway to say and do things that would otherwise not be permitted; parody, satire, caricature and pastiche (PSCP) depend on 'the perceived resolution of incongruities, employing non-seriousness and irony to convey complex meanings … and from the use of nonsense and illogic'.[160] The fashion trends highlighted in the earlier sections often display different degrees and combinations of PSCP evident from the hypermodern trends of logo hacking and *shanzhai* practices and the performatism involving myriad cartoon and comic characters.

A parody must invoke or copy a significant proportion of the original work or mark in order for the parody to be effective. While the critical message in a parody that comments directly on the original work or its author can be easily discerned, the ideas expressed in other forms of humorous works such as satire, caricature and pastiche may be more obtuse. In an oft-quoted passage, the US Supreme Court in *Campbell v Acuff-Rose Music* cryptically mused:

> Parody needs to mimic an original to make its point, and so has some claim to use the creation of its victim's (or collective victims') imagination, whereas satire can stand on its own two feet and so requires justification for the very act of borrowing.[161]

In the evaluation of the degree of transformativeness under the first factor of a fair use analysis, copyright law tends to make a clearer distinction between a parody (which targets the original work) and a satire (which uses the original work as a weapon to target something else). This is a complex fact-intensive inquiry, and by no means an easy feat to discern the requisite degree of transformation needed, as recent cases before the US Supreme Court and Circuit Courts of Appeals have demonstrated.[162]

It appears that the fair use doctrine was designed for maximum flexibility to allow for a case-by-case analysis for the judiciary and was

[160] Conal Condren, Jessica Milner Davis, Sally McCausland and Robert Phiddian, 'Defining Parody and Satire: Australian Copyright Law and Its New Exception: Part 2 – Advancing Ordinary Definitions' (2008) 13 *Media & Arts Law Review* 401, 404–405.

[161] *Campbell v Acuff-Rose Music, Inc*, 510 US 569, 580–581 (1994).

[162] Eg, *Andy Warhol Foundation for the Visual Arts, Inc v Goldsmith*, 598 US 508 (2023) (*Andy Warhol Foundation*); *Google LLC v Oracle America, Inc*, 141 S Ct 1183 (2021); *Dr Seuss Enterprises LP v ComicMix LLC*, 983 F 3d 443 (9th Cir. 2020); *Andy Warhol Foundation for the Visual Arts, Inc v Goldsmith*, 992 F 3d 99, 111 (2d Cir. 2021); *Authors Guild v Google, Inc*, 804 F 3d 202, 220 (2d Cir. 2015);

able to accommodate a kaleidoscope of scenarios from literary criticism to parodic entertainment, from contemporary art to uses on digital and technological platforms. In order to avail oneself of the fair use defence, the commentary on a fashion brand does not have to be direct and critical, can be commercial in nature, but should at least offer some 'new information, new aesthetics, new insights and understandings'[163] vis-à-vis the original work. Second Circuit courts have considered a broader examination of transformation that does not require the presence of comment so long as the purpose in using the original work is 'plainly different from the original purpose for which it was created'[164] and have 'given weight to an artist's own explanation of their creative rationale when conducting the fair use analysis'.[165] It should be noted that in the recent decision of *Andy Warhol Foundation for the Visual Arts Inc v Goldsmith*, the Second Circuit warned against a 'celebrity-plagiarist privilege' and clarified that 'it does not follow, however, that any secondary work that adds a new aesthetic or new expression to its source material is necessarily transformative'.[166] The decision was affirmed on appeal to the Supreme Court, where the majority commented that a use may be justified because copying is reasonably necessary to achieve the user's *new* purpose:

> An independent justification like this is particularly relevant to assessing fair use where an original work and copying use share the same or highly similar purposes, or where wide dissemination of a secondary work would otherwise run the risk of substitution for the original or licensed derivatives of it.[167]

In respect of the first factor, the Supreme Court was careful that one does not adopt an overly broad notion of transformativeness, and that 'the meaning of a secondary work, as reasonably can be perceived, should be considered to the extent necessary to determine *whether the purpose of the use is distinct from the original*, for instance, because the use comments on, criticizes, or provides otherwise unavailable information about

[163] *Blanch v Koons*, 467 F 3d 244, 251-2 (2d Cir. 2006); *Cariou v Prince*, 714 F 3d 694, 706 (2d Cir. 2013).

[164] *Bill Graham Archives v Dorling Kindersley Ltd*, 448 F 3d 605, 609 (2d Cir. 2006); *Blanch v Koons*, 467 F 3d 244, 252–253 (2d Cir. 2006).

[165] *Blanch v Koons*, 467 F 3d 244, 255 (2d Cir. 2006).

[166] *Andy Warhol Foundation for the Visual Arts, Inc v Goldsmith*, 992 F 3d 99, 111, 115 (2d Cir. 2021).

[167] *Andy Warhol Foundation*, 598 US 508, 532 (2023).

the original'.[168] While the Ninth Circuit has rejected a narrow requirement of commenting or criticising the original work in order to qualify as transformative use,[169] it has insisted that the 'new expression must be accompanied by the benchmarks of transformative use'.[170]

What this means for high fashion brands like Gucci, Balenciaga, Vetements and Moschino is that they do not have carte blanche to appropriate iconic copyright-protected works such as Disney characters or Marvel superheroes as part of their performative narratives. They have to clearly evince a different purpose from the original – not simply impose a different aesthetic – and judging from the US Supreme Court's decision in *Andy Warhol Foundation*, some commentary or criticism or new information about the original work is required for the unauthorised use to be a fair one. Digimodernism with its notions of fluidity and multiple authorship, and hypermodernity with its attendant attributes of excessiveness and overconsumption, merit further study on how individuals as *producers* may be adding new information, new aesthetics, new insights and understandings that qualify as transformative uses especially in activities relating to NFTs and the metaverse (eg, creating their own avatars dressed in iconic garments that were shown by luxury fashion brands on the runways of Paris and Milan).

1.4.2 *Trademarks*

Trademark uses that tend to comment on or present a different way of viewing familiar iconography, societal archetypes, public obsessions and majoritarian beliefs are likely to fall within the First Amendment categories of protected speech, such as political speech, art, entertainment and matter of public interest. US courts have resorted to accommodating the First Amendment within doctrinal grounds in trademark laws, primarily in the likelihood of confusion analysis for infringement and the non-commercial use and parody exceptions for dilution actions. US courts have also applied the *Rogers* artistic relevance test to replace a multifactorial likelihood of confusion analysis when there is a trademark

168 *Andy Warhol Foundation*, 598 US 508, 545 (2023) (emphasis added).

169 *Perfect 10 Inc v Amazon.com Inc*, 508 F 3d 1146, 1165 (9th Cir. 2007) (a search engine puts images 'in a different context' so that they are 'transformed into a new creation'); *Kelly v Arriba Soft Corp*, 336 F 3d 811, 819 (9th Cir. 2003) (Arriba's use of thumbnails was transformative because 'Arriba's use of the images serve[d] a different function than Kelly's use – improving access to information on the internet versus artistic expression').

170 *Dr Seuss Enterprises LLP v ComicMix LLC*, 983 F 3d 443, 453–454 (9th Cir. 2020).

challenge to the title or content of an artistic work protected by the First Amendment.[171] In interpreting Article 2.20(2)(d) of the Benelux Convention on Intellectual Property, where a mark owner may sue for the use in the course of trade of a sign that without due cause takes unfair advantage of, or is detrimental to, the distinctive character or the repute of the trademark, the Benelux Court of Justice stated that artistic freedom – as an aspect of the artist's right to freedom of expression – could constitute a 'due cause' when 'there is an artistic expression that is the original result of a creative shaping process'.[172] Artistic freedom, which enjoys protection under Article 10 of the European Convention on Human Rights, could rise to the level of 'due cause', but the artistic expression must not specifically aim at harming the trademark or the proprietor of the trademark.[173]

In the last two decades, luxury fashion brands, particularly Louis Vuitton, are traditionally notorious for aggressively sending cease-and-desist letters and filing claims against parodists, albeit with limited success.[174] The US First Circuit Court of Appeals described parody as 'a humorous form of social commentary and literary criticism . . . [that]

171 Eg, *Rogers v Grimaldi*, 875 F 2d 994 (2d Cir. 1989); *Cliffs Notes, Inc v Bantam Doubleday Dell Publishing Group*, 886 F 2d 490 (2d Cir. 1989); *Westchester Media v PRL USA Holdings, Inc*, 214 F 3d 658 (5th Cir. 2000) *Parks v LaFace Records*, 329 F 3d 437 (6th Cir. 2003); *ETW Corp v Jireh Publishing, Inc*, 332 F 3d 915 (6th Cir. 2003); *Mattel, Inc v MCA Records, Inc*, 296 F 3d 894 (9th Cir. 2002); *E.S.S. Entertainment 2000, Inc v Rock Star Videos, Inc*, 547 F 3d 1095 (9th Cir. 2008); *MGFB Properties, Inc v Viacom Inc*, 54 F 4th 670 (11th Cir. 2022). But the Supreme Court ruled that when the primary mark is used as a mark by the defendant, ie, as a source identifier, the *Rogers* test does not apply: *Jack Daniel's Properties Inc v VIP Products LLC*, 599 US ___ (2023) (Slip Opinion, June 8, 2023) 17–19 (*Jack Daniel's*).

172 *Moët Hennessy Champagne Services v Cedric Art*, Benelux Court of Justice, October 14, 2019, Case A2018/1/8, at [9]. This provision is similar to the Art. 9(2)(c) Regulation 2017/1001 (EUTMR), which allows proprietors of reputable marks to prevent the use of their marks when such use without due cause takes unfair advantage of, or is detrimental to the distinctive character or the repute of their marks. See also Ilanah Fhima, 'Due Cause' (2017) 12 *Journal of Intellectual Property Law & Practice* 897.

173 *Moët Hennessy Champagne Services v Cedric Art*, Case A2018/1/8, at [9].

174 Eg, *Louis Vuitton Malletier, SA v Haute Diggity Dog LLC*, 507 F 3d 252 (4th Cir. 2007) (*Chewy Vuiton*); *Louis Vuitton Malletier, SA v My Other Bag Inc.*, 674 Fed Appx 16, No. 16-241-cv (December 22, 2016) (*My Other Bag*); *Louis Vuitton Malletier, SA v Hyundai Motor America* (2012 WL 1022247 (SDNY March 22, 2012); *Louis Vuitton Malletier, SA v Akanoc Solutions, Inc.*, 591 F Supp 2d 1098 (ND Cal. 2008); *Louis Vuitton Malletier, SA v Dooney & Bourke, Inc., 454 F 3d* 108 (2d Cir. 2006); *Plesner v Louis Vuitton Malletier, SA*, No.KG ZA 11-294 (Court of the Hague, July 21, 2011); Brian Farkas, 'Louis Vuitton v. U Penn', *GS2Law* (March 12, 2012) <http://gs2law.com/louis-vuitton-v-u-penn/>.

seeks to ridicule sacred verities and prevailing mores'[175] thus implicating First Amendment concerns. Parody may thus be seen as contributing valuable commentary and criticism to the marketplace of ideas or advancing democratic debate on matters of public interest through the use of irreverent humour. Typically, the presence of parody makes it difficult for a luxury fashion brand to succeed in both trademark and copyright infringement lawsuits.

The bars for trademark dilution by blurring and tarnishment are also high ones in US law, particularly when First Amendment free speech concerns are triggered by a parody. Regarding blurring, it appears that a parody only serves to *strengthen* the original famous mark. In *Louis Vuitton Malletier, SA v Haute Diggity Dog LLC*, where Louis Vuitton sued a dog toy manufacturer for its Chewy Vuiton product, the Fourth Circuit Court of Appeals held:

> While a parody intentionally creates an association with the famous mark in order to be a parody, it also intentionally communicates, if it is successful, that it is not the famous mark, but rather a satire of the famous mark .... Indeed, by making the famous mark an object of the parody, a successful parody might actually enhance the famous mark's distinctiveness by making it an icon. The brunt of the joke becomes yet more famous.[176]

The US courts generally have found that a trademark may be tarnished when it is 'linked to products of shoddy quality, or is portrayed in an unwholesome or unsavory context', with the result that 'the public will associate the lack of quality or lack of prestige in the defendant's goods with the plaintiff's unrelated goods'.[177] More recent cases narrowed tarnishment to comprise the sale of 'sexual toys, videos and similar soft-core pornographic products'.[178]

Indeed in *Chewy* Vuiton, Louis Vuitton did not take kindly to a range of fluffy dog toys that evoked its 'LV' and Monogram marks; other brands, such as Prada, Chanel and Tiffany & Co, which were similarly parodied, chose to do nothing about it.[179] Louis Vuitton later argued that

175 *LL Bean*, 811 F 2d 26, 29 (1st Cir. 1987).

176 *Chewy Vuiton*, 507 F 3d 252, 267 (4th Cir. 2007). See also *Starbucks Corp. v Wolfe's Borough Coffee, Inc.*, 588 F 3d 97, 112–113 (2d Cir. 2009).

177 *Hormel Foods Corp. v Jim Henson Productions*, 73 F 3d 497, 507 (2d Cir. 1996) (citing *Deere & Co. v MTD Productions, Inc.*, 41 F 3d 39, 43 (2d Cir. 1994)).

178 *V Secret Catalogue v Moseley*, 605 F 3d 382, 388 (6th Cir. 2010).

179 *Chewy Vuiton*, 507 F 3d 252 (4th Cir. 2007)

a tongue-in-cheek reference to its covetable status as a luxury brand in My Other Bag's canvas tote bags was not a type of recoding that should be deemed protectable parody; again, the other brand owners did not sue, and naturally Louis Vuitton did not prevail before the Second Circuit Court of Appeals.[180] The defendant My Other Bag, Inc. (MOB) sells simple canvas tote bags with the text 'My Other Bag . . .' on one side and cartoonish drawings meant to evoke iconic handbags by luxury designers, such as Louis Vuitton, Chanel, and Hermes, on the other. These drawings depict easily recognisable handbags such as the Louis Vuitton Speedy and Hermes Birkin – a reference to hypermodern consumption, performative luxury and the desire for Veblen goods. The New York District Court acknowledged the presence of cultural commentary in MOB's totes:

> Its very name—are a play on the classic 'my other car . . .' novelty bumper stickers, which can be seen on inexpensive, beat up cars across the country informing passersby—with tongue firmly in cheek—that the driver's 'other car' is a Mercedes (or some other luxury car brand). The 'my other car' bumper stickers are, of course, a joke –a riff, if you will, on wealth, luxury brands, and the social expectations of who would be driving luxury and non-luxury cars. MOB's totes are just as obviously a joke.[181]

Louis Vuitton's claims were all dismissed by the court. The court noted that 'MOB markets its bags as "[e]co-friendly, sustainable tote bags playfully parodying the designer bags we love, but practical enough for everyday life"'[182] and found that the parody as 'fair use' defence under 15 U.S.C. § 1125(c)(3) applied. The court further held that even if MOB's use of Louis Vuitton's marks did not qualify as fair use under 15 U.S.C. § 1125(c)(3), the tote bags nevertheless pose no danger of impairing the distinctiveness of Louis Vuitton's marks.[183] On appeal, the Second Circuit unanimously upheld the decision in a brief judgment that endorsed a broad definition of parody (which appears to encompass satire) in trademark law, commenting that the fact that 'the joke on LV's luxury image is gentle, and possibly even complimentary to LV, does not preclude it from being a parody.'[184]

The US decisions have demonstrated a willingness on the part of the courts to accept a semiotic reading of trademarks as cultural signs when

[180] *My Other Bag*, 674 Fed App 16, No 16-241-cv (December 22, 2016).
[181] *Louis Vuitton Malletier, SA v My Other Bag, Inc.*, 156 F Supp 3d 425, 430 (SDNY 2016).
[182] Ibid 431.
[183] Ibid 438–440.
[184] *My Other Bag*, 674 Fed Appx 16, No 16-241-cv (December 22, 2016) at [18].

assessing likelihood of confusion for trademark infringement or evaluating the availability of the non-commercial use exception in a trademark dilution claim for the purposes of parody, satire or political speech. US Circuit Courts of Appeals have consistently declined to find liability against defendants who engaged in non-illegal cultural jamming: Aqua's *Barbie Girl*,[185] Thomas Forsythe's Barbie photographs,[186] Haute Diggity Dog's Chewy Vuiton dog toy[187] and, of course, My Other Bag's tote bags depicting drawings of Louis Vuitton bags.[188]

The post-postmodern frameworks are especially important for the analysis of trademarks. By reclaiming the counterfeit in a hypermodernist manner, heritage brands today are potentially extending their trademark rights into realms where consumers hitherto may not have been confused as to the origin. More recently, we are witnessing obvious efforts by Alessandro Michele (Gucci), Demna Gvasalia (Balenciaga) and Virgil Abloh (Louis Vuitton) to self-disrupt the image that the heritage brands have meticulously cultivated over the decades. Jeanne Fromer calls this 'trade mark ownfringement'.[189] By selling authentic merchandise with *shanzhai*-inspired misspellings such as 'GUCCY' or fake-looking logos that are different from the conventional font used to depict the word mark that consumers are accustomed to, these acts of self-disruption may result in enhancing a finding of a likelihood of confusion or actual confusion for the consumers of Gucci or Balenciaga when they are confronted with *shanzhai* products. If one accepts the view that the inauthenticity of *shanzhai* luxury fashion goods 'strengthens the status hierarchies articulated by possession of 'real' luxury goods and makes those goods more desirable',[190] then the disruption of this sumptuary code by brands like Gucci and Balenciaga will result in a blurring of the distinction.[191] Moreover, a luxury brand engaging in downmarket

185 *Mattel, Inc. v MCA Records, Inc.*, 296 F 3d 894 (9th Cir. 2002).

186 *Mattel, Inc. v Walking Mountain Productions*, 353 F 3d 792 (9th Cir. 2003).

187 *Chewy Vuiton*, 507 F 3d 252 (4th Cir. 2007).

188 *My Other Bag*, 674 Fed Appx 16, No 16-241-cv (December 22, 2016).

189 Jeanne C Fromer, 'Trade Mark Ownfringement' [2023] *Singapore Journal of Legal Studies* 342.

190 Barton Beebe, 'Shanzhai, Sumptuary Law, and Intellectual Property Law in Contemporary China' (2014) 47 *UC Davis Law Review* 849, 864.

191 *Shanzhai* fashion products may arguably be perceived as a commercial parody that is sufficiently robust to 'prevent the confusion necessary for infringement under trade mark law, which requires the observer to be caused to wonder whether the infringing product originates from the registered owner'. See Jani McCutcheon, 'Designs, Parody and Artistic Expression – A Comparative Perspective of Plesner v Louis Vuitton' (2015)

irony and playing with the cultural symbolism of the pedestrian logos such as Ford and DHL without a clear parodic message may expose *itself* to trademark infringement and dilution lawsuits. The altermodernist condition is played out in multiple upcycling efforts that have incurred the ire of mark owners like Louis Vuitton, Chanel and Rolex. Digimodernism is likely to help us understand the behaviour of artists and individuals in the social media and metaverse environments; Rothschild's MetaBirkins will not be the last of such incursions into the alleged province of fashion marks owners.[192]

1.5 Conclusions

It is not surprising that many luxury fashion brands protect their IP rights with great tenacity and rigour, and they will be expected to continue on this path.[193] With deep pockets and an army of top lawyers, brands like Hermes and Louis Vuitton will not even tolerate any parodic or satirical commentary that involve the use of their hallowed marks whether in the physical world or the metaverse, even though they are beginning to redefine their own luxury ideologies.[194] When Haute Diggity Dog and My Other Bag appropriated the LOUIS VUITTON marks to comment on a societal obsession with luxury goods and status symbols, the defendants were relying on the public's understanding of the semiotic values of a fashion cultural icon in order to get the joke – and the critique – behind the merchandise; it is a humorous jab at our hypermodern condition of overconsumption.[195]

41 *Monash. University Law Review* 191, 241 (internal citations omitted) (discussing examples of two- and three-dimensional products parodying familiar trademarks). When luxury brands 'appropriate' these *shanzhai* depictions for themselves, consumers may not be able to easily distinguish a self-parody and a *shanzhai* commercial parody.

[192] The Fashion Law, 'Hermès v. Rothschild: A Timeline of Developments in a Case Over Trademarks, NFTs', *The Fashion Law* (June 23, 2023) <https://www.thefashionlaw.com/hermes-v-rothschild-a-timeline-of-developments-in-a-case-over-trademarks-nfts/>.

[193] However, there are others who may resort to extralegal responses and remedies within their own close-knit communities. The prominence of the 'self-help' phenomenon has been discussed in recent literature. See Amy Adler and Jeanne C Fromer, 'Taking Intellectual Property into Their Own Hands' (2019) 107 *California Law Review* 1455.

[194] Emily Huggard, Patrick Lonergan and Anja Overdiek, 'New Luxury Ideologies: A Shift From Building Cultural to Social Capital' (2022) *Fashion Theory* DOI: 10.1080/1362704X.2022.2117008.

[195] As Furman J so astutely observed: 'In some cases, however, it is better to 'accept the implied compliment in [a] parody' and to smile or laugh than it is to sue . . . MOB's use of Louis Vuitton's marks in service of what is an obvious attempt at humor is not likely

Luxury fashion brands themselves are not immune from lawsuits too. Appropriating all sorts of styles and popular iconography, Demna Gvasalia, designing for Balenciaga and previously Vetements, has redefined the notion of fashion 'placing it within the centre of a Venn diagram of luxury, celebrity, satire, retail, and reality itself'.[196] In his works for both brands, Gvasalia has exhibited various indicia of the post-postmodern condition: mixing of subcultural and popular codes, portraying the grotesque as a powerful alternative to beauty in the fashion system, allowing his own banal designs to be copied in turn thus undermining fashion as an elitist practice, reproducing clearly identifiable uniforms and logos to reiterate the role of fashion as a purely performative act and constantly engaging in the symbolic inversion of high culture to transgress aesthetic hegemony.[197] Therefore, when sued for reproducing a New York City Skyline artwork ubiquitously seen on tourist souvenir bags as a kitschy leather tote bag for Balenciaga priced around US$2,000,[198] and by Car-Freshner Corporation for copying its world-famous LITTLE TREES air fresheners tree design for a US$275 Balenciaga keychain,[199] Gvasalia's entire body of carnivalesque creations that comment on the hypermodern excesses of consumer culture – and his reconstruction of Balenciaga as a fashion brand around the notion that banality and an ugly aesthetic do not compromise desirability – ought to be given significant weight when assessing copyright or trademark infringement.

to cause confusion or the blurring of the distinctiveness of Louis Vuitton's marks; if anything, it is likely only to reinforce and enhance the distinctiveness and notoriety of the famous brand.' *Louis Vuitton Malletier, SA v My Other Bag, Inc*, 156 F Supp 3d 425, 445 (SDNY 2016).

196 Eleonora Dal Bosco, 'Carnivalesque Practices and Cyborg Esthetics: A Study of the Grotesque of Demna' (2022) *Fashion Theory* at 15 (internal citations omitted) DOI: 10.1080/1362704X.2022.2115964.

197 Ibid, at 2–13.

198 *City Merchandise, Inc, v Balenciaga America, Inc, Case 1:18-cv-06748-JSR* (SDNY, complaint filed July 27, 2018); 'Balenciaga, City Merch Settle Lawsuit Over Copycat New York City Bags', *The Fashion Law* (December 11, 2018) <https://www.thefashionlaw.com/home/balenciaga-city-merch-settle-copycat-bag-lawsuit>. The lawsuit was settled.

199 *Car-Freshner Corp v Balenciaga America, Inc*, Case 1:18-cv-09629 (SDNY, complaint filed October 19, 2018); 'Balenciaga and Car-Freshner Corp. Settle Suit Over Fashion Brand's $275 Copycat Keychains', *The Fashion Law* (March 20, 2019) <https://www.thefashionlaw.com/balenciaga-and-car-freshner-corp-settle-suit-over-the-fashion-brands-copycat-keychains/>. The lawsuit was also settled.

One would have to carefully evaluate the zeitgeist and make important – and correct – policy choices when enforcing IP laws and balancing how the freedom of expression features in the manifestations of the post-postmodern condition, such as performativity in brand narratives, multiple authorship, and hyperconsumption. As scholars continue to explore and define new theories to make sense of the twenty-first century, and as lawyers grapple with divergent IP doctrines across jurisdictions, I hope this chapter has introduced sufficient interesting and valuable perspectives for both parties to confidently step into each other's worlds emboldened with new vocabularies to confront the fascinating world of fashion.

2

Intellectual Property Law and the Dream of Post-scarcity Society

BARTON BEEBE*

ABSTRACT

Luxury fashion seeks to aestheticize scarcity and transform its possession into a sign of social distinction. Intellectual property law plays a crucial role in this process. This essay considers the social function that intellectual property law may continue to play in a purportedly 'post-scarcity' society of the future. It asserts that though intellectual property law has long played a technologically progressive role in modern societies, its social function in such societies has been and will continue to be largely reactionary. Even in an otherwise post-scarcity society, intellectual property law will be used, as it is already being used, to preserve 'social scarcity' and regulate signs of social distinction.

> A century ago, scarcity had to be endured; today, it has to be enforced.
>
> —Murray Bookchin, *Post-Scarcity Anarchism*[1]

2.1 Introduction

This chapter considers the potential social role of intellectual property law in a post-scarcity society. My focus will not be on the role of intellectual property law in promoting technological change (a role that is probably already familiar to many readers). Instead, I will consider

* This essay is a revision of 'Intellectual Property Law and Post-Scarcity Society' [2019] *Singapore Journal of Legal Studies* 377, which was itself based on my inaugural EW Barker Centre for Law & Business Distinguished Visitor in Intellectual Property Annual Lecture at the Faculty of Law, National University of Singapore in 2019.

1 Murray Bookchin, *Post-Scarcity Anarchism* (Black Rose Books, 1971) 59 (hereafter Bookchin, *Post-Scarcity Anarchism*).

how, even in a purported post-scarcity society, intellectual property law will likely work to preserve forms of social and cultural differentiation that are based on artificial scarcity, most notable among these the various signs of social distinction produced by the apparel fashion industry. My focus, in other words, will be on the role of intellectual property law in promoting not technological change but social stasis.

I will first discuss some leading examples of economic and social commentary on post-scarcity society and then some recent leading examples of legal commentary on post-scarcity society. I will then turn to the potential social role of intellectual property law in such a society.

2.2 The Dream of Post-scarcity Society

Economic, political and social commentators have spoken of post-scarcity society since at least the 1960s, as Google NGRAM data suggest (see Figure 2.1). It would appear from the data that hopes of post-scarcity society fell off considerably in the late 1970s with the global energy crisis, but the meme is gradually regaining momentum, not just in legal commentary but across the social sciences and in the popular press.[2]

But it would be incorrect to focus only on the specific term 'post-scarcity society', because the dream of such a society has been with us for much longer than the term and arguably stretches back to the earliest religions. An important secular expression of the dream, though no less faith-based, comes to us from the depths of the Great Depression, when, in 1930, John Maynard Keynes penned the essay *Economic Possibilities for Our Grandchildren*.[3] There he explained that his purpose was 'not to examine the present or the near future, but to disembarrass myself of short views and take wings into the future. What can we reasonably expect the level of our economic life to be a hundred years hence? What are the economic possibilities for our grandchildren?'[4] Keynes described the Great Depression and the 'enormous anomaly of unemployment in a world full of wants'[5] as 'a temporary phase of maladjustment'[6] – and in

[2] See Salil K Mehra, 'Competition Law for a Post-Scarcity World' (2016) 4 *Texas A&M Law Review* 1, 2–4, 7–10 (hereafter Mehra, 'Competition Law for a Post-Scarcity World') (surveying current discussions of post-scarcity society).

[3] John Maynard Keynes, 'Economic Possibilities for Our Grandchildren' in *Essays in Persuasion* (Harcourt Brace, 1932) 321(hereafter Keynes, 'Economic Possibilities').

[4] Ibid 322.

[5] Ibid.

[6] Ibid 325.

Figure 2.1 Google Ngram view of 'Post-scarcity', 1900–2010.

Courtesy of Google Ngram Viewer

Google Books, 'Google Ngram View of "Post-Scarcity", 1900–2010' (*Google Ngram Viewer*) <https://books.google.com/ngrams/graph?content=%22post-scarcity>.

the long run, this turned out to be fairly accurate. His diagnosis of the times, quite prescient in some respects, was that 'we are being afflicted with a new disease of which some readers may not yet have heard the name, but of which they will hear a great deal in the years to come – namely, technological unemployment'.[7] But this development 'means in the long run that mankind is solving its economic problem. I would predict that the standard of life in progressive countries one hundred years hence will be between four and eight times as high as it is today'.[8] More generally, he wrote: 'The course of affairs will simply be that there will be ever larger and larger classes and groups of people for whom problems of economic necessity have been practically removed.'[9] This would be 'our destination of economic bliss'.[10]

And yet Keynes recognised that this new stage of economic development would create new challenges. One of these I will detail more fully below. But in general, Keynes predicted that those who have solved the problem of economic necessity will face the ultimate, ethical question of how properly to pursue the art of living: 'Thus for the first time since his creation man will be faced with his real, his permanent problem – how to use his freedom from pressing economic cares, how to occupy the leisure, which science and compound interest will have won for him, to live wisely and agreeably and well.'[11]

Four decades after Keynes' *Economic Possibilities* essay, a decidedly different political-economic thinker took up the theme of post-scarcity society. The American anarchist theorist Murray Bookchin declared in stirring terms that 'for the first time in history we stand on the threshold of a post-scarcity society'.[12] For Bookchin, this was not a matter of Keynes' 'hundred years hence'. Bookchin saw even in what may now strike us as the primitive technologies of the 1960s 'a technology of abundance that is capable of providing for the first time in history the

[7] Ibid.

[8] Ibid 325, 326.

[9] Ibid 331.

[10] Ibid.

[11] Ibid 328. Cf Michael J Madison, Brett M Frischmann, Madelyn R Sanfilippo and Katherine J Strandburg, 'Too Much of a Good Thing? A Governing Knowledge Commons Review of Abundance in Context' (2022) 7 *Frontiers in Research Metrics & Analytics* 1, 4 (hereafter Madison et al, 'Too Much of a Good Thing?') ('What are the social problems associated with abundance – even after we acknowledge harmful externalities and spillovers, such as health, safety, and environmental concerns?').

[12] Bookchin, *Post-Scarcity Anarchism*, above n 1, 12.

material basis for liberation'.[13] But Bookchin emphasised that even though technological developments had already established the material preconditions for post-scarcity, a true 'post-scarcity society' had not yet been achieved.[14] With Keynes, he recognised that the condition of post-scarcity was fundamentally not an economic but an ethical, even aesthetic, condition: 'Scarcity is more than a condition of scarce resources: the word, if it is to mean anything in human terms, must encompass the social relations and cultural apparatus that foster insecurity in the psyche.'[15] For Bookchin the post-Marxist anarchist, this insecurity was a function of the 'exploitative class structure'[16] and the hierarchical property and power relations entailed by such a structure. Only when these were eliminated would post-scarcity society be achieved: 'the word 'post-scarcity' means fundamentally more than a mere abundance of the means of life: it decidedly includes the kind of life these means support. The human relationships and psyche of the individual in a post-scarcity society must fully reflect the freedom, security and self-expression that this abundance makes possible.'[17]

2.3 Legal Commentary on Post-scarcity Society

Keynes spoke in 1930 of 'a hundred years hence', which is 2030 and is not far off. Are we on schedule to have solved our 'economic problem' by then? Recent legal commentators seem to think so. Indeed, with Bookchin, some believe that we have already established the technological preconditions for post-scarcity.

I focus here on two leading examples of post-scarcity legal commentary, both part of the recent wave of legal writing on the development of 3D printing technology. The first is Mark Lemley's article 'IP in a World Without Scarcity'.[18] In it, he predicts a 'coming economy of plenty',[19] an 'economics of abundance'[20] and the emergence of inexpensive, local 3D

[13] Ibid 14.
[14] Ibid 12. See also ibid 14, 'The word "threshold" should be emphasized here for in no way has the existing society realized the post-scarcity potential of its technology.'
[15] Ibid 13.
[16] Ibid.
[17] Ibid.
[18] Mark A Lemley, 'IP in a World Without Scarcity' (2015) 90(2) *New York University Law Review* 460 (hereafter Lemley, 'IP Without Scarcity').
[19] Ibid 496.
[20] Ibid 466.

printing and bioprinting 'not next year, but certainly in our lifetimes'.[21] Lemley focuses on four technologies, 'the Internet, 3D printing, robotics, and synthetic biology,[22] and proposes that 'it is entirely plausible to envision a not-too-distant world in which most things that people want can be downloaded and created on site for very little money – essentially the cost of raw materials'.[23] Such things would include not just standard industrial goods but also biotechnological goods: 'It is certainly possible to imagine a time in which every doctor's office can generate custom genes to order.'[24] Lemley is quick to emphasise that 'this future is not a utopia. None of the technologies I have described is perfect, and each requires physical inputs that will in turn be subject to the laws of scarcity'.[25] But a rhetoric of technological optimism, even boosterism, runs through his article, as does a strain of what might be termed 'threshold rhetoric', consisting of urgent affirmations, as we saw in Bookchin, that we stand just on the threshold of a new technological age.[26] Such rhetoric is typical of legal futurist writing.[27]

A second leading example of post-scarcity legal commentary is Deven Desai and Gerard Magliocca's article 'Patent Meet Napster: 3D Printing and the Digitization of Things'.[28] They assert that 'advances in 3D printing technology are launching an Industrial Counter-Revolution .... The promise of 3D printing is that people will be free to make almost anything they want themselves'.[29] Like Lemley, Desai and Maglioca draw heavily on analogies to internet technology and digital

[21] Ibid 471. See also ibid 504, 'We are still a long way from a post-scarcity world'; ibid 507, 'The technologies I am discussing are still in their infancy.'

[22] Ibid 462.

[23] Ibid.

[24] Ibid 479.

[25] Ibid 502.

[26] Cf Ray Kurzweil, *The Singularity Is Near: When Humans Transcend Biology* (Viking, 2006)(hereafter Kurzweil, *The Singularity Is Near*), 'At the onset of the twenty-first century, humanity stands on the verge of the most transforming and thrilling period in its history.'

[27] See also Barton Beebe, 'Law's Empire and the Final Frontier: Legalizing the Future in the Early Corpus Juris Spatialis' (1999) 108(7) *Yale Law Journal* 1737 at 1751 providing examples of such threshold rhetoric. See generally Barton Beebe, 'Fair Use and Legal Futurism' (2013) 25(1) *Cardozo Studies in Law & Literature* 10 discussing legal futurist analyses of copyright fair use.

[28] Deven R Desai and Gerard N Magliocca, 'Patents, Meet Napster: 3D Printing and the Digitization of Things' (2014) 102 *Georgetown Law Journal* 1691 (hereafter Desai and Magliocca, 'Patents, Meet Napster').

[29] Ibid 1692, 1693.

reproduction in describing the implications of 3D printing. They explain: '3D printing is a general-purpose technology that will do for physical objects what MP3 files did for music.'[30] And like Lemley, they are given to threshold rhetoric: 'In the not-too-distant future, your cell phone will be able to scan objects and produce 3D printer files.'[31]

There are many such articles now in the American law reviews and elsewhere.[32] And there are a few extra-legal sources that they often cite. One is Jeremy Rifkin's 2014 book *The Zero Marginal Cost Society*,[33] whose title speaks for itself. Another is Ray Kurzweil's 2006 book *The Singularity Is Near*.[34] Kurzweil predicts that the 'singularity' will arrive in the 2040s.[35] What is this 'singularity'? As Kurzweil explains, it is the time 'when we will multiply our effective intelligence a billion fold by merging with the intelligence we have created'.[36]

I should admit that I myself have previously addressed the possibility of post-scarcity society and engaged in the same threshold rhetoric. In a 2010 article, I queried whether a 'universal printer' was 'not simply imaginable, but an increasingly realistic possibility'.[37] I further speculated that 'in such an economy of universal printers, printing out a rhetoric of

30 Ibid 1691.

31 Ibid 1696.

32 See Mehra, 'Competition Law for a Post-Scarcity World', above n 2, 2–4, 7–10.

33 Jeremy Rifkin, *The Zero Marginal Cost Society: The Internet of Things, the Collaborative Commons, and the Eclipse of Capitalism* (Palgrave Macmillan, 2014). For examples of citations to Rifkin in the legal literature, see Frank Pasquale, 'Law's Acceleration of Finance: Redefining the Problem of High-Frequency Trading' (2015) 36 *Cardozo Law Review* 2085, 2121; Alexander Peukert, 'Fictitious Commodities: A Theory of Intellectual Property Inspired by Karl Polanyi's "Great Transformation"' (2019) 29 *Fordham Intellectual Property, Media & Entertainment Law Journal* 1151, 1155; Olivier Sylvain, 'Network Equality' (2016) 67 *Hastings Law Journal* 443, 463.

34 See Kurzweil, *The Singularity Is Near*, above n 27. For only a few examples of the many citations to Kurzweil in the legal literature, see James A Dator, 'Futures and Trial Courts' (2009) 18(2) *Widener Journal of Public Law* 517, 521; Deven Desai, 'Privacy? Property? Reflections on the Implications of a Post-Human World' (2009) 18(2) *Kansas Journal of Law & Public Policy* 174; Debora J Halbert, 'Intellectual Property in the Year 2055' (2018) 59(1) *IDEA* 117, 128; John McGinnis, 'How Innovation Makes Us More Equal' (2016) 39(1) *Harvard Journal of Law & Public Policy* 47, 55.

35 Christiana Reedy, 'Kurzweil Claims That the Singularity Will Happen by 2045', *Futurism* (October 5, 2017) <https://futurism.com/kurzweil-claims-that-the-singularity-will-happen-by-2045>.

36 Ibid.

37 Barton Beebe, 'Intellectual Property Law and the Sumptuary Code' (2010) 123(4) *Harvard Law Review* 809, 836 (hereafter Beebe, 'Intellectual Property Law and the Sumptuary Code').

expressions and of things, all goods would be essentially intellectual goods (that is, embodiments of intangible designs) and all property, excluding space and the self, would be essentially intellectual property.[38] And I wondered what role, if any, intellectual property law and policy would play in such a world. In a moment, I will wonder some more about that question.

But before doing so, allow me briefly to register some degree of scepticism about the recent wave of legal writing, including my own, on 3D printing and similar emerging technologies. The Gartner Hype Cycle, albeit unscientific and perhaps a bit hyped itself in its language, is a helpful heuristic for thinking about how expectations regarding new technologies tend to progress over time[39] (see Figure 2.2). The Hype Cycle suggests that soon after a new technology is introduced, there follows a 'Peak of Inflated Expectations' characterised by widespread media attention to the perceived enormous potential of the technology. The bubble then typically bursts as expectations for the technology descend into the 'Trough of Disillusionment' in which 'interest wanes as experiments and implementations fail to deliver' and 'producers of the technology shake out or fail'.[40] Current legal writing on 3D printing and other technologies that herald post-scarcity arguably reflects the 'Peak of Inflated Expectations' phase of legal thinking on such technology, even as media accounts have already entered the phase of disillusionment.[41] No doubt as these technologies mature, expectations will gradually recover along the Hype Cycle's 'Slope of Enlightenment' until they someday level off at the 'Plateau of Productivity'.[42] Nevertheless, the widespread adoption of such technologies – widespread to the degree to constitute a qualitatively new era, a true 'Industrial Counter-Revolution' – now appears to be a far-off prospect.

[38] Ibid.

[39] See Gartner, 'Gartner Hype Cycle' (*Gartner*) <https://www.gartner.com/en/research/methodologies/gartner-hype-cycle> (hereafter Gartner, 'Gartner Hype Cycle'). See also Jackie Fenn and Mark Raskino, *Mastering the Hype Cycle: How to Choose the Right Innovation at the Right Time* (Harvard Business Press, 2008).

[40] See ibid.

[41] See, eg, Signe Brewster, 'Whatever Happened to 3D Printing?', *Techcrunch* (July 10, 2016) <https://techcrunch.com/2016/07/10/whatever-happened-to-3d-printing/>; Nick Allen, 'Why 3D Printing Is Overhyped (I Should Know, I Do It for a Living)', *Gizmodo* (May 18, 2013) <https://gizmodo.com/why-3d-printing-is-overhyped-i-should-know-i-do-it-fo-508176750>.

[42] There is obviously a rough similarity between the Google Ngram graph of the usage of the term 'post-scarcity' and the Gartner Hype Cycle.

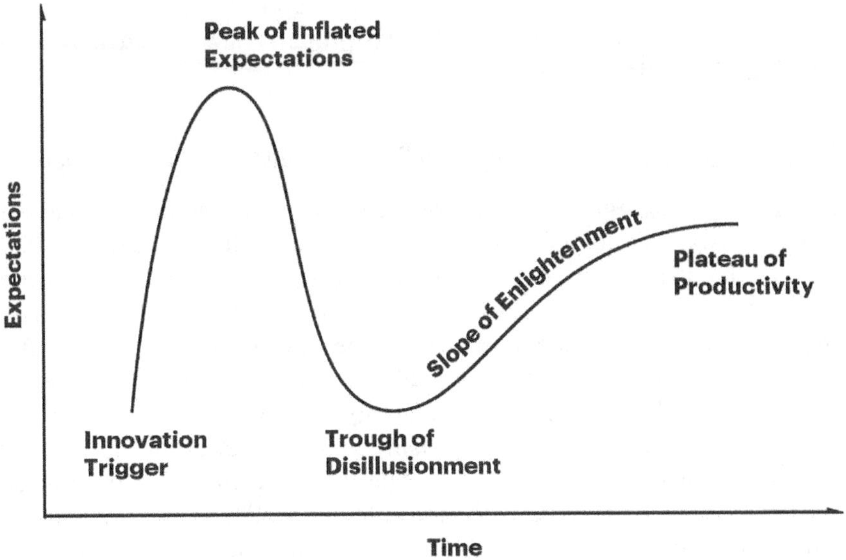

Figure 2.2 The Gartner Hype Cycle.[43]
Courtesy of Gartner, Inc

And yet, it may be worthwhile to be sceptical of one's own scepticism. When assessed retrospectively, most predictions of the future turn out to be laughably wrong. But they are laughable both for what they say will happen that did not – and what they say cannot possibly happen that did. This is all to say that I am not embarrassed finally to ask, if Keynes, Bookchin, Lemley, Desai, Rifkin and Kurzweil (and countless others) are correct (and who am I to question them?), if we are in fact on the verge of a post-scarcity society, what would its implications be for law and specifically for intellectual property law?

2.4 The Role of Intellectual Property Law in Post-scarcity Society

The current conventional method of answering this question focuses on the economy and on technology. Specifically, scholars focus on how, in a post-scarcity society, intellectual property law may foster or impair further economic and technological progress. I will eventually suggest

[43] See Gartner, 'Gartner Hype Cycle', above n 40.

in this section that the more interesting – and also more difficult – question is what social role intellectual property law would play in a post-scarcity society.

2.4.1 *Conventional Views: Intellectual Property Law as Spoiler*

Lemley provides a good example of the scholarship's standard focus on economic and technological progress. With many others, he predicts that current major intellectual property owners will, as he puts it, 'fight the death of scarcity'.[44] Old incumbents will fight the new market disrupters that threaten to institute post-scarcity because these old incumbents profit from scarcity; more essentially and importantly, a regime of scarcity is a regime in which these incumbents have power, and they will seek to hold on to that power by maintaining the conditions of scarcity on which their power is based.[45] These incumbents will try to use restrictive forms of IP law to do so. Specifically, they will seek to strengthen intellectual property laws to inhibit 3D and bio-printing technology.[46] They will seek to impose severe forms of secondary liability on the producers of such technology and severe forms of primary liability on those who use this technology to infringe protected designs.[47]

To ward off this possibility, Desai and Magliocca call for statutory reforms that would limit (or even eliminate) personal liability for 3D printing[48] – though, to be fair, they recognise significant difficulties with such a reform.[49] They also call for a DMCA for patent infringement.[50] Here they are referring to the Digital Millennium Copyright Act of 1998[51] in the United States – and specifically to section 512(c)(1) of the Act.[52] In short, they are calling for a notice-and-takedown system that would limit the liability of digital intermediaries that serve as repositories of patent-infringing 3D printing files. Their proposal is that such intermediaries would not be liable if, upon notice, they expeditiously take down the infringing content.

[44] Lemley, 'IP Without Scarcity', above n 19, 497.
[45] Ibid 497–502.
[46] Ibid.
[47] Ibid.
[48] Desai and Magliocca, 'Patents, Meet Napster', above n 29, 1716, 1717.
[49] Ibid.
[50] Ibid 1718, 1719.
[51] Digital Millennium Copyright Act 1998, 17 USC § 101 (US).
[52] See ibid § 512(c)(1).

In essence, the view of these scholars is that in a post-scarcity society, intellectual property law will largely just be a spoiler. It will just get in the way of innovation, and we should seek to make sure that it does not.

2.4.2 The Social Role of Intellectual Property Law

The conventional view is thus that in a post-scarcity society, intellectual property law will be at least less important to innovation.[53] I remain ambivalent, maybe even pessimistic about this. But set that aside.

2.4.2.1 Intellectual Property Law and Social Scarcity

Instead, I'd like to talk about a different role that intellectual property law might play in a post-scarcity society. And it is not all that different from an important role that intellectual property law is already playing in some neighbourhoods in New York City, Hong Kong, Paris, or Singapore, neighbourhoods where many very affluent individuals already live in something like a post-scarcity world. If food is a problem for them, it is a problem because there is too much of it. And it may be that they have such an abundance of resources (and wisdom) that the only thing they truly feel a scarcity of is time.

But there is perhaps something else that may nevertheless always remain scarce for them. In his essay *Economic Possibilities for Our Grandchildren*, Keynes made an important qualification in his depiction of post-scarcity society:

> Now it is true that the needs of human beings may seem to be insatiable. But they fall into two classes – those needs which are absolute in the sense that we feel them whatever the situation of our fellow human beings may be, and those which are relative in the sense that we feel them only if their satisfaction lifts us above, makes us feel superior to, our fellows. Needs of the second class, those which satisfy the desire for superiority, may indeed be insatiable; for the higher the general level, the higher still are they. But

[53] Dan Burk interestingly proposes a different reason why intellectual property protection may be less important, or at least differently important, to certain forms of innovation in the future: 'The concern with AIs as creators entails a recognition that AI will be transformative at the point of initial creation, where human creativity has typically been the generative mechanism. This shift threatens to sideline the substantive branches of intellectual property law, not rendering them irrelevant, but posing problems that are entirely orthogonal to the problems that patent and copyright were intended to solve.' See Dan Burk, 'Cheap Creativity and What It Will Do' (2023) 57 *Georgia Law Review* 1669 (hereafter Burk, 'Cheap Creativity').

> this is not so true of the absolute needs – a point may soon be reached, much sooner perhaps than we are all of us aware of, when these needs are satisfied in the sense that we prefer to devote our further energies to non-economic purposes.[54]

Keynes imagined a world where our absolute needs would be met. Left to us would be the problem of relative needs, of what he apparently saw as an innate human need to express superiority or at least rank.

One standard way by which humans do so is through the possession of scarcity, or in its aestheticized form, rarity.[55] But how would this work in a society that has overcome scarcity and indeed rarity as well? How would it work in a society where at-home production technologies can easily scan and reproduce an item (or through robots, a service)? How do we distinguish ourselves if much of what is owned and done exists in effectively infinite supply?

Of course, one way is through conduct, through work, through production of what we create and give away, and indeed this is how social distinction is established in the open-source software world (and I think also in the academic world).[56] But at present we live in a global consumer society, where many (certainly not all, but many) distinguish themselves by what they consume rather than by what they produce. And post-scarcity would take this form of consumer society to a whole other level.

How will consumption-based social distinction survive in such a post-scarcity consumer society? Perhaps you will say that it simply will not. Individuals will no longer seek status through the possession of scarcity. But I think this view is one mistake of post-scarcity thinking. Here is an example of this mistake: 'IP has allowed us to cling to scarcity as an organising principle in a world that no longer demands it.'[57] My intuition

54 Keynes, 'Economic Possibilities', above n 4, 326.

55 Beebe, 'Intellectual Property Law and the Sumptuary Code', above n 38, 814–815.

56 See Yochai Benkler, '"Sharing Nicely": On Shareable Goods and the Emergence of Sharing as a Modality of Economic Production' (2004) 114(2) *Yale Law Journal* 273. See generally Yochai Benkler, *The Wealth of Networks: How Social Production Transforms Markets and Freedom* (Yale University Press, 2006).

57 Lemley, 'IP Without Scarcity', above n 19, at 465. In Lemley's defence, he recognises the possibility that post-scarcity society may 'recreat[e] scarcity by declaring certain luxury goods to be off limits to most'. Ibid 514. The crucial point, however, is that individuals in such a society may seek, like individuals in our own society, to differentiate themselves through the possession of commodified scarcities that take forms other than 'luxury goods'. Differentiation is not always hierarchical; for example, street fashion rarely seeks to assert superior wealth. Intellectual property law is what will make such socially differentiating scarcities possible beyond the realm simply of Veblen goods.

is that the world will always demand scarcity. If through our technology we eradicate the scarcities that beset us, we will no doubt seek to invent new ones.[58]

But even if that were true, even if we would give up on the pursuit of rank, consumers will still seek something more essential than status, or superiority or rank. They will seek in the things they consume some form of individuality, identity, some degree of difference as against the crowd, and to do so, they will seek out things that somehow remain rare. Economists (for example Keynes in his talk of the search for 'superiority') seem always to conceive of society as a single vertical, lock-step status hierarchy that everyone is trying to climb. And you may not be surprised that American lawyers (and legal academics) tend to subscribe to a similar social theory.[59] But far more common, I think, particularly in massively multicultural global societies, is the individual's pursuit not of superiority but simply of difference, of distinction understood not hierarchically but more broadly distinction understood qualitatively, as differentiation from sameness – as differentiation from what the French social theorist Jean Baudrillard called 'the hell of the same'.[60] To achieve such difference and individuation in a consumer society, consumers will still turn to rarities and scarcities wherever they can find them. And as Dan Burk has recently emphasised,[61] consumers will continue to seek that greatest rarity of all in a society of superabundance: human authenticity, the sense of connection to and community with other humans, whether that community forms itself around supercars or pick-up trucks – or as Amy Adler has expertly explored, around the possession of non-fungible tokens.[62] And it cannot be emphasised enough,

[58] Cf Madison et al, 'Too Much of a Good Thing?', above n 12, 7 ('Amid abundant information, how do individuals distinguish themselves, positively and negatively?').

[59] See Beebe, 'Intellectual Property Law and the Sumptuary Code', above n 38, 827, 828.

[60] Jean Baudrillard, *The Transparency of Evil: Essays on Extreme Phenomena* (Verso Books, 1993). Cf Eric Mark Kramer, 'Cultural Fusion and the Defense of Difference' in Molefi Kete Asante and Eungjun Min (eds), *Socio-Cultural Conflict between African American and Korean American* (University of America Press, 2000) 181 , 213–217 (discussing the 'relentless drizzle of sameness').

[61] See Burk, 'Cheap Creativity', above n 54.

[62] See Amy Adler, 'Artificial Authenticity' (2023) 98 *New York University Law Review* 706 . Importantly, Adler makes clear that with respect to non-fungible tokens (NFTs), 'as with contemporary art more generally, we see that intellectual property law is not the relevant mechanism for limiting the limitless. Once again, the norm of authenticity – without any operation of law – creates authenticity, even though it's fake'. Ibid 767. It may be that outside of the art world, mass consumer society uses intellectual property law to approximate the workings of the art world's norm of authenticity. It remains to be seen whether

particularly to legal readers, that luxury goods are only a part, and a small part, of this story. Our habitual focus on hierarchical, ordinal status competition and on 'Veblen goods'[63] can blind us to something far more essential, which is individuals' efforts through their consumption somehow to assert horizontal difference in a modern consumer society of mass-produced sameness.

What I am driving at (and if you are in the fashion industry, you already know what I am going to say, because you already live it) is the *social* role of intellectual property law in a post-scarcity society. I refer not to its role in incentivising innovation, but rather its potential role in perpetuating consumption-based social difference and thereby in facilitating identity within a mass global consumer society.

Consider that intellectual property law is the one area of law that at its core is designed to maintain artificial scarcities in the face of superabundance. Intellectual property law is built to restrict access to often near-zero-marginal-cost physical embodiments of intangible works, designs, inventions or trademarks. We have built it in this way to incentivise innovation. But it turns out that intellectual property law is meanwhile perfectly suited to supplying post-scarcity society with the scarcities that individuals in such a society will continue to seek out.[64]

It is as if intellectual property law in its technologically progressive guise, in which it incentivises new technologies, has all along been pushing us towards a post-scarcity society, which is the very form of society where intellectual property law will finally assume a dominant role in social ordering (if not also in technology policy). I am reminded of De Tocqueville's comment on one of the peculiar characteristics of the Americans: 'There is hardly any political question in the United States that sooner or later does not turn into a judicial question.'[65] That was the nineteenth century. In the twenty-first century, if the heralds of post-scarcity society are correct, there may hardly be any question that does not ultimately turn into a question of intellectual property and intellectual property law – and more specifically, of trademark law.

NFTs or similar technologies will evolve to create mass-consumption forms of the 'artificial authenticity' identifies in the art world.

[63] For a thorough and sophisticated critique, grounded in part in First Amendment values, of the role trademark law plays in regulating hierarchical status goods, see Jeremy Sheff, 'Veblen Brands' (2012) 96 *Minnesota Law Review* 769.

[64] See Beebe, 'Intellectual Property Law and the Sumptuary Code', above n 38, 815, 816.

[65] Alexis de Tocqueville, *Democracy in America* (Liberty Fund, 2012).

2.4.2.2 Intellectual Property Law Already Performs This Role

In essence, then, I am arguing that a primary role of intellectual property law in a post-scarcity society will be to perpetuate consumption-based social difference by facilitating the creation of various forms of artificial scarcity. Indeed, it will not just facilitate; it will incentivise the creation of artificial scarcity. Here, intellectual property law will very much be a spoiler. It will restore scarcity to a world that we would have thought could transcend scarcity. If technology is going to strip nature of its ability to enforce scarcity, then culture will do what nature no longer can, and culture will use intellectual property law to do so.

At this point, some proportion of readers may be thinking: this is crazy talk, science fiction, video game thinking, just like talk of post-scarcity society. But on reflection, I do not think that it is.

The social role that I am describing for intellectual property law in a post-scarcity society is very much one of the roles that intellectual property law is already performing in our own society, at least in the economies and cultures of the Global North. As I have explained in much more detail elsewhere,[66] a variety of cases and court opinions from around the world demonstrate intellectual property law's differentiating function.

Take, for example, one of the earliest of such cases, from the United States. In the 1955 case of *Mastercrafters Clock & Radio Co v Vacheron & Constantin-LeCoultre Watches, Inc*,[67] the declaratory plaintiff Mastercrafters produced an electric-powered simulation of the Atmos clock. An Atmos clock is an ingenious device in which the clock is perpetually wound by changes in atmospheric pressure. Apparently, in its day, it was a status symbol – perhaps it still is. Vacheron had threatened suit against Mastercrafters for making electric-powered knockoffs. The cause of action at issue was trademark infringement, and the form of infringement was what is now called in some trademark systems 'post-sale confusion'.[68] No purchaser of the electric-powered clock, costing US$30, was confused into thinking it was an authentic Atmos clock, costing US$175 (or US$2,000 in today's dollars).[69] Still, in

[66] See Beebe, 'Intellectual Property Law and the Sumptuary Code', above n 38, 845–877.

[67] *Mastercrafters Clock & Radio Co v Vacheron & Constantin-LeCoultre Watches, Inc*, 221 F 2d 464 (2d Cir, 1955) (*Mastercrafters*).

[68] See Stacey L Dogan and Mark A Lemley, 'The Merchandising Right: Fragile Theory or Fait Accompli?' (2005) 54 *Emory Law Journal* 461, 491–493.

[69] *Mastercrafters*, above n 68, 465.

the post-sale context, there could be confusion, and the court found that this post-sale confusion would be harmful to Vacheron and its consumers. The American judge reasoned: 'Some customers would buy the plaintiff's cheaper clock for the purpose of acquiring the prestige gained by displaying what many visitors at the customers' homes would regard as a prestigious article.'[70] The judge condemned Mastercrafters' 'intention thus to reap financial benefits from poaching on the reputation of the Atmos clock'[71] and enjoined Mastercrafters' conduct.

There are many such cases like this in American trademark law as well as in American copyright law and design protection law.[72] We also see a plenitude of such cases in European intellectual property law, most notably *L'Oréal SA v Bellure NV*,[73] in which the European Court of Justice (as it then was) explicitly sought to protect L'Oréal's efforts to create and preserve the artificial scarcity of its goods.

We also see such 'post-scarcity cases' in Singapore, though in the most prominent of these cases, *City Chain Stores (S) Pte Ltd v Louis Vuitton Malletier*,[74] the ultimate result, I am happy to say, was altogether different from the American or European case law. In brief, since 2004 Louis Vuitton had been selling in Singapore a watch bearing Louis Vuitton ('LV')'s so-called 'flower quatrefoil' design, which many consumers may recognise from LV's repeating pattern logo. In 2006, City Chain began selling a watch with a very similar design but at a substantially lower price. The Singapore High Court found trademark infringement, passing off, and trademark dilution.[75] Its decision reads very much like the American cases I've just mentioned, particularly when, as the Court of Appeal explained, the trial court took 'judicial notice of the fact that

[70] Ibid 466.

[71] Ibid.

[72] See Beebe, 'Intellectual Property Law and the Sumptuary Code', above n 38, 845–868.

[73] *L'Oréal SA v Bellure NV*, Case C-487/07, ECLI:EU:C:2009:378 (ECJ, February 10, 2009).

[74] *City Chain Stores (S) Pte Ltd v Louis Vuitton Malletier* [2009] SGCA 53, [2010] 1 SLR 382. See also David Tan, 'Differentiating between Brand and Trade Mark: City Chain v. Louis Vuitton Malletier' [2010] *Singapore Journal of Legal Studies* 202; David Tan and Benjamin Foo, 'The Extraneous Factors Rule in Trademark Law: Avoiding Confusion or Simply Confusing?' [2016] *Singapore Journal of Legal Studies* 118. For a discussion of the antidilution issue in City Chain Stores, see Wee Loon Ng-Loy, 'The *Sense and Sensibility* in the Anti-Dilution Right' (2012) 24 *Singapore Academy of Law Journal* 927.

[75] *Louis Vuitton Malletier v City Chain Stores (S) Pte Ltd* [2009] SGHC 24, [2009] 2 SLR (R) 684.

people do get put off certain luxury brands simply because there were so many fakes and cheap look-alikes in the market'.[76]

On appeal to the highest appellate court, the Court of Appeal's unanimous decision, by contrast, reads like a line by line repudiation of the American and European cases. In finding no likelihood of confusion, the Court of Appeal noted, among much else, that luxury goods 'are bought after careful inspection and deliberation,[77] that the substantial price difference between the two watches meant that no LV consumer would be confused into buying a City Chain watch,[78] and more broadly, that the public's mere association between the two products could not form the basis of a finding of likelihood of confusion where there was no confusion as to source.[79] In rejecting LV's passing off claim, the Court of Appeal characterised as 'wholly irrelevant' the possibility that 'the Solvil Flower pattern could be easily mistaken for the Respondent's watches at a glance when worn on the wrist as people do not generally scrutinise another person's watch at close range'.[80] As for the dilution claim, the Court of Appeal found, among other things, that that the flower quatrefoil design was not well-known to the public at large in Singapore.

All in all, it was a wonderfully wise opinion – though its wisdom would no doubt not be appreciated by purveyors of artificial scarcity, such as Louis Vuitton and other luxury fashion brands. City Chain benefitted not just from what was clearly some excellent lawyering but also from a court that was unwilling just yet to endorse an emerging social role of intellectual property law, and particularly trademark law, in an emerging post-scarcity society.

2.4 Conclusion

In brief conclusion, I should say a few words in the nature of review. I began by talking about the dream of post-scarcity society, particularly as envisioned by John Maynard Keynes and Murray Bookchin. I then focused on two leading examples of legal commentary on post-scarcity society and the conventional view that intellectual property law would

[76] *City Chain Stores (S) Pte Ltd v Louis Vuitton Malletier* [2009] SGCA 53, [2010] 1 SLR 382 at [61].
[77] Ibid at [56].
[78] Ibid at [60].
[79] Ibid at [58].
[80] Ibid at [77].

either be a spoiler or just become irrelevant in such a society. Finally, I proposed that intellectual property law would actually become even more important – more relevant – in a post-scarcity society, not for its impact on technological progress but rather for the social function it would play (and that it already does play) in preserving the artificial scarcities that such a society would continue to demand.

We may someday solve Keynes' 'economic problem'. But what will remain is a social problem, the problem that the economist Fred Hirsch called 'social scarcity'.[81] Though intellectual property law has long played a technologically progressive role in modern societies, it may be that its long-term role, as a social matter, will be essentially reactionary. It will function to preserve those structures and habits of social differentiation in our consumer society that are based on the consumption of scarcities. It will be used, as it already is being used, to restore scarcity to post-scarcity society.

[81] Fred Hirsch, *Social Limits to Growth* (Routledge, 2nd edn, 1978).

PART II

Intellectual Property Rights: Copyright, Trademarks, Patents and Registered Designs

3

Fashion's Function in Intellectual Property Law

CHRISTOPHER BUCCAFUSCO AND JEANNE C FROMER*

ABSTRACT

Clothing designs can be beautiful. But they are also functional. Fashion's dual nature sits uneasily in intellectual property law, and its treatment by copyright, trademark, and design patent laws has often been perplexing. Much of this difficulty arises from an unclear understanding of the nature of functionality in fashion design. This chapter proposes a robust account of fashion's function. It argues that aspects of garment designs are functional not only when they affect the physical or technological performance of a garment but also when they affect the perception of the wearer's body. Generally, clothes are not designed or chosen simply to look good. They are also characteristically designed or chosen to look good on. This approach clarifies the appropriate treatment of fashion design in intellectual property, and it exposes the conceptual limitations of the U.S. Supreme Court's copyright decision in *Star Athletica, L.L.C. v Varsity Brands, Inc.*

3.1 Introduction

The creative endeavours of fashion designers have long been celebrated by consumers, journalists and even museums. But despite the widespread recognition of fashion design's artistry, it has always had an uncertain status within intellectual property law. However beautiful a garment may be, it is also functional. It serves to clothe the body, to keep it warm and to enable the wearer to perform particular activities while wearing it.

Copyright, trademark and design patent laws in the United States are deeply anxious about protecting functionality. They each use various

* This chapter is adapted from Christopher Buccafusco and Jeanne C Fromer, 'Fashion's Function in Intellectual Property Law' (2017) 93 *Notre Dame Law Review* 51.

doctrinal devices to block functional content, and they channel that content instead towards the utility patent regime. It should be noted that in Commonwealth common law jurisdictions, the terminology is different. 'Design patents', that protect ornamental designs are known as 'registered designs' or simply 'designs'.[1]

This chapter explains how garments function and how different intellectual property regimes should deal with that functionality. Garments are not simply functional to the extent that they serve the mechanical or technological ends of keeping people properly clothed. They are also functional to the extent that they influence the way the wearer is perceived. When aspects of a design affect the perception of the wearer, for example, by making them look taller, slimmer, broader or curvier, those aspects of the design must be treated as functional.[2]

The US Supreme Court's opinion in *Star Athletica, L.L.C. v Varsity Brands, Inc.*[3] on the copyrightability of cheerleading uniform designs did not recognise this important aspect of the nature of garment design. Because the Supreme Court did not accurately assess the functionality of the cheerleading uniform designs before it, the Court risks conferring a substantial competitive advantage on the designer-plaintiff, one that Congress did not intend to confer[4] and that the designer did not earn. As we explain here, the contested features of these uniform designs – stripes, chevrons, zigzags and colour-blocking – like many features of fashion design, affect the perception of the wearer by drawing attention to certain aspects of the wearer's body over others and by making the wearer seem to be curvier and have a longer torso.

The account of fashion's functionality that we develop here also has important implications for trademark law and design patent law. In this chapter, we explain how trademark and design patent laws can more successfully respond to attempts by claimants to protect functional

[1] Eg Registered Designs Act (Cap 266) (Singapore); Registered Designs Act 1949 (UK); Registered Designs Ordinance (Cap 522) (Hong Kong); Designs Act 2003 (Cth) (Australia); Designs Act 1953 (New Zealand).

[2] For a related analysis of copyrightability of clothing designs, see Giovanna Marchese, 'A Tri-Partite Classification Scheme to Clarify Conceptual Separability in the Context of Clothing Design' (2016) 38 *Cardozo Law Review* 375 (hereafter Marchese, 'Conceptual Separability').

[3] *Star Athletica, LLC v Varsity Brands, Inc*, 580 US 405 (2017).

[4] See Innovative Design Protection Act (IDPA), S Res 3523, 112th Cong (2012) (US); Innovative Design Protection and Piracy Prevention Act (IDPPA), HR Res 2511, 112th Cong (2011) (US).

aspects of garment design without satisfying utility patent law's more strenuous demands.

Section 3.1 describes our account of fashion's function. We explain how, in addition to technical or mechanical functions, fashion design is also functional when it incorporates features that influence the way the wearer is perceived. Section 3.2 explains how copyright law should treat the functional aspects of fashion design in light of copyright law's functionality screening for useful articles, like garment designs, and the law's originality and merger doctrines. In Section 3.3, we illustrate our approach with a case study of the cheerleading uniforms at issue in *Star Athletica* and demonstrate how the Court went wrong. Sections 3.4 and 3.5, respectively, show how our account of fashion's function should affect trademark and design patent laws.

3.2 How Fashion Design Is Functional

Copyright, trademark and design patent laws each limit protection for functional aspects of designs. They each do so in somewhat different ways, as we address. Yet these three legal regimes are unified in limiting functional matter as a way to ensure that those design aspects are protected through utility patent law, if at all. Because of their functionality screens, copyright, trademark and design patent laws each need to identify the functional aspects of otherwise protectable designs.[5]

The features of product designs fall into three mutually exclusive categories. Features can be (1) purely functional, (2) purely non-functional or (3) hybrid. Consider how these features might appear in different parts of an automobile. The car's spark plugs are rarely seen, and their design may be motivated entirely by utilitarian concerns about size and performance. They would fall into the first category. The sculpture of a leaping jaguar that serves as the car's hood ornament has no functional contribution to the car's operation; it exists merely to look good. It falls into the second, purely non-functional, category. Many other aspects of the car's design are simultaneously functional and serve some additional non-functional purpose. The shape of the car's hood both makes it look attractive and influences its aerodynamics. The car's wheels may be designed to look speedy, but they must also be able to

[5] See also Christopher Buccafusco and Mark A Lemley, 'Functionality Screens' (2017) 103 *Vanderbilt Law Review* 1293 (hereafter Buccafusco and Lemley, 'Functionality Screens').

support the car's weight. These and other features of the car's design are hybrid.

Knowing what to treat as functional for purposes of garment design requires understanding how clothing can serve utilitarian ends. In some cases this is fairly simple, while in other cases it is more complex. Decisions about the physical or technological performance of a garment should clearly be treated as functional. For example, a designer's choices to use fabric that provides warmth even in the coldest temperature or fabric that wicks sweat away from the wearer's body are functional.[6]

On the other hand, various aspects of garment design could be purely expressive, or aesthetic. A logo for a sports team emblazoned on a t-shirt is one such example. Similarly, a paisley pattern woven into a necktie is probably a purely expressive element of the tie's design. Two-dimensional pictorial or graphic additions to garment designs are the most plausible candidates of designs for purely expressive elements.

Many of a garment's design features will be at least partially functional and fall into the hybrid category. For example, the incorporation and design of pockets on a pair of trousers may be particularly stylish and visually appealing, but they are also useful because the pockets give the wearer a place for his or her wallet and keys. Thus, the design of pockets and other similar features should also be treated as dual-nature components of garment design. The same might be true for the cut of sleeve that provides a certain degree of warmth, modesty or ease of movement while simultaneously being beautiful to perceive. Many of the aspects of the fit and cut of a garment fall into the hybrid category, because although they may look attractive in their own right, they also affect the garment's technical or physical performance as a piece of apparel.

Designs can importantly also function in ways that go beyond standard mechanical or technological utility. In particular, the designs of many garments are intended to and are purchased because they make their wearers look attractive. A designer's choices about hemline, neckline, darting and, sometimes, fabric prints influence people's perceptions of the wearer. A shopper does not simply ask of a garment, 'Does it look good?' In addition, and more importantly, he or she asks, 'Does it look

[6] If a designer wants to obtain legal protection for the use of a new kind of performance-enhancing fabric, they need to apply for a utility patent and prove that her invention is novel and nonobvious. See, eg, US Patent No 3687754, filed April 29, 1969 (Registered on August 29, 1972) (claiming a 'method of manufacturing an elastic nonwoven fabric').

good on me?' or 'Does it make me look good?'[7] In this way, the garment's design is valued for what it can do when it is being used. Thus, in addition to the mechanical functions of garment designs, another intrinsic – or essential – function garment designs tend to share is that many of their design features are incorporated to affect the perception of the wearer.[8]

Many features of garment design – line, shape, texture, colour and print – exploit features of human visual perception and optical illusions to influence the way in which the wearer's body is perceived.[9] Importantly, these visual effects can be created with both three-dimensional design techniques such as garment shape and cut as well as with two-dimensional design techniques such as patterns, stripes and colour. Thus, the frequent assertion that two-dimensional fabric design is non-functional[10] is in many cases wrong when the design affects how the wearer is perceived. Below, we illustrate a number of these techniques, ranging from camouflage to stripe placement.

As all shoppers know, a certain style or cut of a garment may look good on one person but not on another.[11] And different sorts of designs may affect how people's bodies look. This is not accidental. Design choices create visual effects that can vary the size or shape of the wearer's body or body parts. In this section, we illustrate a number of the most

[7] See, eg, Jintu Fan, 'Perception of Body Appearance and Its Relation to Clothing' in Jintu Fan, Winnie Yu and Lawrance Hunter (eds), *Clothing Appearance and Fit: Science and Technology* (Woodhead, 2004) 1 (hereafter Fan, 'Perception of Body') ('Few people have a perfect body. Most people would like to improve their appearance with appropriate clothing, by camouflaging their less desirable attributes and highlighting the more attractive aspects of their bodies.').

[8] To be sure, there are some instances of haute couture and other fashion designs that are decidedly not about making the wearer look good. In such cases, one can still ask whether particular aspects of such fashion design are incorporated to affect the perception of the wearer. If so, those aspects are just as functional as those that are incorporated to make the wearer look good. Other design aspects of some haute couture and other fashion designs might be purely expressive, with the appearance on the wearer's body being beside the point. Those design aspects are unlikely to be functional in the sense described here.

[9] See Marian L Davis, *Visual Design in Dress* (Prentice Hall, 3rd edn, 1996) 21–23, 33 (hereafter Davis, *Visual Design*); Marilyn Revell Delong, *The Way We Look: Dress and Aesthetics* (Fairchild Books, 2nd edn, 1998) 106–107, 132–133, 166 (hereafter Delong, *The Way We Look*); Marilyn J Horn and Lois M Gurel, *The Second Skin* (Houghton Mifflin, 3rd edn, 1981) 314
(hereafter Horn and Gurel, *The Second Skin*).

[10] Eg, *Galiano v Harrah's Operating Co*, 416 F 3d 411, 419 (5th Cir. 2005).

[11] See, eg, Kat Collings, 'The Complete Guide to Dressing for Your Body Type', *Who What Wear* (April 27, 2017), <http://www.whowhatwear.com/how-to-dress-for-body-type-pear-apple-hourglass>.

prominent design techniques. Our goal here is not to catalogue garment design techniques exhaustively but rather, by choosing common examples, to illustrate the nature of design functionality.

It is common knowledge that the placement of horizontal lines on a garment can make the wearer look shorter and broader, while vertical lines have the opposite effect of lengthening and slimming the wearer's body.[12] Garment design can visually minimise the size of body parts judged to be too large by either appearing to subdivide those body parts or by counterbalancing them to increase the size of surrounding parts.[13] For example, a V-shaped neckline can make the neck look longer and narrower while also making shoulder width narrower.[14] A bodice can be smocked, pleated, draped or gathered at the bust to make the bust appear larger.[15] Similarly, as one design textbook indicates, 'a line continuing around the body, diagonal stripes that are not too dominant, or a reflecting surface smoothly contouring the body call our attention to the rounded contours'.[16]

Designers can also affect the perception of the shape of body parts through design choices. Importantly for our purposes, the combination of colours, shapes and lines can have enormous influence on how the wearer's body is perceived. This is known as colour-blocking, and it was recently made famous by Stella McCartney's line of dresses, garment designs employing a colour-blocked hourglass appearance that made wearers' bodies look both curvier and slimmer. Two examples of these dresses, as worn by actress Kate Winslet, are shown in Figure 3.1. The black colour along the sides, which changes in width at various points, produces a particularly striking hourglass shape.[17] And, in the dress on the right, the brighter colour on the top of the dress produces a larger and more defined bust.[18]

12 See Davis, '*Visual Design*', above n 9, 36–41; Fan, 'Perception of Body', above n 7, 11; Jintu Fan, 'Psychological Comfort of Fabrics and Garments' in Jintu Fan and Lawrance Hunter (eds), *Engineering Apparel Fabrics and Garments* (Woodhead, 2009) 251 , 257 tbl 9.1 (hereafter Fan, 'Psychological Comforts').

13 See Fan, 'Perception of Body', above n 7, 11.

14 Davis, *Visual Design*, above n 9, 339.

15 Ibid 340.

16 Delong, *The Way We Look*, above n 9, 117.

17 Saliha Ağaç and Menekşe Sakarya, 'Optical Illusions and Effects on Clothing Design' (2015) 3 *International Journal of Science, Culture and Sports* 137 , 154–155 (hereafter Ağaç and Sakarya, 'Optical Illusions').

18 Ibid. For a related discussion of this dress design and the implications for the copyrightability of fashion designs, see Marchese, 'Conceptual Separability', above n 2, 406–407.

Figure 3.1 Stella McCartney colour-blocked dresses.[19]
(a) © ABACA/Press Association Images (b) © Action Press / Rex Features

Optical illusions can also be deployed in garment design to influence perceptions of the wearer's body.[20] Consider the Müller-Lyer illusion, as shown in Figure 3.2, which causes a line to look longer if it is bracketed on each end by arrow tails and shorter if it is bracketed on each end by arrow heads.[21] This illusion can be incorporated into garment designs to lengthen or contract the body of the wearer through placement of arrow tails or heads, respectively, as shown in Figure 3.3.[22]

These design techniques are not used just because they look attractive on their own. They are used to make the wearer look more attractive. They are part of what make designs inherently *work* as fashion designs. By manipulating features of human vision, these design techniques alter

[19] Fiona Raisbeck, 'Kate Winslet Wows in Another Body-Con Stella McCartney Dress', *Marie Claire* (November 21, 2011) <http://www.marieclaire.co.uk/news/fashion/532781/kate-winslet-wows-in-another-body-con-stella-mccartney-dress.html#index=1>.

[20] See generally Davis, '*Visual Design*', above n 9, 40–50; Ağaç and Sakarya, 'Optical Illusions', above n 17, 137 (cataloguing various illusions to be used).

[21] Fan, 'Psychological Comforts', above n 12, 257.

[22] Davis, '*Visual Design*', above n 9, 40; Fan, 'Psychological Comforts', above n 12, 257.

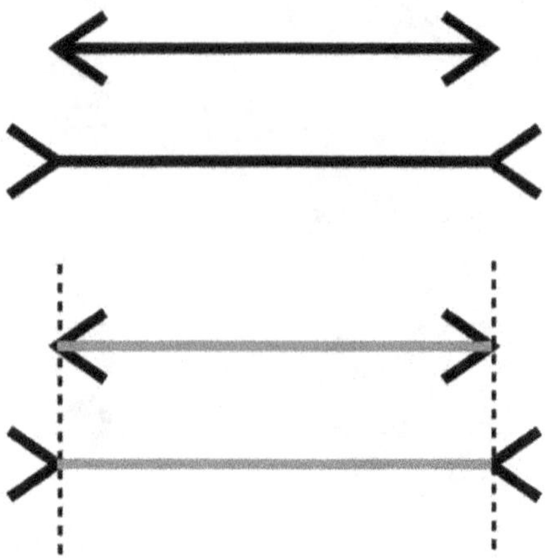

Figure 3.2 Müller-Lyer illusion.[23]
© PsyPhi > SciFi

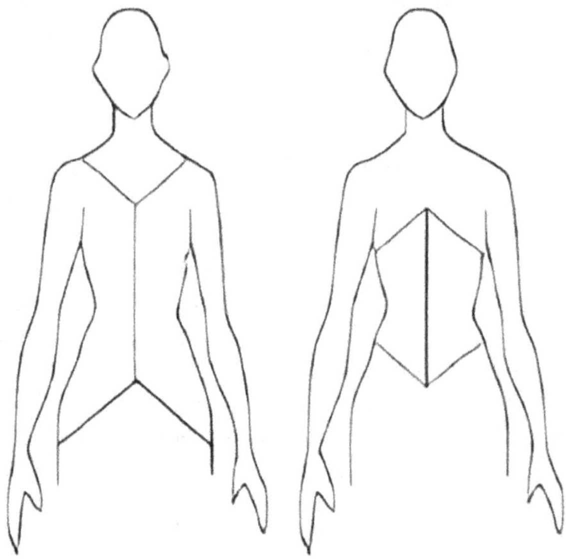

Figure 3.3 The Müller-Lyer illusion applied to garment design.[24]
© International Journal of Science, Culture and Sports

[23] Patric Nordbeck, 'An Ecological Note on the Müller-Lyer Illusion', *PsyPhi > SciFi* (February 22, 2015) <http://pnpsyphi.blogspot.co.uk/2015/02/an-ecological-note-on-muller-lyer.html>.

[24] Ağaç and Sakarya, 'Optical Illusions', above n 17, 143 fig 1e.

the way we see things in the world. As two designers explain, 'By using art components in this way, [designers] can alter the frame of reference in which we see the human form, and in so doing, [they] can create illusions or effects that would not be possible in any other way.'[25] In this sense, they are the same as camouflage or high-visibility patterns that serve a particular function. Unlike a painting or a drawing of a cartoon character, they do not exist merely to portray their own appearance or convey information.

As we argue in Section 3.3, the Copyright Act treats as functional aspects of visual design that influence the perception of another object, including the human body. Accordingly, as a matter of copyright statute and policy, the incorporation of design techniques that produce dependent value are unprotectable. Similarly, trademark and design patent laws must grapple with the issue of whether such functional aspects of fashion designs are unprotectable. We now address these laws in turn, beginning with copyright law.

3.3 Fashion's Function in Copyright Law

Congress and the US courts have long expressed concern about the misuse of copyright law to protect functional objects from market competition.[26] The fashion industry, in particular, has proven a consistent source of consternation in this regard.[27] Over a century ago, one court explained that 'a manufacturer of unpatented articles cannot practically monopolise their sale by copyrighting a catalogue containing illustrations of them'.[28] As the *Star Athletica* case decided by the US Supreme Court indicates, many in the fashion industry are still seeking haven for their designs within copyright law. In this section, we review the general structure of the copyright-patent divide in intellectual property law and the doctrinal techniques that copyright law has historically used to screen out functional content. We then set out how copyright law and policy lead to the conclusion that fashion design features that affect the perception of the wearer are not protectable.

[25] Horn and Gural, *The Second Skin*, above n 9, 314.

[26] *Mazer v Stein*, 347 US 201, 217–218 (1954) (*Mazer*); *Baker v Selden*, 101 US 99, 101–106 (1879); Copyright Law Revision, HR Rep No 94-1476, 94th Cong (1976) (US) 54–55.

[27] Eg, *Fashion Originators' Guild*, 312 US 457 (deeming efforts to stop garment design piracy a violation of the Sherman Act, and emphasising that copyright law, as it then existed, did not provide a basis for preventing such piracy).

[28] *National Cloak & Suit Co v Std Mail Order Co*, 191 F 528, 528 (SDNY 1911).

3.3.1 *The Separate Spheres of Copyright and Patent Laws*

Copyright law and utility patent law address different kinds of creativity. Copyright law protects authors' writings, while patent law protects inventors' discoveries.[29] Put another way, copyright law is the province of expression and aesthetics, while patent law is the province of utility and functionality.[30] Both fields seek to optimise creative production within their spheres, but they both adopt different legal mechanisms to do so.

Patents can confer substantial market power on their owners, enabling them to charge higher prices for access to the protected technology than they otherwise would.[31] These higher prices and diminished market competition are deemed worthwhile, however, because they provide valuable incentives to invest in creating and disseminating new and useful technologies.[32] The world is a better place, so the story goes, when inventors are given incentives to develop and disclose their inventions, even if this comes at the cost of higher prices.[33] But not all 'inventions' are worth this tradeoff. Patent law establishes relatively high standards for obtaining its protection. Inventors who desire patent rights must submit to an expensive patent examination by the Patent and Trademark Office of their inventions' utility, novelty and nonobviousness.[34] Only 75% of utility patents get granted, and the procedure typically costs US$22,000.[35] Moreover, once granted, patent protection lasts only for 20 years from the application date.[36]

Contrast this situation with copyright law. Copyright lasts for much longer than does patent protection. Authors typically receive copyright protection in their works for their entire lives plus an additional 70 years post-mortem.[37] In addition, copyrights are easy to obtain. Under the

[29] Compare Copyright Act 1976, 17 USC § 102 (US) with Patent Act 2012, 35 USC § 101 (US).

[30] Christopher Buccafusco, 'A Theory of Copyright Authorship' (2016) 102 *Virginia Law Review* 1229; Jeanne C Fromer, 'A Psychology of Intellectual Property' (2010) 104 *Northwestern University Law Review* 1441.

[31] Mark A Lemley, 'The Economics of Improvement in Intellectual Property Law' (1997) 75 *Texas Law Review* 989, 996–997.

[32] Ibid 993–996.

[33] Ibid.

[34] Patent Act 2012, 35 USC §§ 101–103, 131 (US).

[35] Jonathan S Masur, 'Costly Screens and Patent Examination' (2010) 2 *Journal Legal Analysis* 687, 695, 700.

[36] Patent Act 2012, 35 USC § 154(a)(2) (US).

[37] Copyright Act 1976, 17 USC § 302(a) (US).

1976 Act, copyright vests without need for further action at the moment that a work is fixed in a tangible medium of expression – as soon as it is filmed, drawn or written down.[38] In contrast to the Patent and Trademark Office, the Copyright Office plays little to no role in screening out inappropriate claims to protection. Moreover, to be protectable, works do not need to be novel and nonobvious but rather only 'original', that is, independently created and that they exhibit a very modest creative spark.[39] This threshold is much lower than the one imposed by patent law.

In light of the differences between obtaining patents and copyrights, there is a sizeable risk that creators will attempt to use copyright law to obtain 'backdoor patents'.[40] Although virtually all areas of copyright are at risk of improperly protecting functional content, these concerns are heightened for certain two- and three-dimensional works. Copyright law has taken a targeted approach to excluding functional aspects of these 'pictorial, graphic, and sculptural works',[41] which we discuss and for which we offer an analytical framework in Section 3.3.2.

3.3.2 Screening Functionality in Pictorial, Graphic and Sculptural Works

To the extent that copyright law protects the aesthetic features of the design, it risks also protecting utilitarian function, the province of patent law. Consistent with this concern, Congress established a general rule against copyright protection for so-called 'useful article[s]', subject to a narrow exception for expressive features of a useful article that are separable from its functional aspects.[42] Specifically, the Copyright Act provides that 'pictorial, graphic, and sculptural works' include 'works of artistic craftsmanship insofar as their form *but not their mechanical or utilitarian aspects are concerned*'.[43] Further, the design of a work that constitutes a 'useful article' is protectable 'only if, and only to the extent

[38] See ibid § 102(a).
[39] Copyright Act 1976, 17 USC § 102(a) (US); *Feist Publications, Inc v Rural Telephone Service Co*, 499 US 340, 345–347 (1991).
[40] *Baker v Selden*, 101 US 99, 102 (1879); Viva R Moffat, 'Mutant Copyrights and Backdoor Patents: The Problem of Overlapping Intellectual Property Protection' (2004) 19 *Berkeley Technology Law Journal* 1473.
[41] Copyright Act 1976, 17 USC § 102(a)(5) (US).
[42] Copyright Act 1976, 17 USC § 101 (US).
[43] Ibid (emphasis added).

that, such design incorporates pictorial, graphic, or sculptural features that can be identified separately from, and are capable of existing independently of, the utilitarian aspects of the article'.[44] In short, to be protectable, a product design must exhibit expressive 'pictorial, graphic, or sculptural features' (we refer to these as 'expressive' features throughout) that are separable from its 'utilitarian aspects'.[45] If a useful article has no expressive features or if the expressive features are inseparable from its utilitarian aspects, it should not receive copyright protection.

Congress was aware that this rule meant many useful works that are visually appealing would be unprotected by copyright, but it considered this appropriate in light of the risks to competition posed by more expansive copyright protection and the availability of design patents for industrial designs.[46] Congress concluded that leaving some works with expressive features unprotected by copyright was preferable to allowing functional objects to gain lengthy legal protection while avoiding the high inventive threshold and careful examination of the patent system.[47]

When dealing with pictorial, graphic or sculptural works, copyright law distinguishes between those works that constitute 'useful articles' and those that do not. According to the Act, a useful article is 'an article having an intrinsic utilitarian function that is not merely to portray the appearance of the article or to convey information'.[48] This definition is vitally important to understanding copyright law's treatment of functionality, and it has two essential purposes. First, the definition explains that only those works that have an intrinsic utilitarian function should be treated as useful articles. 'Intrinsic' in this sense means inherent or essential.[49] The Act differentiates between works that essentially have at least one function and those that do not essentially have any function – that is, those that are essentially expressive.

Second, the definition clarifies how to determine whether some characteristic of a work should be treated as functional or expressive. Aspects of a work that 'merely . . . portray the appearance of the article or . . . convey information' are not functional aspects of the work.[50] They are, instead, expressive features. This distinction is necessary to effectuate the

[44] Ibid.
[45] Ibid.
[46] Copyright Law Revision, HR Rep No 94-1476, 94th Cong (1976) (US) 49–50, 54–55.
[47] Ibid.
[48] Copyright Act 1976, 17 USC § 101 (US).
[49] *Black's Law Dictionary* (9th edn, 2009).
[50] Copyright Act 1976, 17 USC § 101 (US).

statutory requirement that 'the design of a useful article, as defined in this section, shall be considered a pictorial, graphic, or sculptural work only if, and only to the extent that, such design incorporates pictorial, graphic, or sculptural features that can be identified separately from, and are capable of existing independently of, the utilitarian aspects of the article'.[51]

Consider a copyright claim in an original painting. A painting is clearly a 'pictorial, graphic, or sculptural work', so we must then decide whether the painting is a 'useful article'. The answer, in virtually all cases, is that it is not a useful article. Most paintings do not have an intrinsic utilitarian function. Instead, they exist to portray their own appearance. When we think about why most paintings are painted and why they are valued by consumers, we focus on their representational characteristics. Indeed, virtually all of the decisions that an artist makes about the content of a painting are concerned with representational or depictive ends. This is not to say that a painting can have no function. It may successfully cover a hole in the wall, in much the same way that a book can serve as a doorstop. Yet this sort of utilitarian function is one that is shared by all physical objects and is thus not intrinsic, or essential, to a painting or a book in any meaningful way. This sort of non-intrinsic functionality does not magically make paintings or other pictorial, graphic or sculptural works intrinsically utilitarian. Most paintings, then, are by application of the copyright statute, not useful articles.

Now consider the design of a stylish bicycle rack. Although the design may have significant aesthetic features and although it may have won awards for the quality of its design, the bicycle rack has an intrinsic utilitarian function: to hold bicycles securely. The rack was made to hold bicycles, and it is purchased by consumers who want to use it for that purpose. This use is obviously different from typical copyrightable expression, which merely portrays the appearance of an article or conveys information. Similarly, the designs of 'pictorial, graphic, or sculptural' objects like mannequins, floor tiles and, of course, garments, handbags and shoes, are useful articles. They each have an intrinsic function beyond 'portray[ing] the appearance of the article or ... convey[ing] information'.[52] They are, as 'useful articles', then subject to a rigorous separability analysis to determine whether they can support a valid copyright.

---

[51] Ibid.

[52] Copyright Act 1976, 17 USC § 101 (US).

The copyright statute sets out that 'the design of a useful article … shall be considered a pictorial, graphic, or sculptural work only if, and only to the extent that, such design incorporates pictorial, graphic, or sculptural features that can be identified separately from, and are capable of existing independently of, the utilitarian aspects of the article'.[53] This language indicates that Congress intended to extend copyright protection only to some components of a limited class of useful articles – their separable 'pictorial, graphic, or sculptural' (expressive) features. The first step in a separability analysis, then, must involve determining which components of a work are its expressive features and which are its utilitarian aspects. A court cannot determine whether the former are separable from the latter until it has determined which are which.[54]

Prior to the Supreme Court's *Star Athletica* opinion, this inquiry has been the key component to successful application of the useful articles doctrine in fashion design and elsewhere. In effect, a court is asked to parse the various features of a design and to characterise each of those features. The Copyright Act specifically contemplates that a particular design component can fall into one of the three categories like we described in Section 3.1:

1. only pictorial, graphic, or sculptural (or "expressive");
2. only utilitarian (or functional); or
3. both expressive and utilitarian (ie, hybrid).

The first two categories are straightforward. They encompass design features that are either purely expressive or purely utilitarian, respectively. A cartoon character screen-printed on the front of a T-shirt is likely to be purely expressive, for example, while the shape of an internal part of an automotive engine is purely functional.

The existence and content of the third category may seem less clear, but the statute undoubtedly recognises the existence of hybrid components, and it explains how they should be treated. On its face, the Copyright Act recognises the existence of what we call dual-nature components by acknowledging that there are 'pictorial, graphic, or sculptural features' that cannot 'be identified separately from' the 'utilitarian

[53] Ibid.

[54] As we discuss below, we think the United States Supreme Court erred in its *Star Athletica* decision by failing to categorise the design's features, which led in turn to a flawed outcome in the case. See Section 3.3.

aspects of the article'.[55] This language indicates that a component of a design, such as the leg of a chair, may be simultaneously expressive and functional. The back of an Eames chair is both a brilliant work of visual design and a terrific example of functional ergonomic engineering.[56]

Indeed, the fundamental justification for the useful articles doctrine has been to exclude from copyright protection aspects of works that exhibit both expression and function.[57] There would be little need for separability analysis if all components of a design could be designated as either expressive or functional, because copyright law could simply indicate that only the expressive features are protectable. Separability analysis exists precisely because design aspects that are expressive can – and, as discussed in Section 3.3.1, in the case of clothing often will – serve utilitarian purposes.

In sum, it is essential to the policies underlying both copyright and patent laws that copyright law distinguish expression from function in determining protectability. Congress sought to do that with the useful articles doctrine by analysing whether a useful article's expressive features are separable from its functional aspects. We now turn to how to think about fashion designs within this context.

3.3.3 The Functionality of Garment Design Features

Copyright law's useful articles doctrine is intended to handle cases involving works that incorporate both expression and function. Applying this doctrine to fashion designs has proven challenging to courts, as they try to sort and separate the aspects of garments that are expressive from those that are functional. In this section, we offer a robust approach to understanding the nature of fashion's functionality. Our approach is grounded in the current copyright statute and responds to the Supreme Court's *Star Athletica* decision. Correctly applied, it appropriately limits the scope of copyright protection for garment design to only those features that are purely expressive. According to our

[55] Copyright Act 1976, 17 USC § 101 (US).

[56] John R Berry, *Herman Miller: The Purpose of Design* (Rizzoli, 2004) 85.

[57] Copyright law cannot both protect the expressive features of the uniforms and preserve their functional aspects from protection when they are the same. Cf *Morrissey v Procter & Gamble Co*, 379 F 2d 675, 678–79 (1st Cir. 1967) (holding that copyright does not protect expression whose associated idea can be expressed in very few ways, so that the idea effectively merges with the expression, for the reason that in such cases copyright would then unreasonably protect ideas).

approach, components of a garment design should be treated as functional not only if they are mechanically or technologically functional but *also if* they are valued for their ability to influence the way that the wearer is perceived. These components are prevalent in fashion design and, even if they are also expressive, must be screened out of any copyright protection granted to an author.

It is clear that fashion designs are both 'pictorial, graphic, [or] sculptural works' and 'useful articles', so copyright law's separability criteria apply to them.[58] As noted above, the most important step in this analysis involves the identification and categorisation of the components of a claimed design. A court must determine which components of the design are purely expressive, which are purely functional and which are hybrid – that is, that they simultaneously affect the aesthetics and the utility of the garment.

We think that the Copyright Act treats aspects of garment design that influence the perception of the wearer's body as 'utilitarian features' of a useful article, although they may also be expressive 'pictorial, graphic, or sculptural' aspects of the article. The reason is that the copyright statute defines a useful article as one having 'an intrinsic utilitarian function that is *not merely to portray the appearance of the article or to convey information*'.[59] As discussed in Section 3.3.2, the Act distinguishes between useful article features that 'merely portray the appearance of the article or ... convey information' and useful article features that have additional utility. By this distinction, an aspect of a useful article that 'merely ... portray[s] [its] appearance ... or ... convey[s] information' is not considered a utilitarian feature. It is purely an expression of authorship. By contrast, an aspect of a useful article that does not merely portray its appearance or convey information is a utilitarian feature of that article.

In the context of the useful articles doctrine, the Copyright Act establishes a distinction between aspects of designs that are valued inherently for their depictive effect and those whose value is dependent on their effect on other objects. The former it treats as expressive 'pictorial, graphic, or sculptural features', and the latter it treats as 'utilitarian aspects'.[60] Inherently valuable design elements alone may be treated as purely expressive features of a work. Elements that are dependently valuable for their ability to affect the perception of another object

[58] Copyright Act 1976, 17 USC § 101 (US).
[59] Ibid (emphasis added).
[60] Ibid.

are (at least partly) functional, because they do not exist merely to portray their own appearance or convey information. For garments, this dependent visual utility represents an additional way in which aspects of garment design can be utilitarian. In addition to the mechanical utility related to use, warmth and modesty, garments have additional utility under the copyright statute when they incorporate design features that influence the wearer's appearance.

Consider how different sorts of visual figures might be incorporated into the design of a garment. On the one hand, a drawing of a cartoon character on a T-shirt is inherently valuable. It is produced and consumed for the representation it provides. The drawing of the character plays the same role and has the same effect whether it is on a piece of paper, a digital device screen or a garment. On the other hand are useful article designs that are primarily dependently valuable. They produce value when brought into appropriate relationships with other objects and in terms of their effects on those objects: making them look bigger, smaller, different or better. Camouflage offers an ideal example of designs at this end of the spectrum, of those having dependent value. The design of a camouflage pattern achieves its value when it is placed in an appropriate environment. When it is, the pattern works: it functions to cloak the person or object that it covers.[61] Consider, by comparison, the two camouflage patterns in Figure 3.4. The camouflage pattern on the left was worn by soldiers in the US Army deployed in Afghanistan to cloak them well against their surroundings, whereas the camouflage pattern on the right, worn by North Korean soldiers, does not cloak them, but if anything, makes them easier to see.

When a design element, like an effective camouflage pattern, alters the way another object appears, that is, when it works in relation to some other object, that design element should be treated as utilitarian as a matter of copyright law.[62] That is, the design element is 'not merely … portray[ing] the appearance of the article or … convey[ing] information'.[63] Only if a design or an aspect of design exists merely to portray its

[61] Isla Forsyth, 'Subversive Patterning: The Surficial Qualities of Camouflage' (2013) 45 *Environment & Planning* 1037.

[62] Cf *Fulmer v United States*, 103 F Supp 1021 (Ct Cl 1952) (finding no copyright infringement when the US government produced camouflage parachutes from the plaintiff's design showing top and side views of a similar parachute because finding otherwise would be akin to conferring unwarranted patent protection), cited in *Mazer*, above n 26.

[63] Copyright Act 1976, 17 USC § 101 (US).

Figure 3.4 Effective and ineffective camouflage.[64]
(a) © SpaceDaily (b) Courtesy of kotaku.com

own appearance should it be treated by copyright law as purely expressive. One such example would be an image of a character, such as Mickey

[64] The figure on the left can be found in Staff Writers, 'Army Selects New Camouflage for Afghanistan',*Spacewar* (February 24, 2010) <http://www.spacewar.com/reports/Army_Selects_New_Camouflage_For_Afghanistan_999.html>, whereas the figure on the right can be found in Brian Ashcraft, 'North Korean Camo Actually Isn't That Awful', *Kotaku* (October 31, 2013) <http://kotaku.com/north-korean-camo-actually-isnt-that-awful-1455805558>.

Figure 3.5 Pharrell Williams wearing the 'damoflage' print.[65]
Credit: Giovanni Giannoni / WWD / Getty Images

Mouse, printed on a T-shirt. The character exists merely to portray its own appearance. Similarly, Pharrell Williams' so-called 'damoflage' (a pixelated version of Louis Vuitton's damier check print resembling camouflage) – shown in Figure 3.5 – does not serve to camouflage or do anything other than portray its own appearance.

In light of this discussion, we wish to respond to an argument that might be raised to challenge our reading of the Copyright Act: the claim by some courts and scholars that two-dimensional design features are always non-functional, which the Supreme Court recently rejected. It is important to note that expressive techniques that affect the perception of the wearer – and are thus also functional – include both three-dimensional design choices involving the shape and cut of garments as well as two-dimensional design choices involving shapes, colours and patterns. This is essential because some courts and scholars have often

[65] Samantha Tse, 'Pharrell Williams' Louis Vuitton Star-Studded Debut Sparked Joy', *CNN* (June 21, 2023)<https://www.cnn.com/2023/06/21/style/pharrell-williams-louis-vuitton-debut/index.html>.

reflexively treated two- dimensional fabric designs as non-functional.[66] Yet both two- and three- dimensional design features will often be utilitarian in nature. As discussed above, camouflage offers an obvious example of a functional two-dimensional pattern. If the developer of a new camouflage pattern desires intellectual property protection, they must look to the patent system, as some camouflage designers (including the US military itself) have done.[67] High-visibility fabrics or patterns are also functional, even though they are two-dimensional. And the techniques discussed above in Section 3.1 use two-dimensional patterns in similar ways, by altering how the viewer sees the clothed person.[68]

As the Supreme Court emphasised in *Star Athletica*, the Copyright Act clearly anticipates that two-dimensional designs can be functional when it refers to 'pictorial, graphic, or sculptural features' that are inseparable from utilitarian aspects of the design.[69] The first two objects in this list, pictorial and graphic features, are, in fact, two-dimensional design techniques. The statutory scheme thus makes clear that two-dimensional works and features, and not only three-dimensional works and features, can be utilitarian.[70] By stating that 'pictorial, graphic, or sculptural work[s]' can be 'useful article[s]', rather than limiting the statutory text to 'sculptural works', it is apparent that Congress recognised that both two- and three-dimensional works can be utilitarian. Similarly, by indicating that 'pictorial, graphic, or sculptural features' might be inseparable from 'utilitarian aspects' of the design, rather than just referring to 'sculptural features', the copyright statute signifies that both two- and three-dimensional features can be utilitarian.

3.4 The Conceptual Shortcomings of *Star Athletica*

The account presented in Section 3.3 best comports with the Copyright Act's useful articles doctrine as Congress drafted it and the policy goals

66 *Galiano v Harrah's Operating Co*, 416 F 3d 411, 419 (5th Cir. 2005); Melville B Nimmer and David Nimmer, *Nimmer on Copyright* (Matthew Bender Elite Products, rev edn, 2017) § 2.08[B][3]; William F Patry, *Patry on Copyright* (Thomson West, 2017)§ 3:151.

67 Eg, US Patent No 6,805,957 (issued October 19, 2004) ('Camouflage U.S. Marine Corps Utility Uniform: Pattern, Fabric, and Design'); US Patent No 6,499,141 (issued December 31, 2002) ('Multidimensional Camouflage Outer Wear Garment System').

68 Cf Marchese, 'Conceptual Separability', above n 2, 408 (applying another framework to make the case that two-dimensional design features that affect the perception of the wearer only when worn are not truly two-dimensional features).

69 *Star Athletica, LLC v Varsity Brands, Inc*, 580 US 405, 412 (2017) (*Star Athletica*).

70 Ibid (citing Copyright Act 1976, 17 USC § 101 (US)).

undergirding it. In 2017, the US Supreme Court had an opportunity to affirm these principles in *Star Athletica, LLC v Varsity Brands, Inc.*[71] Instead, the Court charted an entirely new path through copyright law, upsetting decades of lower court precedents and altering the nature of copyright's functionality screening. Here we attempt to explain what the Court did and how it went so wrong. We also discuss how our account of fashion's function should still matter for copyright validity and infringement even if its role in the useful articles doctrine is now different.

The case centres on the copyrightability of the cheerleading uniform designs shown in Figure 3.6.[72] The Supreme Court held the arrangement of stripes, chevrons, zigzags and colour-blocking in the garment designs to be separable features of useful articles and potentially copyrightable.[73] In light of our analysis above, we think the Supreme Court came to the wrong conclusion, after failing to recognise that the arrangement of stripes, chevrons, zigzags and colour-blocking in the garment designs at issue – like many components of clothing designs – has both expressive and utilitarian aspects.

Varsity submitted the above designs for registration by the Copyright Office, and Varsity sued Star Athletica for producing uniforms displaying similar designs. The district court granted the defendant's summary judgment motion, ruling that the designs were not protectable because they served the function of identifying their wearers as cheerleaders.[74] The Sixth Circuit Court of Appeals reversed.[75] It is worth spending a moment on the Sixth Circuit's opinion because, even though we think it reached the wrong conclusion, it did so via a logical methodology. The appellate court engaged in the correct set of steps, first determining that the uniform designs were useful articles and then identifying their expressive and functional features.[76] It was only in applying this step that we think the court erred. It concluded that the only features of the uniforms that were functional were those that contributed to their mechanical use as garments, such as enabling wearers to jump and flip or cover their bodies.[77] The Sixth Circuit determined that the stripes,

[71] Ibid.
[72] Ibid.
[73] Ibid 409.
[74] Ibid 410; *Varsity Brands, Inc v Star Athletica, LLC*, No 10-2508, 2014 WL 819422, at *9 (WD Tenn, March 1, 2014).
[75] *Varsity Brands, Inc v Star Athletica, LLC*, 799 F 3d 468, 471 (6th Cir. 2015).
[76] Ibid 487–488.
[77] Ibid 490.

Figure 3.6 Varsity's claimed design.
Courtesy of US Supreme Court opinion and Copyright Office registration image

chevrons and colour-blocking were purely expressive features and were separable from the rest of the uniforms.[78]

The Sixth Circuit understood the basics of the useful articles doctrine and its separability analysis. Its only problem was its failure to grasp that the plaintiff's designs are not purely expressive. Instead, the stripes, chevrons, zigzags and colour-blocking in the claimed designs serve a hybrid purpose, similar to those documented in Section 3.1. They are simultaneously both expressive and functional, serving to accentuate and elongate the cheerleader's body and make it appear curvier in particular areas.[79] We detail some of these hybrid features in light of the discussion in Section 3.1.

In Design 078, the white patches in the colour-blocked pattern help create the visual effect of curviness by creating an hourglass shape with contrasting colours, as in Stella McCartney's dresses.[80] The V-shaped neckline together with the inverted-V-shaped slit on the skirt elongates the body by exploiting the Müller-Lyer illusion. The V-shaped neckline also serves to point to the bust and elongate the neck. The colour-blocking, using contrasting colours, creates contrast and draws attention to the wearer's body. The repeating stripe pattern at the neckline, bust, waist and skirt hem draws viewers' attention from the top of the wearer's neckline all the way to the bottom of the wearer's skirt to see that part of the wearer's body as unified.[81]

Again, in Design 0815, Varsity employs colour-blocking; this time a darker blue colour along the side of the uniform to make the wearer look both more slender in certain places and curvier in others, just as in the Stella McCartney dresses. In addition, the V-shaped striping on the front centre of the uniform serves to further accentuate the bust. The V-shaped neckline both points to the bust and elongates the neck. Designs 299A and 299B have some of the same features associated with the previous

[78] Ibid 491–493.

[79] For a similar observation about these cheerleading uniform designs, see Marchese, 'Conceptual Separability', above n 2, 412; ibid 379 (stating that the designs 'create a trim silhouette shape of the cheerleader').

[80] Giovanna Marchese likewise emphasises that 'the chevrons and stripes are arranged so that the edge of the chevron's "V" frames the cheerleader's chest' and that 'the panels immediately outside the "V" use colors that sharply contrast the color within the "V," which creates a visual effect in the viewer of an hourglass body shape.' Marchese, 'Conceptual Separability', above n 2, 379.

[81] Delong, *The Way We Look*, above n 9, 229 ('Direction can be aided by repetition of similar parts, often called rhythm. Rhythm is defined as the ordered recurrence of parts that leads the eye.').

two designs, plus there is a diagonal striping, which calls attention to the body's rounded contours. Additionally, the chevron at the bottom of the uniform top is cut to display some of the belly and draw attention to it. Design 074 serves to accentuate the curves and elongate the body for many of the reasons discussed with regard to the previous designs. In addition, the colour-blocking serves to highlight the bust by colouring it in white in contrast to the green above it and navy blue below it.

The stripes, chevrons, zigzags and colour-blocking that form the heart of Varsity's uniform designs do not merely portray their own appearance or convey information. They also serve the purpose of influencing the appearance of the uniform's wearer. These features are the reason that the designs succeed as appropriate designs for garments meant to emphasise the fitness, athleticism, and attractiveness of those who don them. It is with these objectives in mind that Varsity here chose to design its uniforms in this fashion, and it is no accident that many cheerleading uniforms share similar design features.[82] Granting copyright protection to these designs would enable Varsity to monopolise functional aspects of garments without satisfying the exacting demands of patent law. Although other designers might be free to produce cheerleading uniforms incorporating features that flatten the bust, widen the waist, and shorten the legs, we suspect that they are unlikely to find a vibrant market for such products. This is not the sort of competitive advantage that copyright law is intended to foster.

Unlike the Sixth Circuit, which misinterpreted what makes a design feature utilitarian or expressive, the Supreme Court thoroughly misunderstood the statute it claimed to be interpreting. Justice Thomas' majority opinion treats the separability criteria as both intellectually simple and doctrinally weak when they are, in fact, neither of these things. He first asks whether the decision maker can 'spot some two- or three-dimensional element that appears to have pictorial, graphic, or sculptural qualities'.[83] He describes this requirement as 'not onerous',[84] as his application of the test to the uniforms proves. According to the majority, an element of a design counts as an expressive feature if it looks like

[82] It is also no accident that Varsity's designs for male cheerleaders often have different design elements from those for female cheerleaders because the physical aspects of male and female bodies that are emphasised differ. '2016 Varsity Spirit Fashion', *Varsity* (2016) 82 <www.varsity.com/publications/Varsity-Spirit-Fashion-2016.html#82>.

[83] *Star Athletica*, above n 69, 414.

[84] Ibid.

something.[85] As we discuss elsewhere in a commentary on the decision, 'considering that this is the area of copyright law that applies to pictorial, graphic, and sculptural works, it is impossible that the claimed works would not have some such features'.[86]

The Supreme Court next asks whether the identified expressive feature can exist apart from the utilitarian aspects of the article.[87] The Court explains that 'the feature must be able to exist as its own pictorial, graphic, or sculptural work . . . once it is imagined apart from the useful article'.[88] Finally, the Court indicates, 'If the feature is not capable of existing as a pictorial, graphic, or sculptural work once separated from the useful article, then it was not a pictorial, graphic, or sculptural feature of that article, but rather one of its utilitarian aspects.'[89] Although we do not find these statements to be entirely clear, we think that they imply that given 'some [expressive] qualities that were spotted in the first step, the second step of the analysis asks whether they could be fixed in some form other than the useful article itself'.[90] Or as we put it more simply elsewhere: 'In effect, the majority's test for separability amounts to: Could you draw it on a sheet of paper?'[91] 'Here, because the [uniform designs] could have been, and actually were, reproduced on other (presumably non-useful) media[– in drawings –]they were separable."[92]

The Supreme Court utterly fails to understand the statute and its requirement that decision makers identify distinct expressive and functional features of the claimed work. In its interpretation of the 'ordinary, contemporary, common meaning'[93] of the statute, the Court asks whether the spotted expressive features can be 'imagined apart from the useful article'.[94] But this is not how the statute reads.[95] Instead, the statute asks whether the work's expressive features can be separated from

[85] Ibid 417.
[86] Christopher Buccafusco and Jeanne C Fromer, 'Forgetting Functionality' (2017) 166 *University of Pennsylvania Law Review Online* 119, 121 (hereafter Buccafusco and Fromer, 'Forgetting Functionality').
[87] *Star Athletica*, above n 69, 417–418.
[88] Ibid 414.
[89] Ibid 414–415.
[90] Buccafusco and Fromer, 'Forgetting Functionality', above n 86, 122–124.
[91] Ibid 122.
[92] Ibid; see *Star Athletica*, above n 69, 414.
[93] *Star Athletica*, above n 69, 414.
[94] Ibid.
[95] Buccafusco and Fromer, 'Forgetting Functionality', above n 86, 122–124.

'the utilitarian aspects of the article'.[96] The difference is not trivial. The Court's statutory misreading substantially lowered the bar for claimants: Rather than distinguishing between and separating the uniform design's pictorial, graphic and sculptural features from its utilitarian aspects, the Court only asks whether the pictorial, graphic and sculptural features were distinct and separate from the uniform itself. Varsity could then claim the stripes, chevrons and colour-blocking because, once they were imaginatively removed from the uniform, a uniform could still exist. That is a different exercise from asking whether a design's pictorial, graphic and sculptural features could be separated from the design's utilitarian aspects.[97]

Under the correct formulation of the test, the Court would have had to determine which components of the design it should treat as utilitarian aspects, something it never asked under the test it conceived for itself.

To make matters worse, the Court failed to appreciate how rigorously Congress intended copyright law to treat functionality. The Court seems to have rejected the notion that copyright law should only be used to protect a work's exclusively expressive features. The majority explains that the imaginatively removed feature of the work 'may not be a useful article', but the majority concludes that the feature is still protectable even if 'the imagined remainder [is not] a fully functioning useful article at all, much less an equally useful one'.[98] This reading of the Act flips the statute on its head. Instead of copyright law protecting only solely expressive features of a work and excluding completely functional and dual-nature aspects, the Court's opinion will prevent copyright from attaching only to purely functional features of the work.

Given the Supreme Court's statutory interpretation, it never had to think carefully about the arguments we have raised above. Because the Court lowered the bar for copyright claimants to protect functional aspects of their designs, it did not significantly interrogate whether the features of the uniform designs that influenced perceptions of wearers' bodies were hybrid. The Court further neglected to rely on the part of the copyright statute that explains what makes a feature utilitarian and which we think requires the classification of many fashion features as utilitarian and therefore inseparable and unprotectable.

[96] Copyright Act 1976, 17 USC § 101 (US).

[97] Buccafusco and Fromer, 'Forgetting Functionality', above n 86, 122–124.

[98] *Star Athletica*, above n 69, 420.

Although this is a shame, it is not a complete catastrophe. The useful articles doctrine is not the only mechanism by which copyright law polices functionality, and we are sanguine that subsequent courts will utilise these tools. For example, for the same reasons as we have articulated as to why these design features are not separable, they likely run afoul of the merger doctrine and ought to be denied protectability on that ground as well. When there are a limited number of ways to express something, the merger doctrine denies copyrightability to that expression, lest it protect the function too.[99] Given the particularities of human vision and human torsos, we suspect that there are only a limited number of ways to express the functions of accentuating the cheerleader's curves, lengthening the cheerleader's torso and so forth. There is thus good basis to deny copyrightability to these features for having merged function and expression.

In addition, when decision makers compare a plaintiff's work with an allegedly infringing work, copyright law demands that they filter out from their analysis aspects of the plaintiff's work that are functional.[100] Accordingly, when decision makers are asked to compare garments like Varsity's to allegedly infringing copies like Star Athletica's, they should be instructed to ignore aspects of the plaintiff's work that contribute to its function, including dual-nature features like the ones discussed above. Doing so will help achieve Congress' goal of limiting copyright protection to functional designs and will minimise costs to consumers and subsequent designers.

3.5 Fashion's Function in Trademark Law

Copyright law is not the only field of intellectual property law that is concerned with screening out functional aspects of product design. Both trademark law and design patent law also cast a wary eye toward

[99] Pamela Samuelson, 'Reconceptualizing Copyright's Merger Doctrine' (2016) 63 *Journal of the Copyright Society of the USA* 417. A canonical case on this doctrine holds that when there is 'one form of expression, [or] at best only a limited number [of ways to express an idea], to permit copyrighting would mean that a party or parties, by copyrighting a mere handful of forms, could exhaust all possibilities of future use of the substance'. *Morrissey v Proctor & Gamble Co*, 379 F 2d 675, 678 (1st Cir. 1967). For that reason, the idea is considered to have merged with the expression, rendering the expression as unprotectable by copyright as the idea. Ibid.

[100] Buccafusco and Lemley, 'Functionality Screens', above n 5.

functionality.[101] Although the doctrines these regimes use to screen functionality differ from those employed by copyright law, their concerns are similar. Accordingly, we analyse how these two fields should respond to the particular issue of fashion design's dependent functionality, considering trademark law in this section and design patent law in Section 3.6.

Unlike copyright law, trademark law is not concerned with encouraging the creation of new aesthetic works. Instead, to promote fair competition and protect consumers, trademark law guards consumers from marketplace confusion by ensuring that certain symbols accurately reflect the source of goods.[102] If a pair of shoes has the distinctive Nike swoosh on it, consumers should be able to trust that the shoes are made by Nike. Trademark law covers more than just words or images that designate source, however. It can also be used to protect features of a product's design or packaging that identify its source.[103] This is known as trade dress.

Trademark law is similar to copyright in at least one important respect: it also needs to be concerned about functionality.[104] Just as features of a pictorial, graphic or sculptural work can have utilitarian features, so too can a product's design or packaging. Moreover, allowing mark owners to protect the functional aspects of their designs can have anticompetitive effects as it does in copyright law.[105] Like copyrights, trademarks do not undergo the substantial ex ante evaluation that patents do to ensure that they are new and nonobvious. In many cases, allowing trademark protection for aspects of garment design that affect the perception of the wearer's body will produce problematic anticompetitive effects.

To ensure that trademark law is not used to provide claimants with an undue competitive advantage, the law excludes functional trademarks

[101] Christopher Buccafusco, Mark A Lemley and Jonathan S Masur, 'Intelligent Design' (2018) 68 *Duke Law Journal* 75.

[102] Mark P McKenna, 'The Normative Foundations of Trademark Law' (2007) 82 *Notre Dame Law Review* 1839, 1841.

[103] *Wal-Mart Stores, Inc v Samara Bros, Inc*, 529 US 205 (2000); *Two Pesos, Inc v Taco Cabana, Inc*, 505 US 763 (1992).

[104] Mark P McKenna, '(Dys)functionality' (2011) 48 *Houston Law Review* 823 (hereafter McKenna, '(Dys)functionality').

[105] Buccafusco and Lemley, 'Functionality Screens', above n 5; McKenna, '(Dys)functionality', above n 104.

and trade dress from protection.[106] Trademark law enables owners to take advantage of the value of their reputations for producing high-quality products, but it seeks to prevent them from using trademarks to gain advantages unrelated to their reputation.[107] This unfair advantage could result if the mark extended to cover useful product features that competitors were then prevented from producing.[108] It could also occur if the mark extended to product features that consumers desired to purchase irrespective of their source-signifying characteristics.

Features of clothing design that influence the way the wearer's body is perceived, such that they make him or her look thinner, bigger, taller or curvier should be treated as bearing on the functionality inquiry in trade dress law. Such features should be treated as functional to the extent that they confer an unfair competitive advantage. Thus, while Burberry's plaid is purely ornamental, a design that used stripes to make the wearer's legs look longer or one that used a pattern to make the wearer's feet look smaller should be treated as functional and unprotectable.

3.6 Fashion's Function in Design Patent Law

Creators of 'any new, original and ornamental design for an article of manufacture' may obtain a design patent.[109] Design patents provide protection from infringement for 15 years from the date of patent grant.[110] To get a design patent, a design's creator must apply to the Patent and Trademark Office, where the application will be examined for patentability.[111] Design patent law does not treat the 'ornamental[ity]' requirement as an affirmative condition that designs be aesthetically pleasing.[112] Rather, the law has long seen this threshold requirement to mean that designs simply be 'non-functional'.[113] The courts have furthermore not understood this requirement to mean that entire designs are necessarily rendered unprotectable for functionality; after all, the 'article[s] of manufacture' that design patent law anticipates will be

106 *TrafFix Devices, Inc v Marketing Displays, Inc*, 532 US 23 (2001).
107 McKenna, '(Dys)functionality', above n 104, 825.
108 *In re Morton-Norwich Prods., Inc*, 671 F 2d 1332, 1339 (CCPA 1982).
109 Patent Act 2012, 35 USC § 171 (US).
110 Ibid §§ 173, 289.
111 Ibid §§ 111, 112, 171.
112 *Seiko Epson Corp v Nu-Kote International, Inc*, 190 F 3d 1360, 1368 (Fed. Cir. 1999).
113 Matthew A Smith, *Design Patents* (2012) 8 (preliminary draft) <http://patentlyo.com/media/docs/2012/12/2012-12-17_design_patents.pdf>.

protected will typically have conventionally functional uses.[114] Instead, courts understand the ornamentality/non-functionality requirement to signify that a 'design patent only protects the novel, ornamental features of the patented design'.[115]

What 'functional' means in the context of design patent law seems less stringent than in copyright and trademark law. A design feature is functional, and therefore unprotectable, only if the feature is '"dictated by" the use or purpose of the article'.[116] By contrast, as the Federal Circuit has explained, 'when there are several ways to achieve the function of an article of manufacture, the design of the article is more likely to serve a primarily ornamental purpose'.[117]

Design patent law ought to take account of hybrid design features in fashion. That is, the law must sort out how to characterise these features: as ornamental or not ornamental. Design patent law must decide whether these features that function to change the appearance of the wearer rather than merely to look attractive in their own right are well accounted for in the calibrations of design patent law or are better addressed by utility patent law. To the extent that design patent law – or the other non-utility patent IP regimes – ignores fashion's function, it risks imposing substantial limits on competition, stifling innovation and increasing costs to consumers.

3.7 Conclusion

The account of fashion's function that we develop in this chapter clarifies how intellectual property law should treat fashion design. It recognises an important way in which designs are functional – when they affect how wearers' bodies are perceived. This is not simply an issue with fashion design, however. As fashion designer and businesswoman Coco Chanel famously said, 'Fashion is not something that exists in dresses only. Fashion is in the sky, in the street. Fashion has to do with the ideas, the way we live, what is happening.'[118] Looking beyond fashion, many visual media can affect the ways that we perceive objects. Trompe l'oeil

[114] Buccafusco and Lemley, 'Functionality Screens', above n 5.

[115] *OddzOn Prods, Inc v Just Toys, Inc*, 122 F 3d 1396, 1405 (Fed Cir. 1997).

[116] *LA Gear, Inc v Thom McAn Shoe Co*, 988 F 2d 1117, 1123 (Fed Cir. 1993).

[117] Ibid.

[118] Rachel Dixon, 'Coco Before Chanel: "She Was Claiming Freedom Through Her Designs"', *The Guardian* (July 31, 2009), <https://www.theguardian.com/lifeandstyle/2009/jul/31/coco-before-chanel>.

painting and camouflage techniques have this effect. The same is true of chemical or physical processes for developing pigments, such as Vantablack, a carbon nanotube surface coating that produces the sensation of perfect blackness.[119] Attempts to gain intellectual property protection for any of these techniques, unless through the patent system, should be met with intense scepticism.

119 Elizabeth Blair, 'Some Artists Are Seeing Red over a New "Black"', *National Public Radio* (March 3, 2016), <http://www.npr.org/sections/thetwo-way/2016/03/03/469082803/some-artists-are-seeing-red-over-a-new-black>.

4

Shape Trademarks Are in Fashion

A Study of Footwear and Sneakers in Australia

VICKI HUANG*

ABSTRACT

The transformation of the sneaker from functional sportswear to a coveted symbol of high-end fashion, represents one of the most significant sartorial shifts in recent history. As demand for sneakers has surged —driven in large part by a renewed interest in fashion among men— competition within the market has intensified. In response, designers have increasingly sought new ways to protect the distinctive appearance of their products. This chapter shows that empirically, the sneaker revolution has increased demand for Australian 3D shape trademarks rather than for registered design rights. This chapter discusses this trend as a cautionary tale for those who might call for a sui generis design right for fashion. This study contends that the lack of demand for Australian design rights arises from a failure to consider aspects of culture, commerce, and the matrix of related rights, particularly trademark rights.

4.1 Introduction

4.1.1 The Sneaker Revolution

Evidence suggests that sneakers were developed in the mid-nineteenth century for privileged elites to play tennis or croquet on grassy British lawns.[1] Since that time, sneakers have transformed from sports

* Thanks to Mitchell Adams, Megan Richardson and David Tan for their comments and assistance. Also, thanks to comments from other authors in this book given at a research roundtable, NUS, Singapore, January 2023.

[1] Elizabeth Semmelhack, 'From Lawn Tennis to Eugenics: A History of Women and Sneakers' (2019) 53(1) *Costume: Journal of the Costume Society* 92, 92.

equipment – to everyday shoe – to fashion object – coveted by both men and women.[2] This transformation is one of the most significant developments in recent sartorial history and, commercially, sneakers now fuel a billion-dollar industry.[3]

A question that arises is why? Why have sneakers become standard footwear for casual use, common on the red carpet and even seen in office wear?[4] Why are we now more likely to talk about 'dress sneakers' than to discuss high heels or lace-up wingtips? The reasons for the shift in aesthetics has triggered examinations from a variety of scholars across different disciplines.[5] For example, feminist scholars have discussed the increased participation of women in the paid workforce and documented the imposition of high heels as a feminist issue.[6] Sociologists and fashion scholars have also written of men's everyday uniform moving away from the suit (and dress shoes) towards a more casual aesthetic.[7] Many have also examined the overall casualisation of the workplace both pre- and post-pandemic.[8] Another significant phenomenon is the emergence of 'sneakerhead culture' – defined as the admiration, collection and trading of sneakers – whose advent is credited to the 1970s hip-hop era in the United States but has since become a

[2] Delisia Matthews, Qiana Cryer-Coupet and Nimet Degirmencioglu, 'I Wear, Therefore I Am: Investigating Sneakerhead Culture, Social Identity, and Brand Preference among Men' (2021) 8(1) *Fashion and Textiles* 1, 2 (hereafter Matthews, Cryer-Coupet and Degirmencioglu, 'I Wear, Therefore I Am').

[3] MarketLine, 'Footwear in Australia, July 2021, Reference Code: 0125–0619' (Research Report) 9 (hereafter Marketline, 'Footwear in Australia, July 2021').

[4] Although note the controversy over wearing sneakers in the US White House: Guy Trebay, 'Do Dress Sneakers Belong in the Oval Office?', *New York Times* (May 19, 2023) <https://www.nytimes.com/2023/05/19/style/do-dress-sneakers-belong-in-the-oval-office.html>.

[5] For an overview of costume and materials history, see Giorgio Riello, 'The Object of Fashion: Methodological Approaches to the History of Fashion' (2022) 152 *Centro de Estudios en Diseño y Comunicación* 121.

[6] See, eg, Marc Linder, 'Smart Women, Stupid Shoes, and Cynical Employers: The Unlawfulness and Adverse Health Consequences of Sexually Discriminatory Workplace Footwear Requirements for Female Employees' (1997) 22(2) *Journal of Corporation Law* 295; and Elizabeth Semmelhack, 'Shoes That Put Women in Their Place', *The New York Times* (May 24, 2015) <https://www.nytimes.com/2015/05/24/opinion/sunday/shoes-that-put-women-in-their-place.html>.

[7] Yuniya Kawamura, *Sneakers: Fashion, Gender, and Subculture. Dress, Body, Culture* (Bloomsbury Academic, 2016) 74 (hereafter Kawamura, *Sneakers*).

[8] See, eg, McKinsey & Company, *The State of Fashion 2023* (November 29, 2022) <https://www.mckinsey.com/industries/retail/our-insights/state-of-fashion> (hereafter McKinsey & Co, *SOF 2023*).

world-wide phenomenon.[9] This increased demand for sneakers (both as everyday footwear and as an object of fashion) has shaken up competition in the traditional sneaker market.

4.1.2 The Major Players in the Sneaker Market

In Australia, traditional sneaker brands such as Nike and Adidas still dominate the performance and lifestyle shoe markets. However, since the sneaker revolution, sneakers are a now a regular offering from many high street and luxury brands, enlarging the lifestyle market with additional (and often more expensive) options. For example, sneakers are now a critical product line from designers such as Balenciaga, Gucci and Alexander McQueen.[10] Conversely, traditional sneaker brands have expanded into more fashion-conscious markets. For example, Nike founded NikeLab[11] to create high end and occasionally avant-garde shoes and apparel. Likewise, Adidas maintains the brand Y-3, which is a long-standing collaboration with renowned avant-garde Japanese designer Yohji Yamamoto (Figure 4.1).[12] Most of the traditional sneaker brands also create capsule collections with successful athletes, for example, Naomi Osaka with Nike.[13] However, many collaborations are now with celebrity designers such as Victoria Beckham (with Reebok),[14] and Stella McCartney (with Adidas).[15] Occasionally, these high-profile relationships experience well-publicised implosions, for example, Adidas' partnership with rapper Ye (formerly known as Kanye West).[16]

[9] Matthews, Cryer-Coupet and Degirmencioglu, 'I Wear, Therefore I Am', above n 2.

[10] Jonathan Hyman, Charlene Azema and Loni Morrow, 'If the IP Fits, Wear It: IP Protection for Footwear—A U.S. Perspective' (2018) 108(3) *The Trademark Reporter* 645 (hereafter Hyman, Azema and Morrow, 'If the IP Fits').

[11] See, eg, Nike, 'Nikelab' (*Nike*) <https://www.nike.com/au/nikelab>.

[12] See, eg, adidas, 'Y-3' (*adidas*) <https://perma.cc/6NYY-T5TF>.

[13] See, eg, Nike, 'Naomi Osaka' (*Nike*) <https://www.nike.com/au/w/naomi-osaka-4an2m>.

[14] Nicole Phelps, 'Victoria Beckham Has Teamed Up with Reebok on a New Athleticwear Collection – And You're Going to Want Everything', *Vogue Online* (January 22, 2019) <https://www.vogue.com/article/victoria-beckham-reebok-collaboration>.

[15] See, eg, Stella McCartney, 'Adidas by Stella McCartney' (*Stella McCartney*) <https://www.stellamccartney.com/au/en/adidas-by-stella-mccartney.html#:~:text=adidas%20by%20Stella%20McCartney%20is,%2C%20yoga%2C%20tennis%20and%20swim>.

[16] Kim Bhasin and Tim Loh, 'Adidas Bet Big on a Volatile Artist, and Lost', *Australian Financial Review* (June 7, 2023) <https://www.afr.com/companies/sport/adidas-bet-big-on-a-volatile-artist-and-lost-20230605-p5de0p#>.

Figure 4.1 Example of cross-market entrants – Adidas' Y-3 Fall/Winter 2022 Collection.[17]
© Thue Norgaard

4.1.2.1 Goliath v Goliath

As fashion designers have entered the lucrative sneaker market, traditional sneaker brands have launched a myriad of lawsuits to protect the distinctive aspects of their shoes including their shape. For example, Adidas are well known for suing any designer using angled stripes on sneakers.[18] Likewise, Converse (now owned by Nike) has filed dozens of

[17] See, eg, Joanna Elizabeth, 'Memories of Orange: Y-3 Fall 2022 Chapter 3 Drops', *Fashion Gone Rogue* (July 18, 2022) <https://www.fashiongonerogue.com/adidas-y-3-fall-2022-memories-orange-campaign/> (where the sneakers are photographed in a high fashion rather than athletic context).

[18] See, eg, Europe: *Shoe Branding Europe BVBA v Adidas and OHIM*, Case C-396/15 P (CJEU, February 7, 2016). See, eg, *Adidas AG v Pacific Brands Footwear Pty Ltd (No 3)* (2013) 308 ALR 74 (Australia); *Adidas America, Inc v Payless Shoesource, Inc*, 546 F Supp 2d 1029 (D Or. 2008) (US).

trademark suits to protect its iconic 'Chuck Taylor' sneaker, which have sold over a billion units since 1917.[19] In the last few years alone, sneaker infringement cases against fashion designers have become almost commonplace. Recently in 2023, Ralph Lauren was sued by NBA hall-of-famer (and Nike collaborator) George Gervin in relation to its high-top basketball sneaker named the 'Gervin Mid'. Gervin alleged violations of his right of publicity, trademark infringement and false designation of origin.[20] The case settled.[21] Also in 2023, Nike sued and settled a trade dress infringement lawsuit against designer John Geiger alleging his GF-01 shoes infringed Nike's Air Force 1 trade dress (see Figure 4.2).[22] In another well-publicised case in 2022, Vans successfully restrained the sale of guerrilla art studio MSCHF's 'Wavy Baby' shoes (a collaboration with singer Tyga), which Vans claimed were a copy of Vans' iconic Sk8 shoes.[23]

4.1.2.2 Approaches Vary across Jurisdictions

These examples demonstrate that it has never been more important for sneaker designers to protect their distinctive trademarks or innovative designs. This competitiveness, coupled with the globalisation of brands, has heightened interest in cross-jurisdictional protection for footwear designs and revealed important differences between legal systems. Of relevance to shoes, this includes the treatment of 3D shape trademarks, the role of design laws, overlap rules and the treatment of functional signs and designs. For example, in the EU, UK, Singapore and Australia, fashion designers have access to both trademark rights and some form of registered or unregistered design rights. In contrast, shoe litigation in the United States typically proceeds as infringement of 'trade dress' – a trademark doctrine originally limited to packaging but that has expanded since the 1980s to 'the

19 Ed Pilkington, 'Converse Blitzes 31 Companies with Lawsuits Over Chuck Imitators', *The Guardian* (October 15, 2014) <https://www.theguardian.com/fashion/2014/oct/14/converse-chucks-imitations-sneakers-companies-lawsuits>.

20 *Gervin v Ralph Lauren Corp*, Case 1:23-cv-1284 (SDNY, complaint filed March 17, 2023), settled with orders published June 6, 2023 at *Gervin v Ralph Lauren Corp*, Case 1:23-cv-1284 (Opinion and Order) (SDNY, June 6, 2023).

21 Ibid.

22 See, eg, *Nike, Inc v La La Land Prod & Design, Inc*, Case 2:21-cv-00443-MCS-PVC (CD Cal, February 8, 2022).

23 *Vans, Inc v MSCHF Prod Studio, Inc*, 602 F Supp 3d 358 (EDNY 2022).

Air Force 1 trade dress	Genuine Air Force 1 Shoes	Infringing/Geiger Products

Figure 4.2 Nike Air Force 1 trade dress vs Geiger's alleged infringing products.[24]
Courtesy of US District Court, Central District of California, opinion

shape and design of the product itself'.[25] The limits of the latter doctrine continue to lead commentators to demand some form of sui generis fashion or design right.[26]

24 *Nike, Inc v La La Land Prod & Design, Inc*, Case 2:21-cv-00443-MCS-PVC (CD Cal, February 8, 2022) at [1] (the court presenting a succinct comparator table of one plane of the sneakers in suit).

25 J Thomas McCarthy, *McCarthy on Trademarks and Unfair Competition* (West Group, 5th ed, 1996–2023) at [§ 8:1] 'Trade Dress Compared to Trademarks'.

26 See, eg, recent commentary from academics, practitioners and media: Cassandra Baloga, 'Copyright & Fashion: The Shoe That Does Not Fit' (2019) 64(3) *New York Law School*

This chapter uses Australia as a case study to illustrate the empirical impact of the sneaker revolution on registered trademark and design rights. This case study also serves as a cautionary tale for those advocating sui generis design rights for fashion designers. This chapter reveals the problems with the Australian system, which implemented a registered design right (without a grace period for self-disclosure) and also allows for concurrent 3D shape trademarks (where there is no statutory bar against functional shapes). In addition to these technical lacunae, this chapter will argue that aspects of culture are relevant in designing an optimal IP framework. This chapter argues that there are unusual aspects of Australian culture as well as IP law that shepherd designers towards registering the overall appearance of a product (such as a shoe) as a 3D trademark but. not as a registered design. This is a problem because in Australia (as with many jurisdictions), a preference for trademark rights over other time-limited rights such as patents or designs can lead to perpetual trademark registrations and anti-competitive monopolies.

4.2 A Culture of 'Casual Piracy'

In comparison to the jurisdictions discussed in this book, Australia is unusual in the sense of being a relatively wealthy country[27] but one that has a notorious attitude of casual piracy towards designer goods.[28] By 'casual piracy', I am not referring to 'frequency of downloads', as that phrase is used in a copyright piracy context.[29] Nor am I referring to so-

Law Review 265; Alice Wickens, 'Design Piracy in the United States: Time to Fashion a Remedy?' (2021) 24(1/2) *Journal of World Intellectual Property* 55; Chavie Lieber, 'Fashion Brands Steal Design Ideas All the Time. And It's Completely Legal. Blame America's Outdated Copyright Laws', *Vox* (April 27, 2018) <https://www.vox.com/2018/4/27/17281022/fashion-brands-knockoffs-copyright-stolen-designs-old-navy-zara-h-and-m>.

27 Credit Suisse, *Global Wealth Databook 2021* (2021) <https://www.credit-suisse.com/about-us/en/reports-research/global-wealth-report.html#:~:text=Total%20global%20wealth%20grew%20by,fastest%20annual%20rate%20ever%20recorded>.

28 Vicki Huang, 'An Empirical Analysis of the Fashion Design Case Law of Australia' (2021) 52(3) *International Review of Intellectual Property and Competition Law* 242, 243: 'A level of benign copying is tolerated in Australia due to the prospect of a net benefit from competition and substitution.'

29 Creative Content Australia, *2021 Australian Piracy Behaviours and Attitudes* (2022) <https://creativecontentaustralia.org.au/wp-content/uploads/2022/04/2021-Australian-Piracy-Behaviours-and-Attitudes.pdf>. See also Australian Government, Attorney General's Department, *Copyright Enforcement Review Issues Paper* (Consultation Paper,

called 'benign copying' done by design-intensive countries, which begets fresh innovation (typically discussed as the piracy paradox).[30] 'Casual piracy' in this context refers to an observation that in Australia, buying and using copies of designer goods is not a hidden shame. Surveys have shown that from a cultural perspective, Australians are more accepting of counterfeit or replica designer products than other developed nations.[31] For example, YouTube videos can be found of Australians instructing others where to buy the best fake bags in Bali (a popular holiday destination for Australians).[32] This kind of 'casual piracy' is often open and frequently normalised. This casual attitude to piracy has been discussed in a copyright context,[33] but I argue that the normalisation of piracy exists in the design context as well.

In a recent IP Australia survey,[34] industry respondents reported 'that consumers and other businesses in Australia do not sufficiently value original design or appreciate the impacts (financial and otherwise) of copying designers, particularly in fashion and furniture'.[35] In reviewing public sentiment, IP Australia found that although designers were concerned about unauthorised copying, this concern was not reflected in the

December 2022) <https://consultations.ag.gov.au/rights-and-protections/copyright-enforcement-review/>.

30 G Noto La Diega, 'Can the Law Fix the Problem of Fashion? An Empirical Study on Social Norms and Power Imbalance in the Fashion Industry' (2019) 14(1) *Journal of Intellectual Property Law & Practice* 18; Kal Raustiala and Christopher Sprigman, 'The Piracy Paradox: Innovation and Intellectual Property in Fashion Design' (2006) 92 *Virginia Law Review* 1687.

31 Tim Golder and Marina Lloyd Jones, 'Unravelling the Threads: Protection for Fashion Designs under Australia's IP Laws' (2009) 4(2) *Journal of Intellectual Property Law & Practice* 95, 108 (discussing a 2005 AC Nielsen Survey and arguing that: 'In Australia, at least it seems that we are willing to fake it').

32 See, eg, Noufy Loves Luxury, 'Louis Vuitton and luxury replica – Bali Market Shopping 2022', YouTube June 9, 2022) <https://www.youtube.com/watch?v=J5LLvZa-qw>, archived at <https://perma.cc/4ASP-R2EE>.

33 Content Café, 'Industry Voices: Liz Bales, The Industry Trust for IP Awareness' (Interview Transcript, August 24, 2021), <https://contentcafe.org.au/chapters-stories-everything/insights-from-industry-insiders-liz-bales-chief-executive-of-the-industry-trust-for-ip-awareness/>. See also '"The Whole Country Pirates": US Comedian Louis CK on Australia – Audio', *The Guardian* (June 6, 2014) <https://www.theguardian.com/technology/audio/2014/jun/06/louis-ck-explains-piracy-australia>.

34 IP Australia is the administrative body for registered IP rights in Australia. See IP Australia, 'About Us' (*IP Australia*) <https://www.ipaustralia.gov.au/about-us>.

35 IP Australia, *Protecting Designs: Design Innovation, Copying and Enforcement in Australia* (Report, 2020) 16 <https://www.ipaustralia.gov.au/sites/default/files/protecting_design_ip_australia_report.pdf>.

broader public conversation.[36] In other words, Australians seem to have a strong appetite for replica goods particularly where the price for the original is much higher than the price for the copy.

In a classical paradigm, a designer might protect their goods from a copier by applying a trademark to the face of the article. However, under common law concepts of trademark law, the equity protected is in the trademark itself and not in the underlying product. Therefore, a counterfeiter could avoid trademark infringement by replicating the underlying article – for example, shoe, bag or dress – but omitting the trademark.[37] In Australia and elsewhere, there would arguably still be a strong demand for this unbranded replica product. This has led some fashion houses to embrace the 'logo-fication' of their goods. For example, some designers with strong trademarks may incorporate or weave their trademarks into the surface of the articles. For example, Burberry's check trademark and Louis Vuitton's monogram trademarks have been incorporated into the entire surface of clothing, handbags and shoes (Figure 4.3).[38] This is a sub-optimal choice for weaker brands and also for well-branded fashion houses who may refuse to confine their creativity to logo-fied goods.

In Australia, for those designers who cannot or will not 'logo-fy' their products but want to protect the overall appearance of their goods, the most attractive option is to pursue protection for the overall appearance of the underlying article, for example, to pursue shoe protection as a 3D shape or as a registered design. In other words, the legal impetus to protect fashion items as 3D IP is important in Australia due to its culture of casual piracy (which happily consumes un-branded 'knock-offs') and where logo-fication is an unavailable or unappealing option.

4.3 Legal Options for Fashion Designers in Australia

If a fashion designer seeks to prevent the copying of an object itself – apparel, shoes, bags, etc – there are many options available to a designer under Australian IP law. For example, a designer can access formal

[36] Ibid.

[37] In Australia and the UK, this could still arguably find an action in common law passing off.

[38] Francesca Montalvo Witzburg, 'Protecting Fashion: A Comparative Analysis of Fashion Design Protection in the United States and the European Union,' (November–December 2017) 107(6) *The Trademark Reporter* 1131, 1131.

Figure 4.3 Logo-fication of designs: (*left*) Burberry's check trademark used upon a sneaker;[39] (*right*) Louis Vuitton quatrefoils and flowers trademarks used upon a sneaker.[40]
(a) © Burberry Limited (b) © Louis Vuitton Australia Pty Ltd.

registered IP rights under the Designs Act 2003 (Cth), Trade Marks Act 1995 (Cth) or Patents Act 1990 (Cth) or unregistered rights under the Copyright Act 1968 (Cth). Designers may also access allied rights under statutory consumer law or the common law tort of passing off.[41] However, this chapter argues that Australian law maintains peculiar lacunae within, and between, copyright, designs and trademark law that shepherd designers towards relying upon 3D trademark rights to protect their designs rather than other types of rights. This is an outcome most jurisdictions try to avoid due to anti-competitive issues specific to trademark law. The concern is that because registered trademarks can be

[39] See, eg, Burberry, 'Vintage Check Cotton and Suede Sneakers Colour: Birch Brown' (*Burberry*) <https://perma.cc/Q8UN-X8MU>. See also Australian Trade Mark No 365299, filed on 7 September 1981 (Registered on September 7, 1981).

[40] See, eg, Louis Vuitton, 'LV Trainer Sneaker' (*Louis Vuitton*) <https://perma.cc/92R2-RRJ9>. See also *Australian Trade Mark No* 8955 (demonstrating the application of high status brand logos upon low status sneakers).

[41] See, eg, *Peter Bodum A/S v DKSH Australia Pty Ltd* (2011) 280 ALR 639.

renewed indefinitely, a perpetual monopoly over a shape (particularly a functional shape) might be granted to a designer/trademark owner. To understand how this sub-optimal situation arose and why designers nevertheless may default to, or strategically use, shape trademarks, a brief overview of relevant aspects of Australian copyright, designs and trademark law is required.

4.3.1 *Copyright and Design Overlap Laws*

In Australia, as with many jurisdictions, copyright subsists automatically once a work assumes material form; registration is not required, and copyright terms are long, typically the life of the author plus 70 years after death of the author.[42] This can make copyright an attractive 'default' if a fashion designer has not, or cannot, obtain other forms of protection, for example, a registered design right. In line with other Commonwealth jurisdictions, the Australian Copyright Act 1968 (Cth) prescribes a closed list of categories for copyrightable works.[43] However, as with the United Kingdom, in Australia the exclusion of utilitarian works is via case law[44] rather than expressly proscribed by statute as in the United States.[45]

In contrast to the United States, Australia also maintains sui generis design laws that were originally modelled on UK legislation.[46] However, unlike the United Kingdom and many EU member states,[47] Australia

[42] See Copyright Act 1968 (Cth), s 10 (Australia) for definitions of 'artistic work' and 'material form'. See also ss 32, 33.

[43] Copyright Act 1968 (Cth), s 32 (Australia), 'Copyright subsists in works: original literary, dramatic, musical or artistic works . . .. Copyright subsists in subject matter other than works: s 85 sound recordings, s 86, cinematograph film, s87 television and sound broadcasts and s 88 published editions of works.' See similar provisions in the UK Copyright, Designs and Patents Act 1988, s 1 (UK). In contrast, EU countries adopt a flexible approach. For example in France, Article L112–1 awards copyright to 'creative products of the mind'.

[44] For example, the High Court, in determining whether a boat hull was protectable under the Copyright Act 1968 (Cth) (Australia) as a work of artistic craftsmanship, held that 'Whether a work is one of artistic craftsmanship . . . turns upon an assessment of the extent to which a work's artistic expression is constrained or unconstrained by functional considerations.' *Burge v Swarbrick* (2007) 232 CLR 336, at [84] (hereafter *Burge*).

[45] Copyright Act 1976, 17 USC § 102 (US).

[46] Collectively, the Designs Act 2003 (Cth) (Australia), Designs Regulations 2004 (Cth) (Australia) and IP Australia, *Designs Examiners' Manual of Practice and Procedure* (Live Manual) <http://manuals.ipaustralia.gov.au/designs/designs_exam_manual.htm>.

[47] Estelle Derclaye, 'A Model Copyright/Design Interface' in Estelle Derclaye (ed), *The Copyright/Design Interface: Past, Present and Future* (Cambridge University Press, 2018) 421; Oliver Church, Estelle Derclaye and Gilles Stupfler, 'Design Litigation in the

pursues a strict approach to demarcation and limits the cumulation of copyrights.[48] The legislative overlap provisions are complex, but essentially designers lose copyright protection if they apply their design industrially, that is, where the design is reproduced 50 times through embodiment into a 3D product.[49] So a sketch of a shoe retains copyright as an artistic work (e.g., as a painting) if it is printed on a T-shirt (a 2D reproduction of an artistic work as surface ornamentation) but loses copyright if the reproduction is as a 3D product, for example, a shoe.[50] In effect, these provisions tacitly encourage designers to use shorter-lived registered design rights rather than rely on lengthy unregistered and unsearchable copyrights for 2D sketched designs.[51] For reasons discussed later, an increased interest in registered designs failed to materialise.

An important exception to the overlap provisions exists for products categorised as works of artistic craftsmanship (WOACs).[52] WOACs

EU Member States: Are Overlaps with Other Intellectual Property Rights and Unfair Competition Problematic and Are SMEs Benefiting from the EU Design Legal Framework?' (2021) 46(1) *European Law Review* 37.

48 See Isabella Alexander, 'The Copyright/Design Interface in Australia' in Estelle Derclaye (ed), *The Copyright/Design Interface: Past, Present and Future* (Cambridge University Press, 2018) 226.

49 Copyright Act 1968 (Cth), s 74 (Australia) and regulation 12 of the Copyright Regulations 2017 (Cth) (Australia) (Copyright Regulations) provides that a design is taken to be 'applied industrially' if it is (inter alia) applied to more than 50 chapters.

50 From 2003, the overlap provisions only apply to the Copyright Act 1968 (Cth), s 74(1) (Australia): corresponding design, in relation to an artistic work, means visual features of shape or configuration, which, when embodied in a product, result in a reproduction of that work, whether or not the visual features constitute a design that is capable of being registered under the Designs Act 2003 (Cth) (Australia). For the purposes of the Copyright Act 1968 (Cth), s 74(1) (Australia): 'embodied in' (in relation to a product) includes being woven into, impressed on or worked into the product. See, eg, *Seafolly Pty Ltd v Fewstone Pty Ltd* (2014) 313 ALR 41, wherein a 2D textile design was not embodied in a garment (swimwear) because the garments did not embody the features of shape or the configuration of the underlying artwork. The artwork retained copyright as an artistic work and did not fall under the ss 74–77 copyright /design overlap provisions.

51 *State of Escape Accessories Pty Ltd v Schwartz* (2022) 166 IPR 242 at [9] (hereafter *State of Escape*): 'The legislative policy is to encourage the use of the registered design system, rather than copyright, for the purpose of protecting artistic works which are applied to industrial products.'

52 Copyright Act 1968 (Cth), s 77 (Australia); Copyright Regulations above n 49 reg 12. Discussion by Full Court in *State of Escape Accessories Pty Ltd v Schwartz* (2022) 166 IPR 242 at [7]–[8]: 'Section 75 of the *Copyright Act 1968* (Cth) provides a defence to copyright infringement in an artistic work where a corresponding design is, or has been, registered as a design. A person will not infringe copyright that subsists in an artistic work by

may receive copyright protection even if registered or registrable under the Designs Act 2003 (Cth).[53] There is no definition of a WOAC in the Copyright Act 1968 (Cth), but UK and Australian courts have cited as examples the works of 'silversmiths, potters, woodworkers, hand embroiderers and many others'[54] whose works are seen as deserving of longer protection due to 'special training, skill and knowledge'.[55] The absence of a strict definition has meant designers of more modern products, such as boat hulls,[56] corkscrews[57] and handbags[58] have tried to shoehorn themselves into copyright in the absence of registered design right protection.

In relation to fashion, in a 1998 case,[59] the knitwear brand Coogi successfully argued that a length of its highly textured knitted fabric (which featured three-dimensional elements) was a work of artistic craftsmanship.[60] However, it failed to make out that copyright in this

reproducing the work in three-dimensional form when applying a corresponding design to a product. Section 77 of the *Copyright Act 1968* (Cth) also provides a defence to copyright infringement in an artistic work where a corresponding design is applied industrially, and the design is not registered or is not registrable under the *Designs Act 2003* (Cth). However, these defences do not operate where the artistic work is a work of "artistic craftsmanship". A work of artistic craftsmanship may still be afforded copyright protection, even if it is capable of protection by registration under the *Designs Act 2003* (Cth), and even if a corresponding design has been industrially applied.'

53 Explanatory Memorandum to the Copyright Amendment Bill 1988 (Cth) (Australia) at [24] states that works of artistic craftsmanship 'are more appropriately protected under the Act whether industrially applied or not'. The High Court in *Burge* above n 44 at [43] approved the observations of Drummond J in *Coogi Australia Pty Ltd v Hysport International Pty Ltd* (1998) 86 FCR 154, 168 (hereafter *Coogi*): 'What may justify the special status conferred on works of artistic craftsmanship by ss 74–77 is recognition that the real artistic quality that is an essential feature of such works and the desirability of encouraging real artistic effort directed to industrial design is sufficient to warrant the greater protection and the accompanying stifling effect on manufacturing development that long copyright gives, in contrast to relatively short design-protection.'

54 Eg, the High Court in *Burge* above n 44 discussed the history for the inclusion of WOAC at [45]–[62], including discussions of the report of the Gregory Committee at 260, and Lord Simons' discussion of applied and decorative arts emerging from the Arts and Crafts movement 1862–1910 in *George Hensher Ltd v Restawile Upholstery (Lancs) Ltd* [1976] AC 64, 77, 80–1, 84, 88, 96 (hereafter *Hensher*).

55 *Burge* above n 44 at [61], citing *Hensher*, above n 54, 91, per Lord Simon. For an in-depth analysis, see Patrick Masiyakurima, 'Copyright in Works of Artistic Craftsmanship: An Analysis' (2016) 36(3) *Oxford Journal of Legal Studies* 505.

56 *Burge*, above n 44.

57 *Sheldon and Hammond v Metrokane* (2004) 61 IPR 1.

58 *State of Escape*, above n 51.

59 Prior to the substantial reforms of the Designs Act 2003 (Cth) (Australia).

60 *Coogi v Hysport* (1998) 86 FCR 154.

WOAC had been infringed.[61] Unlike Coogi, most other fashion plaintiffs have failed in subsistence arguments, that is, that their products rose to being works of artistic craftsmanship. For example in 2003, a court held in *Muscat v Le*[62] that mundane black pants lacked the requisite artistry and artistic intent to be classed as a WOAC.[63] In a more recent case, the handbag designer of Escape's popular[64] neoprene tote bag failed to convince the Federal Court of Australia that the prototype for the bag was a WOAC (Figure 4.4).[65] In that case, the court held that 'whether the bag is a work of artistic craftsmanship turns on the extent to which the Escape Bag's artistic expression, in its form, was unconstrained by functional considerations'.[66] The court could not equate the designer's choices, for example, of neoprene fabric or using sailing rope for handles, to that of an 'artist-craftsperson';[67] instead, they were considered 'an evolution in styling'[68] rather than an act of artistic craftsmanship.

These cases indicate that copyright protection for a 3D object is theoretically possible *if* the work expresses the necessary artistry and artistic intent to be considered a work of artistic craftsmanship. However, the bar for such classification is extremely high. In *Coogi*, there was significant evidence of artistic decision-making in Coogi's unusual stitch structures and colours.[69] There was much evidence of conscious design choices incorporated into the 3D forms of the knitted textiles. Designers of less unusual forms will likely fail to qualify their products as WOACs and (as the legislature intended) should consider alternative rights, such as a registered design right. Unfortunately, as discussed below, Australian design law has had significant limitations.

61 Ibid at 615.
62 *Muscat v Le* (2003) 204 ALR 335.
63 Ibid at [48]–[49].
64 State of Escape, *As Seen In* (August 30, 2016) <https://www.stateofescape.com/pages/press>.
65 *State of Escape* above n 51.
66 Ibid at [37], affirming lower court at [109], which in turn cited *Burge*, above n 44, at [83].
67 *Burge*, above n 44, at [63], [66].
68 Ibid at [67].
69 *Coogi* above n 53.

Figure 4.4 State of Escape neoprene bag.[70]

4.3.2 Design Laws

In Australia, the Designs Act 2003 (Cth) seeks to protect the interests of designers for up to ten years.[71] The scope of the registrable interest is limited to the 'overall appearance of the product' where that appearance results from 'one or more visual features',[72] so long as it is 'new' and

70 *State of Escape*, above n 51, 23 (where the court discussed the features of the bag that might indicate artistic expression such as the use of sailing rope).

71 The term of protection for a design is five years from the filing date, with one allowable extension of five years upon payment of a single renewal fee: Designs Act 2003 (Cth), ss 46–47 (Australia).

72 Designs Act 2003 (Cth) (Australia): s 5 (design), s 6 (definition of a product), s 7 (definition of a visual feature).

'distinctive'[73] when compared with the prior art base.[74] Fashion, including apparel and shoes, is theoretically well suited for registrations as designs. In addition, Australia differs from many other TRIPS members by allowing functional features to be registered as designs.[75] Liability for infringement is found if a design is 'identical to' or 'substantially similar to' the overall impression of a registered design.[76] An online application starts from A$250, with additional fees required if a designer elects to have their design examined and certified.[77]

4.3.2.1 Design Registrations

Design applications are underused in Australia, particularly by Australian residents. Recent studies show that applications have stagnated and are relatively low in number (2,500–3,000 applications a year between 2001 and 2017).[78] In contrast, the number of design applications worldwide has doubled each year.[79] Indeed, non-residents constitute the majority of applicants for Australian design registrations.[80] An exception to this trend is for clothing manufacturing, where applications from Australians outnumber those from non-residents. Indeed 20% of all

[73] To be distinctive, a design must not be 'substantially similar' in overall impression to a design that forms part of the prior art base: Designs Act 2003 (Cth), pt 4 (Australia).

[74] The prior art base for a design consists of designs publicly used in Australia or published in a document anywhere in Australia or abroad: Designs Act 2003 (Cth) s 15(2) (Australia).

[75] Designs Act 2003 (Cth), s 7(2) (Australia). A visual feature may, but need not, serve a functional purpose. For a discussion of the legislative history behind the allowance of functionality, see Sam Ricketson, Megan Richardson, Mark J Davidson and Vicki Huang, *Intellectual Property: Cases, Materials and Commentary* (LexisNexis Butterworths, 6th edn, 2020) 574–576.

[76] Designs Act 2003 (Cth), s 71 (Australia). See also the exclusive rights of registered owners in s 10.

[77] A design must be examined and certified to commence infringement proceedings under Designs Act 2003 (Cth) s 73 (Australia). Approximately 15.9% of registered designs are certified. Michael R Falk et al, *Design Law and Practice: Design within Australia and How Australia Compares to Its International Peers* (Economic Research Paper No 08, IP Australia and IPRIA, 2019) (hereafter Falk et al, *Design Law and Practice*).

[78] Falk et al, '*Design Law and Practice*', above n 77, 10: Data from 2002–2017 shows a 'declining trend in the average number of design rights (applications) per employee since 2004–05 across the economy. This decline was less marked for the design rights-intensive industries'.

[79] IP Australia, *Valuing Designs: The Economic Impact of Design Rights in Australia* (Report, 2020) 7. <https://www.ipaustralia.gov.au/sites/default/files/defining_design_ip_australia_report.pdf>.

[80] Ibid.

Australian design registrations in 2016 were for clothing manufacturing with just 4% coming from non-residents.[81] The most prolific applicant is Australian designer Zimmermann with 668 applications primarily for dress designs.[82]

A question that emerges is – where are the *foreign* fashion designers? It seems paradoxical that foreign applicants dominate the Australian designs register except with regard to clothing manufacturing. One explanation is likely to be the historical absence of a grace period in Australia. That is, Australia (until recently) did not allow a grace period prior to the file date, meaning that if a designer staged a live fashion show or posted images onto social media, this would populate the prior art base and prevent design registrations of those exposed designs. While Australian-based designers would be aware of this trap, foreign designers may be less aware of Australian law, or they may consider Australia too small a market, or a season (and a hemisphere) outside the collections shown in Paris, Milan, London and New York to prioritise a design registration.

4.3.2.2 No Grace Period – Impact and Reforms

Different government reviews of the designs system found that Australia was one of the few industrialised countries without a 'grace period'[83] and this was a major deterrent from using the design system.[84] For example, the Australian Council for Intellectual Property (ACIP) found that designers would 'inadvertently or due to ignorance of the law' publish or reveal their design and thereby 'forfeit all possible rights in that design' by seeding the prior art base.[85] In IP Australia's 2020 survey, designers complained that the linear design rights system was in conflict with good design practice that 'is iterative, with rounds of ideation and prototyping based on different inputs'.[86] Designers complained about having to

[81] Falk et al, *Design Law and Practice*, above n 77, 15, reporting that 'It is worth noting that in Australia, 20 per cent of resident filings were in clothing manufacture in 2016. By comparison, in Germany, Italy and the UK, clothing has been the focus of both resident and non-resident design filers.'

[82] See, eg, *Zimmermann* Registered Design No. 202213209, June 3, 2022.

[83] Falk et al, '*Design Law and Practice*', above n 77, 8.

[84] See Advisory Council on Intellectual Property, *Review of the Designs System* (Final Report, March 2015) 28 (*Review*) (hereafter Advisory Council on Intellectual Property, *Review*). See also Falk et al, '*Design Law and Practice*', above n 77.

[85] Advisory Council on Intellectual Property, *Review*, above n 84, 8.

[86] IP Australia, *Talking Design: Views from Australia's Visual Design Ecosystem* (Report, January 2020) 12 <https://www.ipaustralia.gov.au/sites/default/files/talking_design_ip_australia_report.pdf>.

register a design before disclosing it (to test market demand), and this dissatisfaction was compounded by the inability to change that design after applying to register it.[87]

It is argued that for many designers with concerns about prior disclosures, registering a shape trademark for an object, such as a shoe, would be an attractive option. Trademarks are not tested for 'newness' against the prior art making any prior exposure of a design irrelevant. In addition, there are no cumulation bars to dual design/trademark rights (nor patent/copyright and trademark rights) in Australia.[88] Therefore, while the copyright/design overlap provisions would typically expel a fashion designer from copyright and towards designs protection, the limitations on design rights (particularly the historic lack of a grace period) might shepherd fashion designers, particularly international designers, to seek a shape mark for 3D objects.

Recent reforms to the Designs Act 2003 (Cth) in effect from September 2021 have introduced a 12-month grace period (prior to filing) and brings Australia closer to international norms.[89] This, and other changes designed to provide flexibility and simplicity, may influence the patterns of registrations from September 2021.[90] Nevertheless, the inherent benefits of securing a shape mark (discussed in Section 4.3.3) would likely still attract designers to trademarks, though the reforms might mean that more dual design and trademark rights are applied for post-reforms.

4.3.3 Trademarks

The advent of the Trade Marks Act 1995 (Cth) introduced major changes to comply with Australia's obligations under the TRIPS Agreement.[91]

[87] Ibid.

[88] The Productivity Commission, *Intellectual Property Arrangements, Inquiry Report* (Final Report no 78, September 23, 2016) 339–340 <https://www.pc.gov.au/inquiries/completed/intellectual-property#report>.

[89] Explanatory Memorandum, Designs Amendment (Advisory Council on Intellectual Property Response) Bill 2020 (Cth) (Australia), at [10], discussing the World Intellectual Property Organisation, *Industrial Design Law and Practice—Draft Chapters* (SCT/33/2, January 16, 2015) Art 6 <https://www.wipo.int/meetings/en/doc_details.jsp?doc_id=295316>.

[90] The new Act includes changes relating to relief from infringement before registration, to the right of the exclusive licensee to bring infringement proceeding and to formalities.

[91] See discussion at *Registrar of Trade Marks v Woolworths Ltd* (1999) 93 FCR 365, [19]. See also Mark J Davison and Ian Horak, *Shanahan's Australian Law of Trade Marks and*

The definition of a 'sign'[92] was broadened to expressly include shapes, sounds, colours and scents.[93] The protection of 3D shapes therefore has a different foundation to US trade dress law, which was influenced by state-based unfair competition law.[94] In Australia, unlike the United States, there is no requirement to show actual use or an express intention to use at the time of application; instead marks can be subject to removal for non-use after registration.[95] Indefinite renewals are permitted (without re-examination) so long as the renewal fees are paid.[96]

As with other TRIPS member countries, there were concerns that the express codification[97] of shape trademarks could have an anti-competitive effect if mark owners were to have monopolies over functional shapes.[98] A classic example is a basic bottle shape, or in a fashion context, the shape of a basic T-shirt. Both have an opening and a shape

Passing Off (Lawbook Co, 5th edn, 2012) [85.25] (hereafter Davison and Horak, *Shanahan's*).

92 'Sign' is defined in the Trade Marks Act 1995 (Cth), s 6 (Australia): '"Sign" includes the following or any combination of the following, namely, any letter, word, name, signature, numeral, device, brand, heading, label, ticket, aspect of packaging, shape, colour, sound or scent.'

93 In contrast, the Trade Marks Act 1955 (Cth), s 6 (Australia) defined a sign as a 'device, brand, heading, label, ticket, name, signature, word, letter or numeral, or any combination thereof'.

94 For example, see J Thomas McCarthy, *McCarthy on Trademarks and Unfair Competition* (West Group, 5th edn, 1996–2023) at [§ 7:54]. See also [§ 8:1]: 'Early in the development of the law, a distinction was made between the law of registered "trademarks" and the law of "unfair competition," with the latter encompassing, among other things, unregistered "trade dress." Today, these kinds of distinctions have disappeared. Today, many types of deigns and shapes protectable as "trade dress" can be registered as "trademarks."'

95 Trade Marks Act 1995 (Cth), pt 9 (Australia).

96 Ibid ss 75, 77.

97 Under the earlier Trade Marks Act 1995 (Cth) (Australia) shapes were not excluded from registration, but successful applicants usually relied on two-dimensional representations of their distinctive products or packaging. See, eg, the 2D shape of the Coca-Cola contour bottle and *AU Trade Mark No 63697*, filed on April 24, 1934 (Registered on April 25, 1934); *AU Trade Mark No 767355*, filed on July 14, 1998 (Registered on July 14 1998); *AU Trade Mark No 1160893*, filed on February 12, 2007 (Registered on February 12, 2007); and *AU Trade Mark No 1160894*, filed on February 12, 2007 (Registered on February 12, 2007).

98 See Julia Baird, 'The Registrability of Functional Shape Marks' (2002) 13(4) *Australian Intellectual Property Journal* 218, 225; Jani McCutcheon, 'Monopolised Product Shapes and Factual Distinctiveness under s.41(6) of the *Trade Marks Act* 1995 (Cth)' (2004) 15(1) *Australian Intellectual Property Journal* 18; Mark Davison, 'Shape Trade Marks: The Role and Relevance of Functionality and Aesthetics in Determining Their Registrability' (2004) 15(2) *Australian Intellectual Property Journal* 106, 108–109; Michael Handler, 'Disentangling Functionality, Distinctiveness and Use in Australian

designed to contain a substance, for example, a liquid or a human torso. These basic shapes serve a critical utilitarian function and to grant a trademark monopoly over such shapes might inhibit competition.

Most jurisdictions proscribe against registration of functional shapes though express statutory bars.[99] However, for reasons that remain 'obscure',[100] there are no express legislative provisions in Australia to refuse functional shapes despite inclusion of such provisions in earlier drafts of the current Act[101] and in similar Commonwealth jurisdictions.[102] Instead, functionality is dealt with as an aspect of distinctiveness at registration or when assessing an infringer's impugned use (ie, where use of functional aspects of the mark are considered non-infringing).[103] In his comparison of different jurisdictions, Michael Handler has argued that this is a 'suboptimal way of managing the problems raised by functional marks'.[104]

The Australian Trade Marks Office (ATMO) tries to factor in functionality into the assessment of distinctiveness, that is, whether 'other persons, trading in goods of the relevant kind and being actuated only by proper motives ... will think of the sign and want to use it in connexion with similar goods'.[105] If a shape mark has 'significant functional features there is a strong likelihood that other traders will need to use that shape for their similar goods' in the context of fair competition.[106] However, evidence of use can be presented to show that a functional shape has

Trade Mark Law' (2018) 42(1) *Melbourne University Law Review* 55, 75–76 (hereafter Handler, 'Disentangling').

99 Handler, 'Disentangling', above n 98, 58–61, comparing EU and US approaches. See also Qadir Qeidary, 'Shape Mark (Trade Dress) Distinctiveness: A Comparative Inquiry into US And EU Trademark Law' (2021) 13(1) *William & Mary Business Law Review* 71.

100 See Handler, 'Disentangling', above n 98, 62 for historical analysis.

101 However, a functionality bar was included in the Trade Marks Act 1994 (Cth), s 39 (Australia) now repealed. This Act was hastily enacted by Parliament, but it was never commenced and was eventually replaced by the Trade Marks Act 1995 (Cth) (Australia).

102 See, eg, Trade Marks Act 1994 s 3(2) (UK): 'A sign shall not be registered as a trade mark if it consists exclusively of (b) the shape or another characteristic, of goods which is necessary to obtain a technical result.' See similar provision in Singapore: Trade Marks Act (Cap 332), s 7(3)(b) (Singapore).

103 *Koninklijke Philips Electronics NV v Remington Products (Aust) Pty Ltd* (2000) 100 FCR 90, confirmed in *Kenman Kandy (Aust) Pty Ltd v Registrar of Trade Marks* (2002) 122 FCR 494.

104 Handler, 'Disentangling', above n 98, 63.

105 *Clark Equipment Co v Registrar of Trade Marks* (1964) 111 CLR 511, 513 (Kitto J).

106 IP Australia, *Trade Marks Office Manual of Practice and Procedure* (Live Manual, July 2022) pt 3.4 <https://manuals.ipaustralia.gov.au/trademark/3.-shape-three-dimensional-trade-marks>.

become in fact distinctive[107] or has acquired 'distinctiveness through use'.[108] Nevertheless, it appears that using distinctiveness as a filter against functional marks is 'imperfect'.[109] In his analysis of the Australian Register, Handler identified a 'significant number' of shape and colour marks that were prima facie functional. Conceding that it was impossible to know if functionality was considered by the ATMO as such records are not publicly available, Handler identified several shape marks that were rejected in other jurisdictions on functionality grounds but were accepted for registration in Australia by the ATMO.[110]

4.3.3.1 Australian Shoe Shape Litigation

In *Global Brand Marketing Inc v YD Pty Ltd*[111] (*Global Brand*) – the only reported shoe shape infringement case in Australia – details of the prosecution history were discussed in the judgment. In that case, Diesel S.p.A (Diesel) the licensee of Global Brand Marketing, was able to register the 'Shape' trademark (#986713) for the overall appearance of its popular square toed sneaker and the 'Sole' trademark (#986709) for the embossed under-sole of the shoe (Figure 4.5).

The Federal Court of Australia noted that the ATMO examiner originally objected to the shape mark on the grounds that: '[The] trade mark consists of the shape of a shoe. The shape is an ordinary shoe shape. Other traders should be able to use an ordinary shoe shape in connection with goods or services similar to yours.'[112] In response, Diesel limited the registration with an endorsement emphasising distinctive aspects of the registration such as the 'stylised letter D', and the registration was accepted.[113]

In evaluating the validity of the shape mark, the court reviewed the authorities and gave its support to the principle that non-functional shapes can operate as Australian trademarks. Moreover, the court in construing the infringement claim, declared that YD were also using its own shoe shape and sole as shape trademarks of YD. The court held that

[107] Ibid pt 3.9.

[108] *Marrakesh Agreement Establishing the World Trade Organization*, opened for signature April 15, 1994, 1869 UNTS 299, 33 ILM 1197 (signed April 15, 1994), annex 1C (*Agreement on Trade-Related Aspects of Intellectual Property Rights* [TRIPS]), ch 15: Where signs are not inherently capable of distinguishing the relevant goods or services, Members may make registrability depend on distinctiveness acquired through use.'

[109] Handler, 'Disentangling', above n 98, 83–84.

[110] Ibid.

[111] *Global Brand Marketing Inc v YD Pty Ltd* (2008) 76 IPR 161.

[112] Ibid at [10].

[113] Ibid.

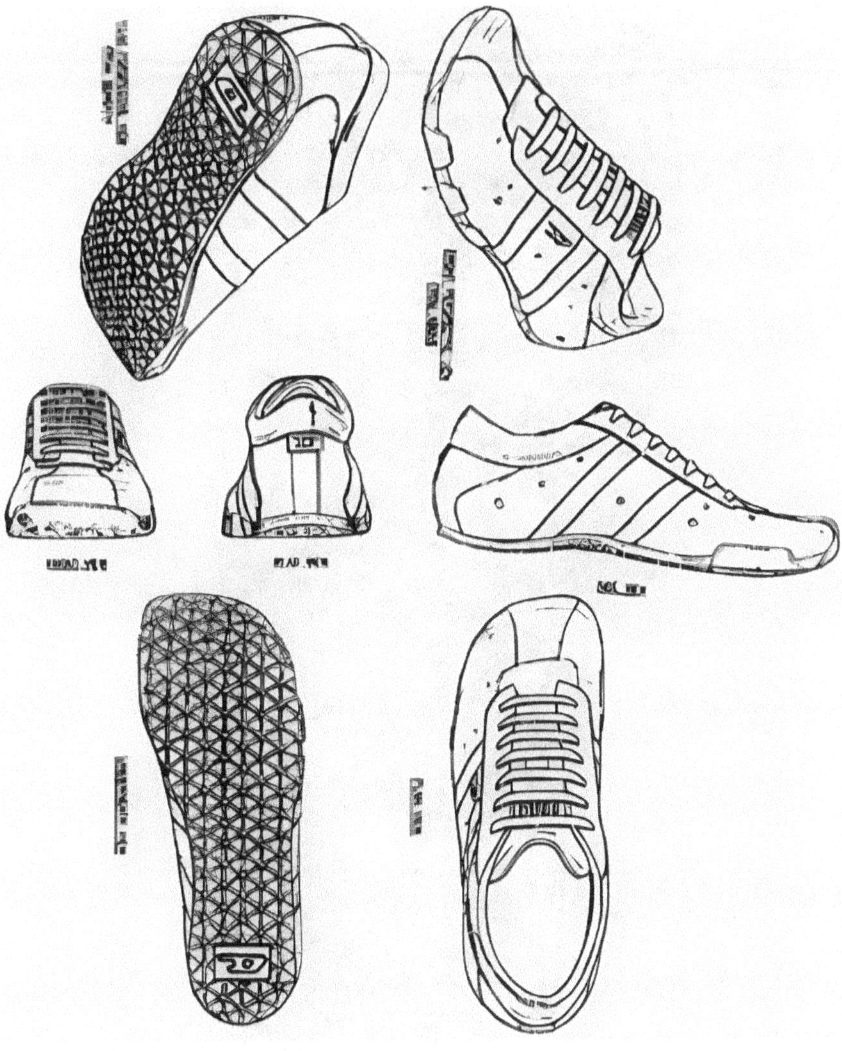

Figure 4.5 Registered shape marks of Diesel:[114] (*left*) shape mark (#986713); (*right*) sole mark (#986709).
(a) © Federal Court of Australia (b) © Federal Court of Australia

YD's trademarks as used by YD were not deceptively similar to Diesel's Shape and Sole marks and therefore not infringing. Although the

[114] Ibid at [4] (where the court focussed on these representations of the shoes as depicted on the trademark register).

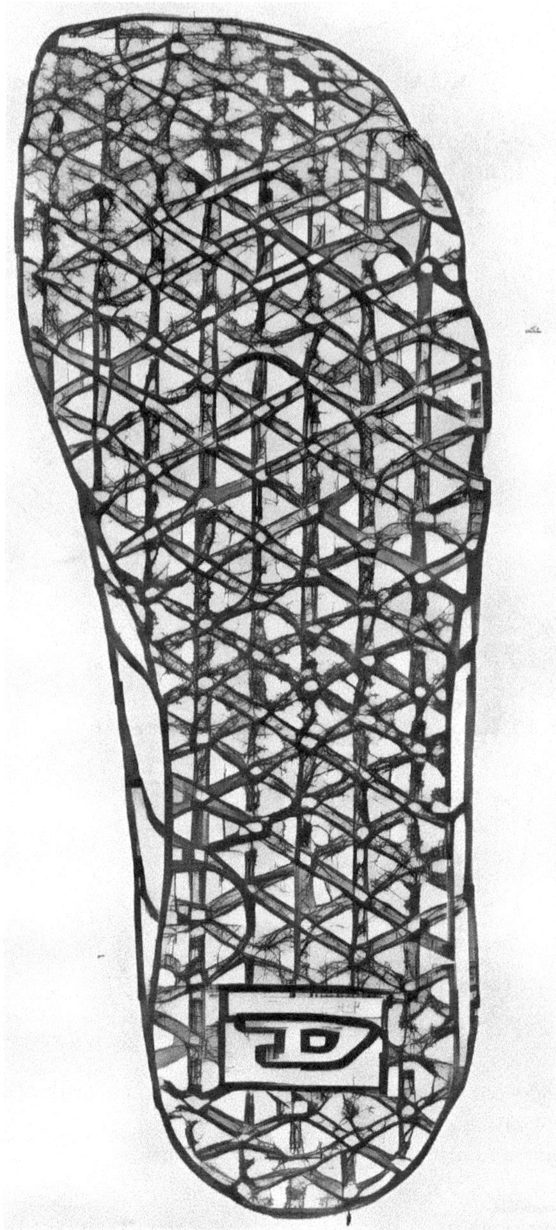

Figure 4.5 (*cont.*)

plaintiffs were not successful, it was significant that Justice Sundberg found that both parties had valid trademark rights in the shape of their shoes as well as the soles of those shoes. In relation to the plaintiff's registered marks, his Honour found that the non-functional and non-descriptive features overwhelmed the functional and common features of the marks.[115] This decision likely gave traders some confidence to apply for trademark registrations for distinctive shapes related to footwear.

Given all the factors discussed above – increased demand for sneakers, a culture of casual privacy, limitations of copyright and designs law and favourable trademark courts – it is hypothesised that shoe designers are increasingly reliant on protecting footwear by registering them as 3D shape trademarks. Although causation is not argued, it is suggested that 3D shoe registrations may be on the increase due to these various factors.

4.4 Method

To examine whether and how fashion designers have employed Australian trademark and design registrations in relation to shoes, publicly available trademark and design registration data from IP Australia was extracted. In relation to trademarks, this study uses two sources of data. First, trademark application data from IPGOD2021[116] was extracted by a research assistant for the period January 1, 1996 (commencement of the Trade Marks Act 1995 (Cth)) until December 31, 2021 (25 years).[117] This data was used to identify trends over time. Second, in order to examine specific trademark applications in detail, the author located these via the online Australian Trade Marks Register (the Register).[118] Additional data was retrieved from the online Australian Designs Register.[119] All coding was done by the author.

115 In relation to the sole mark see ibid at [66]–[68]; in relation to the shape mark see ibid at [70]–[73].

116 IP Australia, *Intellectual Property Government Open Data (IPGOD) 2022* (Online Data Set, June 21, 2022) <https://data.gov.au/dataset/ds-dga-49017fd0-e7be-4fc0-88c8-046fc366d980/details?q=>.

117 A grace period was introduced by Royal Asset on September 11, 2021; see Designs Amendment (Advisory Council on Intellectual Property Response) Act 2021 (Cth) (Australia). Given the data at hand, it was more practical to include the three-month period from September to December 2021 in the study than to exclude it.

118 IP Australia, *Australian Trade Mark Search* (Web Page) <https://search.ipaustralia.gov.au/trademarks/search/quick>.

119 See, eg, IP Australia, *Australian Designs Search* (Web Page) <https://search.ipaustralia.gov.au/designs/search/>.

A key limitation of the study is that the number of applications in the dataset is small. Descriptive statistics based on a small number of applications are sensitive to change if a small number of new applications are added to the dataset. Nevertheless, the applications cover the entire population of available applications in the period of inquiry, so are in this sense representative. Still, this study does not make any predictive statements and inferences are only drawn with caution.

4.5 Results and Discussion

4.5.1 Overview of Trademark Application and Registration Data

4.5.1.1 Shape Relative to All Applications

Over the 25-year period (January 1, 1996–December 31, 2021) there were 1,486,174 trademark applications to IP Australia. Of these, only 3,631 were for shape trademarks, that is, less than 1% (on average only 0.24%). The bars of Figure 4.7 show that while there was some enthusiasm for shape mark applications in the first 10 years of the Trade Marks Act 1995 (Cth), the number of shape applications slightly declined after 2015. This decline is significant in light of the fact that trademark applications in general (ie, for non-shape marks) increased dramatically over the same period.[120] The *relative* proportion of shape to total marks (line) can therefore be seen to decline over time. In other words, Figure 4.6 shows that both the nominal and relative popularity of shape trademarks fell after their initial popularity. This is consistent with previous findings by Amanda Scardamaglia and Mitchell Adams.[121]

4.5.1.2 Applications Related to Fashion

Fashion designers can apply for marks across a wide range of goods and services. For the purpose of this chapter, the focus was on shape

[120] IP Australia, 'Australian Intellectual Property Report, 2023' (Research Report, April 2023) 23–24 <https://www.ipaustralia.gov.au/tools-and-research/professional-resources/data-research-and-reports/australian-ip-report-2023 > showing general upward trend but a fall of 1.3% in 2022 from a record high in 2021.

[121] Amanda Scardamaglia and Mitchell Adams, 'Registering Non-traditional Signs as Trade Marks in Australia: A Retrospective' (2016) 26(3) *Australian Intellectual Property Journal* 149, 156 (hereafter Scardamaglia and Adams, 'Registering Non-traditional Signs').

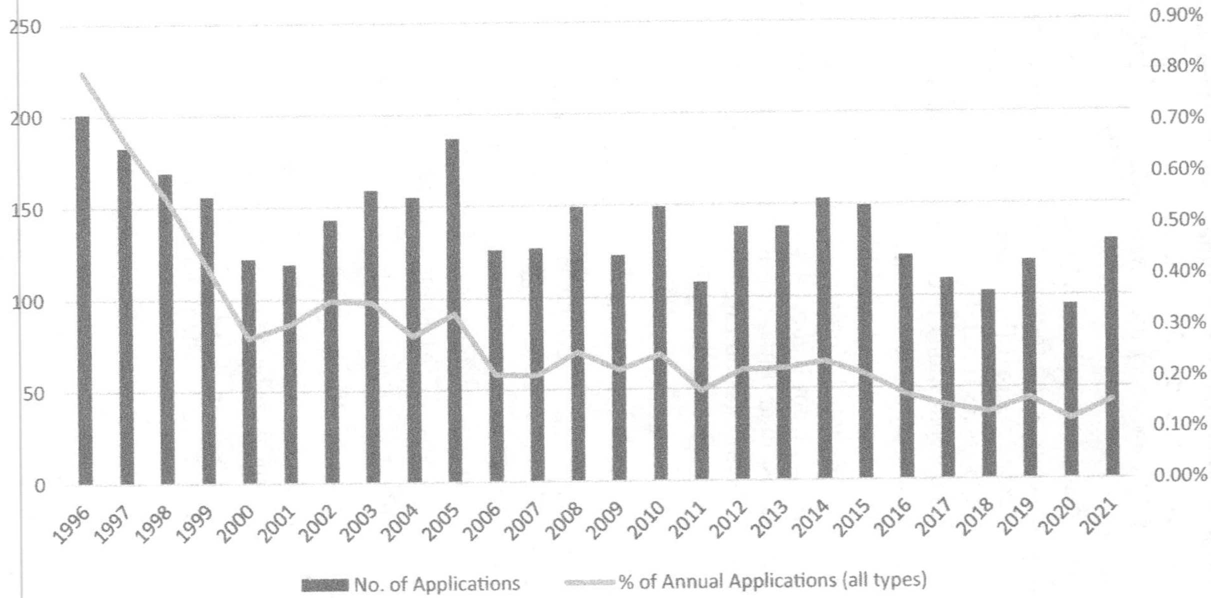

Figure 4.6 Shape trademark applications (actual) and relative to annual trademark applications per year (Janaury 1, 1996–December 31, 2021).

Credit: Vicki Huang

applications under Nice Class 25 (clothing, headgear and footwear)[122] between January 1, 1996, and December 31, 2021. Fashion designers also applied for shapes under other classes but in much smaller numbers. For example, under Class 18 (bags and wallets) there were 92 shape applications, and under Class 14 (jewellery) there were 105 shape applications for the same period.

Of the 3,631 shape mark applications, 226 (6.2% or 226/3,631) were for Class 25 (clothing, headgear and footwear). Figure 4.7 plots the total number of shape applications per year (bars) and the percentage of shape applications that were in Class 25 (line). Figure 4.7 shows that while the nominal number of shape applications declined over time (descending dotted trend line), the proportion that were shape applications in fashion (Class 25) grew over time (ascending dotted trend line).

Bearing in mind the small population size of 3,631 shape mark applications with 226 in Class 25, from Figures 4.7 and 4.8 we can infer that while shape applications lost their initial popularity, the interest in shape trademarks for Class 25 (ie, the fashion industry) grew in both nominal and relative terms.

4.5.2 A Closer Look at Shape Marks and Class 25 – Footwear

Of the 226 shape trademark applications in Class 25, there were 117 shape mark applications specific to footwear. That is, 52% (117/226) of all shape applications in Class 25 were for shoes. Of these 117 shoe applications, 55 (47%) were for 3D representations of the whole shoe as a shape trademark; 23 (19%) for the sole, 37 (31%) for a 3D device or badge and 2 (2%) for a toe cap or filigree.

4.5.2.1 What Kinds of Whole Shoes and Success Rates?

Of these 55 whole shoe applications, Figure 4.8 shows that there were 7 categories of shoes, with sneakers being the most popular at 36% (20/55 applications) followed by boots (22% or 12/55). Birkenstock submitted 7 (13% or 7/55) applications in 2019. The outcomes of these applications

[122] IP Australia uses the 45 classes of goods and services from the International Classification of Goods and Services (commonly referred to as the 'Nice Classification'). IP Australia, 'The Purpose of Classification', *Trade Marks Manual of Practice and Procedure* (Live Manual, November 6, 2021) <https://manuals.ipaustralia.gov.au/trademark/1.-the-purpose-of-classification>.

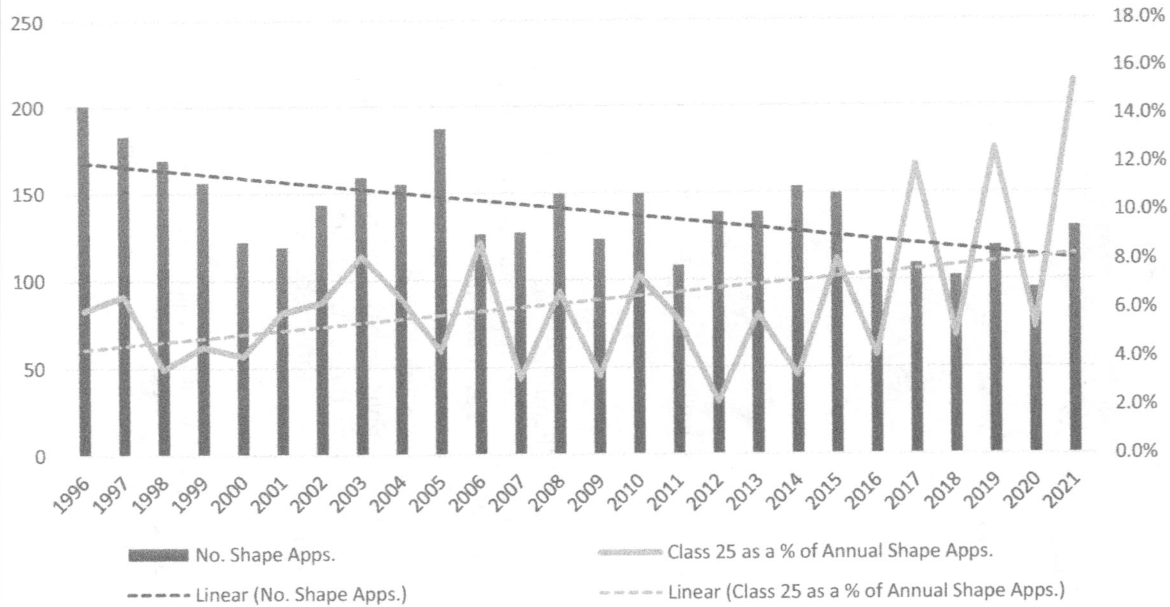

Figure 4.7 Class 25 shape trademark applications (actual) and relative to annual shape trademark applications per year (January 1, 1996–December 31, 2021).
Credit: Vicki Huang

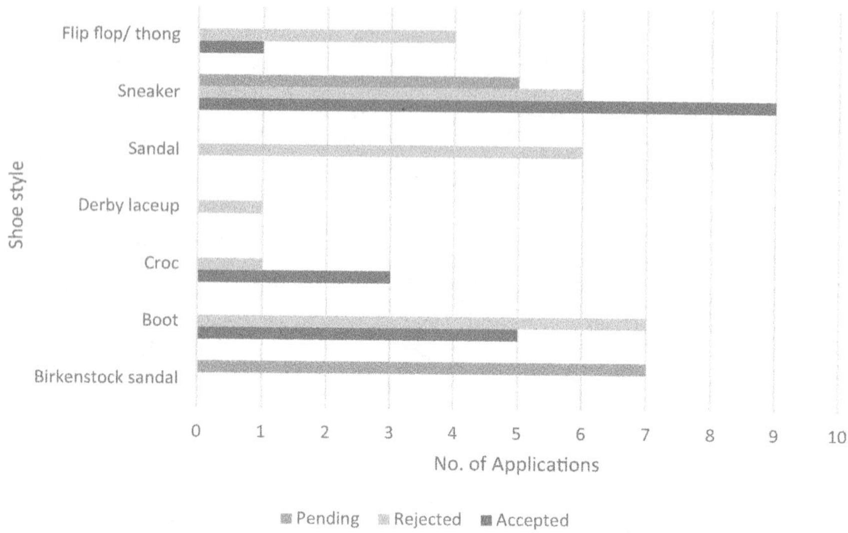

Figure 4.8 Whole shoe trademark applications and status ($n = 55$, January 1, 1996–December 31, 2021).
Credit: Vicki Huang

were coded as 'Accepted',[123] 'Pending'[124] or 'Rejected'[125]. Scardamaglia and Adams studied 975 shape mark applications over a 20-year period (January 1, 1996–December 31, 2015) and found that the registration of shape marks had a 37.3% success rate.[126] In this smaller sample of 55 whole shoe applications, excluding 12 pending applications, the success rate was 42% or (18/43 applications). The top three applicants in terms of number of filings were Birkenstock, Action Africa and Vans. The majority of all applicants were foreign companies.

[123] Coded as 'Accepted' where the status of the application was 'Registered: Registered/ protected', 'Protected: Registered/protected', 'Protected: Renewal due', 'Ceased -Not renewed: Renewal fee not paid', 'Removed - Not renewed: Renewal fee not paid' or 'Registered: Renewal due''.

[124] Coded as 'Pending' where the status of the application was 'Published: Awaiting examination'.

[125] Coded as 'Rejected' where the status of the application was either 'Lapsed: Not accepted' or 'Not protected: Not accepted'.

[126] Scardamaglia and Adams, 'Registering Non-traditional Signs', above n 121, 156 stating that during this period, 975 shape trademarks were registered (37.3% of the total shape mark applications) from January 1, 1996 to December 31, 2015 (20 years).

The 55 whole shoe applications represented 18 different designers. There were a cluster of dominant international applicants, including Birkenstock (sandals) (13% or 7/55 applications), Vans (sneakers) (11% or 6/55 applications) and Action Africa (sandals) (11% or 6/55 applications).

4.5.2.2 Trademark and Design Rights Overlap

As discussed above, between January 1, 1996, and December 31, 2021, there were 226 shape trademark applications in Class 25 (clothing, footwear, headgear). Looking at each application, there were 117 shape mark applications specific to footwear. That is, 52% (117/226) of all shape applications in Class 25 or 3.2% (117/3631) total shape applications were for footwear. Examining IP Australia's Designs Register[94] between January 1, 2004 (the commencement of the Designs Act 2003 (Cth)) and December 31, 2021 (19 years), there were 120,355 design applications. Of these, 1.4% or 1,697 were applications relating to shoe designs in in class (02-04Z).[95]

Of the 18 shoe designers with trademark applications for shapes, 7 had similar or overlapping design applications for at least one of their designs. Five were international designers – Birkenstock IP GmbH, Crocs, Diesel/World Brands, Bolt Premium Workwear and Globe International. Two were Australian – RM Williams and Sole Surfer. Therefore, it cannot be said that shoe designers are totally ignoring the registered designs system; however, it is clear that a growing number are seeking out trademark protection as an adjunct to or in lieu of registered design protection.

4.6 Discussion

The empirical data reveals that while overall demand for Australian shape trademarks is low and declining, the demand for such marks for fashion goods has increased in real and relative terms. A significant portion of this demand has come from the fashion industry, particularly from shoe applicants seeking a 3D shape trademark. This would suggest that shoe designers (particularly some sneaker designers) view shape trademarks favourably. As discussed earlier, this demand could be a response to Australia's culture of casual piracy and/or the perceived limitations of other IP rights such as design rights.

A more general explanation for the increased demand for shoe trademarks is an overall increase in the aggregate demand for shoes.

In relation to Australia, the footwear market has grown significantly. For example, in 2004, the retail value of the market was US$1.3 billion.[127] By 2017, the Australian footwear market reached a value of US$3.6 billion.[128] This mirrors global trends, where shoe sales have grown exponentially, becoming a critical product category for fashion designers and sportswear brands.[129] A key driver of this growth has been sneakers. MarketLine Australia reported in 2017[130] and 2021[131] that the 'growing popularity of sports footwear is driving growth in the market, thanks to the "athleisure" trend that has swept across the world'. Significantly in 2021 they noted, 'The cultural shift of athletic footwear being repurposed as everyday wear has changed the dynamics of the footwear market.'[132] This is not just an Australian phenomenon. McKinsey & Company have reported that globally, fashion leaders predict that casual wear, sportswear and sneakers are the categories with the greatest growth potential.[133] This trend began before the global pandemic but no doubt accelerated during stay-at-home work mandates in Australia as well as other countries.

There are also fascinating, systematic cultural changes that are impacting the growth in demand for sneakers. In particular, the growth of 'sneakerhead culture' and the increased interest by men for fashion (typically expressed through an interest in sneakers). Yuniya Kawamura argues that 'men are reclaiming adornment and fashion', expression men had abandoned due to the adoption of the business suit as 'uniform since the Industrial Revolution'.[134] However, 'to avoid being "effeminate," girls and women are shut out from the community' leading to a male dominant sub-culture of 'sneaker-heads' or 'sneaker-holics'.[135] This gendered

[127] Datamonitor, 'Footwear in Australia, October 2005, Reference Code: 0125–0619' (Research Report) 8.

[128] MarketLine, 'Footwear in Australia, November 2018, Reference Code: 0125–0619' (Research Report, November 2018) 2 (Marketline, 'Footwear in Australia, November 2018').

[129] Hyman, Azema and Morrow, 'If the IP Fits', above n 10, 647, reporting that in 2017, Gucci's shoe sales were up from 12% (since 2013) to 19% of its total revenue. Kering group reported that 45% of sports and lifestyle revenues were attributable to shoes.

[130] MarketLine, 'Footwear in Australia, November 2018', above n 128, 7.

[131] MarketLine, 'Footwear in Australia, July 2021', above n 3, 23.

[132] Ibid.

[133] McKinsey & Co, *SOF 2023*, above n 8, 16.

[134] Kawamura, *Sneakers*, above n 7, 74.

[135] Ibid at 77.

demand is reflected in economic studies that show the footwear market is also pivoting male. For example, in Australia in 2017, the ratio of women's to men's footwear was 53.4% to 34% of the dollar value of the overall market.[136] In 2020, this gender gap closed with the ratio of women's to men's footwear becoming 42% to 41.4% of the market.[137]

Admittedly, it is difficult to parse out how much of this gender swing relates to the pandemic. Australia has an uneven labour force participation between genders,[138] and the confinement of both male and female office workers may have increased demand for sneakers unevenly. Nevertheless, even pre-pandemic, the popularity and marketing of sneakers towards men was evident. Kawamura, points out that 'boys and young men are the biggest consumers of sneakers' and this is reflected in the supply of sneakers where 'there are far more varieties and choices for male sneakers than female sneakers'.[139] As sneakerhead culture becomes more visible,[140] and profitable, how designers respond to the increased influence of the male customer will be fascinating.

The increase in competition in the global sneaker market shows no sign of slowing down. With that there will likely be increased demand for IP protection in all jurisdictions. This study has shown that in Australia shoe designers have sought out 3D shape trademarks as an addition to (or instead of) registered designs. Other jurisdictions are dealing with shoe designers pressing other types of rights. For example, difficulties with enforcing trade dress rights in the United States has led to interesting strategies from some designers. The brand Off-White has successfully been granted a US registration of the ironic trademark 'FOR WALKING', which is used on its sneakers and other shoes.[141] Nike, has amassed over

[136] MarketLine, 'Footwear in Australia, November 2018', above n 128, 7.

[137] MarketLine, 'Footwear in Australia, July 2021', above n 3, 9.

[138] In Australia, the 2022 labour force participation rate was 71.3% male and 62.1% female; see Australian Bureau of Statistics, 'Gender Indicators, Participation in the Labour Force February 2023' (*Australian Bureau of Statistics*) <https://www.abs.gov.au/statistics/people/people-and-communities/gender-indicators#work>.

[139] Ibid.

[140] For example, Netflix broadcast a television series named *Sneakerheads*, depicting a man's obsession with an elusive pair of kicks. See Internet Movie Database (IMDb), 'Sneakerheads: TV Series, 2020' (*IMDb*) <https://www.imdb.com/title/tt10151772/>.

[141] *US Trademark Registration No 7077829* (Registered on June 13, 2023).

34,000 patents globally[142] and recently sued Lululemon for infringement of textile patents used in Nike's flyknit sneaker range.[143]

Nevertheless, for many designers, it is the overall appearance of the product, that is, the shoe design, that is seen as warranting protection. The increase in shoe demand and alleged copying of designs will undoubtedly lead to further calls for the United States to adopt a form of sui generis design right for fashion. Such advocates should view Australia as a cautionary tale. This chapter has argued that the success of fashion design rights requires a holistic consideration of the culture, commerce and the matrix of related rights. A problem for jurisdictions such as Australia where the matrix allows for and tacitly encourages the registration of shoes as shape trademarks, may be the anti-competitive effects of this demand. As with other jurisdictions, trademarks in Australia can be registered indefinitely without substantive re-examination. Although the dataset in this study is fairly small, it is clear that many significant brands are using the Australian trademark system to protect the overall appearance of their goods. In Australia, the majority of footwear trademark applicants are foreign companies. Given a concern of the government is the stimulation of the domestic design industry, an increase in foreign-owned trademarks over shapes is an issue that requires particular vigilance. And it will be interesting to observe whether demand for more time limited design rights increases now that changes (including the inclusion of a grace period) have been implemented.

[142] Insights by Greys, 'Nike Patents – Insights & Stats (Updated 2023)' (Web Page) <https://insights.greyb.com/nike-patents/>.

[143] Daphne Howland, 'Nike Sues Lululemon Over Shoe Manufacturing Patents', *Retail Dive* (February 1, 2023) <https://www.retaildive.com/news/nike-sues-lululemon-design-shoe-patents-lawsuit/641738/>.

5

Non-traditional Trademarks, Distinctiveness and the Fashion Industry

SUSANNA H S LEONG AND IRENE CALBOLI*

ABSTRACT

This chapter analyses the use of non-traditional trademarks (NTTMs) in the fashion industry. With reference to selected cases in the United States, the European Union and Singapore, the authors study the arguments for and against the protection of these signs as trademarks, as well as the appropriate test for the evaluation of distinctiveness. Although some fashion designers and enterprises have celebrated victories in court, it has been widely noted that the registration and protection of these NTTMs can be problematic and potentially detrimental to innovation in the fashion industry. The authors also critically examine the different tests of 'association' and 'reliance' as discussed in recent court decisions on acquired distinctiveness of NTTMs and conclude with a recommendation that the 'reliance' test is the preferred test.

5.1 Introduction

In its simplest form, the fashion industry may be described as the business of making apparel. Yet most will agree that the term 'fashion' goes beyond mere functionality in apparel to incorporate other attributes such as identities in styles, personal tastes and cultural biases. As an industry, it spans a wide range of offerings from haute couture, luxury fashion, bridge brands and diffusion lines to high street, fast fashion and economy brands,[1] providing the market with a plethora of fashion

* The authors would like to thank Professor David Tan for his editorial suggestions and contributions to the manuscript of this chapter. We have benefitted greatly and are grateful for David's support and assistance, as always.

[1] For an explanation of the different fashion offerings, see 'The market levels of fashion', *Alicia Amy Jones* (2023) <https://aliciaamyjones.co.uk/the-market-levels-of-fashion>.

products at varying price points and other attributes. To survive and thrive in the fashion industry, designers and artisanal craftsmen must constantly innovate and create iconic and memorable designs and fashion concepts to differentiate their products from those of others, towards the ultimate objective of establishing a loyal customer base. Originality in designs and fashion concepts is thus the lifeblood of fashion designers. The mass market covets celebrated designs, many of which have originated from talented designers in haute couture and luxury fashion as well as lesser-known freelancers, because of their aesthetic appeal and exclusivity. The prevalent use of social media has contributed significantly to the extent and speed that unique and distinctive designs are able to reach vast consumer markets. A few notable design concepts have transcended mere commercial merchandise, successfully permeating popular culture. As such, fashion designers are driven to claim ownership in their designs and design concepts with the objective of preventing others from copying and exploiting them without attribution or due compensation.

Unfortunately, such protection is not always easy to achieve. While registered design rights may provide the means to protect designs, which are novel (not common to the trade) and not functional in nature, for a limited number of years (on average between 15 and 25 years depending on the country), many designs in the fashion industry, in particular designs of apparels, shoes, bags and other fashion accessories, often fall short of the requisite standard of novelty because they are common to the trade. Yet it has been noted that certain aspects or features of these designs are able to capture consumers' attention and create lasting impressions. Examples of such memorable designs often cited include the eye-catching red on the bottom of a Christian Louboutin heel,[2] the intrecciato weave pattern and knot adornment on a Bottega Veneta product, the specific placement of buckles and zippers on a Balenciaga handbag, the red-green-red racing stripes of Gucci, the Adidas three-stripes design and the protruding 'pocket tab' in the form of a folded ribbon sewn with its ends captured in the seam of a rear patch pocket on a pair of Levi's jeans, just to mention a few. The lack of adequate legal protection of fashion designs and design concepts continues to be a major source of dissatisfaction for fashion designers and is deeply rooted in a palpable sense of inequity.

[2] *US Trademark Registration No 3361597*, filed on March 27, 2007 (Registered on January 1, 2008).

At the same time, the modern fashion industry has grown into a huge lucrative global business and is a far cry from the bespoke artisanal craft business model of centuries past. At the outset of the twenty-first century, the modus operandi of fast-fashion conglomerates is the pursuit of profitable styles that can be translated, with the help of competitive technology, into timely in-season merchandise for the global mass apparel market. Aesthetically appealing designs and original design concepts are often the targets of cheap knock-offs almost immediately after they are presented to the public at fashion shows and on the catwalks. This has further fuelled the need for fashion designers and fashion houses to find effective ways to obtain property rights in their fashion designs and concepts in a bid to stop unauthorised exploitations.

There is a discernible trend in the fashion industry to obtain property rights by filing trademark applications for iconic design features applied on products, such as single colours, monograms and patterns, commonly referred to as non-traditional trademarks (NTTMs), and by defending vigorously the validities of these registered trademarks in courts. Recent examples of fashion houses going to court to lay claims over NTTMs that they consider distinctive of their goods and services include Bottega Veneta's intrecciato weave and knot marks, Christian Louboutin's red sole mark, the Adidas three-stripes design and the Levi's protruding 'pocket tab'.

The surge in registrations of NTTMs globally is the result of several factors. Following the 1994 Agreement on Trade-Related Aspects of Intellectual Property Rights (TRIPS), the world has seen the growth of the trademark universe. The broader definition of a trademark in TRIPS and the willingness of policymakers across all continents to facilitate the registration of traditional marks and NTTMs alike have contributed to the expansionist trend observed. In particular, modern branding and marketing strategies (which have had success in educating consumers to make a connection between a specific colour, design feature or smell and a particular origin of goods and services) have convinced businesses to seek exclusive rights over NTTMs. Yet it could be said that the protection of NTTMs have not been harmonised at the multilateral level despite their widespread acceptance and use. Indeed, courts in different countries have not always been consistent with the treatments of NTTMs, often resulting in differing judgments and creating uncertainties for trademark proprietors when protecting their NTTMs.

This chapter examines the use of NTTMs in the fashion industry. In particular, the authors study the arguments for and against the protection of NTTMs with reference to selected cases in the United States and the European Union. Although some fashion designers and enterprises have celebrated victories in court, it has been widely noted that the registration and protection of these NTTMs as trademarks can be problematic and potentially detrimental to continued innovations in the fashion industry. Closely connected to the conferral of trademark rights in NTTMs is the countervailing policy to ensure market competition and public accessibility to common design features and shapes in the fashion industry. Because of this, central to the discussion of where the appropriate balance ought to be struck is the element of distinctiveness of NTTMs, that is, their ability to distinguish goods and services, and consequently whether they should be conferred trademark rights. As it is generally accepted that NTTMs are inherently devoid of distinctiveness, the criteria in the assessment of whether they have *acquired distinctiveness through use* (in the alternative) becomes critical for proprietors seeking trademark protection of their NTTMs. To this end, the authors critically examine the different tests of 'association' and 'reliance' as discussed in recent court decisions on acquired distinctiveness of NTTMs and conclude with a recommendation that the 'reliance' test is preferred and ought to be adopted.

5.2 NTTMs in the United States and the European Union

As a starting point, there is no internationally agreed-upon and accepted definition of NTTMs.

Under Article 15.1 of TRIPS, any sign, or any combination of signs, capable of distinguishing a business's goods or services from those of others is a trademark. This definition is expansive in scope and identifies the most important and universally accepted function of a trademark, that is, its ability to distinguish and to serve as a badge of origin for goods or services. In fact, an all-encompassing reference to 'any sign' in the definition of a trademark without qualification in Article 15.1 paves the way for the registrability of unconventional signs, including those that are not visually perceptible. As such, any signs outside of the traditional categories of words and images may be considered NTTMs and they possibly include visually perceptible signs like single colours, shapes, video clips, holograms, gestures and position marks, as well as non-visually perceptible ones like sounds and smells.

The broad definition of a trademark provided in TRIPS has opened up a whole new universe of possible signs, that of NTTMs, which may be protected through trademark registrations. Furthermore, registrations of NTTMs received a significant booster from post-TRIPS treaties such as the Singapore Treaty on the Law of Trade Mark 2006, which has provided the international trademark community with some degree of clarity and certainty in the registration procedure for novel types of trademarks, including non-visible signs. This has in turn facilitated the increase in registrations of NTTMs globally, including by prominent fashion houses and fashion designers. Indeed, over the years, fashion house and designers have not only taken advantage of the increasingly liberal and expansive legal norms in trademark protection to secure protection for NTTMs with regard to their fashion products but have also resulted in a marked increase in litigation in the fashion industry all over the world.

5.2.1 The United States

In US law, a trademark is defined to include 'any word, name, symbol, or device, or any combination thereof – used by a person . . . to identify and distinguish his or her goods . . . from those manufactured or sold by others and to indicate the *source of the goods*'.[3] The terms 'symbol' or 'device' would seem appropriate for protecting various aspects of fashion design such as the use of a distinctive colour, configurations of colour, pattern or even shape, so long as they do not fall under what is specifically listed as unregistrable under the Lanham Act.[4]

The US Lanham Act does not define 'descriptive', but it prohibits the registration of marks that are 'merely descriptive' of the goods or services for which the marks are sought to be registered.[5] Registration always requires that an applicant prove the mark is distinctive.[6] The courts have interpreted this requirement to be satisfied by showing the mark (i) is either inherently distinctive, or has acquired distinctiveness through secondary meaning and (ii) is not functional.[7] The functionality doctrine

[3] Lanham Act 2006, 15 USC § 1127 (US) (emphasis added).
[4] Ibid § 1052.
[5] Ibid § 1052 (e)(1), (f).
[6] Ibid § 1052.
[7] Eg, *Qualitex Co v Jacobsen Products Co*, 514 US 159, 165 (1995); *Two Pesos, Inc v Taco Cabana, Inc*, 505 US 763, 768 (1992); *Inwood Labs, Inc v Ives Labs, Inc*, 456 US 844, 851 fn 11 (1982); *Christian Louboutin SA v Yves Saint Laurent America Holding, Inc*, 696 F 3d 206, 216–228 (2nd Cir. 2012); *Moldex-Metric Inc v McKeon Products Inc*, 891 F 3d 878, 883–888 (9th Cir. 2018); *Bliss Collection LLC v Latham Companies LLC*, 82 F 4th 499, 514–515 (6th Cir. 2023).

in US law encompasses both utilitarian/traditional functionality and aesthetic functionality and can be a significant hurdle for fashion brands seeking to register colours and shapes; its discussion unfortunately is beyond the scope of this chapter.[8]

In the context of the fashion industry, secondary meaning arises when a descriptive – or otherwise unprotectable – symbol or device has been used in such a manner, for a sufficient duration and frequency, that it becomes uniquely identified with the user and/or the user's product.[9] Depending on a mark's eligibility for trademark registration, an owner of a mark may seek federal protection under either the principal or supplemental register.[10] To qualify as a trademark, a NTTM has to satisfy all three requirements: (i) the mark exists in a tangible form as a symbol, device or any combination of these, and is distinctive; (ii) the particular aspect of the symbol or device (eg, colour or shape) is adopted and used as a *mark* by a manufacturer or seller of goods or services and (iii) it identifies and distinguishes the seller's good or services from those made or sold by others.[11]

5.2.1.1 Christian Louboutin – the Red Sole Mark

The 'Red Sole Mark'[12] of French fashion house Christian Louboutin is a famous example of a NTTM, the validity and exclusive trademark rights of which were upheld by the US Second Circuit Court of Appeals. Over three decades ago, in 1992, French designer Christian Louboutin first made and sold women's high heels shoes with a unique feature – the

[8] Ibid. See also Christopher Buccafusco and Jeanne C Fromer, 'Fashion's Function in Intellectual Property Law' (2017) 93 *Notre Dame Law Review* 51; Justin Hughes, 'Cognitive and Aesthetic Functionality in Trademark Law' (2015) 36 *Cardozo Law Review* 1227; Mark P McKenna, '(Dys)functionality' (2011) 48 *Houston Law Review* 823.

[9] American Law Institute, *Restatement (Third) of Unfair Competition* (1993) § 13, cmt. e; Anthony L Fletcher, 'Separating Descriptive Sheep from Generic Goats' (2013) 103 *Trademark Reporter* 487, 487.

[10] See J Thomas McCarthy, *McCarthy on Trademarks and Unfair Competition* (West Group, 4th edn, 2013) § 19.36 (June 2018 update). A supplemental registration confers no benefits of validity beyond those gained at common law. Principal registration receives the strongest federal trademark protection providing 'prima facie evidence of the validity of the registered mark ... and of the owner's exclusive right to use the registered mark'. Lanham Act 2006, 15 USC § 1057(b) (US). See also Lanham Act 2006, 15 USC § 1091(c) (US).

[11] McCarthy, *McCarthy on Trademarks and Unfair Competition* § 3.1.

[12] The trademark was granted by USPTO in January 2008, and stated: 'The color(s) red is/are claimed as a feature of the mark. The mark consists of a lacquered red sole on footwear.' The description of the trademark was accompanied by a diagram indicating the placement of the colour.

outsole of the shoe was painted with a high-gloss red lacquer, contrasting with the colour of the remainder of the shoe. Since then, Christian Louboutin has invested substantial capital in creating a global brand based on this 'red sole' feature of his women's high-heeled shoes,[13] so much so that the 'flash of a red sole' is today 'instantly' recognisable, to 'those in the know', as Louboutin's handiwork.[14] In 2008, Christian Louboutin obtained trademark registration of the 'Red Sole Mark' in the United States.

Another venerable French fashion house Yves Saint Laurent (YSL) began to market, in 2011, a line of 'monochrome' shoes in purple, green, yellow and red. As the YSL shoes in the monochrome style featured the same colour on the entire shoe including matching soles, the red version was therefore all red, including a red insole, heel, upper, and outsole. Christian Louboutin claimed that YSL's red monochrome shoes infringed his 'Red Sole Mark' and took YSL to court after negotiations to settle the dispute between the parties failed. The US District Court for the Southern District of New York denied a preliminary injunction to restrain YSL's alleged use of the 'Red Sole Mark', and Christian Louboutin appealed to the US Second Circuit Court of Appeals.

Central to the Second Circuit's decision in *Christian Louboutin S.A. v. Yves Saint Laurent Am. Holding, Inc.*[15] is the question whether a single colour may serve as a legally protected trademark in the fashion industry. In the decision, US Circuit Judge Cabranes rejected the District Court's conclusion that a single colour can never serve as a trademark in the fashion industry because single-colour marks are considered inherently functional, as this is inconsistent with the Supreme Court's decision in *Qualitex Co. v Jacobsen Products Co.*[16] As such, there is no *per se* rule of functionality for colour marks in the fashion industry that would effectively deny trademark protection to any deployment of a single colour in an item of apparel. This ruling effectively paved the way for single

[13] Louboutin also sells women's flat shoes or men's shoes with red-lacquered outsoles. For a picture of Louboutin's Greggo flat shoe, see Jeanne C Fromer and Mark P McKenna, 'Claiming Design' (2018) 167 *University of Pennsylvania Law Review* 123 (hereafter Fromer and McKenna, 'Claiming Design').

[14] *Christian Louboutin SA v Yves Saint Laurent America Holding, Inc*, 778 F Supp 2d, 488 (SDNY, 2011)

[15] *Christian Louboutin SA v Yves Saint Laurent America Holding, Inc*, 696 F 3d 206 (2nd Cir. 2012).

[16] *Qualitex Co v Jacobson Products Co*, 514 US 159, 162, 115 S Ct 1300, 131 L Ed 2d 248 (1995).

colours to be registered as trademarks in the fashion industry as long as the single-colour marks are found to have acquired 'secondary meaning' and are not aesthetically functional. Having done so, the Second Circuit did not think it was necessary to address whether the 'Red Sole Mark' was indeed functional and whether YSL could avail itself of this defence. This was because the court concluded, based on the evidence adduced by Christian Louboutin, that the 'Red Sole Mark' had acquired a limited 'secondary meaning' to become a distinctive source indicator of Christian Louboutin's footwear.[17] Therefore, Christian Louboutin's 'Red Sole Mark' was ruled to be valid and enforceable.

However, the Second Circuit found that 'secondary meaning' of the mark held by Christian Louboutin extended only to the use of a lacquered red outsole that contrasted with the adjoining portion of the shoe. The court held that 'it is the contrast between the sole and the upper that causes the sole to "pop," and to distinguish its creator'.[18] Accordingly, the scope of the property rights conferred on Christian Louboutin's 'Red Sole Mark' were limited to only those situations in which the red lacquered outsole contrasted in colour with the adjoining 'upper' of the shoe.[19] The red soles of YSL's monochrome red shoes therefore did not constitute trademark infringement of Christian Louboutin's 'Red Sole Mark' as they were used in situations where there were no contrast between the red outsoles and the remaining 'uppers' of the YSL shoes.

In the assessment of whether the 'Red Sole Mark' has acquired a 'secondary meaning', the Second Circuit reiterated that the relevant factors to consider included '(1) advertising expenditures, (2) consumer studies linking the mark to a source, (3) unsolicited media coverage of the product, (4) sales success, (5) attempts to plagiarize the mark, and, (6) length and exclusivity of the mark's use'.[20] Christian Louboutin adduced extensive evidence in terms of advertising expenditures, media coverage

[17] See Fromer and McKenna, 'Claiming Design' above n 14; David Tan, 'Aesthetic Functionality Back in Vogue: Clash of the Fashion Titans' (2013) 18 *Media & Arts Law Review* 164.

[18] *Christian Louboutin SA v Yves Saint Laurent America Holding, Inc*, 696 F 3d 206, 227 (2nd Cir. 2012).

[19] Modification of the Red Sole Mark was made pursuant to Section 37 of the Lanham Act (2006), 15 USC §1119 (US) insofar as it is sought to be applied to any shoe bearing the same colour 'upper' as the outsole.

[20] *Christian Louboutin SA v Yves Saint Laurent America Holding, Inc*, 696 F 3d 206, 226 (2nd Cir. 2012).

and sales success before the lower court. Based on the evidence, the court approved the lower court's finding that the 'Red Sole Mark' had gained secondary meaning that caused it to be '*uniquely associated*' with the Christian Louboutin brand.

5.2.1.2 The Levi Strauss 'Pocket Tab' Mark

One of the most celebrated, and perhaps oldest, NTTMs in the US apparel industry is Levi Strauss & Co's 'pocket tab' device,[21] 'a folded ribbon sewn with its ends captured in the seam of a rear patch pocket'[22] on a pair of Levi's jeans. Since 1936, Levi Strauss & Co has used its famous pocket tab device in an array of colours, the very first being red tabs bearing the company's LEVI'S word mark in white, to distinguish its jeans by sight identification in a crowded denim market. Levi Strauss & Co has obtained US federal trademark registrations in respect of its 'pocket tab' device.[23] Over the years, the company has waged numerous court battles against other enterprises that have used protruding pocket tabs on jeans.

Levi Strauss & Co's 'pocket tab' trademark is an example of a NTTM applied on an apparel as it is the tab's *location* (attached to the seam of a rear patch pocket) and its defined *shape* (a folded ribbon sewn with ends captured in the seam of a rear patch pocket) in which the company Levi Strauss & Co has obtained property rights (trademark protection) and is seeking to enforce against third parties.

The likes of LEVI'S 'pocket tab' marks are also often referred to as 'position trademarks'. The idea of affixing a label, visible externally, consistently upon the back pocket of a pair of jeans as a distinguishing feature was indeed a novel one when Levi Strauss & Co first conceived of it and used it as a trademark in the apparel industry in 1936. Yet the

21 For an image of Levi Strauss & Co's celebrated 'pocket tab' device, please see Tracey Panek, 'Celebrating 85 Years of the Levi's Red Tab', *Levi Strauss & Co* (September 1, 2021) <https://www.levistrauss.com/2021/09/01/85-years-of-the-levis-red-tab/>.

22 *Levi & Strauss & Co* v *Blue Bell Inc*, 632 F 2d 817, 818 (9th Cir. 1980).

23 The pocket tab coloured red, *US Trademark Registration No 356701*; The pocket tab carrying 'LEVI'S', Reg No 516,561; The pocket tab coloured red and located in the left-hand vertical seam of the right rear patch pocket, *US Trademark Registration No 577490*; The pocket tab coloured white and located at the left-hand vertical seam of the right rear patch pocket, *US Trademark Registration No 720376*; The pocket tab coloured black and located at the left-hand vertical seam of the right rear patch pocket, *US Trademark Registration No 774625*; The pocket tab carrying 'LEVI'S', coloured white, and located at the left-hand vertical seam of the right rear patch pocket, *US Trademark Registration No 775412*. See *Levi & Strauss & Co* v *Blue Bell Inc*, 632 F 2d 817, 819 (9th Cir. 1980).

trademark registration of such a sign may still be strongly objected to on the ground that the LEVI'S 'pocket tab' lacked inherent distinctiveness, a fundamental requirement of trademark registration.[24] After all, LEVI'S 'pocket tab' is, for all intent and purposes, a simple apparel label, albeit a protruding one that has been placed in an unconventional location for apparel –at the external seam of the back pocket of a pair of jeans, as opposed to being attached to the inside seam of the apparel, where consumers usually expect labels to be affixed.[25] In other words, it may be argued that the average consumer is not accustomed to this *location* of garment labels as a source indicator, but instead they are likely to pay greater attention to the distinctive LEVI'S word mark on the 'pocket tab'. This is because consumers would *not* appreciate the trademark significance of such a position mark, the protruding 'pocket tab', without first being educated that it is used by the proprietor Levi Strauss & Co for that purpose.

However, Levi Strauss & Co was successful in its trademark registrations for the 'pocket tab' device, as it was able to show, at the time of application, that although the 'pocket tab' device lacked inherent distinctiveness when it was first adopted in 1936, it had acquired distinctiveness through substantial use, a phenomenon referred to in US trademark law as the acquisition of a 'secondary meaning'.[26] The US Court of Customs and Patent Appeals in *Levi & Strauss & Co v. Blue Bell Inc.* explained that the basic element of 'secondary meaning' in US trademark law is 'is a

[24] It should be noted that a trademark that lacks inherent distinctiveness and is not generic may still be protected if it is shown to have acquired distinctiveness in the sense of an acquisition of a 'secondary meaning'. Whether a trademark has acquired a 'secondary meaning' is a question of fact. This was precisely what Levi & Strauss & Co has successfully demonstrated in *Levi & Strauss & Co* v *Blue Bell Inc*, 632 F 2d 817 (9th Cir. 1980).

[25] See Mark A Lemley and Mark P McKenna, 'Trademark Spaces and Trademark Law's Secret Step Zero' (2023) 75 *Stanford Law Review* 1.

[26] *In re Levi Strauss & Co*, 165 USPQ 348 (TTAB 1970), the Trademark Trial and Appeal Board recognised trademark significance in the pocket tab's location and defined shape. The evidence presented by Levi Strauss & Co was found sufficient to establish secondary meaning in those features. In a subsequent case, *Levi & Strauss & Co vs Blue Bell Inc*, the Ninth Circuit Court of Appeals accepted the evidence presented by Levi Strauss & Co to the lower District Court as sufficient to establish 'secondary meaning' of the 'pocket tab' device. The direct and circumstantial evidence adduced included, amongst others, 'use of the mark continuously for 44 years, sales of products bearing the mark of $500,000,000 in the one year before suit, a use on 500,000,000 garments between 1969 and 1977, and widespread advertising directed to the mark, were among the facts of record'. *Levi & Strauss & Co vs Blue Bell Inc*, 632 F 2d 817, 821 (9th Cir. 1980).

mental recognition in buyers' and potential buyers' minds that products connected with the symbol or device emanate from or are *associated* with the same source'.[27] In that case, Levi Strauss & Co sued Blue Bell Inc. (the maker and seller of WRANGLER jeans) for trademark infringement of LEVI'S 'pocket tab' device for affixing a horizontally disposed, protruding label bearing the mark 'HONDO' at the top of an inset pocket for its HONDO line of jeans. The US Court of Customs and Patent Appeals ruled in favour of Levi Strauss & Co and upheld the registration of LEVI'S 'pocket tab' device trademark. The court recognised that Levi Strauss & Co had, through extensive use and advertising of the 'pocket tab' device, built the device into a mark that prospective customers *associated* with only one particular seller of jeans in spite of the initial lack of inherent distinctiveness. Blue Bell Inc (WRANGLER) was thus found to be liable for trademark infringement on the ground that prospective buyers upon seeing the protruding HONDO mark on the back pockets of a pair of WRANGLER jeans would conclude that these jeans originated or were in some ways connected with the proprietor of *the* 'pocket tab' device mark, that is Levi Strauss & Co. In other words, the court found that prospective buyers of jeans would be confused by the use of the protruding HONDO mark on a pair of WRANGLER jeans, especially when the assessment was based on an imperfect recollection of the competing marks by prospective buyers.

The fact that the WRANGLER jeans were clearly labelled to indicate source by another label and a paper billboard bearing the distinctive WRANGLER word mark provided no assistance to Blue Bell Inc. in avoiding a finding of confusion on the part of the prospective buyers. The US Court of Customs and Patent Appeals further rejected the argument by Blue Bell Inc that Levi Strauss & Co 'may not use the trademark laws to obtain a perpetual monopoly on the idea of a protruding pocket label for pants, when the alleged trademark is not limited to any size, colour, or precise location of label, or to any wording on the label, simply because (Strauss) was the first to use this type of label'. It is clear that the court was of the view that the property right conferred on the LEVI'S 'pocket tab' trademark was not simply premised on a 'first-to-use' basis of a novel fashion concept. Rather, it was based on the finding by the court that the LEVI'S protruding 'pocket tab' mark gave the public a reliable indication of source and facilitated responsible marketplace competition.

27 *Levi & Strauss & Co v Blue Bell Inc*, 632 F 2d 817, 820 (9th Cir. 1980) (emphasis added).

As a result, Levi Strauss & Co was effectively conferred a property right in the use of a protruding label affixed at a particular location on garments as a distinguishing source indicator. Others are thus prohibited from using a similar label in a similar location on their apparel even if their labels bear a different, clear and distinctive word mark and the apparel is clearly labelled to indicate a different source as demonstrated in *Levi & Strauss & Co v Blue Bell Inc.*[28] More recently, Levi Strauss & Co, in a continuing quest to assert its property rights, had sued fashion houses Saint Laurent[29] and Kenzo,[30] respectively, for alleged trademark infringement of its signature protruding 'pocket tab' mark.

5.2.2 The European Union

Across the Atlantic in the European Union (EU), the European Union Trade Mark Regulation (EUTMR), together with the European Union Trade Mark Implementing Regulation (EUTMIR) and the European Union Trade Mark Delegated Regulation (EUTMDR)[31] constitute the main legislation governing trademark protection–related aspects in the European Union.[32] Broadly speaking, the EUTMDR covers procedural rules relating to opposition, revocation and invalidity actions, appeals to the Boards of Appeal, the organisation of the Boards of Appeal, notifications from the

[28] 'To stake a claim in its tab design, Levi's allegedly prints a certain number of products with a red tab bearing just the ® symbol on it. Levi's claims that this shows that Levi's owns trademark rights in the red tab, and not just the wording. The rumour is that one out of every 10 jeans has a plain red tab.' See Mari-Elise Paul, 'Levi's Keeps Tabs on YSL's Pockets', *Stites & Harbison PLLC* (September 24, 2019) <https://www.stites.com/resources/trademarkology/levis-keeps-tabs-on-ysls-pockets>.

[29] *Levi Strauss & Co v Yves Saint Laurent America Inc*, Case No 18-cv-06977-JSC. Levi Strauss & Co ultimately settled the trademark infringement dispute with Saint Laurent in 2019. See <https://sourcingjournal.com/denim/denim-business/levis-settlement-yves-saint-laurent-red-tabs-patent-164147/>.

[30] *Levi Strauss & Co v Kenzo Paris USA LLC et al*, Case No. 18-cv-02106-LB. This dispute also seemed to settle in 2018.

[31] Commission Delegated Regulation (EU) No 2017/1430 of May 18, 2017, supplementing Council Regulation (EC) No 207/2009 on the European Union trade mark and repealing Commission Regulations (EC) No 2868/95 and (EC) No 216/96 [2017] OJ L 205/1. Since May 13, 2018, repealed by Commission Delegated Regulation (EU) No 2018/625 of March 5, 2018, supplementing Regulation (EU) 2017/1001 of the European Parliament and of the Council on the European Union trade mark, and repealing Delegated Regulation (EU) 2017/1430 [2018] OJ L 104/1.

[32] Full EU trademark legal texts can be found here: 'EU trade mark legal texts', *European Union Intellectual Office* (2023) <https://euipo.europa.eu/ohimportal/en/eu-trade-mark-legal-texts>.

Office and communications with the Office, time limits and suspensions and certain procedures concerning international registrations. On the other hand, the EUTMIR covers matters such as the contents of EU trademark applications, representation of EU trademarks, rules on publication and registration, language and translation issues, priority and seniority, transfers and surrenders, EU collective and certification marks and certain procedures concerning international registrations.

Since 2016, new amendments to the EUTMR have been brought forth by amending Regulation (EU) No 2015/2424 of the European Parliament and the Council, which came into force on March 23, 2016 and is now codified as 2017/1001.[33] As it stands, Recital 10 of the EUTMR indicates that 'a sign should be permitted to be represented in any appropriate form using generally available technology, and *thus not necessarily by graphic means*, as long as the representation is clear, precise, self-contained, easily accessible, intelligible, durable and objective' (emphasis added). Article 4 of the EUTMR that once contained the 'graphical representation' requirement has since been amended to remove this requirement.[34]

Art 3(1) of the EUTMIR further reflects Recital 10 and Art 4 (b) of the EUTMR[35] demonstrating flexibility about NTTMs, but with a willingness to uphold the legal certainty for the parties involved. The latter aspect is reflected by the emphasis given in Art 3(1) EUTMIR on the necessity that the representation of a trademark must conform with the seven prerequisites established in the *Sieckmann* judgment.[36] Art 3(3) of the EUTMIR also contains a *non-exhaustive* list of types of trademarks: (a) word, (b) figurative, (c) shape, (d) position, (e) pattern, (f) colour, (g) sound, (h) motion, (i) multimedia and (j) hologram marks. Amongst the absolute grounds for refusal are those mentioned in Article 7 of the EUTMR.[37]

33 Regulation (EU) No 2017/1001 of the European Parliament and of the Council of June 14, 2017, on the European Union trade mark [2017] OJ L154/1.

34 Regulation (EU) No 2017/1001 of the European Parliament and of the Council of June 14, 2017 on the European Union trade mark [2017] OJ L154/1 art 4.

35 Ibid ('an EU trademark may consist of any signs . . . that are capable of being represented on the Register of European Union trade marks (the Register), in a manner which enables the competent authorities and the public to determine the clear and precise subject matter of the protection afforded to its proprietor').

36 *Siecknann v Deutsches Patent- und Markenamt*, Case C-273/00 ECLI:EU:C:2002:748 at [55] (December 12, 2002) ('a trade mark may consist of a sign which is not in itself capable of being perceived visually, provided that it can be represented graphicly, particularly by means of images, lines or characters, and that the representation is clear, precise, self-contained, easily accessible, intelligible, durable and objective').

37 Regulation (EU) No 2017/1001 of the European Parliament and of the Council of June 14, 2017 on the European Union trade mark [2017] OJ L 154/1, art 7.

These legislative amendments in EU trademarks protection provided legal bases for fashion houses and designers to seek stronger and more extensive protection for the use of NTTMs.

5.2.2.1 Christian Louboutin – the Red Sole Mark

Unsurprisingly, in May 2013, French fashion house Christian Louboutin, armed with its victory in the US courts, initiated proceedings before the District Court in The Hague, Netherlands, against Van Haren (a shoe retailer operating numerous outlets in the Netherlands) for selling high-heeled women's shoes with red soles and as such, alleged that Van Haren had infringed Christian Louboutin's registered NTTM, namely the 'Red Sole Mark'.[38] The District Court in The Hague ruled in favour of Christian Louboutin, upholding in part the claims of Christian Louboutin. Van Haren challenged the judgment of the District Court in The Hague under Article 2.1(2) of the Benelux convention,[39] claiming that the mark at issue was invalid on the basis that the mark is a two-dimensional figurative mark that consists of a red coloured surface and that the red sole gives *substantial value* to the shoes marketed by Christian Louboutin since that colour forms part of the appearance of those shoes and plays an important role in a consumer's decision to purchase them. One issue of contention was whether the concept of 'shape', within the meaning of that provision, is limited solely to three-dimensional properties of a product, such as its contours, measurements and volume, or whether that concept also covers properties that are not three-dimensional. In this regard, as the District Court was uncertain, it therefore decided to stay the proceedings and referred the following

[38] Christian Louboutin's NTTM was registered on January 6, 2010, for goods in Class 25, namely 'footwear (other than orthopaedic footwear)' of Benelux trade mark No 0874489. On April 10,2013, the registration was amended so as to limit the goods covered to 'high-heeled shoes (other than orthopaedic shoes)'. The description of Christian Louboutin's registered NTTM consisted 'of the colour red (Pantone 18 1663TP) applied to the sole of a shoe as shown (the contour of the shoe is not part of the trade mark but is intended to show the positioning of the mark)'.

[39] The Benelux convention on intellectual property (trademarks and designs) was signed in The Hague on February 25, 2005, by the Kingdom of Belgium, the Grand Duchy of Luxembourg and the Kingdom of the Netherlands (the Benelux convention). Article 2.1 of the Benelux Convention, headed 'Signs capable of constituting a Benelux trade mark' provides inter alia that: 'Nevertheless, signs consisting exclusively of the shape which results from the nature of the goods themselves, which gives *substantial value to the goods*, or which is necessary to obtain a technical result *shall not be regarded as trade marks*' (emphasis added).

question to the Court of Justice of the European Union (CJEU) for a preliminary ruling:

> Is the notion of 'shape', within the meaning of Article 3(1)(e)(iii) of [Directive 2008/95], limited to the three-dimensional properties of the goods, such as their contours, measurements and volume (expressed three-dimensionally), or does it include other (non-three-dimensional) properties of the goods, such as their colour?

In *Christian Louboutin and Christian Louboutin Sas v van Haren Schoenen BV*,[40] the CJEU held that, because Directive 2008/95 provides no definition of the concept of 'shape', the meaning and scope of that concept must, as the Court consistently held, be determined by considering its usual meaning in everyday language, while also taking into account the context in which it occurs and the purposes of the rules of which it is part. In general, under EU law, the concept of 'shape' is usually understood as a set of lines or contours that outline the product concerned. Accordingly, it does not follow from Directive 2008/95, the case-law of the Court, or the usual meaning of that concept, that a colour per se, without an outline, may constitute a 'shape'. Notably, the CJEU held that, although the shape of the product, or of a part of the product, plays a role in creating an outline for the colour, it cannot, however, be held that a sign consists of that shape in the case where the registration of the mark did not seek to protect that shape but sought *solely to protect the application of a colour to a specific part of that product.*

Christian Louboutin's NTTM, as it was described in the trademark registration, cannot be regarded as consisting 'exclusively' of a shape because the main element of that sign is a specific colour designated by an internationally recognised identification code. In answering the question by the Hague's District Court, the Court clarified that Article 3(1)(e)(iii) of Directive 2008/95 must be interpreted as meaning that a sign consisting of a colour applied to the sole of a high-heeled shoe, such as that at issue in *Christian Louboutin and Christian Louboutin Sas v van Haren Schoenen BV*, does not consist exclusively of a 'shape', within the meaning of that provision. French fashion house Christian Louboutin was victorious once again.[41]

[40] *Louboutin and Christian Louboutin*, Case C-163/16, ECLI:EU:C:2018:423 (CJEU, February 6, 2018).

[41] Christian Louboutin had pursued numerous actions for trademark infringement in several jurisdictions but it was not always successful. For a comprehensive discussion of Christian Louboutin's legal suits, see Irene Calboli, 'Hands Off "My" Colors, Patterns, and

5.2.2.2 Louis Vuitton – the Checkerboard Pattern Mark

Despite these wins, other fashion houses and designers have encountered headwinds in their claims for exclusive rights in NTTMs. Louis Vuitton Malletier (LV) is one of them.[42] In August 1998, LV sought and was granted registration of the 'checkerboard pattern' NTTM (also called 'chequerboard').

The 'checkerboard pattern' is popularly known as the 'Damier' and today adorns the surface of many LV products such as bags, wallets, shoes and clothing.[43] More than a decade later in 2009, Nanu-Nana filed an application for declaration of invalidity of LV's registered 'checkerboard pattern' NTTM on the grounds that it was descriptive, devoid of distinctive character, had become customary in current language/bona fide and established practices of trade, consists exclusively of shape giving substantial value to goods, contrary to public policy or morality[44] and/or registered in bad faith.[45] The Cancellation Division in the Office of Harmonization in the Internal Market (OHIM) approved the application for declaration of invalidity on the bases of Art 7(1)(b) ('devoid of any distinctive character'), read with Arts 52(1)(a) and 7(3) and 52(2) of the EUTMR. This decision was upheld by the First Board of Appeal of OHIM. LV's appeal to the European Union General Court (EUGC)[46] was dismissed. The General Court upheld OHIM's decision invalidating LV's registered 'checkerboard pattern' NTTM.

Regarding the claim that LV's NTTM lacked inherent distinctiveness, the EUGC held that the relevant public's perception is not necessarily the same in the case of a three-dimensional mark (which also consists of the

Shapes! How Non-traditional Trademarks Promote Standardization and May Negatively Impact Creativity and Innovation' in Irene Calboli and Martin Senftleben (eds), *The Protection of Non-Traditional Trade Marks* (Oxford University Press, 2018) 296–299 (hereafter Calboli, 'Hands Off').

42 *Louis Vuitton Malletier v Office for the Harmonisation in the Internal Market (Trade Marks and Designs) (OHIM)*, Case T-359/12 (General Court, April 21, 2015).

43 'Louis Vuitton Damier', *Louis Vuitton* (2023) <https://us.louisvuitton.com/eng-us/recommendations/louis-vuitton-damier>; Kristian Burt, 'Pharrell Williams Sets Off a New Dazzling Era for First Louis Vuitton Men's SS24 Show', *VMan* (June 22, 2024) <https://vmagazine.com/article/pharrell-williams-sets-off-a-new-dazzling-era-for-first-louis-vuitton-mens-show/>.

44 Council Regulation (EC) No 207/2009 of February 26, 2009 on the Community trade mark [2009] OJ L 78/1 arts 52(1)(a), 7(1)(b), (c), (d), (e)(iii), (f).

45 Ibid arts 52(1)(b).

46 The European Union General Court was formerly known as the European Union Court of First Instance, which was first established in 1989. The renaming took place following the entry into force of the Treaty of Lisbon in 2009.

product's appearance) as compared to a word or figurative mark, which is unrelated to the appearance of products that the mark denotes. In particular, average consumers are not in the habit of making assumptions about a good's origins based on the shape or packaging in the absence of graphic or word elements. Therefore, it is more difficult to establish distinctiveness in such cases. The more the shape to be protected as a trademark resembles the shape most likely to be taken by the product, the more likely that the trademark is devoid of distinctive character in accordance with Art 7(1)(b) of the EUTMR. The EUGC held that to possess distinctive character, the mark must depart significantly from the norm or customs of the sector to fulfil an essential function-indicating origin. In the present case, LV's 'checkerboard pattern' NTTM has no notable variations as it is the same as traditional form. The weft and warp 'pattern within a pattern' are also not notably varied from the conventional presentation.

As to LV's claim that the 'checkerboard pattern' NTTM has acquired distinctiveness, the EUGC held that in the case of a (then) Community trademark, acquired distinctiveness of a mark must be established in all the member states of the European Union before it may be validly registered. In this case, the EUGC was of the view that LV was unable to discharge the requisite burden of proof in respect of acquired distinctiveness in its 'checkerboard pattern' NTTM.

5.2.2.3 Adidas – the Three-Stripe Design

Similarly, Adidas has not always been successful in securing exclusivity for its 'three-stripe' NTTM in the European Union.

In 2009, Belgian footwear company Shoe Branding Europe BVBA ('Shoe Branding') applied to register its two-stripe design as a trademark in the EU. Adidas initiated trademark opposition proceedings alleging that Shoe Branding's two-stripe design is 'confusingly similar' to its well-known three-stripe trademark. Adidas had secured registration of a mark that was described to 'consists of three parallel equidistant stripes of identical width, applied on the product in any direction' in Class 25 for clothing, footwear, headgear.

The litigation about the three-stripe and two-stripe NTTMs took the parties all the way to the CJEU[47] in 2016 and saw the CJEU affirming the lower EUGC's decision: 'The difference between two and three stripes

[47] *Shoe Branding Europe BVBA v Adidas AG*, Case C-396/15 P (General Court, February 17, 2016).

placed on a shoe [is] not sufficient to affect the similarities arising from the configuration of the signs at issue and from their position on the side of the shoe [so that] that difference [does] not influence the overall impression produced.' As such, Adidas was successful in its opposition of Shoe Branding's application for registration of its two-stripe NTTM.

However, it is interesting to note that sometime in 2014 and in the midst of the two-stripe/three-stripe opposition battle, Shoe Branding filed an application for declaration of invalidity of one of Adidas' registered three-stripe NTTM.[48] The Cancellation Division of the European Union Intellectual Property Office (EUIPO)[49] granted the application for declaration of invalidity, on the ground that Adidas' NTTM was devoid of any distinctive character, whether in terms of inherent distinctiveness or acquired distinctiveness through use. This decision was affirmed by the Second Board of Appeal of the EUIPO.[50] Adidas' appeal to the EUGC to annul the EUIPO's decision was dismissed.[51] An important issue before the courts was whether Adidas' three-stripe NTTM had acquired distinctiveness through use throughout the EU. Agreeing with the EUIPO, the EUGC held that there was hardly any relevant evidence[52] to substantiate Adidas' claim that its three-stripe NTTM has acquired distinctiveness throughout the EU. Accordingly, Adidas' three-stripe NTTM was also invalidated.

Clearly, there were no winners in the long legal battles between Adidas and Shoe Branding. More recently, in 2021, Adidas sued luxury designer

[48] Based on Council Regulation (EC) No 207/2009 of February 26, 2009, on the Community trade mark [2009] OJ L 78/1 art 52(1)(a) (now Regulation (EU) No 2017/1001 of the European Parliament and of the Council of 14 June 2017 on the European Union trade mark [2017] OJ L 154/1 art 59(1)(a)) in conjunction with Council Regulation (EC) No 207/2009 of February 26, 2009, on the Community trade mark [2009] OJ L 78/1 art 7(1)(b) (now Regulation (EU) No 2017/1001 of the European Parliament and of the Council of June 14, 2017, on the European Union trade mark [2017] OJ L 154/1 art 7(1)(b)).

[49] European Union Intellectual Property Office (EUIPO) was formerly known as The Office of Harmonization in the Internal Market (OHIM). The OHIM was rebranded as the EUIPO in 2016.

[50] *adidas AG v European Union Intellectual Property Office (EUIPO)*, R 1515/2016-2 (EUIPO 2nd BoA, March 7, 2017).

[51] Ibid; *Adidas AG v EUIPO and Shoe Branding Europe BVBA*, Case T-307/17, ECLI:EU:T:2019:427.

[52] Relevant evidence includes market share held by mark; how intensive, geographically widespread and long-standing use of mark has been; amount invested in promoting mark; proposition of relevant class of persons who, because of the mark, identify goods as originating from a particular undertaking; and statements from chambers of commerce and industry or other trade and professional associations.

Thom Browne in the US over the latter's use of a four-stripe design on the ground that it was too similar to Adidas' three-stripe design. On January 12, 2023, the eight-person jury in the US District Court for the Southern District of New York ruled in favour of Thom Browne.[53]

5.3 The Protection of NTTMs – Problems and Objections

As the above cases demonstrate, the protection of NTTMs is not without difficulties. In certain jurisdictions, the range of registrable NTTMs is limited by the requirement that, in order to be protected as a mark, a sign must be 'capable of graphic representation' or be 'visually perceptible'. Based on this requirement, it becomes practically impossible, or considerably more difficult, to protect non-visual signs such as smells and sounds unless they could be visually represented in some way.

Moreover, from a public policy perspective, some, including one of the authors,[54] have argued that granting registered trademark rights to NTTMs is problematic and ought to be discouraged or disallowed based on competition and freedom of expression concerns.

For one, NTTMs are signs that often consist of features in product designs such as shapes, patterns or colours that may be common or functional in nature and thus ought to remain in the public domain and be available for use by others in the course of trade. In trademark law lingo, NTTMs are either 'devoid of distinctive character' or descriptive of 'the kind, quality, intended purpose … or other characteristics of good or services' and as such it is in the public's interest (in particular, from the perspective of fair competition) to keep them free for all to use. To use the examples referred to above, granting trademark protection to the Bottega Veneta Intrecciato pattern, LV Damier Checkerboard pattern or Louboutin red-sole shoes means that, in practice, no one can copy these designs or produce similar-looking ones. One key reason is because registered trademark protection is potentially indefinite, since marks can be renewed after a 10 year period. As a result, consumers are denied the opportunity to purchase other products with the same features (often with a much lower price tag). Some may argue that this

[53] 'Thom Browne Beats out Adidas in Stripe-Centric Trademark Battle', *The Fashion Law* (January 12, 2023) <https://www.thefashionlaw.com/thom-browne-beats-out-adidas-in-stripe-centric-trademark-battle/>. See also *adidas America, Inc, et al, v Thom Browne,* Inc, Case 1:21-cv-05615 (SDNY).

[54] Calboli, 'Hands Off', above n 41, 304–307.

may not be of major concern as consumers are still offered a large number of alternative choices in a market economy – several types of bags or shoes, even without these designs. Still, competitors are foreclosed from producing *those* product features and consumers cannot be offered less costly, or merely other, alternatives. This runs fundamentally against the principles of the trademark right, whose ultimate objective is to promote market competition, not to protect a monopoly on aesthetic and appealing features.

An additional concern is that the protection of NTTMs ultimately encourages prolonged repetitive use of iconic or popular design features of a product so as to secure and maintain trademark registrations under the concept of distinctiveness acquired through use, forgoing alternative novel and innovative design features. In particular, once a feature receives trademark protection, companies need to continue to replicate it 'as is', lest they lose protection because they would be using the 'marks' inconsistently. In turn, this may have a chilling effect on creativity and innovation of the enterprises that are proprietors of the NTTMs, with the result that society is worse off overall. For example, every pair of Louboutin shoes, be they for women or men, use the famed red soles today. Likewise, the LV Damier checkerboard pattern is omnipresent across most LV products, particularly its bags. The same applies to the intrecciato weave – albeit in different widths – at Bottega Veneta. Of course, these companies are eager to repeatedly use their marks because doing so drives more consumers to purchase their products. Yet, should companies desire to change their products, consumers would struggle to recognise them because they have become used to the same features in all products. Precisely because of this, LV's recent attempts to innovate its products has been largely based on reproducing its signature monogram and checkerboard patterns on different materials such as transparent plastic, or as the new menswear designer Pharrell Williams had done, rendering the Damier pattern to resemble pixels and jungle camouflage. Likewise, Bottega Veneta has introduced products with the intrecciato weave in different larger sizes, but this innovation arguably does not depart significantly from the brand's strategy of using the same iconic pattern on all its products.

In other words, granting excessive protection to NTTMs can also result in limiting investments in product innovation and quality. In particular, the possibility to continue to extract value from the same shapes, colours and patterns protected on an exclusive basis – without competitors being able to copy these features – may lead producers to avoid investing in new products as the above examples demonstrate. This is a serious concern. IP laws are supposed to promote innovation, yet NTTMs could become vehicles to promote standardisation and commercialisation of non-innovative products. This may lead to a loss of creativity, innovation and investment in product quality in the long term with negative consequences for everyone.

5.4 NTTMs and the Legal Requirement of Distinctiveness

The preceding sections discussed the approaches in the United States and European Union on assessing distinctiveness. In Singapore, the highest appellate court, the Court of Appeal, has observed that 'the criteria for assessing distinctiveness character are the *same* for all categories of marks. Nevertheless, the perception of the relevant public may not always be the same for all categories of marks, and it may therefore be more difficult to establish distinctive character in relation to some categories (such as shapes, colours, personal names, advertising slogans and surface treatments) than others'.[55] Regarding colour, for instance, one has witnessed protracted litigation by Cadbury to protect the use of the colour purple for its chocolates, with courts being cautious about granting too wide a monopoly should the trademark registration be approved.[56]

A mark's inherent distinctiveness must be assessed by reference to the goods or services in respect of which registration is sought as well as the perception of relevant persons, namely the consumers of those goods or services, who is deemed to be reasonably well-informed, observant and circumspect.[57] The critical question to ask is whether the average consumer would appreciate the trademark significance of the mark in question without being educated that it is used for that purpose.

It is surmised that the most significant objection to NTTMs as registered trademarks relates to the subsistence (or absence) of the element of distinctiveness, which is the cornerstone of a trademark registration. After all, the primary function of a trademark is that of an indicator of origin and distinctiveness, that is, the attribute in a trademark to distinguish goods or services having one business source from goods or services having a different business source. Conventional signs such as

[55] *Société des Produits Nestlé SA v Petra Foods Ltd* [2016] SGCA 64 at [22(c)].

[56] Eg, *Société des Produits Nestlé SA v Cadbury UK Ltd* [2013] EWCA Civ 1174; *Société des Produits Nestlé SA v Cadbury UK Ltd* [2022] EWHC 1671 (Ch).

[57] *Société des Produits Nestlé SA v Petra Foods Ltd* [2016] SGCA 64 at [22(b)].

words or figurative devices, in particular coined or invented words and unique, one-of-a-kind logos, are examples of trademarks that possess the innate ability to distinguish goods or services. The law refers to such trademarks as possessing inherent distinctiveness.

In contrast, except in rare circumstances, NTTMs are generally found not to be inherently capable of distinguishing the relevant goods and services because it has been widely acknowledged by the courts that the average consumer is not normally accustomed to perceive these marks, such as shapes and single colours, as badges of trade origins before the products have been sold in the marketplace for some time. In other words, the average consumer does not, *by reason alone of the mark* (a shape, sound or a colour), perceive the goods in question as originating from a particular trader. To qualify for trademark protection, proprietors of NTTMs should thus adduce evidence to show that these signs, though lacking in inherent distinctiveness, have nonetheless acquired distinctiveness through extensive use and substantial market investments.

Indeed, Article 15.1 of TRIPS acknowledges the important distinction between signs that are inherently capable of distinguishing the relevant goods and services and those that are not. In the case of the latter, Article 15.1 provides that member states may make registrability dependent on distinctiveness acquired through use. The concept of 'distinctiveness acquired through use' and the applicable test for factual distinctiveness are thus the linchpin of the registrability of NTTMs and constitutes the basis of the validity of the registrations.

Based on this, this chapter now turns to the critical question of distinctiveness of NTTMs and the exposition of the test for acquired distinctiveness by the courts in Singapore and the United Kingdom in recent NTTM decisions with particular attention to shapes.

5.4.1 NTTMs and the Test of Distinctiveness Acquired through Use – Reliance vs Association

Nestlé's four-finger KitKat chocolate bar has been the subject of multiple legal disputes, particularly concerning its shape and attempts to register it as a trademark. Indeed, in the last decade, Nestlé has been engaged in various trademark opposition and infringement proceedings in the European Union, the United Kingdom and Singapore over its NTTM – a three-dimensional trademark in the shape of its four-finger and two-finger chocolate bar marketed under the name KIT KAT.

In all of these proceedings, Nestlé has persistently argued that its NTTM, although devoid of inherent distinctiveness, has nevertheless acquired factual distinctiveness through use. It is Nestlé's contention that the correct approach to the assessment of acquired distinctiveness is to show 'that a significant proportion of the relevant class of consumers *perceives* the goods designated exclusively by the mark in issue, as opposed to any other trademark which might also be present, as originating from the applicant. This does not require any finding that consumers have, in the past, placed *any reliance* upon the mark in their transactional behaviour'.[58] In other words, there is no need to show that the NTTM has played a role in the consumer's purchasing decision or behaviour. It follows that a '*mere association*' of the NTTM with the trademark proprietor's goods, in the sense that if the consumer is to consider who marketed the goods bearing the NTTM, he would identify the trademark proprietor, which is sufficient for a finding by the court that the NTTM has acquired distinctiveness through use. However, Nestle has not found British courts to be receptive to this argument, which has been rejected to date.

Although US courts in cases such as *Levi & Strauss & Co v. Blue Bell Inc.* and *Christian Louboutin S.A. v. Yves Saint Laurent Am. Holding, Inc.* appear to have adopted the 'mere association' test in the determination of distinctiveness in NTTMs, courts in Singapore and the United Kingdom are of a different view. In particular, the Singapore Court of Appeal in *Société des Produits Nestlé SA v Petra Foods Ltd* (the KitKat case) has unequivocally stated that the correct test for acquired distinctiveness of a trademark in Singapore is the 'reliance' test and not the 'mere association' test. Under the 'reliance' test, the inquiry is whether, *by reason alone of the mark*, consumers perceive the goods in question as emanating from a particular trader.[59] The 'reliance' in this context is reliance in the specific sense that consumers *perceive the mark in question as a trademark* and must be contrasted with reliance in the sense that 'consumers had in the past gone out and made purchasing decisions on that basis'.[60] The 'reliance' test is similarly adopted by the CJEU and the Court of Appeal in the UK.

[58] *Societe Des Produits Nestlé SA vs Cadbury UK Ltd* [2017] EWCA Civ 358 at [67] (emphasis added).

[59] *Société des Produits Nestlé SA v Petra Foods Ltd* [2016] SGCA 64 at [47].

[60] *Nestlé SA v Cadbury UK Ltd (No 2)* [2016] EWHC 50 (Ch) at [59].

5.4.2 *The 'Reliance' Test as the Preferred Test to Assess the Acquired Distinctiveness of NTTMs in the Fashion Industry*

The authors are of the view that, even though the KitKat case addressed only shape marks, the Singapore Court of Appeal's judgment should be applicable to NTTMs beyond merely shapes on the issues of inherent distinctiveness and acquired distinctiveness as the threshold for trademark protection. As such, the 'reliance' test propounded by both the English and Singapore Courts of Appeal can, and should, be applied in the assessment of acquired distinctiveness of other NTTMs, such as design features in the form of single colours or combination of colours, monograms, patterns, forms of packaging and trade dress commonly used in the fashion industry.

This test may seem conservative, and even restrictive, to fashion houses and other trademark proprietors, yet it also represents the best compromise between granting trademark protection while still considering the impact of such protection on competition and, in general, expression. Accordingly, the authors support that, between the 'reliance' test and the 'mere association' test, the 'reliance' test is the preferred test to follow in assessing the acquired distinctiveness of NTTMs in the fashion industry. This test accords with both general trademark principles and trademark policy.

5.4.3 *Principles*

As it is well-known, but it is worth repeating, the registration of a sign or indicia as a trademark confers on the proprietor exclusive rights in perpetuity that effectively impinge other traders' freedom to operate in the same or similar markets. For well-known signs, this impingement virtually extends to all markets. This legal monopoly is not only lengthy but also extensive and powerful. For example, in the case of an alleged infringement of identical marks on identical goods, there would be no need to show a likelihood of confusion about the origin of a defendant's goods because, subject to certain defences, confusion is normally presumed (at least in the European Union and several other jurisdictions including the United Kingdom and Singapore) in such cases of 'double identity'. In turn, the public interest is served if *all signs* seeking registration fulfil the essential function of a trademark, which is to guarantee the identity of the origin of the marked goods or services to the consumer or end user by enabling him, without the possibility of confusion, to distinguish the goods or services from others that have another origin.[61] In other words, only those signs that are either inherently distinctive or have acquired distinctiveness through use can perform this important function, that is, to permit consumers to make informed decisions between competing goods from different undertakings in the course of trade, and ought to be registered as trademarks and protected as such.

The application of the 'reliance' test to assess acquired distinctiveness through use ensures that the sign or indicia to be registered is worthy of protection by focusing on the need for the proprietor to prove that it has played a role in the consumer's perception of the sign or indicia in question *as a trademark*. In the words of the Singapore Court of Appeal in the KitKat case, accepting evidence of 'mere association' as sufficient would 'detract from and undermine the essential function of trademarks, which is to *guarantee* the origin of goods and services'.[62]

The need to ensure that the sign or indicia seeking registration fulfils the essential function of trademarks is made that much more acute in the case of NTTMs because of a common attribute they all share despite their diverse nature.

More often than not, NTTMs are signs that have never been used as the sole means of identifying trade origin. Instead, they are always used alongside other distinctive trademarks, such as words, logos and other figurative devices. To use the Louboutin red sole as an example, the mark is used along with the word mark on the shoe and the shoe box. As such, courts have referred to these NTTMs as 'limping' trademarks as they rely on the presence of other, traditional trademarks, which serve as 'crutches'.[63] In the KitKat case, this lengthy passage is worth noting:

> There is no absolute rule that a mark that has only been used with other trademarks cannot also on its own distinguish the relevant goods or services ... ultimately, the question is whether the mark can stand up on its own as an indicator of trade origin, and in each case, this will depend on the evidence. Nonetheless, where a mark has never been used as a sole badge of origin ... this might lend weight to the inference that the trader does not depend on the mark standing alone to serve as a trademark. This is a factor that the trader would have to overcome in proving that the mark has indeed acquired distinctiveness.[64]

[61] *Koninklijke Philips Electronics NV v Remington Consumer Products Ltd* [2003] Ch 159.

[62] *Société des Produits Nestlé SA v Petra Foods Ltd* [2016] SGCA 64 at [38].

[63] Ibid at [59].

[64] Ibid.

The recognition of the 'limping' nature of NTTMs is significant, as it affects the evaluation of whether NTTMs, although lacking in inherent distinctiveness, have acquired distinctiveness through substantial use. The adoption and the application of the 'reliance' test effectively and aptly places the onus on the proprietor of NTTMs to prove that they are truly able to function as trademarks and, as such, deserving of protection. This first accords with the general principles of trademark law.

5.4.4 Policy

As mentioned, the protracted and often acrimonious legal disputes between fashion businesses, as shown in the cases above, bring to focus the tension that has been created in a particular sector like the fashion industry in which seemingly common shapes, patterns and or a combination of these indicia are conferred intellectual property rights in the form of NTTMs owned by one proprietor to the exclusion of others in the same trade. It is thus accepted that trademark law, as with all other intellectual property laws, requires a careful balancing of the interests of various stakeholders.

Long usage, and often first use, of a particular NTTM, for example, the shape of a product (Bottega Veneta's intrecciato weave and knot bags), a colour (Christian Louboutin's red sole shoes), a pattern (Adidas three stripes) or a trade dress (LEVI's protruding 'pocket tab') might result in a substantial degree of market recognition, such that consumers are quick to call to mind or to *associate* that NTTMs with a particular trader because they have become familiar with that NTTM and therefore recognise it. However, it is submitted that such recognition or association on the part of the consumer does not necessarily guarantee that the consumer is actually relying on the NTTMs as a badge of origin – in other words, that the consumer treats that sign as a trademark or a badge of origin.

Instead, in the authors' view, the 'reliance' test sets an appropriately high bar in the assessment of acquired distinctiveness as compared to the 'mere association' test. Consequently, the adoption of this test accords with policy, as it avoids striking a balance too far in favour of the private proprietary interests of trademark owners to the detriment of fair access, market competition and expressive trademark uses in general. As argued above, the problem and danger of overprotection are very real. To conclude the chapter, it is worth repeating what Jacob J (as he then was) adroitly explained in *Nestlé v Unilever*:

> There is a bit of sleight of hand going on here and in other cases of this sort. The trick works like this. The manufacturer sells and advertises his product widely and under a well-known trademark. After some while the product appearance becomes well known. He then says the appearance alone will serve as a trademark, even though he himself never relied on the appearance alone to designate origin and would not dare to do so. He then gets registration of the shape alone. Now he is in a position to stop other parties, using their own word trademarks, from selling the product, even though no-one is deceived or misled.[65]

5.5 Conclusion

Because of their nature, there are unique and serious competition-related and expression-associated problems, which may result from affording overbroad protection to NTTMs. With the various safeguards identified and mentioned, courts around the world have tried, on the one hand, to meet the needs of business for novel branding and marketing strategies in the form of NTTMs (at least in shape marks), while, on the other hand, minimising the ills that NTTMs bring about so as to strike a balance in order to ensure market competition, minimise the overlaps of IP rights and prevent abuses of the trademark system. In our view, the sensible solution adopted by the Singapore Court of Appeal with the 'reliance' test strikes the correct balance in protecting trademarks while also safeguarding the general trademark principles and the objectives of trademark policy.

[65] *Société des Produits Nestlé SA v Unilever Plc* [2003] RPC 35 at [32].

6

Utility Patents and the Fashion Industry

ROGER ALLAN FORD

ABSTRACT

This chapter reviews the fashion industry's uses of utility patents. It first provides an overview of the fashion industry's patenting activities, looking at how many patents are granted for fashion-related inventions and how large apparel companies obtain those patents. It then examines companies' use of patents, looking at how patent litigation in the fashion industry compares to other industries. Finally, it turns to the uneasy tension in fashion between function and aesthetics, examining the specific technologies and inventions being claimed in fashion patents to see what can be inferred about the relationship between fashion and intellectual property

6.1 Introduction

Fashion is not the first industry that comes to mind as depending on patent law. Other, higher-tech industries like semiconductors and pharmaceuticals occupy much more of the time of patent lawyers and judges. Yet every year, large apparel manufacturers apply for and obtain patents, and every year patent offices issue thousands of patents in 'wearing apparel', 'weaving' and other categories relevant to the fashion industry.[1] Many of these patents are directed to the sorts of fashion that seem obviously technological or routinely subjected to technological

[1] This is not a new phenomenon; some of the earliest patents covered inventions that helped enable the development of the fashion industry. Eg, US Patent No 72X (Issued on March 14, 1794) (ginning cotton); US Patent No 8,294 (Issued on August 12, 1851) (improvement in sewing-machines). Isaac Singer's sewing-machine patent, for instance, played a key role in one of the first patent pools. See Adam Mossoff, 'The Rise and Fall of the First American Patent Thicket: The Sewing Machine War of the 1850s' (2011) 53 *Arizona Law Review* 165. For more on technological innovation and adaptation in the fashion industry, see, eg, Phyllis G Tortora, *Dress, Fashion and Technology: From*

innovation, like athletic wear or watches. Others are directed towards new materials and construction techniques that can be used in a variety of garments. But still more are directed to garments that employ traditional methods of design and construction.

This chapter examines the fashion industry's uses of utility patents. It first provides an overview of the fashion industry's patenting activities, looking at how many patents are granted for fashion-related inventions and how large apparel companies obtain those patents (Section 6.2). It then examines companies' use of patents, looking at how patent litigation in the fashion industry compares to other industries (Section 6.3). Finally, it turns to the uneasy tension in fashion between function and aesthetics, examining the specific technologies and inventions being claimed in fashion patents to see what can be inferred about the relationship between fashion and intellectual property (Section 6.4).

Before we dive in, a quick note on scope. This chapter focuses on utility patents, the type of patent most people think of when they think 'patent'. Utility patents cover inventions – 'any new and useful process, machine, manufacture, or composition of matter, or any new and useful improvement thereof', as it is put in US law.[2] Utility patents are not, however, the only kind of patent; in addition to plant patents (which cover, well, plants), in the United States there are also design patents, which cover 'any new, original and ornamental design for an article of manufacture'.[3] Similar rights are protected in other countries under other names, like 'registered designs'. Whatever the name, design protections are a more conventional fit for fashion, since they can apply to purely aesthetic creations without any showing of utility. Those rights, however, are covered elsewhere in this volume; our focus here will be utility patents only.[4]

6.2 Obtaining Patents: Patenting Fashion Inventions

6.2.1 Patents by Classification

Fashion may not be the most obvious industry to rely on patents, but numerous technologies are critical to the industry. Apparel itself has for

Prehistory to the Present (Bloomsbury, 2015); Andrew Godley, 'The Development of the Clothing Industry: Technology and Fashion' (1997) 28 *Textile History* 3.

2 Patent Act 2012, 35 USC § 101 (US).

3 Patent Act 2012, 35 USC § 171(a) (US).

4 On design protection, see Chapters 7 and 11.

centuries reflected technological change; otherwise, today clothing would be made without synthetic fibres, modern dyes or even the sewing machine. Some of these technological developments are relevant to almost every fashion house; consider new fabrics, new fabric dyes and treatments or new methods of construction. Others are specific to market segments like athletic wear or jewellery.

For an initial sense of how important patents are to fashion, we can look at how many patents are granted that appear to relate to fashion. This is not a trivial task, for a few reasons. Patents can at times be written in impenetrable language only occasionally resembling English. Even when read by a patent practitioner, though, it is not always obvious what are the different applications an invention might have. For instance, the original US patent for hook-and-loop fasteners (more commonly known as Velcro) mentioned use as 'closing devices for clothing, blinds or the like' but didn't mention the countless other uses to which Velcro has been applied.[5] So it is impossible to get a definitive list of fashion-related patents.

Helpfully, the patent offices of different nations have agreed on standard classification schemes that make it possible to filter patents for those related to particular technologies. These classification schemes have numerous limitations: many of the categories are broad, the schemes have changed over the years and they rely on the patent applicant or patent examiner to identify a particular use as a possibility. Perhaps most critically, most patents fall within multiple technology classifications, and the fashion-related classifications may be minor, niche or hypothetical uses of a technology. For instance, US Patent No. 7,627,451, titled 'movement and event systems and associated methods', was granted to Apple Inc. in 2009. The patent explains that the invention 'relates to sensing systems monitoring applications in sports, shipping, training, medicine, fitness, wellness and industrial production' and includes 76 separate technology classifications, one of which – A43B3/34, for 'footwear characterised by the shape or the use with electrical or electronic arrangements' – relates to fashion. If Apple ever made use of the invention covered by this patent, it apparently did not do so in footwear. Yet the patent comes up in a search for patents falling within fashion-related classifications. Still, despite these limitations in using technology classifications and their potential to produce overly broad results, they can provide a helpful overview of fashion-related patenting activity.

[5] US Patent No 3,009,235 (Issued on November 21, 1961), describing and claiming a 'separable fastening device' and originally assigned to International Velcro Co.

To examine fashion-related patenting activity, the most comprehensive classification scheme – the Cooperative Patent Classification, which is maintained jointly by the US Patent and Trademark Office and the European Patent Office – was used to identify technology classifications related to fashion. The CPC contains approximately 250,000 classification entries, which are organised into nine sections (like 'human necessities' and 'physics') that are divided into classes, subclasses, groups and so forth. Ten classes were identified as being most likely to cover most fashion-related inventions:[6]

- A41: Wearing Apparel
- A42: Headwear
- A43: Footwear
- A44: Haberdashery; Jewellery
- A45: Hand or Travelling Articles [which includes umbrellas, purses, luggage, handbags, and walking sticks, among other things]
- D01: Natural or Man-Made Threads or Fibres; Spinning
- D02: Yarns; Mechanical Finishing of Yarns or Ropes; Warping or Beaming
- D03: Weaving
- D04: Braiding; Lace-Making; Knitting; Trimmings; Non-Woven Fabrics
- D05: Sewing; Embroidering; Tufting

Each of these classes contains numerous specific classification entries. For instance, A41, the group covering 'wearing apparel', contains six subclasses, including 'shirts; underwear; baby linen; handkerchiefs'; 'corsets; brassieres'; 'outerwear; protective garments; accessories' and so forth. Each subclass contains dozens of specific classifications like 'collars with supports for neckties or cravats', 'reversible collars', 'chemically stiffened collars' and so forth.

The number of US patents granted each year containing any classification entry falling within one of these ten classes was determined from the US Patent and Trademark Office's PatentsView database.[7] The results show a general upward trend in the number of patents granted each year, with recent years showing more than 5,000 patents a year (Figure 6.1):

[6] These are not the only classes that could relate to fashion. Other potentially relevant classes include D06, which covers various flexible materials and treatments for them, including fabric treatments and laundry but also carpet cleaning and methods of turning tubes inside out; and C14, which covers skins, hides, pelts and leather. But arbitrary lines must sometimes be drawn.

[7] PatentsView, 'Patent Search' (United States Patent and Trademark Office) <https://patentsview.org/>.

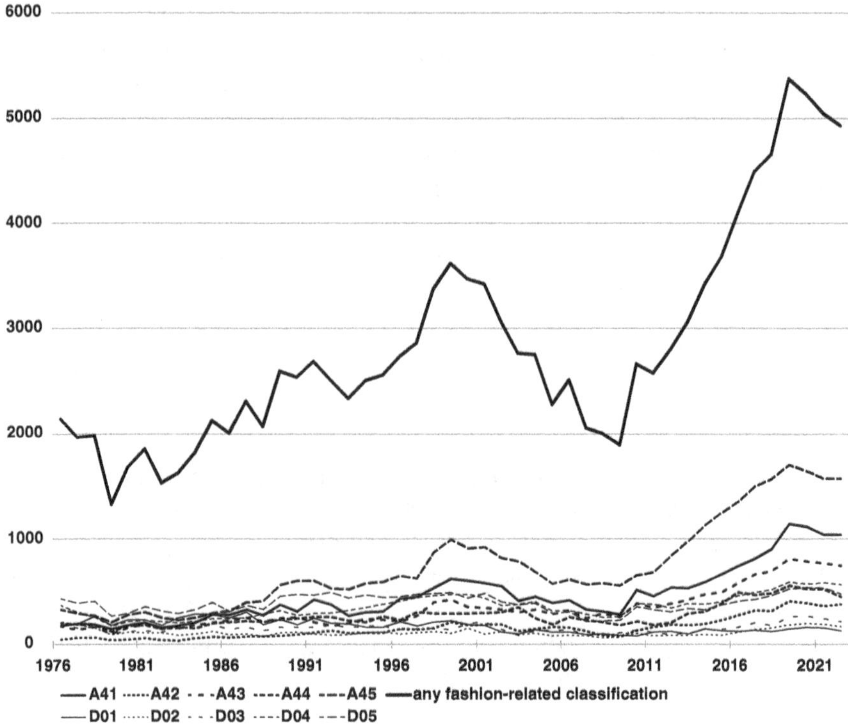

Figure 6.1 Upward trend in fashion-related patents.[8]
Credit: Roger Allan Ford

This trend, though, does not appear to be due to any growing importance of patents to the fashion industry. Instead, it appears to track the general growth in the number of patents issued each year, which increased from around 70,000 patent grants (in the United States) in 1976 to around 350,000 in 2020.[9] Indeed, the proportion of all patents with any classification entry from the ten fashion-related classes has

[8] Lines for each class, A41 through A45 and D01 through D05, represent the number of patents granted each year containing any classification entry falling within that class, using PatentsView data. The line for total fashion-related patents represents the number of patents granted each year containing any classification entry falling within the 10 classes. Because many patents contain classification entries from more than one of these classes, the counts for the 10 classes do not add up to the count for all fashion-related patents.

[9] There are varying explanations for the broader growth in patents, including general economic growth, increasing globalisation of the patent system, improvements in management of research and development, growth in patent litigation and other options for

fallen from just over 3% in 1976 to around 1.5% in 2020, suggesting that fashion has relied comparatively less on patents than have other industries over the last four decades.

Still, thousands of fashion-related patents a year is not a trivial number; it represents around 100 fashion-related inventions a week. It may seem like a lot for a field that isn't especially technological. But compare it to the number of patent grants in 2022 in some other technology classes (Table 6.1).

Many of these classes cover far more patents than the fashion-related classifications. That is not surprising, since some of these classes are quite broad (A61, for instance, covers inventions as varied as surgical techniques, dental implements, veterinary tools, cardiac stents, devices to accommodate the disabled and radiation treatments, among others). But as Table 6.1 shows, even narrowly drawn classes in niche areas like wastewater treatment (C02) and nuclear physics (G21) have similar numbers of patents granted as the fashion-related classes.

Patents in the fashion-related classes are obtained by a wide array of applicants, ranging from expected firms like fashion houses and manufacturers to individual inventors and firms with no obvious link to fashion. Although patents are issued to inventors – individual humans – rather than companies, most patents are assigned to a company when issued, and that information is listed on the face of the patent. Between 2000 and 2022, 78,212 patents were issued that included one or more fashion-related classification entry, with 36 different firms accounting for 100 or more patents (Table 6.2).

In addition to apparel manufacturers, these firms include electronics makers like Apple, Samsung and Sony; consumer-goods makers like

monetising patents and procedural changes in the patent system that made it advantageous to obtain families of multiple related patents for inventions that might otherwise have been covered by one patent. For some of the relevant literature, see, eg, Georg von Graevenitz, Stefan Wagner and Dietmar Harhoff, 'Incidence and Growth of Patent Thickets: The Impact of Technological Opportunities and Complexity' (2013) 61 *Journal of Industrial Economics* 521; David L Schwartz, 'The Rise of Contingent Fee Representation in Patent Litigation' (2012) 64 *Alabama Law Review* (2012) 335; Allen W Wang, 'Rise of the Patent Intermediaries' (2010) 25 *Berkeley Technology Law Journal* 159; Bronwyn H Hall, 'Exploring the Patent Explosion' (2004) 30 *Journal of Technology Transfer* 35; Nancy T Gallini, 'The Economics of Patents: Lessons from Recent US Patent Reform' (2002) 16 *Journal of Economic Perspectives* 131; Samuel Kortum and Josh Lerner, 'What Is Behind the Recent Surge in Patenting?' (1999) 28 *Research Policy* 1; Francis Narin, Elliot Noma and Ross Perry, 'Patents as Indicators of Corporate Technological Strength' (1987) 16 *Research Policy* 143.

Table 6.1 *Patent grants within selected technology classes (2022)*

CPC Class	Grants
A61: Medical or Veterinary Science; Hygiene	40,327
B33: Additive Manufacturing Technology [e.g., 3D printing]	2,658
B60: Vehicles In General	18,428
C01: Inorganic Chemistry	2,427
C02: Treatment of Water, Waste Water, Sewage, or Sludge	1,544
C07: Organic Chemistry	11,046
C08: Organic Macromolecular Compounds; Their Preparation or Chemical Working-Up; Compositions Based Thereon	6,717
G06: Computing; Calculating or Counting	83,820
G11: Information Storage	6,206
G21: Nuclear Physics; Nuclear Engineering	731
H03: Electronic Circuitry	7,122
H04: Electronic Communication Technique	69,774
H10: Semiconductor Devices; Electric Solid-State Devices Not Otherwise Provided For	9,077

Procter & Gamble and Kimberly-Clark; materials and chemical companies like 3M, du Pont and Dow; even large industrial manufacturers like Honeywell and Boeing. Some of these non-fashion firms are patenting inventions with fashion-related applications, like inventions related to the Apple Watch, while others are patenting materials that happen to overlap in the fashion-related technology classes, like novel fabrics for aerospace purposes. Still, the firms listed in Table 6.2 accounted for less than 15% of the fashion-related patents, suggesting that the vast majority of fashion-related patents are issued to small firms, individual inventors and non-fashion firms with a small number of inventions that may peripherally touch on fashion.

Even though other technologies account for far more patents than those related to fashion, there are still thousands of fashion-related patents granted each year, and many of those patents are nevertheless granted to large fashion companies, as discussed in Section 6.2.2.

6.2.2 *Large Fashion Firms*

Companies in the fashion industry have a variety of approaches to utility patents. Some obtain many, while others obtain very few or none. Of those patents, some fall within the fashion-related classifications discussed in Section 6.2.1, while others relate to other aspects of their

Table 6.2 *Companies with more than 100 patents in fashion-related technology classes (2000–2022)*[10]

Company	Grants
Nike, Inc.	3,273
The Procter & Gamble Co.	707
L'Oreal	684
YKK Corporation	631
Kimberly-Clark Worldwide, Inc.	575
3M Innovative Properties Co.	509
Brother Kogyo Kabushiki Kaisha	505
E. I. du Pont de Nemours and Co.	458
Apple Inc.	331
Toray Industries, Inc.	251
adidas AG	227
Under Armour, Inc.	209
Honeywell International Inc.	196
Milliken & Company	194
Groz-Beckert KG	187
Illinois Tool Works Inc.	182
Toyota Jidosha Kabushiki Kaisha	181
Maschinenfabrik Rieter AG	181
Shima Seiki Mfg., Ltd.	177
Salomon S.A.S.	166
Reebok International Limited	146
Trutzschler GmbH & Co. KG	143
Janome Sewing Machine Co., Ltd.	134
Unicharm Corporation	134
Velcro Industries B.V.	133
Samsung Electronics Co., Ltd.	121
Johns Manville	120
Sony Corporation	120
Otter Products, LLC	112
Invista North America S.a.r.l.	109
Kao Corporation	108
BASF SE	108
The Boeing Company	104
Teijin Limited	103
Braun Gmbh	102
Dow Global Technologies LLC	101

[10] Companies are taken from the initial assignee field in PatentsView and do not include patents that were later assigned to another firm. The data also does not group companies with similar names, including subsidiaries, patents with misspelled assignees and the like. Accordingly, this data should be treated as a minimum estimate.

Table 6.3 *Patents obtained by fashion-sector firms with market cap of more than $10bn*[11]

Company	Country	Market Cap	Grants
LVMH	France	$386 billion	814
Nike	United States	$186 billion	5,694
Hermès	France	$171 billion	81
Christian Dior	France	$138 billion	198
TJX Companies	United States	$91 billion	0
Inditex	Spain	$84 billion	2
EssilorLuxottica	France	$81 billion	5,031
Kering	France	$65 billion	35
Fast Retailing	Japan	$63 billion	65
Lululemon	Canada	$41 billion	26
Ross Stores	United States	$40 billion	1
Adidas	Germany	$26 billion	1,772
H&M	Sweden	$19 billion	3
Prada	Italy	$15 billion	7
Burlington Stores	United States	$13 billion	0
VF Corp.	United States	$11 billion	7
Zalando	Germany	$10 billion	0

business. This diversity is seen even in the largest firms, as seen in this table of the worldwide number of patents obtained between 2000 and 2022 by apparel firms with market capitalisations of US$10 billion or more (Table 6.3).

[11] The listed market capitalisations are as of January 2023. The source for patent information switches here to Google Patents. See 'Google Patents' (*Google*) <https://patents.google.com/>. The datasets available through Google Patents have two major advantages over PatentsView: they include patents from more than 100 countries, including all the major fashion markets, and they include information about patent assignments that occur after a patent is granted rather than just assignment at the time of grant, like PatentsView. (The classification information available through Google Patents, however, is less reliable and harder to work with than that in PatentsView.) The number of patents listed for each firm is a rough estimate, based on assignments to entities that I was able to associate with each company, excluding design patents (which made up a significant fraction of several companies' portfolios). It may undercount patents that are assigned to subsidiaries with names that do not immediately reveal the association between subsidiary and parent. Table 6.3 excludes one large apparel firm, Cintas, which sells work uniforms and similar goods falling outside of most definitions of 'fashion'. Cintas, which is based in the United States, had a market cap of around US$45 billion in January 2023 and received 32 patents between 2000 and 2022.

Several observations can be made about this data. First, there is a vast disparity in different firms' patenting activities, which corresponds to differences in their underlying businesses. Just 4 of the 17 companies – LVMH, Nike, EssilorLuxottica and Adidas – account for almost 97% of the patent grants. What these four companies have in common is that their businesses are not limited to traditional apparel but include other categories of goods and services, both within the fashion industry (such as leather goods and jewellery) and in other markets. These non-apparel businesses account for most of their patents. Two of the companies, Nike and Adidas, are sportswear companies that make sneakers and a variety of sports equipment. EssilorLuxottica makes glasses, lenses and other optical goods. And LVMH is a conglomerate with dozens of luxury brands across numerous categories including wine and spirits (Dom Pérignon, Hennessy, Krug, Moët & Chandon, among others), watches and jewellery (Bulgari, Hublot, TAG Heuer, Tiffany & Co.), makeup and perfume (Acqua di Parma, Fenty Beauty, Sephora), even yachts and luxury trains. Moreover, the trend continues beyond the top four patent recipients: Christian Dior, the company with the fifth-most patent grants (and which has a complicated ownership structure that overlaps substantially with LVMH) sells a lot of perfume, which accounts for most of its patents.

Second, the number of patents obtained by firms is larger than the number of *fashion-related* patents obtained by the same firms, as discussed in Section 6.2.1.[12] This may seem obvious given the first observation, but the two points are distinct, because there may or may not be a correspondence between a firm's patenting activity and its business activity. Indeed, firms patent many technologies that come out of research without ever intending to commercialise them.[13] Still, large fashion firms obtain many non-fashion patents in addition to patents falling within the fashion-related technology classes. Sometimes, they obtain these patents because they are also engaged in non-fashion businesses, like LVMH's wine and spirits business. Sometimes, these patents cover underlying technologies that may be used in fashion goods without being listed within those classes. And sometimes, these patents relate to

[12] This is not a perfect comparison, since the firm-by-firm patent numbers in this section are worldwide, not limited to the United States, and since the firm-by-firm numbers account for assignments after a patent is issued. But the comparison still holds true even if the firm-by-firm numbers are limited to US patents and assignments at issuance.

[13] See, eg, Ted Sichelman, 'Commercializing Patents' (2010) 62 *Stanford Law Review* 341.

business operations or infrastructure, even if they don't relate directly to the firm's products. Fast Retailing, for instance, has several patents that cover retail equipment, like one on a 'reading apparatus and commodity sales data processing apparatus'.[14] That patent's classification entries fall within classes G06 ('computing; calculating or counting') and G07 ('checking-devices'), not any of the fashion-related classes, even though the invention is closely related to the company's operations. Similarly, Ross Stores has one patent, which describes and claims a 'real estate management system and method' that has nothing to do with fashion and everything to do with running a large retail chain.[15]

Third, among the long tail of firms that do not have hundreds or thousands of patents, there are still differences between different types of firms. For instance, those that sell their own goods have more patents than those who are retailers principally selling third-party goods. And this is true whether or not those brand sellers manufacture their own goods in house or rely on contract manufacturers. The pure retailers on the list – TJX (TJ Maxx and Marshalls, among others), Ross Stores, Burlington Stores and Zalando (a European e-commerce firm modelled on Zappos) – have only one patent between them, and it's the Ross Stores real-estate patent mentioned above. Compare that to Hermès, Inditex (Zara), Kering (Gucci, Saint Laurent and Balenciaga, among others), Fast Retailing (Uniqlo), Lululemon, H&M, Prada and VF Corp., which have 226 patents combined. Some of these patents claim glasses, shoes or their components, like the companies with the most patents, and some claim business processes or technologies like retail point-of-sale terminals. But others claim traditional items of sewn apparel, like the jacket sleeves with built-in ventilation flaps covered by one Lululemon patent (Figure 6.2).

Fourth, other than being largely based in Europe and the United States, this collection of companies shows no particular correlation between geography and patent strategy. The same is true when breaking down patent grants by issuing nation or patent office. Across all the companies listed, 54% of patents were obtained from the United States; 25% were issued by the European Patent Office or one of the national patent offices in Europe; 13% were issued by China; and the rest came from Canada (3%), Japan (3%), Australia (2%) and a smattering of other nations (1% combined).

[14] US Patent No 9,519,897 (Issued on December 13, 2016).

[15] US Patent No 8,341,089 (Issued on December 25, 2012).

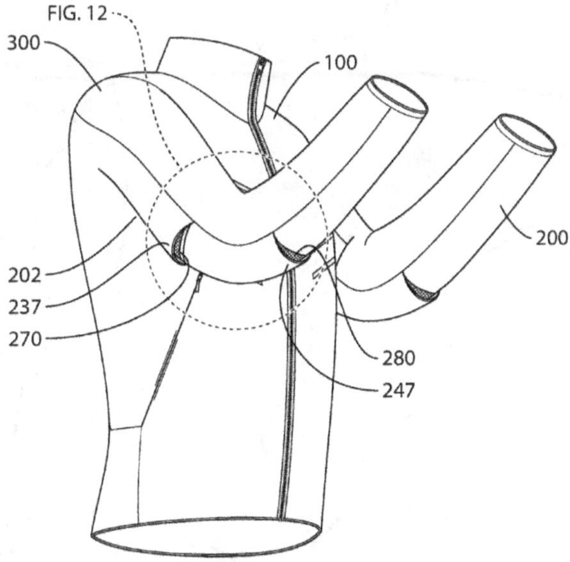

Figure 6.2 Lululemon sleeve patent.[16]
Courtesy of United States Patent and Trademark Office

Individual companies also acted globally when obtaining patents: other than Inditex's two Spanish patents and Ross Stores' one US patent, every company that obtained patents obtained them from multiple nations. Hermès' 81 patents, for instance, were obtained from China, Denmark, France, Germany, Spain, Taiwan, the United States and the European Patent Office. And though a few companies have obtained a disproportionate number of patents from their home nations, that home-nation bias was small compared to the bias in favour of large markets like the United States and China.

Finally, just as the number of fashion-related patents issued has increased over time, so has the number obtained by these large firms. Different firms, though, reflect different patterns, as seen in a graph of patents issued to the large fashion firms each year between 2000 and 2022 (Figure 6.3).

While every company except Christian Dior has increased its patenting activity over time, some have increased far more quickly than

[16] US Patent No 11,425,947 (Issued on August 30, 2022), as seen in fig. 11, assigned to Lululemon Athletica Canada Inc, and describing and claiming a 'sleeve for a garment'.

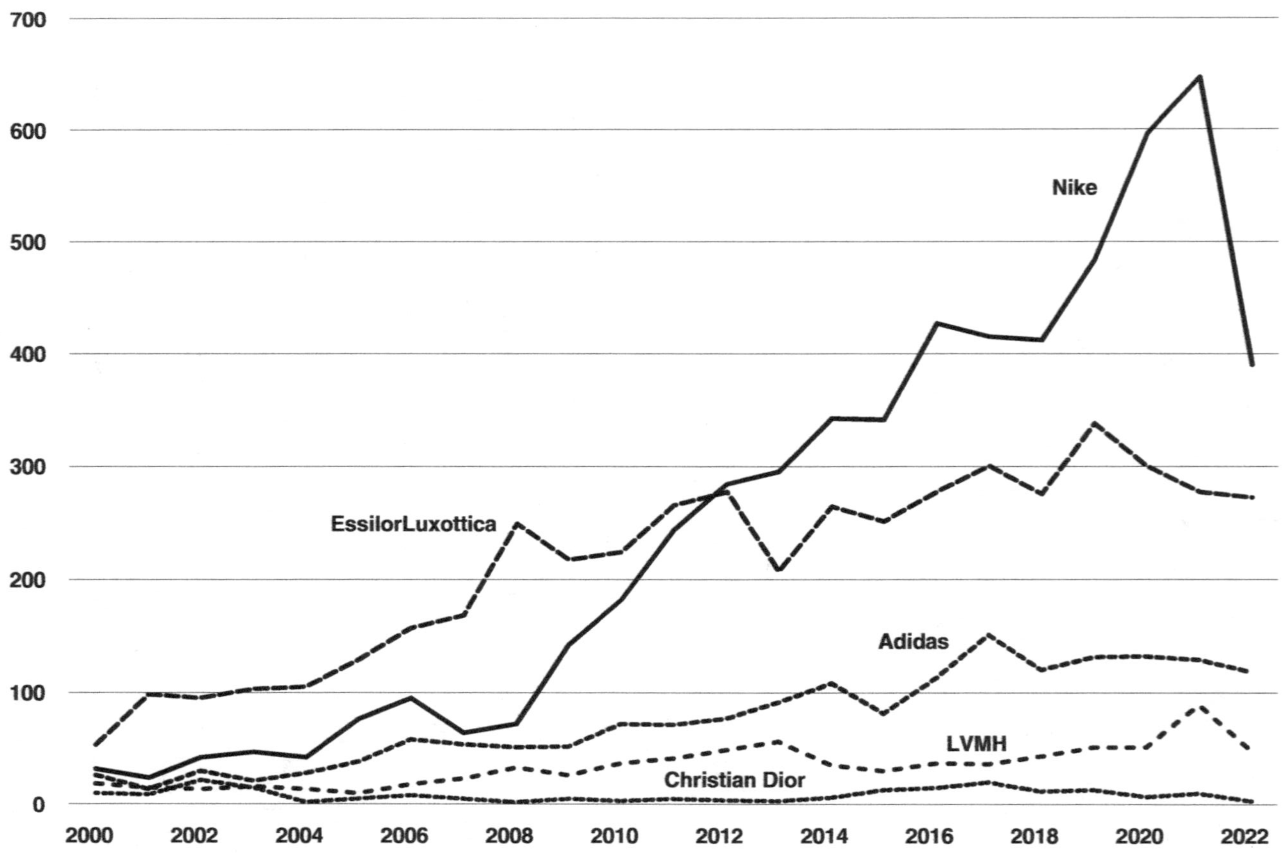

Figure 6.3 Patents issued to large fashion firms by year (2000–2022).
Credit: Roger Allan Ford
Patent counts are from Google Patents, following the same methods as Table 6.3.

others; compare, for instance, Nike and EssilorLuxottica.[17] This suggests that patenting growth is more likely to reflect individual companies' growth, strategies and other circumstances more than broader trends in the fashion industry.

There are limitations to how much we can infer from patenting activity, since the act of obtaining a patent doesn't say anything about how that patent is used. But patent activity does provide tentative indications that the fashion industry does make use of patents, albeit to a lesser degree than some other fields. That use is concentrated among firms that make athletic wear, watches, eyewear and other accessories more than traditional apparel manufacturers. It is also clear that not all fashion-related patents are obtained by fashion firms; plenty of other companies obtain patents that are classified, in part, in classes that relate to fashion. Likewise, not all patents obtained by fashion companies cover fashion-related inventions; others cover the full array of things these companies do, like Ross Stores' real-estate patent. But to move beyond these inferences, it is helpful to widen the scope beyond just the act of acquiring patent rights to the use of those patents once acquired.

6.3 Using Patents: Patent Litigation

Patent scholars generally think about three broad ways that a patent can be valuable to a company: as an asset to be monetised (whether through infringement litigation, licensing or the rents that come from a legal monopoly), as a signalling tool (whether to investors, competitors, potential clients or employees or others) or as a defensive tool (in the event that a competitor brings a patent lawsuit).[18] These different sources of value

[17] Another interesting pattern is the dip in patents obtained in 2022 by some companies compared to prior years. This does not appear to reflect data-quality limitations, since it only applies to some companies and the data were reconfirmed in July 2023. It may instead reflect changes in corporate strategy, random noise or delayed effects of the COVID-19 pandemic.

[18] For a necessarily small and incomplete selection from the relevant literature, see, eg, Annamaria Conti, Jerry Thursby and Marie Thursby, 'Patents as Signals for Startup Financing' (2013) 61 *Journal of Industrial Economics* 592; Andrei Hagiu and David B Yoffie, 'The New Patent Intermediaries: Platforms, Defensive Aggregators, and Super-Aggregators' (2013) 27 *Journal of Economic Perspectives* 45; Knut Blind, Katrin Cremers and Elisabeth Mueller, 'The Influence of Strategic Patenting on Companies' Patent Portfolios' (2009) 38 *Research Policy* 428; Dan L Burk, 'The Role of Patent Law in Knowledge Codification' (2008) 23 *Berkeley Technology Law Journal* 1009; John R Allison, Mark A Lemley, Kimberly A Moore and R Derek Trunkey, 'Valuable Patents'

can make it difficult to understand a firm's patent strategy, since some, like litigation, are fairly transparent, while others, like licensing, may be entirely opaque to outsiders.

Still, there are ways to obtain insights about a firm's patent strategy from its visible patent activities. Looking at litigation is maybe the simplest, since the possibility of infringement litigation is the implicit threat even in a friendly license agreement, so that a firm with significant licensing activity will generally also have significant litigation activity.

A surface look at patent-litigation activity by the large apparel companies discussed above shows a wide array of litigation activities, with some firms frequently litigating their patents and others never doing so, as seen in Table 6.4, showing the number of patents with related litigation activity.

On the whole, compared to other industries traditionally seen as depending on patents, the fashion industry obtains fewer patents and is less likely to litigate the patents it does get. For instance, the three largest pharmaceutical companies – Eli Lilly, Johnson & Johnson and Novo Nordisk – have collectively obtained more than 5,000 patents that had litigation activity, amounting to 14% of their patent portfolios. Similarly, the tech companies Apple, Microsoft and Samsung have collectively obtained more than 6,500 patents that had litigation activity, making up 11% of their patent portfolios. By these standards, Adidas is the only large apparel company that compares.

Even though these statistics suggest that patent litigation is not driving fashion firms' patenting activities, they nevertheless likely overstate the degree to which large fashion firms assert their patents in litigation, for a few reasons. For one, the related litigation activity reflected in Table 6.4 refers to any litigation over any patent in a patent's global family, which can be scores of patents from numerous countries. At the same time, a single patent-infringement lawsuit may assert many patents, even if only one or two are core to the dispute between the parties. Consequently, a large number of patents with related litigation may reflect only a small number of live patent disputes.

(2004) 92 *Georgetown Law Journal* 435; Clarisa Long, 'Patent Signals' (2002) 69 *University of Chicago Law Review* 625; Zvi Griliches, Ariel Pakes and Bronwyn H Hall, 'The Value of Patents as Indicators of Inventive Activity' in Partha Dasgupta and Paul Stoneman (eds), *Economic Policy and Technology Performance* (Cambridge University Press, 1987).

Table 6.4 *Share of patents obtained by large apparel companies with associated litigation activity*[19]

Company	Patent Grants	Patents With Litigation Activity	Percentage
LVMH	814	28	3%
Nike	5,694	273	5%
Hermès	81	0	0%
Christian Dior	198	7	4%
TJX Companies	0	0	—
Inditex	2	0	0%
EssilorLuxottica	5,031	397	8%
Kering	35	0	0%
Fast Retailing	65	0	0%
Lululemon	26	0	0%
Ross Stores	1	0	0%
Adidas	1,772	253	14%
H&M	3	0	0%
Prada	7	0	0%
Burlington Stores	0	0	—
VF Corp.	7	0	0%
Zalando	0	0	—

To obtain a better understanding of how fashion firms use patents in litigation, the Stanford NPE Litigation Database[20] and PACER[21] were used to identify US lawsuits in which these firms asserted patents. Although the count is not exhaustive due to older cases with incomplete files, remarkably, only twelve cases were identified in which these companies asserted utility patents (Table 6.5).[22]

These cases fall into two broad categories. The main category is lawsuits against large competitors, in which patented technologies are

[19] Litigation activity is based on Darts-IP's global IP litigation dataset, as incorporated into Google Patents. All columns refer to patents granted from 2000 to 2022.

[20] See Stanford Program in Law, Science and Technology, 'Stanford NPE Litigation Database' (*Stanford Law School*) <https://npe.law.stanford.edu/>.

[21] See 'PACER: Public Access to Court Electronic Records' (*Administrative Office of the US Courts*) <https://pacer.uscourts.gov/>.

[22] In comparison, many more cases were identified in which these firms asserted *design* patents.

Table 6.5 *Share of patents obtained by large apparel companies with associated litigation activity in the United States*

Company	Patent Grants	US Patent Lawsuits
LVMH	814	0
Nike	5,694	6
Hermès	81	0
Christian Dior	198	0
TJX Companies	0	0
Inditex	2	0
EssilorLuxottica	5,031	2
Kering	35	0
Fast Retailing	65	0
Lululemon	26	0
Ross Stores	1	0
Adidas	1,772	4
H&M	3	0
Prada	7	0
Burlington Stores	0	0
VF Corp.	7	0
Zalando	0	0

the core of the dispute; Adidas, for instance, has filed patent lawsuits against competing shoemakers Asics, Nike, Skechers and Under Armour,[23] while Nike, in turn, has filed patent lawsuits against Adidas, Hummel and Puma.[24] (Indeed, a significant chunk of these cases are part of a long-running dispute between Nike and Adidas, which extended beyond federal litigation to proceedings before the Patent and Trademark Office and the International Trade Commission, before it settled in 2022.)[25] But considering the size of the fashion industry, there are not

[23] See *Adidas AG v Under Armour Inc*, No 1:14-cv-00130 (D Del filed February 4, 2014); *Adidas America, Inc v Skechers USA, Inc*, No 3:16-cv-01400 (D Or filed July 11, 2016); *Adidas AG v Asics Am Corp*, No 1:17-cv-00285 (D Del filed March 17, 2017); *Adidas AG v Nike, Inc*, No 2:22-cv-00198 (ED Tex filed June 10, 2022).

[24] See *Nike, Inc v Adidas Am Inc*, No 9:06-cv-00043 (ED Tex filed February 16, 2006); *Nike, Inc v Hummel Sport USA*, No 1:16-cv-11559 (D Mass filed July 28, 2016); *Nike, Inc v Puma N Am, Inc*, No 1:18-cv-10876 (D Mass filed May 3, 2018); *Nike, Inc v Adidas AG*, No 3:21-cv-01780 (D Or filed December 8, 2021).

[25] In addition to the cases cited in the two previous footnotes, see, eg, *Nike, Inc v Adidas AG*, No 2021-1903, 2022 WL 4002668 (Fed Cir September 1, 2022); *Adidas AG v Nike, Inc*,

very many of these cases; they all appear to involve shoes or glasses. Beyond these cases, there are a few lawsuits against companies selling knockoffs, in which the asserted patents are sideshows to claims asserting trademarks, design patents, and other causes of action like unfair competition.[26]

The small number of patent lawsuits brought by fashion companies doesn't necessarily mean that the fashion industry is failing to get value out of its patent portfolios. Not all the industries that are traditionally seen as dependent on patents litigate large numbers of them. Semiconductor manufacturing, for instance, is an intensely competitive industry that obtains many patents and considers them strategically important yet litigates very few of them. Intel, Nvidia and TSMC, for instance, have collectively obtained 995 patents that had related litigation, accounting for just 2% of their collective portfolios. One possible explanation is that these firms are more likely to rely on licensing – especially cross-licensing agreements with competitors – because the industry is fairly concentrated and has high barriers to entry. Since there are fewer players to worry about, it is easier to focus on resolving disputes without litigation. (It helps that semiconductor manufacturing is a classic patent thicket – a field with many overlapping patents that make it almost impossible to operate without practicing *some* patented invention – which gives firms a strong incentive to reach cross-licensing agreements and avoid becoming defendants in litigation.)[27]

The technology-centric portions of the fashion industry, like athletic wear and glasses, resemble the semiconductor-manufacturing industry in a key way: both have a small number of firms that account for most of the market share. But there are also critical differences. Fashion firms mostly sell to consumers, not businesses like semiconductor manufacturers, and

963 F 3d 1355 (Fed Cir 2020); *Nike, Inc v Adidas AG*, 955 F 3d 45 (Fed Cir 2020); *Adidas AG v Nike, Inc*, 894 F 3d 1256 (Fed Cir 2018); *Nike, Inc v Adidas AG*, 812 F 3d 1326 (Fed Cir 2016); *In re Certain Knitted Footwear*, No 337-TA-1289 (USITC instituted January 10, 2022). See also Blake Brittain, 'Nike, Adidas Settle Patent Fights Over Shoe Technology', *Reuters* (August 19, 2022) <https://www.reuters.com/legal/litigation/nike-adidas-settle-patent-fights-over-shoe-technology-2022-08-19/>.

[26] See, eg, *Nike Inc v Fashion Accessories Plus Inc*, No 4:02-cv-02904 (SD Tex filed July 30, 2002); *Nike, Inc v Saso Golf, Inc*, No 3:06-cv-01250 (D Or filed August 31, 2006).

[27] See, eg, James E Bessen, 'Patent Thickets: Strategic Patenting of Complex Technologies' (Working Paper, Technology and Research Policy Initiative Boston University School of Law, 2003) <https://ssrn.com/abstract=327760>; Carl Shapiro, 'Navigating the Patent Thicket: Cross Licenses, Patent Pools, and Standard Setting' (2000) 1 *Innovation. Policy and Economy* 119.

they depend more on marketing and style to sell their products, compared to the continual technological innovation of semiconductor manufacturing. So, we should expect these fashion companies to rely less heavily on patents, whether through infringement litigation or cross-licensing. And that is consistent with the relatively few patent lawsuits brought by the fashion industry.

6.4 Patents and the Nature of Utility in Fashion

As discussed before, most of the patents obtained by large fashion companies don't actually claim *apparel*; instead, they often claim sporting equipment or accessories or retail strategies and tools or constituent technologies for these things. But there are patents, like the Lululemon sleeve patent mentioned above (Figure 6.1), that claim traditional forms of apparel.

In addition to revealing information about the fashion industry and its strategic decision-making, these patents tell us something about the nature of utility in fashion and the relationship of fashion to different forms of intellectual-property protections. Intellectual property traditionally draws a distinction between utilitarian or functional creations – which are protected by utility patents – and creations that are creative or aesthetic or artistic rather than functional – which are protected by copyrights and design patents. Fashion, though, makes a mess of this traditional dichotomy, since even basic questions like what counts as utility versus aesthetics are debated and disputed. Fashion firms, policymakers, courts and others have responded to this uncertainty by attempting to use a wide array of protections – traditional ones like patents and copyright and more novel ones like design rights and trade dress claims within trademark law – and by using these protections in new ways, as when a designer plasters a logo all over a product to gain stronger trademark protections.

The US Supreme Court confronted these difficulties in 2017, concluding in *Star Athletica, LLC v. Varsity Brands, Inc.* that designs of cheerleader uniforms could be protected by copyright law notwithstanding that the uniforms were 'useful articles'.[28] At issue was whether elements of clothing designs, such as stripes, chevrons or zigzags, were protectable as aesthetic elements of an otherwise useful article of clothing. Under US

[28] *Star Athletica, LLC v Varsity Brands, Inc*, 580 US 405, 137 S Ct 1002 (2017).

copyright law, to be protectable, the uniforms' 'pictorial, graphic, or sculptural features' must be capable of being 'identified separately from' and 'existing independently of the utilitarian aspects of the article'.[29] By concluding that the design of the uniforms could be copyrighted, the court necessarily concluded that the graphic features of the uniform could exist 'independently of the utilitarian aspects' of the uniform.

The court's resolution of *Star Athletica* suggests that patent law would not cover those graphic features because they are separate and independent of the uniform's utility. Indeed, in an important trademark case in 2001, the court adopted this reasoning, concluding that a company could not obtain trademark protections for a product feature – which, like copyright law, requires that the feature not be functional – precisely because that feature had been protected by a utility patent:

> A utility patent is strong evidence that the features therein claimed are functional. If trade dress protection is sought for those features the strong evidence of functionality based on the previous patent adds great weight to the statutory presumption that features are deemed functional until proved otherwise by the party seeking trade dress protection.[30]

So, if a utility patent is strong evidence of functionality, and the graphic features of a cheerleader uniform can exist separately from the utilitarian aspects of the uniform, then those features should not be patentable (assuming functionality and utility are synonyms).

Remarkably, however, a review of patents obtained by fashion companies shows that graphic features of apparel are frequently patented, precisely because of the aesthetic characteristics of those features. These patents generally claim methods of using two-dimensional clothing design to make clothing that creates a favourable three-dimensional shape or a favourable perception of a person's body shape. For instance, one patent obtained by VF Corp., for a 'body-enhancing garment and garment design',[31] describes the invention like this:

> Many garments are constructed with visible patterns on the fabric. These patterns typically utilize symmetrical, straight, and/or repeating details or pattern elements and have no intentional brightness gradients when the garments are laid flat. Additionally, patterns may include illusory details or lines created within the negative space between the pattern elements,

[29] Copyright Act 1976, 17 USC § 101 (US).
[30] *TrafFix Devices, Inc v Marketing Displays, Inc*, 532 US 23, 29–30 (2001).
[31] US Patent No 10,327,487 (Issued on June 25, 2019).

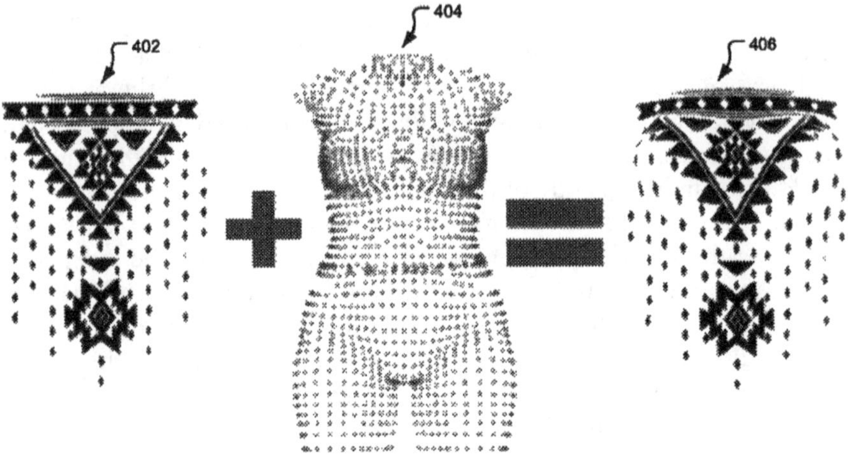

Figure 6.4 Body-enhancing garment patent.[32]
Courtesy of United States Patent and Trademark Office

and serve as an informative element of the pattern itself. These patterns become curved and shaded when worn on the body. The visual system assumes that the curvature and/or brightness gradients of those patterns is attributed entirely to the body shape (i.e., that curved lines of the pattern on the garment would be straight lines if the garment was laid flat). Thus, using the rules of perception, the visual system constructs a three-dimensional body shape based in part on the curvature, size, and shading of the pattern.

* * *

When a person wears clothing, he or she voluntarily puts patterned clothing on his or her body. The brain interprets the lines, spacing, sizing and other elements of the pattern using the rules discussed above and other rules known within the field of vision science. Current clothing designs do not take into account that the brain uses these patterns on garments to construct a 3D shape of the wearer. As such, a problem with existing garment construction or design is that it can create garments that make an individual's form less attractive to others, a result that is typically not desired by the individual wearing the garment. While the rules of perception have been heavily studied, these rules have not been applied to clothing. Further, the rules of perception have not been utilised on a garment to change the perception of a human feature to fall within or move towards known attractive size and shape ranges and/or desired size and shape ranges when worn.

[32] Ibid fig. 4.

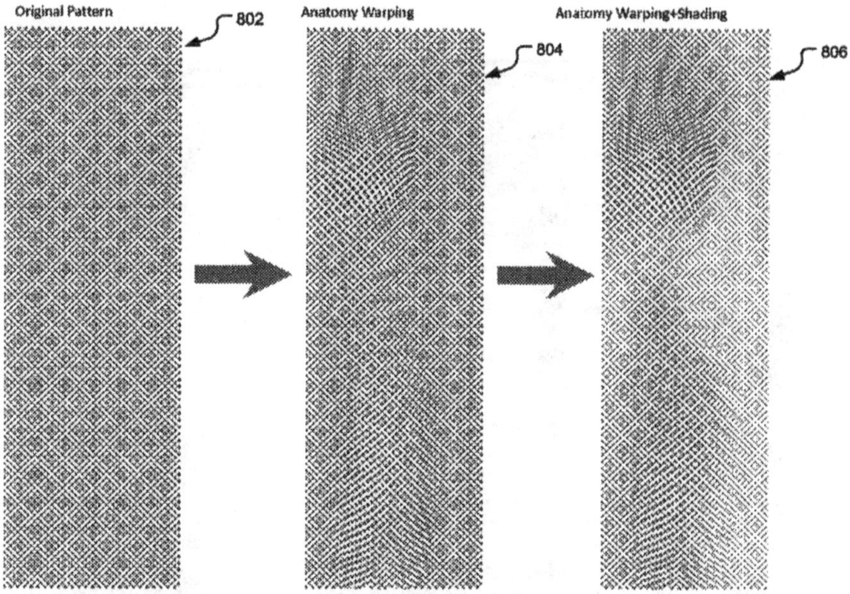

Figure 6.5 Shading patent for aesthetic effects via optical illusions.[33]
Courtesy of United States Patent and Trademark Office

The patent goes on to describe and claim various methods for using shading, curved lines and other optical tricks on clothing to tweak how the shape of a person's body will be perceived by others. For instance, if a garment has a pattern of dots, then the position of those dots could be shifted in a way that reflects the desired 3D body shape of the wearer. A viewer's eye will assume that the dots reflect a fixed pattern and will see the tweaked pattern as reflecting the intended shape. The patent shows this concept in Figures 6.4 and 6.5.

And other patents describe and claim similar illusions. A European patent jointly obtained by VF Corp. and the University of California, for instance, describes and claims a 'method for anatomy shading for garments' that uses shading instead of pattern distortion to accomplish the same sort of optical tricks (Figure 6.6).

The use of optical tricks to affect how clothes look on a person is, of course, not a new concept in fashion; designers have been doing similar

[33] Ibid fig. 6.

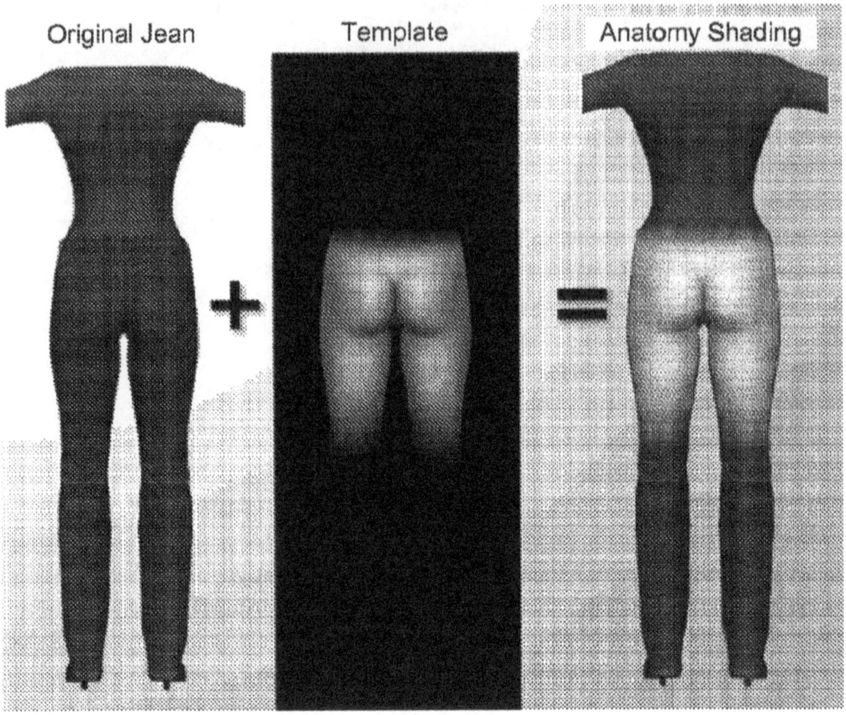

Figure 6.6 Anatomy-enhancing shading on jeans.[34]
Courtesy of the European Patent Organisation

things for centuries. Indeed, the cheerleader uniforms at issue in *Star Athletica* have the designs they do precisely because they create certain impressions when worn by cheerleaders, as discussed elsewhere in this volume (Figure 6.7).[35]

The combinations of colour blocking, chevrons, diagonal lines, inward-pointing angles and other features aren't just artistic choices by the designer; they're choices designed to make the wearer – a cheerleader – look better. As Christopher Buccafusco and Jeanne C Fromer have

[34] See fig. 5: EU Patent No 3,060,075 (issued April 3, 2019).

[35] See Chapter 3. See also Brief of Professors Christopher Buccafusco and Jeanne Fromer as *Amici Curiae* in Support of Petitioner, *Star Athletica, LLC v Varsity Brands, Inc*, No 15-866 (US filed July 22, 2016).

Figure 6.7 Cheerleader uniforms at issue in *Star Athletica v. Varsity Brands*. Courtesy of US Supreme Court opinion and Copyright Office registration image

explained elsewhere, clothing is not generally designed to look good in isolation; it's designed to look good *when worn by someone.*[36]

The fact, then, that companies have sought, and obtained, utility-patent protection for inventions designed to change the visual perception of a person wearing a particular garment provides additional evidence, if more were needed, that the aesthetic design of fashion has functionality. And in turn it bolsters the case, contra *Star Athletica*, against protecting fashion designs using copyright law or novel forms of intellectual-property protections. Instead, it suggests that utility patents may be a better fit, despite the small amounts of patent litigation engaged in by fashion companies.

6.5 Conclusion

Fashion is not an obvious fit for utility patents, since the things that make a fashion firm successful are generally not the sorts of things protectable by patent law. Yet despite that poor fit, thousands of patents are granted each year for fashion-related technologies, and large fashion companies have obtained thousands of patents between them. At the same time, evidence of how the industry uses these patents is hard to come by since few are litigated and the industry lacks the sort of cross-licensing arrangements that some more patent-dependent industries use.

[36] Christopher J Buccafusco and Jeanne C Fromer, 'Fashion's Function in Intellectual Property Law' (2017) 93 *Notre Dame Law Review* 51.

The kinds of inventions patented by the fashion industry range from traditional apparel to athletic wear to fashion-adjacent technologies like business methods and retail equipment. The most interesting ones, however, provide insights into a core issue in fashion law: the line between functionality and aesthetic or artistic expression. These patents claim and protect ways of tweaking the aesthetic designs of clothing to change how they look on their wearers. The availability of utility patents for these inventions suggests that aesthetic choices in fashion do serve functional purposes, and therefore that that the law should look more sceptically upon efforts to extend copyright and other non-patent protections to aesthetic choices made by fashion designers.

7

Barriers to Enforcing Design Rights over Fashion in the United Kingdom

ROBERT BURRELL AND EMILY HUDSON

ABSTRACT

Working from the premises that fashion designers ought to enjoy some form of intellectual property protection over their creations and that they benefit from such protection, this chapter explores the problems that fashion designers are likely to face when seeking to enforce their rights in the United Kingdom. Like other commentators, we conclude that designs law in the United Kingdom is a mess and is in need of reform. We also argue that Brexit has made the problems faced by designers worse, without necessarily creating the policy space for meaningful national reform. One consequence may be that designers are likely to rely even more heavily on the copyright system, but this merely shifts the tensions of Brexit from the legislative and political realms to the judicial realm.

7.1 Introduction

This chapter asks whether the United Kingdom's intellectual property regime is adequate to meet the needs of fashion designers. As such, it rests on two assumptions: first, that fashion designers ought to enjoy some IP protection over their creations and, second, that fashion designers benefit from having rights to enforce against third party interlopers. Neither of these assumptions is unproblematic. In relation to the first, it is notable that design protection is generally justified by reference to a standard market failure account.[1] However, if one engages with this justification seriously, one might query whether there is any meaningful

[1] See, eg, Council Regulation (EC) No 6/2002 of 12 December 2001 on European Union designs (EUDR), Recital 7 to the original text; *Nintendo Co Ltd v BigBen Interactive GmbH*, Joined Cases C-24/16 and C-25/16) at [73] (ECDR 3, September 27, 2017); *Ferrari SpA v*

danger of undersupply in the fashion industry that the law needs to guard against. This chimes with observations that fashion is characterised by a strong culture of design innovation that has not obviously been held back by widespread imitation and copying. Indeed, on at least one prominent account, the 'low-IP equilibrium' of the fashion industry may help spur innovation.[2] An alternative justification for IP protection might derive from appeals to distributive justice. For instance, those concerned about the under-protection of fashion often point to the position of emerging and lesser-known designers whose works are copied by larger, more powerful, industry players.[3] But this puts into focus the second assumption, in relation to enforcement: even if the *content* of the law was entirely fit-for-purpose, designers would gain little if they lack the resources or knowledge to seek legal redress. Indeed, attempts to strengthen rights may backfire if the practical effect of any new or 'improved' regime is to provide large industry players with even more capacity to pursue smaller players, while themselves continuing to copy with impunity.

If this chapter rests on questionable assumptions, why write it at all? Part of the answer is that there is an active debate about IP protection for fashion.[4] There is therefore value in doctrinal work that engages closely

Mansory Design Holding GmbH, Case C-123/20, at [31]–[32] (ECDR 2, October 28, 2021); C Scott Hempill and Jeannie Suk, 'The Law, Culture, and Economics of Fashion' (2009) 61 *Stanford Law Review* 1147; Katie Mullane, 'Setting a Trend for Design Rights: An Analysis of Whether the United States Should Follow the European Union's Model for Fashion Design Protection' (2018) 21 *Trinity College Law Review* 276. That said, it has been observed that the rationales for the protection of designs have not been as well elucidated as those for, say, copyright and patents: Lionel Bently, Brad Sherman, Dev Gangjee and Phillip Johnson, *Intellectual Property Law* (Oxford University Press, 6th edn, 2022) 732.

2 Kal Raustiala and Christopher Sprigman, 'The Piracy Paradox: Innovation and Intellectual Property in Fashion Design' (2006) 92 *Virginia Law Review* 1687. The authors published a follow-up piece considering changes in the fashion industry: Kal Raustiala and Christopher Jon Sprigman, 'Faster Fashion: The Piracy Paradox and Its Perils' (2021) 39 *Cardozo Arts & Entertainment Law Journal* 535.

3 See, eg, Lauren Howard, 'An Uningenious Paradox: Intellectual Property Protections for Fashion Designs' (2009) 32 *Columbia Journal of Law & the Arts* 333; Tiffany din Fagel Tse, 'Coco Way before Chanel: Protecting Independent Fashion Designers' Intellectual Property against Fast-Fashion Retailers' (2016) 24 *Catholic University Journal of Law and Technology* 401.

4 See, eg, Vicki T Huang, 'An Empirical Analysis of the Fashion Design Case Law of Australia' (2021) 52 *International Review of Intellectual Property and Competition Law* 242; William van Caenegem and Violet Atkinson, 'Observing Creativity in Fashion: Implications for Copyright' (2021) 16 *Journal of Intellectual Property Law & Practice* 1398; Francesca M Witzburg, 'Fashion Forward: Fashion Innovation in the Era of Disruption' (2021) 39 *Cardozo Arts & Entertainment Law Journal* 705.

with the existing legal infrastructure so that we properly understand fashion's 'law in books'. Although some scholarship – in particular, that emanating from the United States – focuses on the lack of IP protection for fashion,[5] in the United Kingdom, there are a number of rights that are relevant to the sector. In fact, far from being an IP wasteland, the legally astute UK designer might wonder why there are so many overlapping and, by and large, cumulative regimes that might protect their creations:[6] the UK registered design system;[7] the (new, EU-derived) supplementary unregistered design right;[8] the (old, UK-created) sui generis unregistered design right;[9] copyright; and (although outside the scope of this chapter) registered trade marks and passing off. This preponderance of regimes is part of the second reason why this topic is worth exploring: that design law in the United Kingdom is in need of a wide-ranging review.[10] One way of feeding into this process is by asking how the current system might operate for one community of designers. As we note at various points, the sort of doctrinal analysis in this chapter might

[5] See, eg, Susan Scafidi, 'Intellectual Property and Fashion Design' in Peter K Yu (ed), *Intellectual Property and Information Wealth: Issues and Practices in the Digital Age* (Greenwood, 2007); Hempill and Suk, above n 1; Howard, above n 3. Although we problematise the current model of protection in the UK, this should not distract from the fact that the UK is starting from a much higher base of protection.

[6] By cumulative, we mean that the starting point is that the same subject matter can be protected by more than one regime. For instance, registration of a design does not preclude reliance on unregistered design rights or prevent registration of a trade marks. Some overlaps may be prevented indirectly by rules in relation to subsistence or registrability; for instance, the functionality exclusion in section 3(2) of the Trade Marks Act 1994 (UK) might prevent certain design features from being registered as trade marks. As discussed in Section 7.3, the Copyright, Designs and Patents Act 1988 (UK) (CDPA) originally had a series of provisions intended to exclude certain designs from copyright protection, thus directly responding to overlap concerns; these provisions have been watered down due to European harmonisation.

[7] Governed by the Registered Designs Act 1949 (UK).

[8] The legislative regulation of the SUD is complicated, but in essence, the new UK right retained (with some modification) the content of the unregistered EU right found in what was then known as the Community Designs Regulation (CDR) (now EUDR). The SUD was created by The Designs and International Trade Marks (Amendment etc.) (EU Exit) Regulations 2019 (SI 2019/638), as amended by The Intellectual Property (Amendment etc.) (EU Exit) Regulations 2020 (SI 2020/1050).

[9] Governed by the CDPA.

[10] A matter recognised by the UK Intellectual Property Office ('UKIPO'), which in 2022 ran a review of the designs system: see 'IPO Launches Call for Views on Designs System', *UKIPO* (January 25, 2022) <https://www.gov.uk/government/news/ipo-launches-call-for-views-on-designs-system. The outcome of the review is available at 'Reviewing the Designs Framework: Call for Views', *UKIPO* (updated July 12, 2022) <https://www.gov.uk/government/consultations/reviewing-the-designs-framework-call-for-views>.

be helpfully supplemented by empirical work in relation to creative norms and enforcement practices in the fashion sector.

The thesis of this chapter is as follows. UK designs law is widely regarded as being highly unsatisfactory. It has been described as 'multi-layered, complex and lacking in logic'.[11] The problems with the system have become more pronounced following the UK's departure from the European Union. We start in Section 7.2 by summarising registered and unregistered design protection in the United Kingdom. We observe that prior to Brexit, it was often assumed that the EU's unregistered design right offered the most appropriate form of protection for the fashion industry.[12] Protection is short, lasting a maximum of three years, but it was said that any downsides in relation to duration were of lower concern in a fast-moving sector and were offset by the benefits of avoiding the need for registration. However, there are a number of matters that may limit the relevance of the UK's new supplementary unregistered design right (the SUD), all of which may cause designers to consider other IP options. First, a three-year term of protection may not be suitable for designs that are intended or turn out to have longer market presence. Second, infringement of the SUD requires proof of copying, in contrast with registered designs, for which liability is strict. Finally, the lack of reciprocity between the SUD and the equivalent EU regime, now known as the UEUD, means that UK designers who would previously have enjoyed unregistered design rights across the EU no longer do so, unless the rules on first disclosure are interpreted in a way that permits simultaneous publication.

There are a number of ways that the UK government could address the issues identified in relation to the SUD. However, there are political, legal

[11] Bently et al, above n 1 at 738. Concerns about unnecessary complexity also appeared in responses to the UKIPO review: 'Calls for Views on Designs: Analysis of Responses', *UKIPO* (updated July 12, 2022) <https://www.gov.uk/government/consultations/reviewing-the-designs-framework-call-for-views/outcome/calls-for-views-on-designs-analysis-of-responses> [30]–[40].

[12] In particular, one finds this assumption in publications produced by UK law firms. See, eg, 'How Intellectual Property Rights Can Protect Fashion Products in the UK: Now and Post-Brexit', *Stewarts Law* (September 12, 2018) <https://www.stewartslaw.com/news/intellectual-property-rights-can-protect-fashion-products-uk-now-post-brexit/> noting: 'The use of registered designs has sometimes been limited to high-value, premium and iconic designs that are most likely to be copied, with many designers relying on unregistered design rights to protect short-lived, seasonal designs . . .. The Community unregistered design right is often of much greater assistance to designers . . .. As the right arises automatically (without the need to register it), it gives good short-term protection over creations.'

and philosophical impediments to each of these options, raising the question of what UK fashion designers will do in the absence of any (meaningful) reform. One option is to pro-actively register their designs before novelty-destroying disclosures are made. However, another option – and the focus of Section 7.3 – is to rely more heavily on copyright as part of their protection strategy. The viability of this approach increased following case law from the Court of Justice of the European Union (CJEU), which suggests that the EU understanding of a 'work' is incredibly broad. We observe that UK judges have sought to interpret the CDPA in a way that respects this case law, while also recognising that the CJEU's approach maps awkwardly onto (1) the closed list of subject matter in the CDPA and (2) the policy imperative, expressed in much existing UK case law, to limit the copyright protection of designs. Our concern is that if UK judges expand the ambit of an 'original artistic work' too far, it may not be possible to correct for the overshoot at other points in the copyright system. That is, if we agree that certain designs (especially functional ones) are not the sort of works that copyright ought to protect, the more principled and effective way to achieve that state of affairs is for such designs to be excluded by a subject matter limitation, not for courts to seek to manipulate other rules (for instance, in relation to infringement or exceptions) to bring protection within reasonable bounds.

7.2 Protected Designs in the United Kingdom

7.2.1 Overview of Legal Framework

As noted in the introduction, there are three regimes in the United Kingdom that relate specifically to designs: (1) a registered system, (2) the supplementary unregistered design right (SUD) and (3) the sui generis unregistered design right governed by the CDPA. In this sub-section, we provide a brief overview of each of these regimes.

The registered system is administered by the Designs Registry at the UK Intellectual Property Office (UKIPO).[13] The registration process is inexpensive and light-touch, in that there is no examination or opposition process but merely a review of the application. Thus, for the disgruntled competitor or designer who believes that a design ought never to have been registered,[14] the only course of action is to launch

[13] For an overview of the registration process, see Bently et al, above n 1 at 741–746.

[14] The grounds for which are in Registered Designs Act 1949 (UK), s 11ZA.

invalidity proceedings or (if they have been sued for infringement) file a counterclaim against the registered proprietor. A registered design receives an initial five-year term of protection, which can be renewed a further four times, resulting in a maximum term of 25 years.[15] During that time, the registered proprietor enjoys 'the exclusive right to use the design and any design which does not produce on the informed user a different overall impression'.[16] This right applies not just to products mentioned in the application but to any product.[17]

The authors of *Intellectual Property Law* suggest that 'while registration has been popular in the electronics and furniture industries, the textile and fashion industries have tended to rely more on unregistered design right[s]'.[18] This could reflect a lack of knowledge of the existence, mechanics or benefits of the registered system or that those benefits are not perceived to outweigh the costs of applying for and maintaining registrations.[19] Importantly for this chapter, one of these benefits is that the protection conferred by a registered design is strict, in that proof of copying is not required in order to establish infringement.[20] Other commonly cited benefits to registration include the longer term of protection when compared with unregistered design rights (as noted above, up to 25 years) and the fact that registration confers priority over later designs.[21] That said, Brexit means that UK designers can no longer obtain a Registered European Union Design (REUD) that includes the United Kingdom. Designers who desire UK *and* Community protection must therefore register their design at both the UKIPO and the EU Intellectual Property Office (EUIPO). Such applications must be made within six months of one another to take the benefit of Paris Convention priority.[22]

[15] Ibid at s 8.

[16] Ibid at s 7(1).

[17] *Green Lane Products v PMS International* [2008] EWCA Civ 358.

[18] Bently et al, above n 1 at 742.

[19] See generally Anna Tischner, 'The Role of Unregistered Rights – a European Perspective on Design Protection' (2018) 13 *Journal of Intellectual Property Law & Practice* 303; 'Designs Framework Survey: Analysis of Responses', *UKIPO* (updated July 12, 2022) https://www.gov.uk/government/consultations/reviewing-the-designs-framework-call-for-views/outcome/designs-framework-survey-analysis-of-responses (especially the analysis of Question 9 – reasons for not registering your design). As noted in the introduction, this is an area that might benefit from further empirical work.

[20] Discussed in Bently et al, above n 1 at 798–799.

[21] Ibid at 742.

[22] Paris Convention for the Protection of Industrial Property as amended on September 28, 1979, Art 4; see also Agreement on Trade-Related Aspects of Intellectual Property Rights, Art 2.

Second, there is the supplementary unregistered design right. The SUD was established in 2020 and is intended to 'mirror', in the post-Brexit landscape, what was known at the time as the unregistered Community design right (UCD).[23] To be protected, a 'design'[24] must be 'new' and have 'individual character'.[25] The SUD has a duration of three years from the date the design 'was first made available to the public within' the United Kingdom.[26] As will be seen, there is currently uncertainty in relation to this requirement.

The UCD – and by extension, the SUD – has been justified on the grounds that many designers will benefit more from a shorter and more limited unregistered right than a longer and fuller right that requires registration. Fashion designers have been identified as a group that will benefit in particular from an unregistered right, including because of the relatively short length of the seasonal fashion cycle and the presence of many individual designers and smaller fashion houses that lack the resources to maintain registered design portfolios.[27] However, a trade-off for those relying on the UCD (now UEUD) or SUD is that the right is qualified: to sustain an infringement action, the holder of the right must prove copying.[28] The right does not, therefore, apply to independent creation. Furthermore, in the absence of reciprocal arrangements with the EU, the SUD applies only within the United Kingdom. As mentioned

[23] See 'Guidance: Changes to Unregistered Designs', IPO and Government Digital Service (January 30, 2020). As part of Brexit IP arrangements, recognition was also given in the UK to UCDs that existed *prior* to January 2021 through a 'continuing unregistered design' right (or CUD). In line with the term of protection for UCDs, all CUDs expired by the end of 2023 <https://www.gov.uk/guidance/changes-to-unregistered-designs>. Since that time, there has been some shift in EU designs law through the revision of Council Regulation (EC) No 6/2002 to what is now known as the EUDR, above n 1. One change is that registered and unregistered Community designs have been renamed EU designs: EUDR Art 1.

[24] Defined to mean 'the appearance of the whole or a part of a product resulting from the features of, in particular, the lines, contours, colours, shape, texture and/or materials of the product itself and/or its ornamentation': Retained CDR, above n 8, at Art 3(a).

[25] Ibid at Arts 4–6.

[26] Ibid at Art 11. The text of retained Art 11 refers not only to making available in the UK but in 'a qualifying country or a qualifying territory'. However, the Secretary of State has not designated any such countries or territories: Bently et al, above n 1 at 746.

[27] See, eg, Tischner, above n 19 at 304, 305; Philippa Bailey, 'Copyright and Designs in Fashion', The Chartered Institute of Trade Mark Attorneys (October 21, 2021), <https://www.citma.org.uk/resources/trade-marks-ip/intellectual-property-blog/copyright-and-designs-in-fashion-blog.html> ('protection is potentially available without registration as some forms of design protection arise automatically. This is perfect for the fashion industry because collections come and go, and generally have a short shelf life which means it's simply not practical or affordable to register everything').

[28] EUDR, above n 1 and Retained CDR, above n 8, at Art 19(4).

in the introduction, this changes the state of play for UK designers who previously enjoyed an EU-wide unregistered right.

Finally, there is the UK's sui generis unregistered design right. This right first appeared with the passage of the CDPA as part of efforts to provide greater intellectual coherence to the treatment of designs, such that subject matter was placed in its most appropriate IP 'box'. The CDPA placed limits on the circumstances where a design could be protected by copyright on the basis that copyright often over-protected such subject matter.[29] It also created a new, short, unregistered right that included functional designs.[30] This sui generis right defines 'design' as 'the design of . . . the shape or configuration . . . of the whole or part of an article'[31] and excludes 'surface decoration'.[32] This limits the relevance of the sui generis right to fashion design – for instance, it will not apply to two-dimensional features such as patterns and colour combinations (these being neither shape nor configuration)[33] or ornamentation (if this is excluded as surface decoration).[34] That said, it would be an

[29] CDPA s 51 and 53. These provisions are included in the list of 'permitted acts' and, as such, can be characterised as exceptions. However, like many of the UK's permitted acts, they do not so much reflect some overriding public policy goal where copyright norms must give way to another value (such as freedom of speech) but rather serve to adjust the rules of copyright subsistence and duration to make sure that copyright 'fits' different types of subject matter. See Robert Burrell and Allison Coleman, *Copyright Exceptions: The Digital Impact* (Cambridge University Press, 2005) 5. As originally enacted, the CDPA also contained a further provision in section 52 that served to reduce the term of protection for artistic works that had been exploited by means of an industrial process. This provision was repealed in 2016 in light of the decision of the CJEU in *Flos SpA v Semeraro Casa e Famiglia SpA*, C-168/09 (ECDR 8, January 27, 2011).

[30] For a summary, see Bently et al, above n 1 at 824. The duration of the design right is up to 15 years: CDPA, s 216(1).

[31] CDPA, s 213(2).

[32] Ibid at s 213(3)(c).

[33] Eg, *Lambretta Clothing v Teddy Smith* [2004] EWCA Civ 886 (the sui generis right did not protect a combination of colours used in a sports-themed garment as these were not an aspect of shape or configuration; in addition, the combination would be caught by the exclusion for surface decoration).

[34] This exemption can apply to two- and three-dimensional decorations. Its application can require an assessment of whether a particular feature is better classified as decorative or functional. A feature whose primary purpose is decorative will not fall outside the exemption merely because it has some, limited, functional purpose: *Dyson v Qualtex* [2006] EWCA Civ 166, at [83].

overstatement to suggest it is irrelevant to fashion.[35] Like the SUD, infringement of the sui generis right requires proof of copying.

7.2.2 *Appropriateness of the UK Regime for Fashion Designers*

A question for anyone considering design protection is whether to register their design, bearing in mind that registration does not preclude concurrent reliance on unregistered rights.[36] As mentioned in the introduction, prior to Brexit, it was often assumed that the EU's unregistered design right (then known as the UCD) offered the most appropriate form of protection for the fashion industry. Protection is short, lasting a maximum of three years, but any downsides in relation to duration were thought to be of relatively little concern in a fast-moving sector and were offset by the benefits of avoiding the financial and other costs of registration.

However, it is worth pausing to reflect on the operation of the (now) UEUD and its post-Brexit 'mirror' right, the SUD. This analysis discusses three features that might limit the relevance of these rights to fashion designers, these being features that also differentiate the UEUD and SUD from the registered system:[37] first, their duration; second, the need to prove copying in order to establish infringement; and third, the rules for creation and the resulting post-Brexit challenges for designers who wish UK *and* EU protection.

Starting with duration, there is the question of whether a three-year term is too short. As mentioned above, a shorter right is said to be appropriate for fashion due to the rapid turnover of designs and collections, which suggests that consumer demand in fashion markets tends to be time-bound – bearing in mind there are exceptions, as exemplified by certain collectable luxury brand items such as the Hermès Birkin and Chanel 2.55 handbags. It is also uncontroversial that, within the fast fashion sector, there are copyists who can turn around knock-off versions within weeks of the public exposure of the original item on the fashion

[35] Eg, the sui generis right was relied upon successfully in *Freddy v Hugz Clothing* [2020] EWHC 3032 (IPEC) in relation to the configuration of elastic panels in buttock-enhancing jeans, although it did not apply to the same design when worn (as the shape would differ from one person to another and was not, therefore, a protectable design).

[36] Discussed above in n 6.

[37] On the latter point, see, eg, *Rothy's Inc v Giesswein Walkwaren AG* [2020] EWHC 3391 (IPEC), at [100] (listing the three main issues in which the law on unregistered Community designs departs from that in relation to registered Community designs).

runways in Paris or Milan or on social media feeds. The business model of many such merchants is to satisfy the immediate public demand for a garment just like the one [X] wore or [Y] designed.[38] Thus, there is good evidence that commercial-level copying can coincide with the market for source designs and certainly occur well within the three-year term of the unregistered right.

However, when thinking about duration, the question is not just when copying occurs – after all, the fashion cycle is also characterised by the old coming back (often to the horror of those who survived acid wash jeans or ultra low-slung trousers to begin with).[39] Rather the question is the length of time for which the designer should enjoy exclusivity in their design. There are a number of matters that might inform this, including the typical commercial life of the products in question, but also the desirability of copying in order to satisfy consumer demand and support design innovation. Of course, it might be asked whether smaller and lesser-known designers – apparently key beneficiaries of an automatic right – have similar experiences to those described above. For instance, one can imagine that unlike established luxury fashion houses with celebrity designers who want to set a new trend with every runway show, emerging designers might wish to maintain consistency in their range so as to develop a clear voice or point of view as a designer. However, taken in the round, the three-year term suggests that for the UEUD and SUD, it has been decided that problematic copying – that is, that for which a legal response is appropriate – is that which occurs relatively quickly. For designers who want longer rights, there is the registered system. We can see the logic in this, although as discussed in Section 7.3, there is a fear that, on current trends, UK designers may in fact be channelled towards the turbo-charged protection offered by copyright.

[38] For discussion of fast fashion, see, eg, din Fagel Tse, above n 3, at 417–422; Witzburg, above n 4, at 706–707 and 726–728; Howard, above n 3, at 341–344. There is some variation in the business models adopted within the fast fashion sector, including in relation to (i) speed (eg, some online-only retailers are able to produce new designs even faster than those who operate bricks-and-mortar stores) and (ii) what is copied (eg, some fast fashion brands replicate the general look and trends of other designers, whilst other seek to replicate, sometimes very closely, particular styles).

[39] See, eg, Mehera Bonner, '50 Fashion Trends That We Hope Never Come Back in Style: The Only way 2020 Could Get Worse? Low-rise Jeans', *Cosmopolitan* (May 21, 2020) <https://www.cosmopolitan.com/style-beauty/fashion/g32553844/outdated-fashion-trends/>; 'The Worst Fashion Trends of Every Decade: Some Things Are Better Left in the Past', *Harper's Bazaar* (May 26, 2020) <https://www.harpersbazaar.com/fashion/trends/g7627/worst-trends-of-every-decade/>.

Second, for both the UEUD and SUD, it is necessary to prove copying in order to establish infringement.[40] The significance of this is illustrated by *Rothy's v Giesswein Walkwaren*,[41] in which the UCD claim failed because copying could not be established. In legal circles, this case has been said to illustrate not only the benefits of registration[42] but that 'rights holders who rely mainly on unregistered rights [should] think twice about their protection strategy'.[43]

Rothy's concerned shoe designs. The claimant was a Californian company that had registered a Community design for its 'Pointed Loafer' shoe. The Pointed Loafer was a ballerina shoe with a pointed toe and a protruding loafer-style tongue. Its upper components were made with a knitted yarn derived from recycled plastic. The claimant alleged that the defendant had infringed its registered Community design (RCD) *and* its UCD through the latter's 'Pointy Flat' shoe.[44] In addition to similarities in the shapes of the shoes, the upper parts of the defendant's shoe were made from a knitted meshwork fabric produced from recycled plastic. For images of each shoe, see Figure 7.1.

Rothy's is important for a number of reasons. A key aspect of the claimant's case was that the protected design included the knitted material on the upper surface of the shoe. To establish this for the RCD, it was necessary to show that the fabric was apparent in the images included in the registration[45] (it being impermissible to look to the Pointed Loafer itself to determine what the registration means).[46] Here, HHJ Stone (sitting as a

[40] EUDR, above n 1, and Retained CDR, above n 8, Art. 19(4).

[41] *Rothy's* [2020] EWHC 3391 (IPEC).

[42] See, eg, Lucy Flascher, 'Court Finds Infringement of Registered Community Design for Sustainable Ballerina Shoe', *Mishcon de Reya* (January 18, 2021) <https://www.mishcon.com/news/court-finds-infringement-of-registered-community-design-for-sustainable-ballerina-shoe>; Sean Ibbetson, 'Rothy's v Giesswein: IPEC Finds Rothy's RCD for a Pointed Loafer Has been Infringed', *Bristows* (February 5, 2021) https://www.bristows.com/viewpoint/articles/rothys-v-giesswein/>; Darren Smyth, 'Final Decision from a UK Community Design Court Clarifies How to Interpret a Registered Design' (2021) 16 *Journal of Intellectual Property Law & Practice* 203.

[43] Gregory Carty-Hornsby, 'Registered Design Enforcement: The Key Lessons from Rothy's v. Geisswein', *Marks & Clerk* (February 16, 2021) <https://www.marks-clerk.com/insights/articles/key-lessons-from-rothy-s-v-geisswein/>.

[44] The claimant was able to bring this claim in the UK as the case was heard during the Brexit transition period, meaning that the territory of the UCD included the UK, and the IPEC was able to sit as a Community Design Court: *Rothy's*, above n 37, at [9].

[45] Ibid at [54] (citing *Magmatic Ltd v PMS International Ltd* [2016] UKSC 12 ('*Trunki*'), at [30]).

[46] Ibid at [60].

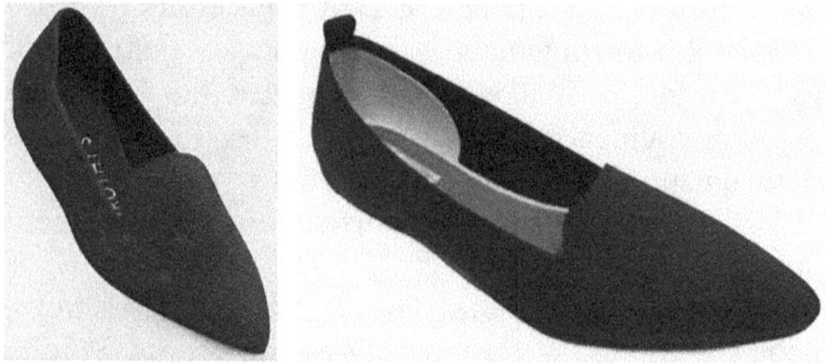

Figure 7.1 (*left*) The claimant's Pointed Loafer and (*right*) the defendant's Pointy Flat.
Credit: Open Justice License v1.0

Deputy High Court Judge) was willing to zoom in on the images of the RCD in finding that the designer claimed a knitted fabric rather than a shape or textured appearance more generally.[47] Another significant aspect of the case was that HHJ Stone had little difficulty in rejecting the attack on the validity of the RCD or in finding that the RCD had been infringed. The knitted upper stood out to the 'informed user' (a strange individual even when judged against English law's other fictional legal characters). It conferred both the necessary 'individual character' for validity *and* ensured that the defendant's shoe produced the same 'overall impression'.[48]

For present purposes, however, the key thing to note is that although the registered design case succeeded, the claimant was unable to make out a case for infringement of its UCD because it could not demonstrate that the defendant had copied its Pointed Loafer. It was clear from documents disclosed by the defendant that its designers had used shoes of the claimant as inspiration for its Pointy Flat. However, amongst all those materials, there was no reference to the Pointed Loafer – and two of the designers gave evidence that they had never seen that design. The similarity in the material of the upper was explained as being the result of one of the designers viewing an article that described the claimant's use of recycled plastic material in its shoes.

It would be going too far to claim that this case illustrates that, for the UCD (and, by implication, the UEUD and SUD), it is more difficult to prove copying or derivation than in copyright. As a general matter, the CJEU has clarified that Member States are entitled to apply national rules

[47] Ibid at [57]–[59].
[48] Ibid at [83]–[99].

relating to the reversal of the burden of proof such that copying can be inferred from objective similarity alone in appropriate circumstances.[49] In essence, the defendant in *Rothy's* was able to present a plausible narrative that the Pointy Flat was 'an independent work of creation' vis-à-vis the Pointed Loafer. The plausibility of the defendant's account – that is, that no one had seen the Pointed Loafer – was strengthened by the fact that the Pointed Loafer was a limited-edition product that was on the claimant's website for a short period of time.

There are, moreover, copyright cases in a similar vein. Most famously, in *Mitchell v BBC*,[50] the BBC was able to defend a copyright infringement action in relation to the animated characters in a children's television programme. The claimant had pitched a show to the BBC. Subsequently, the BBC broadcast a programme featuring characters that displayed some striking similarities with the claimant's drawings. However, the BBC prevailed as it was able to provide a convincing explanation to account for these similarities (including that characters aimed at young children tend to have certain common – and, given the idea/expression dichotomy, unprotectable – features).[51] Also important to the outcome in that case, much like in *Rothy's*, was that the claimant was not able to make out a convincing case of access by the BBC animators, despite his pitch.

The point is therefore not that there is a different legal or evidential standard to be applied between copyright and designs cases but more that some combination of functional constraints, design norms and the possibility of inspiration from a common third party source in a sector where referencing and imitation are the norm mean that the requirement to prove copying acts as a much more formidable hurdle in designs law than in does in the *typical* copyright action.[52] As HHJ Stone observed in a designs case involving an allegation of copying of dress designs, 'absent

[49] *H Gautzsch Großhandel GmbH & Co KG v Münchener Boulevard Möbel Joseph Duna GmbH* (C-479/1213) (ECDR 14 (Third Chamber), February 13, 2014).

[50] *Mitchell v BBC* [2011] EWPCC 42.

[51] Something similar can also be seen in cases in which copyright is being claimed in a logo. Many logos tend to be relatively simple, seek to communicate something about the goods or services and feature elements that are common to the trade. A tribunal may well, for example, refuse to draw an inference of copying if similarities lie in commonly used elements such as a simple star and circle device, cursive writing sloping up left to right, and the use of the colours of the Italian flag on marks registered in relation to foodstuffs: *AIA Agricola Italiana Alimentare SpA v Borgo Developments Pty Ltd as trustee for The L Borgo Trust* [2018] ATMO 184.

[52] This is a point that some commentators anticipated many years ago, see, eg, Lionel Bently, 'Requiem for Registration? Reflections on the History of the UK Registered

striking closeness between the designs in relation to features that were not well known', a tribunal may not be willing to draw an inference of copying from other factors (such as the defendant's 'design process').[53]

Rothy's therefore helps highlight the significance of the requirement for copying and raises questions about the inferences that can be drawn in the absence of unambiguous evidence of access. Lawyers responded to *Rothy's* by emphasising the desirability of designers registering their designs. We might, however, ask whether the rules on infringement undermine the stated aims of the UEUD and SUD. To put it another way, if there is consensus that a short but strong *unregistered* design right is best for fashion designers such that we *don't* want them to have to bother with registration, should the UEUD and SUD be strengthened by removing the requirement that infringement requires copying?

This would, of course, involve abandoning the view that 'absolute' or 'true' monopolies are only justified for registered forms of IP. This view is often said to rest on the proposition that liability for independent creation can be justified because the act of registration provides public notice of the existence of a right. Whether this proposition withstands close scrutiny is open to question. For instance, it ignores the fact that registered rights can often be difficult to locate, sometimes deliberately so. Moreover, it is an idea that already has no application in the trade-mark sphere, where liability for passing off is not conditional on proof of copying or derivation.

However, even if agreement could be reached regarding the intellectual case for removing the copying requirement in the United Kingdom, it would be necessary to contend with post-Brexit arrangements. In particular, the ability of the United Kingdom to amend the SUD is constrained by Article 247(1) of the Trade and Cooperation Agreement between the EU and UK, which provides:

> Each Party shall confer on holders of an unregistered design the right to prevent the use of the unregistered design by any third party not having the holder's consent only if the contested use results from copying the unregistered design in their respective territory.[54]

Design System' in A Firth (ed), *Perspectives on Intellectual Property Vol 1: The Prehistory of Intellectual Property Law* (Sweet & Maxwell, 1996).

53 *Original Beauty Technology v G4K Fashion Ltd* [2021] EWHC 294 (Ch), at [117].

54 Trade and Cooperation Agreement between the European Union and the European Atomic Energy Community, of the one part, and the United Kingdom of Great Britain and Northern Ireland, of the other part (OJ L 149, 30.4.2021, p 10) (as amended; version at December 1, 2021).

Given the Brexit goal of 'taking back control',[55] it might have been thought that the UK government would maximise its freedom to strike out in a different direction with its domestic laws, especially vis-à-vis the EU. However, when the Trade and Cooperation Agreement (which has relatively few provisions in relation to IP) is read alongside other new trade agreements (such as the Free Trade Agreement with Ukraine),[56] we see a pattern of the United Kingdom limiting – at times significantly – its legislative freedom in the IP space. In relation to unregistered designs, while it is still open for the United Kingdom to extend the duration of the SUD,[57] changing the rules around infringement is off the table.[58]

One explanation for the loss of regulatory freedom in Article 247 might have been to pave the way for reciprocal recognition of unregistered design rights. However, no such reciprocity has been established. And herein lies the issue for the UK designer who wishes to rely on *unregistered* rights in the UK *and* EU. Under Art 11(1) of the EUDR, the unregistered right comes into existence on the date the design 'was first made available to the public within the Union'. However, the EUDR has not provided a clear resolution to the question of whether disclosures in other territories can nevertheless satisfy this requirement.[59] The position in the United Kingdom is likewise unclear: although guidance issued by the UKIPO states that a SUD 'is

[55] See, eg, The Prime Minister, 'EU Exit: Taking Back Control of Our Borders, Money and Laws While Protecting our Economy, Security and Union' (2018) (Her Majesty's Stationery Office, Cm 9741).

[56] Political, Free Trade and Strategic Partnership Agreement between the United Kingdom of Great Britain and Northern Ireland and Ukraine (2020).

[57] See Trade and Cooperation Agreement, above n 54 Art 247(2) (the term of protection shall be 'at least' three years from the date the design was first made available); UK-Ukraine FTA, ibid, at Art. 204(2).

[58] See also UK-Ukraine FTA, above n 56, Art 203(5) (also requiring copying for infringement of unregistered designs). Interestingly, although the sui generis right is expressly outside of Art 247(1) of the Trade and Cooperation Agreement, no such limit appears in the UK-Ukraine FTA.

[59] Discussed in detail in Sara Ashby and Catriona Smith, 'Unregistered Design Law: The Good, the Bad, and the Ugly' (2018) 13 *Journal of Intellectual Property Law & Practice* 315, 321–323; Annette Kur, 'Finally Back to TRIPS-Compliance? EU Design Law and the Criterion of Publication "within EU Territory"' (2023) 18 *Journal of Intellectual Property Law & Practice* 11. Originally, the CDR stated in Art 110a(5) that 'Pursuant to Article 11, a design which has not been made public within the territory of the Community shall not enjoy protection as an unregistered Community design.' One question was whether and how this qualified the text of Art 11(2) which stated that making available, as described in Art 11(1), will be deemed to have occurred 'if it has been published, exhibited, used in trade or otherwise disclosed in such a way that, in the normal course of business, these

established by first disclosure in the UK',[60] the United Kingdom did not retain all the relevant provisions of the CDR on this matter.[61] Thus, it is open to question whether disclosure in the United Kingdom can establish the UEUD, and likewise whether disclosure in the EU (and indeed elsewhere) might establish the SUD.[62] Against this backdrop, well-advised parties are exploring ways to publish simultaneously in both jurisdictions. The success of such efforts is difficult to predict. Simultaneous here means truly simultaneous – there is no equivalent to the 30-day rule under the Berne Convention.[63] The obvious step of placing a design on a website accessible in both jurisdictions may not result in simultaneous publication, given the emphasis that has been placed on the need for websites to 'target' a jurisdiction in order for there to be a relevant connection.[64] In any event, for smaller market actors – said to be important recipients of automatic rights – it is almost inevitable that they will at times inadvertently lose their ability to access the unregistered design right system.

One practical response to all three issues is for designers to register their designs: this will give them protection for up to 25 years, means they do not have to prove copying to establish infringement and allows them to rely on the six-month priority period to register their designs in the UK and the EU. But as already mentioned, one of the main rationales for an unregistered right is that the knowledge and resources required for registration are outside the reach of large swathes of the fashion industry.

events could reasonably have become known to the circles specialised in the sector concerned, operating within the Community'. As Ashby and Smith observe, there was a good argument that, taken on its own, Art 11(2) included disclosures made *outside* the EU that become known to professional circles within the Community. However, Art 110a (5) was understood to oust that approach: see, eg, the German Federal Supreme Court in Case *Gebäckspresse II* (2008) I ZR 126/06. As discussed by Kur, although the above text from Art 110a(5) was removed in the EUDR, the reason for this deletion was not discussed in the explanatory memorandum, and the ambiguity of Art 11 remains.

60 'Guidance: Changes to Unregistered Designs', UKIPO and Government Digital Services (January 30, 2020) <https://www.gov.uk/guidance/changes-to-unregistered-designs>.

61 The UK did not retain Art 110a(5), discussed above n 59. Instead, Art 110a was omitted: see SI 2019/638, above n 8, at Sched 1, item 50.

62 Compare the advice of UKIPO at n 60, where it is said that 'first disclosure in the EU does not establish a SUD' and 'first disclosure in the UK may not establish a UCD'.

63 Berne Convention Art 3(4).

64 For instance, as seen in *Warner Music UK Ltd v TuneIn Inc* [2019] EWHC 2923 (Ch), in relation to whether foreign radio streams were 'communicated to the public' by TuneIn when UK users could access those streams via TuneIn's app. The answer was yes, as various indicators suggested the streams were targeted to UK users, including that UK advertisements were played and TuneIn's premium service was priced in pounds sterling.

In sum, although the UK designs system is in need of reform, there are a number of matters that stand in the way of revising the SUD. In addition to the usual issues for law reform – limits in legislative bandwidth, challenges in reaching consensus amongst diverse stakeholders, etc – there is the fact that the United Kingdom is operating within a network of trade agreements in which it has agreed to certain standards for IP protections, including agreements that preserve numerous standards from EU law. For those who believe that fashion is under-protected by the SUD, one response might therefore be to bolster calls for fashion designers to rely on the registered system. However, another response might be to encourage designers to seek redress by reference to another unregistered right: copyright. We believe that this is far from obviously desirable, as reliance on copyright risks massively over-correcting for problems associated with the SUD and UEUD. We explore this in Section 7.3.

7.3 Copyright

In this section, we discuss our concerns about copyright playing a more prominent role in designs protection in the United Kingdom. We start with a brief examination of why copyright might be attractive to designers and why, in our view, copyright is an inappropriate IP 'box' for many designs. This includes discussion of case law from the CJEU that seems to have taken a very expansive approach to the definition of an original 'work' in European copyright law, such that many designs will have dual protection in copyright and designs law. We then discuss the reception of that case law in the United Kingdom and argue that UK judges should be slow to follow the approach of the CJEU, including due to the difficulties in sufficiently reining in rights, for instance, via infringement or exceptions, once subject matter has been expanded.

We start with the reasons why UK designers might be attracted to copyright, which are straightforward and can be dealt with relatively swiftly. In short, reliance on copyright not only avoids issues in relation to the SUD but also the registered design right. Copyright protection is automatic and, given the principle of national treatment that underpins the international copyright system, makes the time and place of creation (or first public exposure) less significant. To the extent that there are concerns about the short duration of the SUD, such concerns clearly do not apply to copyright, as the default rule for artistic works is that copyright subsists for the life of the author plus 70 years.[65] This is also

[65] CDPA, s 12.

far longer than the maximum term of the registered right. Finally, although infringement of copyright requires that the defendant copied the claimant's work, UK judges are willing to draw inferences about this based on the level of objective similarity between and the character of the two works and the defendant's familiarity with the claimant's work.[66]

Our concern with recourse to copyright is that copyright provides an unduly long and inappropriate form of protection over designs in a range of fields, including fashion. For avoidance of doubt, we are not saying that fashion should be excluded from copyright protection. We can imagine haute couture and avant garde creation in which the craftmanship and visual appeal are such that copyright protection is appropriate (or at least defensible). We can also imagine instances in which individual features might justifiably be protected by copyright, for instance, where the image on a T-shirt is an original drawing.[67] However, we have concerns about clothing and footwear being protected by copyright, for reasons of doctrine and policy including that (1) the creative choices in fashion design are limited by the nature of the item and the function it serves; (2) clothing and footwear are basic human needs, which only reinforces the need for restraint in the exclusive rights thrown around such creations; (3) to the extent clothing goes beyond basic needs and is a vehicle for personal expression (of the designer, wearer, or both), imitation is baked-in to an industry known for being cyclical, referential and trend-driven; and (4) the designs of younger designers may enjoy a copyright term that is 5 times as long as the maximum protection of a registered design and over 40 times as long as the unregistered design right.

Some of these concerns can be illustrated by reference to the ballerina shoe, the subject of the *Rothy's* case, discussed in Section 7.2. Expert evidence was given in relation to the 'basic anatomy' of ballerina shoes, their design heritage, their 'important characteristics' (e.g., toe shape, heel height, outsole profile, vamp and trim) and the types of materials they comprise (e.g., leather, suede and canvas).[68] On the one hand, one can see the potential for creative decision-making in relation to each element.

[66] See, eg, *Francis Day & Hunter v Bron* [1963] 1 Ch 587 (CA); *Designers Guild Ltd v Russell Williams (Textiles) Ltd* [2000] 1 WLR 2416 (House of Lords); *Mitchell v BBC*, above n 50 esp. at [38]–[39].

[67] As was the case in *Elwood Clothing Pty Ltd v Cotton On Clothing Pty Ltd* [2008] FCAFC 197. That said, we have doubts about the conclusion on infringement in that case, which was made out due to similarities in the overall 'look and feel' of the designs.

[68] *Rothy's*, above n 37, at [47]–[52].

On the other hand, the product has to function as a shoe. Although the designer has choices, many relate to how the characteristics of the shoe manifest, not whether those characteristics are present to begin with. Furthermore, when thinking about each such manifestation, the designer may have to work within fairly limited parameters. For instance, the toe shape of a ballerina shoe can, according to the expert evidence in *Rothy's*, be pointed, square, round or almond shaped.[69] It may be that there are infinite, minute gradations between and within these options – for instance, a pointed toe can be sharper or more rounded.[70] But ultimately, designers are using their creativity to make choices that are bounded to greater and lesser degrees by practical and technical considerations.

In *Rothy's*, the elements of the claimant's Pointed Loafer admitted by the defendant to be different from the relevant design corpus were the heel height, the material of the upper and the presence of a counterline.[71] These were held by HHJ Stone to be enough for the shoe to have a different overall impression to the informed user, meaning that the RCD (and, under the same reasoning, UCD) was valid. What might have happened if the claimant argued that the Pointed Loafer was an original work? To explore this in the European context, we consider two design-oriented judgments from the CJEU: *Cofemel v G-Star Raw*[72] and *Brompton Bicycle.*[73] Those cases concerned the definition of a work under the Information Society Directive (ISD). To understand the significance of those cases, it is useful to understand the legal backdrop when they were handed down.

Prior to *Cofemel*, there had been a long line of CJEU case law stating that, to be protected, a work must be original in terms of being its 'author's own intellectual creation'.[74] In applying this standard, relevant questions included whether the author was able to make 'free and creative choices'[75] or had, through their choices, put their 'personal

[69] Ibid at [49](a).

[70] Ibid.

[71] Ibid at [67]–[90].

[72] *Cofemel – Sociedade de Vestuário SA v G-Star Raw CV*, Case C-683/17) (ECDR 9 (Third Chamber), September 12, 2019).

[73] *Brompton Bicycle v Chedech/Get2Get*, Case C-833/18 (ECDR 10 (Fifth Chamber), June 11, 2020).

[74] This case law commencing with *Infopaq International A/S v Danske Dagblades Forening*, Case C-5/08, at [33]–[37] (ECDR 16 (Fourth Chamber), July 16, 2009).

[75] *Funke Medien NRW GmbH v Germany*, Case C-469/17, at [23] (ECDR 25 (Grand Chamber), July 29, 2019).

touch' on the work.[76] In *Levola Hengelo*,[77] handed down ten months prior to *Cofemel*, it was held that 'two cumulative conditions must be satisfied for subject matter to be classified as a "work"':[78] first, that it passes the European originality standard and, second, that it is 'the expression of the author's own intellectual creation',[79] being an expression that is 'identifiable with sufficient precision and objectivity.'[80] Applying this test, it was held that the taste of a food product – in that case, a spreadable cheese dip – was not a work as it 'cannot . . . be pinned down with precision and objectivity'.[81]

Levola Hengelo generated numerous questions about the European approach to the meaning of 'work'.[82] On the one hand, the CJEU recognised that, as a party to the WCT, the European Community must comply with Articles 1 to 21 of Berne.[83] It referred to the definition of 'literary and artistic works' in Berne[84] and statements in the WCT and TRIPS that copyright may be granted to expression but not to ideas.[85] However, in considering the significance of the international copyright framework, the CJEU focused on the need for the claimed expression to be objectivity identifiable, not the nature of the expression to begin with. That is, the problem with the taste of food was not that it was outside the subject matter in Article 2 but that it was not sufficiently certain: people experience taste very subjectively, and there is currently no technology by which a machine can make that assessment objectively.[86]

Our concern with this approach is that, if taken seriously, it suggests the only thing standing in the way of tastes being 'works' is the lack of technology to objectively measure them – that there was no separate reason, coming from doctrine or policy, for them to be excluded from copyright

[76] *Painer v Standard Verlags GmbH*, Case C-145/10 (ECDR 6 (Third Chamber), December 1, 2011).

[77] *Levola Hengelo BV v Smilde Foods BV*, Case C-310/17 (ECDR 2 (Grand Chamber), November 13, 2018).

[78] Ibid at [35].

[79] Ibid at [37].

[80] Ibid at [40].

[81] Ibid at [42].

[82] See, eg, Jani McCutcheon, 'Levola Hengelo BV v Smilde Foods BV: The Hard Work of Defining a Copyright Work' (2019) 82 *Modern Law Review* 936; Jani McCutcheon, 'The Concept of a Copyright Work under EU Law: More Than a Matter of Taste' (2019) 44 *European Law Review* 767.

[83] *Levola Hengelo*, above n 77 at [38] (citing WCT, Art 1(4)).

[84] Ibid at [39] (citing the Berne Convention, Art 2(1)).

[85] Ibid (citing WCT, Art 2 and TRIPS, Art 9(2)).

[86] Ibid at [42].

protection. In his Opinion in *Levola Hengelo*, AG Wathelet discussed three additional reasons why tastes of foodstuffs are not works: (1) all the illustrative subject matter in Berne Article 2 are works that are perceived visually or aurally;[87] (2) no multilateral treaties have been made or revised to confer copyright protection on tastes (as has occurred for other contentious subject matter, such as computer programs);[88] and (3) the *recipe as such* of a foodstuff is not protectable, being an idea.[89] However, the Grand Chamber focused mainly on another proposition discussed by AG Wathelet: (4) that the expression needs to be sufficiently precise.[90] It also seemed to depart from AG Wathelet's observation that originality should be considered *in addition to* whether the subject matter is a work, that is, that they are distinct concepts and should not be conflated.[91]

This brings us to *Cofemel*, where the relevant legal uncertainty related to whether Member States could include additional requirements for subject matter to be a protected 'work' or otherwise have their own gloss on that question. G-Star had instituted proceedings in Portugal alleging that, inter alia, Cofemel had infringed its copyright in its ARC design for jeans and ROWDY design for sweatshirts and T-shirts. The Portuguese copyright statute only protected works of applied art and design 'which constitute an artistic creation'.[92] The Supreme Court of Portugal referred to the CJEU two questions in relation to the permitted content of local subsistence rules: was it compatible with the ISD for a Member State to protect designs that 'create their own visual and distinctive effect from an aesthetic point of view' or to require that designs be 'artistic creation[s]' or 'work[s] of art'.

The CJEU repeated the two-limb definition of work set out in *Levola Hengelo*.[93] In doing so, it observed that there will be no originality where 'the realisation of a subject matter has been dictated by technical considerations, rules or other constraints, which have left no room for creative

[87] Ibid at [AG51].
[88] Ibid at [AG52]–[AG54].
[89] Ibid at [AG55].
[90] Ibid at [40]. See also ibid at [AG56] (citing *Sieckmann v Deutsches Patent- und Markenamt*, Case C-273/00 (Ch 487 (Court of Justice), December 12, 2002) (a scent is unable to be registered as a trade mark as it cannot be represented graphically on the register)).
[91] Ibid at [AG44], [AG46].
[92] *Cofemel*, above n 72, at [15] (quoting from Art 2 of the *Código do Direito de Autor e dos Direitos Conexos* (Code on Copyright and Related Rights) (PT)).
[93] Ibid at [29].

freedom'.[94] We pause here to note that if this is intended as exhaustive of the situations in which technical imperatives oust originality, and is read literally, it would seem to operate in very narrow circumstances. To return to the ballerina shoe in *Rothy's*, it would be going too far to suggest that matters such as the shape of the toe or the height of the heel are dictated *solely* by technical considerations: there may be a range of choices that all result in functional shoes, and aesthetic matters might help mediate the choice between them. The CJEU also observed that if the two limbs in *Levola Hengelo* are met, the work 'must, as such, qualify for copyright protection'.[95] This suggests that additional requirements are not permitted, for instance, that a work be an 'artistic creation'. Finally, the case suggests that Member States should take care in adding their own gloss by rewriting or reimagining European requirements. In the latter stages of the judgment, the CJEU observed that the Berne-compatible approach in Europe was that copyright and designs give separate and cumulative protection, albeit that concurrent protection 'can be envisaged only in certain situations'.[96] However, it said that copyright protection may not be linked to the 'aesthetic effects' produced by a design as (1) such effects produce intrinsically subjective internal experiences and (2) just because a design generates an aesthetic effect does not mean that it constitutes its author's own intellectual creation.[97]

Taken to its logical conclusion, the approach in *Cofemel* suggests that any requirement that a work be 'artistic' is straight-out incompatible with European copyright law, unless a convincing way can be found to distinguish artistic nature from an aesthetic effect. Furthermore, the CJEU's two-limb approach suggests that, under European copyright law, a work is an objectively certain expression that is the result of an intellectual process in which free and creative choices are made. In such a world, it is not obvious that the design of a Pointed Loafer is outside the scope of copyright protection as being the wrong sort of expression. Furthermore, the CJEU stated that the degree of protection afforded a work 'does not depend on the degree of creative freedom exercised by its author' – that is, works involving fewer creative choices do not get 'inferior' protection.[98]

[94] Ibid at [31].
[95] Ibid at [35].
[96] Ibid at [52].
[97] Ibid at [53]–[54].
[98] Ibid at [35].

As noted above, originality may provide some handbrake to the protection of functional and utilitarian items. However, this will depend on the circumstances in which courts find that technical considerations oust creative choices. This was considered by the CJEU in the *Brompton Bicycle* case. Brompton bicycles are marketed by an English company and contain a mechanism that allows them to exist in three different positions: folded, unfolded and on stand-by. Because of their compact size, they are attractive for those who need to take their bicycles onto England's excellent public transport system as part of their commute. The question was whether Brompton could bring an action *in copyright* against a competitor who produced its own folding bike that resembled Brompton bicycles. The CJEU clarified that a work may be original despite its realisation being 'dictated by technical considerations', so long as these considerations have not 'prevented the author from reflecting his personality in that subject matter, as an expression of free and creative choices'.[99] It stated that the existence of other shapes that achieve the same technical result is not decisive.[100] The CJEU left it to the national court to apply this guidance to the facts. The clear lesson is that copyright can protect functional shapes.

The approach in *Cofemel* and *Brompton Bicycle* conflicts with UK law in a number of ways. First, it sits awkwardly – although not necessarily irreconcilably – with the UK's closed list of protected subject matter.[101] We say 'not necessarily' because a closed list might nevertheless permit expansive definitions that end up including all the subject matter that meets the CJEU two-limb test. However, when we look at the drafting of the UK closed list and interpretations developed by judges, we struggle to see a principled and intellectually compelling way that the UK approach can be completely aligned with that in Europe without the CDPA being amended.

In the CDPA, artistic work is defined exhaustively – it means '(a) a graphic work, photograph, sculpture or collage, irrespective of artistic quality, (b) a work of architecture being a building or a model for a building, or (c) a work of artistic craftsmanship'.[102] A conflict can

[99] *Brompton Bicycle*, above n 73, at [26].

[100] Ibid at [35].

[101] In the UK, section 1 of the CDPA states that copyright subsists in 'the following descriptions of work', being original literary, dramatic, musical or artistic works, sound recordings, films or broadcasts and the typographical arrangement of published editions.

[102] CDPA, s 4(1).

immediately be seen between the European approach and the category works of artistic craftsmanship, unless the word 'artistic' – which in the UK has traditionally required some visual or aesthetic appeal[103] – is interpreted to refer to the nature of the work, for instance, that the relevant expression has a visual rather than a semiotic function. A further conflict arises when one considers interpretations in the case law. As mentioned earlier, the UK struggled for many decades with the boundary between copyright and designs. One cause was case law in which plaintiffs were able to successfully claim copyright in utilitarian objects such as the moulds for the heating plates of a sandwich toaster.[104] These cases seemed to take very seriously the qualification that things like sculptures and engravings are protected 'irrespective of artistic quality', such that the focus was almost exclusively on the method of creation.

There was pushback against this trend, including because it was allowing the development of a definition of 'sculpture' that was entirely divorced from the ordinary meaning of the term and causing a significant expansion in the subject matter protected by copyright.[105] Judges therefore sought to read some limiting principles into words like 'sculpture', for instance, by agreeing that a sculpture is not any work made through sculpting but one that is 'made by an artist's hand'.[106] The meaning of sculpture was considered by the UK Supreme Court in 2011 in *Lucasfilm v Ainsworth*, which concerned the copyright status of Stormtrooper helmets and other artefacts made for the Star Wars movies.[107] A key principle affirmed by the Supreme Court was that while judges should not assess artistic *quality* (this being precluded by the text of the CDPA), it was entirely acceptable to consider artistic *purpose*.[108] The Supreme Court therefore endorsed the legal analysis of the trial judge, Mann J, who developed a list of factors relevant to the meaning of sculpture, the key elements of which were that (1) the ordinary usage of sculpture is

[103] See, eg, the summary of Mann J in *Lucasfilm Ltd v Ainsworth* [2008] EWHC 1878 (Ch), at [124]–[135].

[104] *Breville Europe Plc v Thorn EMI Domestic Appliances Ltd* [1995] FSR 77. See also the New Zealand case, *Lincoln Industries v Wham-O* [1985] 3 IPR 115 (Court of Appeal) (the wooden prototype for a Frisbee was a sculpture, and the moulds to create the plastic disks and the disks themselves were engravings).

[105] See, eg, *J&S Davis (Holdings) Ltd v Wright Health Group Ltd* [1988] RPC 403; *Metix (UK) Ltd v GH Maughan (Plastics) Ltd* [1997] FSR 718.

[106] *Metix*, above n 105, at 722.

[107] *Lucasfilm Limited v Ainsworth* [2011] UKSC 39.

[108] Ibid at [37].

relevant but not determinative, (2) artistic worth is not relevant and (3) the essence of a sculpture is that it is intended to have visual appeal (although it may also have other purposes).[109] The Supreme Court observed that this definition was supported as a matter of policy:

> It is possible to recognise an emerging legislative purpose (though the process has been slow and laborious) of protecting three-dimensional objects in a graduated way .... Different periods of protection are accorded to different classes of work. Artistic works of art (sculpture and works of artistic craftsmanship) have the fullest protection .... Although the periods of protection accorded to the less privileged types have been progressively extended, copyright protection has always been much more generous. There are good policy reasons for the differences in the periods of protection, and the Court should not, in our view, encourage the boundaries of full copyright protection to creep outwards.[110]

The Court stated that it would 'not accord with the normal use of language' to describe a helmet used in the making of a film as a 'sculpture' and that the Stormtrooper helmet 'was utilitarian in the sense that it was an element in the process of production of the film'.[111] As such, the Court was not prepared to disturb the conclusions of the trial judge that the artefacts were not sculptures, as that term is used in the CDPA.[112]

UK courts have now begun to explore the question of how the two-limb test in *Cofemel* maps onto the closed-list approach in the CDPA and the meaning of categories such as sculpture and works of artistic craftsmanship. For instance, in *Response Clothing v Edinburgh Woollen Mill*, which was handed down during the Brexit transition period, it was held that a wave fabric pattern constituted a work of artistic craftsmanship irrespective of whether the relevant test was the British one or the European test in *Cofemel*.[113] HHJ Hacon did not, therefore, need to determine what would happen if the fabric was a work under *Cofemel* but not a work of artistic craftsmanship as traditionally understood in the United Kingdom. That said, he expressed the view that the task of the British judge is not to determine whether the ISD has removed all gaps in protection; rather, the judge must ask whether it

[109] Ibid at [36] (agreeing with the list of factors of Mann J in *Lucasfilm Ltd v Ainsworth*, above n 103, at [118]).

[110] Ibid at [48].

[111] Ibid at [44].

[112] Prior to the UK litigation, George Lucas had obtained default judgment against Andrew Ainsworth in California: ibid at [4].

[113] *Response Clothing v Edinburgh Woollen Mill* [2020] EWHC 148 (IPEC).

is possible to interpret the CDPA in conformity with the ISD. This would seem to reflect the view that there are limits to the *Marleasing* principle, under which national courts must seek to interpret national law in conformity with EU directives.[114] If it is simply not possible to interpret a local statute in accordance with EU law (bearing in mind the looser rules for statutory construction that govern that process), it is for the legislature to fix the situation.[115] Thinking about this in the context of copyright subsistence, it is one thing for UK judges to define the protected categories of work as broadly as possible but another for them to abandon the closed list entirely or push the boundaries of the statutory language in such a dramatic way that it amounts to much the same thing.

The position has now been further clarified by the decision in *WaterRower v Liking*,[116] which also considered the meaning of work of artistic craftsmanship. It was held that a series of water resistance rowing machines (an example of which appears in Figure 7.2) were *not* protected as original artistic works under the CDPA, meaning that the claimant's action for copyright infringement failed. However, in the course of the reasoning, HHJ Forsyth concluded that each of the WaterRower iterations *was* a work under the European test.

This meant that unlike *Response Clothing*, it was necessary for HHJ Forsyth to reach a view on the potential conflict between European and UK copyright law. On the European approach – which remained relevant as cases such as *Cofemel* and *Brompton Bicycle* form part of assimilated CJEU case law – HHJ Forsyth was not prepared to find that the technical constraints inherent in the device (for instance, that it needs runners, a seat with padding, footrests, and so forth) left no room for creative freedom, applying

[114] *Marleasing SA v La Comercial Internacional de Alimentacion SA*, Case C-106/89, [1992] 1 CMLR 305.

[115] For further discussion of this in the copyright context, see Kitchin J (as he then was) in *Football Association Premier League Ltd v QC Leisure* [2012] EWHC 108 (Ch), especially [22]–[27], [73]–[74]. As mentioned in the main text, judges are not bound by the usual rules of statutory interpretation when applying the *Marleasing* principle and can, for instance, depart from the literal words of a statute or imply words into a provision. It is not, however, possible to adopt an interpretation that is in clear conflict with the statute. The *Marleasing* principle ceased to be part of UK law from January 1, 2024, as a consequence of the Retained EU Law (Revocation and Reform) Act 2023. For discussion, see *Makeality Ltd v City Doggo Ltd* [2025] EWCA Civ 400.

[116] [2024] EWHC 2806 (IPEC). For other cases to consider the relationship between the European case law and the subject matter listed in the CDPA, see *Equisafety Limited v Woof Woof* [2024] EWHC 2478 (IPEC) (discussed further below) and *Rinkoff v Baby Cow Productions Ltd* [2025] EWHC 39 (IPEC).

Figure 7.2 A WaterRower machine.
Credit: Open Justice License v1.0

statements from *Brompton*.[117] In contrast, on the UK approach, he indicated that the device failed to qualify as a work of artistic craftsmanship within the meaning of s.4(1)(c) of the CDPA. HHJ Forsyth considered indications from a number of authorities, including *Hensher* and *Response Clothing*, in reaching this conclusion. The problem for the claimant was that even though Mr Duke, the creator of the WaterRower, had constructed the prototype with the requisite craftsmanship and with care and consideration as to its appearance, it would be going too far to suggest he was ever acting an artist-craftsman. To qualify as a work of artistic craftsmanship, the work has to have an 'an artistic justification' and not merely a commercial rationale.[118] With the prototopye held not to be protected, the modified WaterRowers fared no better as none of the changes were driven by any artistic rationale.

At first sight, the decision in *WaterRower* might seem to lessen the danger of copyright coming to play a major role in protecting fashion design. It now seems clear that, despite CJEU case law to the contrary, it will still be necessary for the work to be of an artist's hand or have some artistic quality or appeal.

On further reflection, however, the position may not be as clear cut. One question, on which we shall not dwell, is whether a higher court might take a different approach to HHJ Forsyth in how to deal with case

[117] Ibid at [168].
[118] Ibid at [182].

law such as *Cofemel*, being one which does much more to read away the language of the CDPA's closed list. HHJ Forsyth attempted to find a way forward that both recognised the case law from the CJEU and paid respect to the UK drafting environment. If the goal was to achieve genuine reconciliation, his solution clearly fell short. However, we see merit in his choice to respect the words of the UK statute and to present a decision-making framework that centres the EU test.

However, even if future judges are likewise disinclined to ignore the language and interpretations of the CDPA, the decisions in *Response Clothing* and *WaterRower* are consistent with other cases that have applied a relatively lax definition of works of artistic craftsmanship. For instance, in *Bonz Group*, Tipping J held that handmade woollen sweaters and cardigans were works of artistic craftsmanship.[119] Mrs Rodwell, the principal designer of the garments, was said to have 'brought sufficient artistry to the task', such that the designs have 'more than sufficient aesthetic appeal' and Mrs Rodwell could 'fairly be described as an artist'.[120] In the Australian case, *Coogi Australia v Hysport International*,[121] it was held that brightly-coloured knitted fabric was also a work of artistic craftsmanship. The outcomes in these cases can be contrasted with that in *Equisafety and Woof Wear*,[122] in which it was held that high-visibility equestrian products, including a waistcoat, were not protected works of artistic craftsmanship. Focusing on the waistcoast, although the designer had choices in where to apply new elements to an existing waistcoat design, those elements did not 'reflect the author's personality as required [by *Cofemel*].'[123] This meant that the new features did not themselves comprise a work in the EU sense, and it was further held that they were not protected under the 'older' UK law either, as they were not the product of a craftsman.[124] Given the particular facts of this case, and the brevity of the reasoning, it would be unwise to suggest it has moved the dial on the copyright status of clothing in general.[125]

The upshot of the foregoing analysis is that anyone who can demonstrate that aesthetic considerations were a significant consideration

[119] *Bonz Group (Pty) Ltd v Cooke* [1994] NZHC 1004.

[120] Ibid at p. 14 of the version available at www.nzlii.org/nz/cases/NZHC/1994/1004.pdf.

[121] (1998) 41 IPR 593.

[122] Above n 116.

[123] Ibid [49].

[124] Ibid.

[125] To similar effect, see *WaterRower*, above n 116, at [209]–[212].

throughout the creative process will be in a relatively strong position to claim copyright in their creations. In the context of fashion, the fact that a garment has some functional elements will not preclude it being protected, although the simpler the design and/or the more it is dictated by function, the less likely this will be the outcome. In that regard, we agree with the result in *Equisafety*, and indeed believe that judges should take great care before concluding that everyday items of clothing are protected by copyright.

Of course, even if a designer can establish copyright subsistence, this is not the end of the matter in relation to enforcement, as the claimant still needs to establish infringement and the defendant may point to an exception. However, we have concerns about relying on infringement and exceptions to deal with the inevitable overshoots in protection that will arise from a broad, European-inspired approach. One set of concerns relate to the suitability of infringement principles for functional works. For instance, in a world of ubiquitous online availability, there may be plenty of evidence to suggest access, meaning that much will turn on similarity and substantial part. We wonder whether differences that may be highly significant as a technical matter might result in works that remain highly similar as a visual matter. Another set of concerns relate to whether the current suite of exceptions will provide adequate breathing space for design innovation. For instance, the CJEU's approach to the quotation exception suggests that it may be inapplicable in most designs cases, as the Court has defined quotation to relate to uses to illustrate a point or enter into a dialogue with the source work.[126] This sort of intellectual engagement is likely to be lacking in most fashion design.

Finally, the more fundamental point is that if we agree that certain designs (especially functional ones) are not the sort of works that copyright ought to protect, the more principled and effective way to achieve that state of affairs is for such designs to be excluded by a subject matter limitation, not for courts to seek to manipulate other rules to bring protection within reasonable bounds. If we were to suggest any reform to the CDPA, it would be to re-instate the schema that was set up in 1988, for instance, by reviewing the decision to repeal section 52.

[126] See, especially, *Pelham GmbH v Hütter*, Case C-476/17, at [71] (ECDR 26, July 29, 2019).

7.4 Conclusion

We wish to conclude our chapter with some brief remarks on post-Brexit lawmaking in the United Kingdom. The analysis presented in this chapter is far from uplifting. Designs law in the United Kingdom is in need of reform and fashion designers are one community that might benefit from a root-and-branch review of the current legislative framework (at least if one accepts the two premises set out in the introduction). However, as with much IP policymaking, we fear that positive reform is a distant prospect. The process of withdrawing from the EU saw the UK agree to limit its policy freedom, such that radical reform is no longer on the cards – but at the same time, Brexit has produced genuine friction and difficulties for creative communities. There is scope for good faith disagreement about the relative importance of policy freedom versus frictionless trade, but in the IP field at least, this trade-off has proven to be largely illusory. The terms on which the UK left the EU are such that the space for meaningful reform is limited, but the costs of the exclusion from EU-wide arrangements are real.

The irony is that in the design field, the costs of divergence are likely to provide a further reason for pushing designers towards reliance on copyright. This creates a conundrum for judges, who will have to decide whether to diverge from CJEU case law on copyright subsistence. Considered in isolation, divergence might seem an attractive option as the CJEU has taken EU copyright law in a strange and difficult to justify direction. At the same time, it is hard to imagine that a judge would not be conscious of the fact that the UK's relationship with the EU remains far from settled and that divergence now would be undesirable as long as closer trade relations remains a real possibility.

PART III

Current Trends

8

Fashion Upcycling and Trademark Infringement

A Circular Economy/Freedom of the Arts Approach

MARTIN SENFTLEBEN

ABSTRACT

Fashion upcycling offers unprecedented opportunities for the sustainable reuse of clothing: using second-hand garments as raw materials for new creations, upcyclers can transform used pieces of clothing into new fashion products that may become even more sought-after than the source material. Considering the overarching policy objective to ensure a circular economy, the use of trademark-protected fashion elements for upcycling purpose can be qualified as a particularly important form of artistic expression. The reference to products of the original trademark owner is made for the socially valuable purpose of providing a vision of better, more sustainable production and consumption practices.

8.1 Introduction

Fashion upcycling offers unprecedented opportunities for the sustainable reuse of clothing: using second-hand garments as raw materials for new creations, individuals and businesses can transform used pieces of clothing into new fashion products that may become even more sought-after than the source material.[1] The Merriam-Webster Dictionary defines 'upcycling' as the act of 'recycl[ing] (something) in such a way that the resulting product is of a higher value than the original

[1] For a detailed description of different upcycling practices, see J B Schenerman, 'One Consumer's Trash Is Another's Treasure: Upcycling's Place in Trademark Law' (2020) 38 *Cardozo Arts and Entertainment Law Journal* 745, 755–762 (hereafter Schenerman, 'Upcycling's Place'). Cf N Q Dorenbosch, 'Upcycling – op het snijvlak van duurzaamheid en intellectuele eigendom' (2022) *Intellectuele eigendom en reclamerecht* 147 (hereafter Dorenbosch, 'Upcycling'); Andie Bain, '"Dank" Customs, Bootlegs, and Reworked Pieces' (2020) 23 *Journal of World Intellectual Property* 375, 383–384 (hereafter Bain, 'Customs').

item: to create an object of greater value from (a discarded object of lesser value)'.[2] Wikipedia describes upcycling as 'the process of transforming by-products, materials, useless, or unwanted products into new materials or products perceived to be of greater quality, such as artistic value or environmental value'.[3] Obviously, the transformation of pre-existing source materials, such as second-hand clothing in the case of fashion upcycling, lies at the core of upcycling initiatives.

The productive reuse of garment components in upcycling projects is socially desirable in the light of the overarching policy goal to achieve environmental sustainability. With rapid product cycles – new collections each season, at least eight seasons for menswear and womenswear luxury brand designers each year – the fashion industry produces a highly problematic fashion garbage heap every year.[4] Fashion upcycling that adds new value to worn pieces of clothing can contribute to the reduction of fashion waste.[5]

The more individual fashion elements and garment components enjoy trademark protection, however, the more legal obstacles arise. Upcycling may trigger allegations of consumer confusion and unfair freeriding when fashion elements bearing third-party brand insignia become elements of the upcycled product. Once it is assumed that the display of third-party trademarks on upcycled products constitutes an actionable form of use in the sense of trademark law, the exhaustion of trademark rights after the first sale does not necessarily offer a solution because the change and rearrangement of branded garment components may render the first

2 See 'Upcycle', *Merriam Webster* <https://www.merriam-webster.com/dictionary/upcycle>. Cf Dorenbosch, 'Upcycling', above n 1, 147; Martin Senftleben (2022), 'Robustness Check: Evaluating and Strengthening Artistic Use Defences in EU Trademark Law' (2022) 53 *International Review of Intellectual Property and Competition Law* 567, 572 (hereafter Senftleben, 'Robustness'); Bain, 'Customs', above n 1, 383; A M Keats, 'Trendy Product Upcycling: Permissible Recycling or Impermissible Commercial Hitchhiking?' (2020) 110 *The Trademark Reporter* 712 (hereafter Keats, 'Trendy Product'); Elisha Teibel, 'Waste Size: The Skinny on the Environmental Costs of the Fashion Industry' (2019) 43 *William and Mary Environmental Law and Policy Review* 595, 624–625 (hereafter Teibel, 'Waste Size').

3 See 'Upcycling', Wikipedia <https://nl.wikipedia.org/wiki/Upcycling>.

4 Ashly Riches, 'The Fashion Industry Is Not as "Green" as It Would Like You to Believe' (2022) 33 *Duke Environmental Law and Policy Forum* 83, 84–86; Ariele Elia, 'Fashion's Destruction of Unsold Goods: Responsible Solutions for an Environmentally Conscious Future' (2020) 30 *Fordham Intellectual Property, Media & Entertainment Law Journal* 539, 541–551 (hereafter Elia, 'Fashion's Destruction'); Teibel, 'Waste Size', above n 2, 597–598.

5 Elia, 'Fashion's Destruction', above n 4, 576–577. See also the examples given by Schenerman, 'Upcycling's Place', above n 1, 755–762.

sale doctrine inapplicable and give the trademark proprietor ammunition to oppose the resale (Part II). Therefore, the question arises whether other defences are available in trademark law to escape the verdict of infringement. In the EU, the referential use defence seems capable of offering a robust basis for upcycling (Part III). To fully develop this defence, however, it is important to go beyond circular economy arguments and include lines of reasoning that consider the particular importance of the message that is conveyed with the sale of upcycled products: the urgent need for a change of production and consumption patterns (Part IV). Despite the societal value of this statement, labelling guidelines are necessary to ensure compliance with the overarching requirement of honest practices in industrial or commercial matters (Part V). By attaching their own logos to upcycled products and clearly displaying these logos in shops, upcyclers can ensure sufficient clarity about the commercial source of their products and successfully rebut allegations of misleading behaviour and misappropriation (Part VI).

8.2 Use as a Mark and Exhaustion

Trademark law offers several starting points for trademark infringement actions against the use of trademarked garment elements in fashion upcycling projects. In the EU, general gatekeeper criteria set forth in the Trade Mark Regulation (EUTMR)[6] and the Trade Mark Directive (TMD)[7] – requiring use 'in the course of trade' and 'in relation to goods or services'[8] – may fail to prevent trademark owners from establishing *prima facie* infringement. As the Court of Justice of the European Union (CJEU) applies these general infringement criteria flexibly, they are incapable of providing a reliable shield against allegations of trademark infringement. According to CJEU jurisprudence, the

[6] Regulation (EU) 2017/1001 of the European Parliament and of the Council of June 14, 2017, on the European Union Trade Mark (codification) [2017] OJL 154/1.

[7] Directive (EU) 2015/2436 of the European Parliament and of the Council of December 16, 2015, to approximate the laws of the Member States relating to trade marks [2015] OJL 336/1.

[8] Regulation (EU) 2017/1001 of the European Parliament and of the Council of June 14, 2017, on the European Union Trade Mark (codification) [2017] OJL 154/1 art 9(2); Directive (EU) 2015/2436 of the European Parliament and of the Council of 16 December 2015 to approximate the laws of the Member States relating to trade marks [2015] OJL 336/1 art 10(2).

requirement of use 'in the course of trade'[9] implies that unauthorised use is only actionable where it occurs 'in the context of commercial activity with a view to economic advantage and not as a private matter'.[10] This formula confines EU trademark rights to use that takes place in a commercial context. The use of a trademark for the purposes of private study, political debate, teaching or academic research is unlikely to constitute use in the course of trade as long as it does not occur against a commercial background.[11] If use for upcycling purposes does not enter the commercial sphere, the requirement of use in the course of trade can serve as an effective gatekeeper that blocks access to trademark protection from the outset.[12] However, use of a trademark in an upcycling context will be qualified as use in trade the moment it is combined with a commercial activity.[13] When upcycled fashion products are placed on the market, the assumption of use in the course of trade will be inescapable.[14]

[9] Regulation (EU) 2017/1001 of the European Parliament and of the Council of June 14, 2017, on the European Union Trade Mark (codification) [2017] OJL 154/1 art 9(2); Directive (EU) 2015/2436 of the European Parliament and of the Council of December 16, 2015, to approximate the laws of the Member States relating to trade marks [2015] OJL 336/1 art 10(2).

[10] *Google France SARL, Google Inc v Louis Vuitton Malletier SA*, Cases C-236/08 to 238/08, ECLI:EU:C:2010:159, at [50] (CJEU, March 23, 2010); *Arsenal Football Club plc v Matthew Reed*, Case C-206/01, ECLI:EU:C:2002:651, at [40] (CJEU, November 12, 2002).

[11] Annette Kur and Martin Senftleben, *European Trade Mark Law – A Commentary* (Oxford University Press, 2017) para 5.24–5.25 (hereafter Kur and Senftleben, *European Trade Mark Law*).

[12] Łukasz Żelechowski, 'Invoking Freedom of Expression and Freedom of Competition in Trade Mark Infringement Disputes: Legal Mechanisms for Striking a Balance' (2018) 19 *European Research Area Forum* 115, 118–119 (hereafter Żelechowski, 'Invoking Freedom of Expression').

[13] See case law on trademark reuse in parody scenarios, such as *Lila Postkarte*, Case I ZR 159/02, 583 (German Federal Court of Justice, February 3, 2005); *Greenpeace v Esso*, Case 06-10961 (French Supreme Court, April 8, 2008); *Greenpeace France and Greenpeace New-Zealand v Areva*, Case 07-11251 (French Supreme Court, April 8, 2008). For commentary, see Żelechowski, 'Invoking Freedom of Expression', above n 12, 119–120; Kur and Senftleben, *European Trade Mark Law*, above n 11, para 6.59–6.70; Sabine Jacques, 'A Parody Exception : Why Trade Mark Owners Should Get the Joke' (2016) 38 *European Intellectual Property Review* 471, 471–472 and 479; Christophe Geiger, 'Trade Marks and Freedom of Expression – the Proportionality of Criticism' (2007) 38 *International Review of Intellectual Property and Competition Law* 317 (hereafter Geiger, 'Proportionality of Criticism').

[14] Cf Katya Assaf, 'The Dilution of Culture and the Law of Trademarks' (2008) 1 *IDEA: The Intellectual Property Law Review* 49, 56, for a similar conclusion based on US trademark law.

This does not mean that the trademark owner will automatically succeed in an infringement lawsuit. In addition to use in the course of trade, EU trademark law also requires use 'in relation to goods or services'.[15] In principle, this further prerequisite for protection could be understood to require 'use as a trademark'. It may be applied to confine the scope of trademark rights to instances where another's trademark is employed as an identifier of commercial source with regard to one's own goods or services.[16] Following this approach, access to trademark protection in fashion upcycling cases could be confined from the outset.[17] The gatekeeper requirement of 'use in relation to goods or services' – understood in the sense of 'use as a trademark' – would serve as a filter to exclude claims that do not concern use for the purpose of identifying the commercial source of upcycled products. Trademark infringement claims would be doomed to fail as long as a fashion designer only makes decorative use of fashion elements bearing third-party brand insignia and refrains from including third-party trademarks as indications of the commercial origin of her own, upcycled products.

Instead of adopting this approach, however, the CJEU opted for a much more flexible application of the gatekeeper criterion of use in relation to goods or services.[18] In *Bayerische Motorenwerke AG (BMW) and BMW Nederland BV v Ronald Karel Deenik*, the Court concluded that use for the purpose of informing the public about repair and maintenance services offered with regard to trademarked products satisfied the criterion of 'use

[15] Regulation (EU) 2017/1001 of the European Parliament and of the Council of June 14, 2017, on the European Union Trade Mark (codification) [2017] OJL 154/1 art 9(2); Directive (EU) 2015/2436 of the European Parliament and of the Council of December 16, 2015, to approximate the laws of the Member States relating to trade marks [2015] OJL 336/1 art 10(2).

[16] *Adam Opel AG v Autec AG*, Case C-48/05, ECLI:EU:C:2007:55, at [24] (CJEU, January 25, 2007), pointed in this direction. The course adopted in this judgment, however, was not followed in further decisions.

[17] Graeme B Dinwoodie and Mark D Janis, 'Confusion Over Use: Contextualism in Trademark Law' (2007) 92 *Iowa Law Review* 1597, 1599–1600; S L Dogan and M Lemley, 'Trademarks and Consumer Search Costs on the Internet' (2004) 41 *Houston Law Review* 777, 809–811.

[18] Cf Angsar Ohly, 'Schutz von Kulturgütern durch das Markenrecht?' in Franz Hacker and Frederik Thiering (eds), *Festschrift für Paul Ströbele zum 75. Geburtstag* (Carl Heymanns, 2019) 335 (hereafter Ohly, 'Schutz'). For an overview of developments in this area, see Annette Kur, 'Confusion over Use? – Die Benutzung "als Marke" im Lichte der EuGH-Rechtsprechung' (2008) 1 *Gewerblicher Rechtsschutz und Urheberrecht – International* 11 (hereafter Kur, 'Confusion').

in relation to goods or services' – even though Deenik had not used the trademark BMW to pass off his second-hand cars and repair services as offers stemming from BMW. In advertising, Deenik had merely referred to BMW as the owner of the car brand that was central to his own activities.[19] The CJEU also qualified use in comparative advertising as use in relation to goods or services on the ground that the advertiser made use of a competitor's trademark to distinguish her own products from those of the competitor.[20]

Summarising the current broad notion of 'use in relation to goods or services', the Court stated that for satisfying this precondition for an infringement action, it was sufficient that a link was established with goods or services. This formula can also be found in the fashion-related decision in *Céline SARL v Céline SA* where the Court held with regard to the interface between trademark and trade name rights that once a link was established between the company, trade or shop name and the goods or services offered by the alleged infringer, trademark use in relation to goods or services could no longer be denied – even where the name was not affixed to marketed goods as such.[21] The formula of a link with goods or services, then, became established case law in later decisions dealing with keyword advertising. In *Google France SARL, Google Inc v Louis Vuitton Malletier SA* the CJEU confirmed that relevant use in relation to goods or services existed 'in any event' where a third party used a conflicting sign in such a way that a link was established between that sign and the goods or services offered by the third party.[22] In *L'Oréal SA v eBay International AG*, the Court found that the criterion of a link was satisfied because eBay's advertisements created 'an obvious association

[19] *Bayerische Motorenwerke AG (BMW) and BMW Nederland BV v Ronald Karel Deenik*, Case C-63/97, ECLI:EU:C:1999:82, at [42] (CJEU, February 23, 1999). For an overview of the development of the trademark use requirement in CJEU jurisprudence, see Kur, 'Confusion', above n 18, 1–11.

[20] *O2 Holdings Limited and O2 (UK) Limited v Hutchison 3G UK Limited*, Case C-533/06, ECLI:EU:C:2008:339, at [35]–[36] (CJEU, June 12, 2008). As to keyword advertising on the basis of services offered by a search engine, use of a competitor's trademark as a keyword for a sponsored link with one's own advertising has been found to constitute trademark use on similar grounds. See *Google France SARL, Google Inc v Louis Vuitton Malletier SA*, Case 236/08 to 238/08, at [71] (CJEU, March 23, 2010).

[21] *Céline SARL v Céline SA*, Case C-17/06, ECLI:EU:C:2007:497, at [23] (CJEU, September 11, 2007).

[22] *Google France SARL, Google Inc. v Louis Vuitton Malletier SA*, Cases C-236/08 to 238/08, ECLI:EU:C:2010:159, at [72] (CJEU, March 23, 2010); *L'Oréal SA v eBay International AG*, Case C-324/09, ECLI:EU:C:2011:474, at [92] (CJEU, July 12, 2011).

between the trade-marked goods which are mentioned in the advertisements and the possibility of buying those goods through eBay'.[23] The CJEU thus adopted a low threshold requirement with regard to the connection with goods or service: a mere 'link' or 'association' is sufficient.[24]

As a result, the gatekeeper criterion of 'use in relation to goods or services' does not prevent a trademark claim against references to the trademark that are only made to identify goods or services as those of the trademark owner and are not perceived by the public as indications of commercial source. The CJEU has brought several forms of referential use – references to the trademark as being the distinctive sign of the trademark owner – within the scope of EU trademark rights.[25] This elastic interpretation can have a deep impact on fashion upcycling. In the absence of a strict requirement of use as a trademark – understood in the sense of use for the purpose of identifying and distinguishing the goods of the fashion upcycler – the threshold criterion of use in relation to goods or services loses its gatekeeper function.[26] The moment a mere link with trademarked fashion elements is sufficient to bring unauthorised use within the scope of trademark rights, the Court erases the boundary line between non-actionable use for upcycling purposes and actionable use as a trademark. A trademark claim can no longer be excluded when upcycled products merely display trademarked fashion elements that have served as raw material (e.g. buttons or parts of dresses bearing the logos of luxury fashion houses), and even when these upcycled products are sold under the prominent mark of the upcycler. In the EU, the mere use of a trademark in some relation to the upcycled product can already serve as a starting point for an infringement claim.[27]

[23] Ibid at [93].

[24] As to the debate on this development, see the summary in Roland Knaak, Annette Kur and Alexander von Mühlendahl (2011), 'Study on the Functioning of the European Trade Mark System', *Max Planck Institute for Intellectual Property & Competition Law Research Paper No. 12–13*, 2011, para 2.178 <http://ec.europa.eu/internal_market/indprop/tm/index_en.htm>.

[25] Cf Ohly, 'Schutz', above n 18, 335; Kur and Senftleben, *European Trade Mark Law*, above n 11, para 5.50–5.54.

[26] Kur and Senftleben, *European Trade Mark Law*, above n 11, para 5.14–5.15 and 5.49–5.56.

[27] Cf Estelle Derclaye and Matthias Leistner, *Intellectual Property Overlaps – A European Perspective* (Hart, 2011) 328; Ilanah Simon Fhima, 'Embellishment: Trademark Use Triumph or Decorative Disaster?' (2006) 28 *European Intellectual Property Review* 321; Kur, 'Confusion', above n 18, 12.

As a result, fashion upcyclers are exposed to confusion and dilution claims that cannot be dismissed as evidently unfounded from the outset. Once the trademark proprietor has surmounted the hurdles of 'use in the course of trade' and 'use in relation to goods or services',[28] she can establish *prima facie* infringement by arguing that the display of brand insignia on upcycled products is confusing because it indicates a commercial connection with the trademark owner.[29] A confusion claim may also be based on post-sale confusion. Even if the true commercial origin is clearly indicated at the point of sale, the trademark owner may argue that confusion may arise once the purchaser leaves the store. The public seeing upcycled goods outside – without a shop environment ensuring clarity about the upcycling – may misinterpret third-party trademarks as indications of commercial source.[30] The trademark proprietor may also argue that use on the upcycled product constitutes unfair freeriding because it exploits the positive image evoked by the third-party brand.[31] In the case of marks with a reputation, this line of argument seems promising. In *L'Oréal SA and Others v Bellure NV and Others*, the CJEU confirmed that, in contrast to blurring and tarnishment, the freeriding branch of the EU dilution doctrine does not require proof of damage[32] – in the sense of providing evidence of a change in the

[28] Regulation (EU) 2017/1001 of the European Parliament and of the Council of June 14, 2017, on the European Union Trade Mark (codification) [2017] OJL 154/1 art 9(2); Directive (EU) 2015/2436 of the European Parliament and of the Council of December 16, 2015, to approximate the laws of the Member States relating to trade marks [2015] OJL 336/1 art 10(2).

[29] *Adidas AG and Adidas Benelux BV v Marca Mode CV and Others*, Case C-102/07, ECLI:EU:C:2008:217, at [30]–[34] (CJEU, April 10, 2008). As to the broad concept of confusion in modern trademark law, cf Anna Tischner and Katarzyna Stasiuk, 'Spare Parts, Repairs, Trade Marks and Consumer Understanding' (2023) 54 *International Review of Intellectual Property and Competition Law* 26, 35–36 (hereafter Tischner and Stasiuk, 'Spare Parts'); Dorenbosch, 'Upcycling', above n 1, 148–149; Keats, 'Trendy Product', above n 2, 713–714 and 718–719; Mark Lemley and Mark McKenna, 'Irrelevant Confusion' (2010) 62 *Stanford Law Review* 413, 414–422.

[30] *Arsenal Football Club plc v Matthew Reed*, Case C-206/01, ECLI:EU:C:2002:651, at [57] (CJEU, November 12, 2002). Cf Dorenbosch, 'Upcycling', above n 1, 148–149; Schenerman, 'Upcycling's Place', above n 1, 766–767 and 778–779; Kur and Senftleben, *European Trade Mark Law*, above n 11, para 5.131–5.146.

[31] *L'Oréal SA and Others v Bellure NV and Others*, Case C-487/07, ECLI:EU:C:2009:378, at [49] (CJEU, June 18, 2009). Cf Tischner and Stasiuk, 'Spare Parts', above n 29, 38–39. As to the additional risk of tarnishing that may arise under specific circumstances, see Keats, 'Trendy Product', above n 2, 719–720.

[32] *L'Oréal SA and Others v Bellure NV and Others*, Case C-487/07, ECLI:EU:C:2009:378, at [47]–[49] (CJEU, June 18, 2009).

economic behaviour of the average consumer.[33] The doors to trademark infringement claims are thus wide open.[34]

To create breathing space for upcycling, it is thus important to explore defences that may immunise upcycling initiatives from allegations of trademark infringement. Considering the specific context in which the use takes place – the reuse of garments that have previously been sold with the consent of the trademark proprietor – the exhaustion of trademark rights after the first sale immediately comes to mind. Article 15(1) TMD and Article 15(1) EUTMR state in this regard that:

> [a] trade mark shall not entitle the proprietor to prohibit its use in relation to goods which have been put on the market in the Union under that trade mark by the proprietor or with the proprietor's consent.[35]

Evidently, it is tempting to jump to the conclusion that the use of second-hand clothes for upcycling purposes does not amount to infringement in the light of this exhaustion rule. The crux, however, lies in the focus on goods 'put on the market ... by the proprietor'. Rightly understood, the exhaustion rule is intended to cover the resale of goods in the specific form in which these goods have been marketed by the trademark owner. Changes can render the exhaustion doctrine inapplicable.[36] More specifically, Article 15(2) TMD and Article 15(2) EUTMR stipulate that the exhaustion of the rights conferred by a trademark shall not occur:

> where there exist legitimate reasons for the proprietor to oppose further commercialisation of the goods, especially where the condition of the goods is changed or impaired after they have been put on the market.[37]

[33] *Intel Corporation Inc v CPM United Kingdom Ltd*, Case C-252/07, ECLI:EU:C:2008:655, at [77] (CJEU, November 27, 2008); *Environmental Manufacturing LLP v Office for Harmonisation in the Internal Market (Trade Marks and Designs) (OHIM) and Société Elmar Wolf*, Case C-383/12, ECLI:EU:C:2013:741, at [37], [43] (CJEU, November 14, 2013).

[34] Martin Senftleben, *The Copyright/Trademark Interface – How the Expansion of Trademark Protection Is Stifling Cultural Creativity* (Wolters Kluwer, 2020) 156–170 (hereafter Senftleben, *The Copyright Trademark Interface*).

[35] Directive (EU) 2015/2436 of the European Parliament and of the Council of December 16, 2015, to approximate the laws of the Member States relating to trade marks [2015] OJL 336/1 art 15(1).

[36] Dorenbosch, 'Upcycling', above n 1, 148.

[37] Directive (EU) 2015/2436 of the European Parliament and of the Council of December 16, 2015, to approximate the laws of the Member States relating to trade marks [2015] OJL 336/1 art 15(2).

This configuration of the exhaustion rule renders the doctrine inapplicable in many upcycling scenarios. As explained above, changes to the goods are inherent in the concept of upcycling. The transformation of pre-existing source materials, such as second-hand clothing in the case of fashion upcycling, lies at the core of upcycling initiatives. As a result, trademark proprietors will often have the opportunity to rebut exhaustion arguments by pointing out that the condition of the goods has been changed or that elements of the original goods have become part of new and different, upcycled goods.[38]

These counterarguments need not always have success. As indicated above, the EU exhaustion rule requires that the trademark proprietor have a 'legitimate reason' for opposing the further commercialisation of the goods after the first sale. Considering the societal interest in a sustainable circular economy, it is conceivable to assume that in upcycling cases, arguments based on the change/transformation of goods must be deemed illegitimate from the outset unless the trademark proprietor manages to substantiate an unusual necessity to oppose the commercialisation of upcycled products containing protected brand insignia. For instance, the trademark proprietor could be obliged to produce evidence of use that deliberately aims at misleading consumers, damaging the mark, denigrating the business of the trademark proprietor etc.[39] This approach could be based on Article 37 of the EU Charter of Fundamental Rights (Charter or CFR) that brings the strong societal interest in environmental protection and sustainable development into focus:

> [a] high level of environmental protection and the improvement of the quality of the environment must be integrated into the policies of the Union and ensured in accordance with the principle of sustainable development.[40]

[38] Dorenbosch, 'Upcycling', above n 1, 148–149; A Kur, '"As Good as New" – Sale of Repaired or Refurbished Goods: Commendable Practice or Trade Mark Infringement?' (2021) 70 *Gewerblicher Rechtsschutz und Urheberrecht - International* 228, 232–233 (hereafter Kur, 'Sale of Repaired Goods'); Keats, 'Trendy Product', above n 2, 715–716. Cf *Gefärbte Jeans*, Case I ZR 210/93, 726 (German Federal Supreme Court, December 14, 1995), stating that the exhaustion rule did not cover the resale of 'stonewashed' second-hand jeans.

[39] Cf *The Gillette Company and Gillette Group Finland Oy v LA-Laboratories Ltd Oy*, Case C-228/03, ECLI:EU:C:2005:177, at [42]–[45] (CJEU, March 17, 2005).

[40] Charter of Fundamental Rights of the European Union [2000] OLJ 364/1 art 37.

Additional support for this approach may follow from the Circular Economy Action Plan[41] which the European Commission adopted in 2020 as a pillar of the European Green Deal – Europe's agenda for sustainable growth.[42] The Action Plan seeks to make the EU economy fit for a green future, strengthen its competitiveness whilst protecting the environment, and give new rights to consumers. An important element of the Action Plan is the objective to establish a legal framework that makes product policies more sustainable, in particular by enhancing the sustainability and repairability of goods in the European market. Evidently, legal solutions that shield upcycling initiatives from allegations of trademark infringement are compliant with these goals.[43]

Nonetheless, doubts about the robustness of this solution remain. Even if particular importance is attached to the objective to protect the environment and support sustainable development, it must not be overlooked that the protection of intellectual property also enjoys protection under the Charter. Article 17(2) CFR explicitly offers protection for intellectual property rights under the umbrella of the right to property.[44] The environmental protection clause in Article 37 CFR, thus, does not constitute a carte blanche for overriding trademark rules. By contrast, it follows from Article 52(1) CFR that limitations of the trademark proprietor's right to property are subject to the principle of proportionality. While Article 37 CFR shows clearly that environmental protection constitutes an objective of general interest in the EU, this interest must be weighed against the trademark proprietor's interest in trademark protection and

[41] European Commission, Communication, 'A New Circular Economy Action Plan for a Cleaner and More Competitive Europe', *COM* (March 11, 2020)98 (hereafter European Commission, 'Circular Economy').

[42] European Commission, Communication, 'The European Green Deal', *COM* (December 11, 2019) 640.

[43] European Commission, 'Circular Economy', above n 41, 7–9. Cf Tischner and Stasiuk, 'Spare Parts', above n 29, 28; Charlotte Vrendenbarg, 'IE en de circulaire economie: Stimulans of obstakel?' (2023) *Nederlands Juristenblad* 971, 971–972 (hereafter Vrendenbard, 'IE').

[44] For a more detailed discussion of this provision, see D J W Jongsma, *Creating EU Copyright Law – Striking a Fair Balance* (Hanken School of Economics, 2019) 163–168; J Griffiths and L McDonagh, 'Fundamental Rights and European IP Law – the Case of Art 17(2) of the EU Charter' in C Geiger (ed), *Constructing European Intellectual Property Achievements and New Perspectives* (Edward Elgar, 2013) 75; C Geiger, 'Intellectual Property Shall Be Protected!? Article 17(2) of the Charter of Fundamental Rights of the European Union: A Mysterious Provision with an Unclear Scope' (2009) 31 *European Intellectual Property Review* 113.

the broader societal interest in a well-functioning trademark system.[45] According to the above-described rules of EU trademark law, a change of the condition of branded goods is a standard scenario in which the trademark proprietor has the opportunity to oppose the resale of goods on the basis of the exhaustion doctrine. While the societal goal of environmental protection and sustainable development supports the position of fashion upcyclers in trademark infringement procedures, it is unclear whether this overarching objective, which has found its way into Article 37 of the Charter, will allow upcyclers to prevail routinely in infringement cases.[46] Therefore, it is important to look beyond the exhaustion rule and assess the potential of other defences to provide stronger support for upcycling initiatives.

8.3 Referential Use Defence

As the foregoing analysis has shown, general gatekeeper criteria in EU trademark law – use ;in the course of trade; and ;in relation to goods or services'[47] – are incapable of immunising fashion upcycling projects effectively against allegations of trademark infringement. In addition, trademark proprietors may have success in demonstrating prima facie infringement by relying on broad concepts of confusion and dilution that include confusion about an economic connection with the trademark owner and protection against unfair freeriding. The doctrine of exhaustion can offer only limited support for fashion upcycling. To arrive at a robust solution, however, it would be necessary to declare trademark owner arguments against the further commercialisation of trademarked fashion elements *a priori* illegitimate after the first sale. As upcycled products, by definition, present trademarked fashion elements in an altered and transformed way, the success of this strategy is unclear. Article 15(2) TMD and Article 15(2) EUTMR explicitly afford trademark proprietors the opportunity to oppose the further commercialisation of trademarked goods if their condition has been changed.

[45] For an overview of the rationales of trademark protection, see Kur and Senftleben, *European Trade Mark Law*, above n 11, para 1.06–1.15.

[46] Bain, 'Customs', above n 1, 402–403.

[47] Regulation (EU) 2017/1001 of the European Parliament and of the Council of June 14, 2017, on the European Union Trade Mark (codification) [2017] OJL 154/1 art 9(2); Directive (EU) 2015/2436 of the European Parliament and of the Council of December 16, 2015, to approximate the laws of the Member States relating to trade marks [2015] OJL 336/1 art 10(2).

Luckily, EU trademark law contains additional limitations of exclusive rights that may support fashion upcycling projects. The referential use defence and the descriptive use defence are of particular relevance. In line with Article 17 TRIPS which explicitly refers to 'fair use of descriptive terms', Article 14(1)(b) TMD and Article 14(1)(b) EUTMR permit the unauthorised use of:

> signs or indications which are not distinctive or which concern the kind, quality, quantity, intended purpose, value, geographical origin, the time of production of goods or of rendering of the service, or other characteristics of goods or services.

Arguably, the inclusion of trademarked fashion elements in upcycled products can constitute permissible *decorative* use. As long as consumers do not perceive the third-party trademark as an indication of commercial source,[48] the use can be qualified as non-distinctive or descriptive: fashion elements bearing third-party trademarks appear as mere embellishments.

The success of this defence argument, however, is unclear. CJEU jurisprudence indicates that the descriptive use defence is unavailable when a third-party trademark becomes a central element of the very contents of a product. Decorative use of this nature is unlikely to fall within the scope of the descriptive use concept.[49] As the CJEU concluded in *Adidas AG and Adidas Benelux BV v Marca Mode CV and Others*, the purely decorative use of a two-stripe motif on sports clothing 'is not intended to give an indication concerning one of the characteristics of those goods'.[50] Constituting design features, the stripes were not intended to indicate the characteristics of the sports and leisure garments.[51] Similarly, the Court denied descriptive use in *Adam Opel AG v Autec AG* on the ground that the faithful reproduction of the Opel logo on a scale model car could not be regarded as an indication of product characteristics. Instead, the logo became part of the product itself:

[48] *Adidas-Salomon AG and Adidas Benelux BV v Fitnessworld Trading Ltd*, Case C-408/01, ECLI:EU:C:2003:582, at [39]–[41] (CJEU, October 23, 2003); *Adidas AG and Adidas Benelux BV v Marca Mode CV and Others*, Case C-102/07, ECLI:EU:C:2008:217, at [34] (CJEU, April 10, 2008); *Medusa*, Case I ZR 175/09, at [23]–[30] (German Federal Court of Justice, November 24, 2011). Cf Senftleben, *The Copyright Trademark Interface*, above n 34, 158–161.

[49] Kur and Senftleben, *European Trade Mark Law*, above n 11, para 6.23–6.27.

[50] *Adidas AG and Adidas Benelux BV v Marca Mode CV and Others*, Case C-102/07, ECLI: EU:C:2008:217, at [48] (CJEU, April 10, 2008).

[51] Ibid.

> However, the affixing of a sign which is identical to a trade mark registered, inter alia, in respect of motor vehicles to scale models of that make of vehicle in order to reproduce those vehicles faithfully is not intended to provide an indication as to a characteristic of those scale models, but is merely an element in the faithful reproduction of the original vehicles.[52]

Quite clearly, this case law may render the descriptive use defence inapplicable in fashion upcycling cases. For example, sewing buttons bearing the Chanel double-C logo onto a distressed denim jacket may be deemed a central element of the product itself, even if the garment clearly bears the logo of a new upcycling designer. According to prevailing CJEU case law, such a use is unlikely to be regarded as a descriptive use.

It is an open question whether the CJEU is willing to give the second branch of Article 14(1)(b) TMD – the non-distinctive use defence – an independent meaning in upcycling cases. The reference to signs or indications 'which are not distinctive' in Article 14(1)(b) TMD is the result of the 2015 trademark law reform. It extends the scope of the traditional descriptive use concept to non-distinctive signs and indications. Theoretically, it is possible to qualify the inclusion of third-party trademarks in upcycled products as a form of non-distinctive use.[53] In this specific context, third-party brand insignia only serve non-distinctive, decorative purposes. They are not intended to indicate the commercial source of the product. The CJEU, however, has not clarified the concept of 'which are not distinctive' yet.[54] In particular, it remains unclear whether a sign or indication that actually enjoys trademark protection could be found non-distinctive in certain contexts, such as the particular circumstances arising from upcycling.

In the light of these legal uncertainties, it is important to explore further defence arguments, in particular the referential use defence. Referential use arguments may provide stronger and more robust support for fashion upcycling. The defence of referential use is laid down in

[52] *Adam Opel AG v Autec AG*, Case C-48/05, ECLI:EU:C:2007:55, at [44] (CJEU, January 25, 2007).

[53] Cf Tischner and Stasiuk, 'Spare Parts', above n 29, 39–40.

[54] For a more detailed discussion of the field of application of this defence, see Senftleben, *The Copyright Trademark Interface*, above n 34, 510–512; Annette Kur, 'Yellow Dictionaries, Red Banking Services, Some Candies, and a Sitting Bunny: Protection of Color and Shape Marks from a German and European Perspective' in Irene Calboli and Martin Senftleben (eds), *The Protection of Non-Traditional Trademarks – Critical Perspectives* (Oxford University Press, 2018) 101 (hereafter Kur, 'Protection of Color').

Article 14(1)(c) TMD and Article 14(1)(c) EUTMR. It defines referential use as use 'for the purpose of identifying or referring to goods or services as those of the proprietor of that trade mark'. For instance, a parody using a trademark to symbolise and criticise the business conduct and policies of the trademark proprietor may fall within the scope of the referential use defence.[55] Prior to the 2015 trademark law reform, EU law only exempted the unauthorised use of trademarks to 'indicate the intended purpose of a product or service'.[56] The law reform broadened the referential use defence substantially. It introduced the more general concept of use for the purpose of identifying and referring to the trademark proprietor's goods or services.[57]

Arguably, the display of trademarked fashion elements on upcycled products can fall within the scope of the referential use defence. To fully develop this line of argument, however, it is necessary to identify the specific message which upcyclers convey when they include third-party trademarks in their creations as decorative references to the original fashion products of brand owners. As the following discussion based on freedom of artistic expression and cultural sciences will show, the statement made with the inclusion of third-party trademarks contributes significantly to the achievement of the societal goal of moving towards a sustainable circular economy.

8.4 Environmental Sustainability and Artistic Expression

As already pointed out, overarching goals of environmental sustainability, including the aim to reduce fashion waste, support freedom of upcyclers to include fashion items even if these items bear third-party trademarks. Article 37 CFR reflects the objective to achieve a high level of environmental protection. Upcycling projects contribute to the realisation of this objective. To cultivate the referential use defence in this

[55] Senftleben, 'Robustness', above n 2, 581–582. For non-infringement arguments based on a parallel between parody cases and upcycling, see Schenerman, 'Upcycling's Place', above n 1, 772–775.

[56] Directive 2008/95/EC of the European Parliament and of the Council of October 22, 2008, to approximate the laws of the Member States relating to trade marks [2008] OJL 299 art 6(1)(c). Cf *The Gillette Company and Gillette Group Finland Oy v LA-Laboratories Ltd Oy*, Case C-228/03, ECLI:EU:C:2005:177, at [49] (CJEU, March 17, 2005).

[57] As to the considerations underlying the broadening of the referential use concept as a result of the trademark law reform, see Kur and Senftleben, *European Trade Mark Law*, above n 11, para 6.39–6.41.

context, however, it is necessary to explain why freedom to refer to the goods of third-party brand owners plays a crucial role. If it can be demonstrated that, by reworking fashion elements bearing third-party trademarks, upcyclers make a statement that has particular societal value, it becomes possible to substantially broaden the arsenal of constitutional arguments that can be invoked to support the application of the referential use defence: not only the general goal of environmental protection (Article 37 CFR) but also freedom of artistic expression (Articles 11 and 13 CFR) militate in favour of employing the referential use defence as a legal tool to exempt upcycling from the control of trademark owners.

In literature, the free expression dimension of upcycling has already been pointed out. As Andie Bain explains, upcycling is not only an act of adding particular value to second-hand garments; it also constitutes an act of communication. The reworked goods 'are reinterpreting the initial communicative act of a trademark'.[58] Therefore, robust defences against allegations of trademark infringement appear desirable not only from the perspective of the goal of environmental protection, but also as a tool to preserve freedom of expression and freedom of the arts.[59] Upcycling goes far beyond a neutral reinterpretation of brand messages. A foray into cultural sciences yields the important insight that the reinterpretation resulting from upcycling has particular societal importance. To explore this societal value, the 'Aeneous Peer Coat' created by the Amsterdam-based artist Duran Lantink – sold for €3.500 (Figure 8.1)[60] – can serve as a reference point:

Evidently, the iconic LV logo – stemming from Louis Vuitton leather bags – is featured on this upcycled fashion product. Lantink's creation

[58] Bain, 'Customs', above n 1, 389. As to the initial communicative act to which Bain refers, it has been demonstrated that luxury fashion brands in particular carry important semiotic connotations. Arguably, their recoding can be classed as acts of communicative expression that merit protection in the light of freedom of expression. See David Tan, 'The Semiotics of Alpha Brands: Encoding/Decoding/Recoding/Transcoding of Louis Vuitton and Implications for Trademark Laws' (2013) 32 *Cardozo Arts & Entertainment Law Journal* 221 (hereafter Tan, 'Semiotics').

[59] Bain, 'Customs', above n 1, 406. As to the independent role of the guarantee of freedom of the arts in intellectual property cases, see *Pelham GmbH and Others v Ralf Hütter and Florian Schneider-Esleben*, Case C-476/17, ECLI:EU:C:2019:624, at [29]–[35] (CJEU, July 29, 2019). Cf C Geiger and E Izyumenko, 'The Constitutionalization of Intellectual Property Law in the EU and the Funke Medien, Pelham and Spiegel Online Decisions of the CJEU: Progress, but Still Some Way to Go!' (2020) 51 *International Review of Intellectual Property and Competition Law* 282, 293–294.

[60] See the information provided at 'Coats', *Duran Lantink* <https://duranlantink.com/ssaw21>.

Figure 8.1 Upcycled coat by Duran Lantink
Credit: Duran Lantink

offers a suitable point of reference because it constitutes not only upcycled fashion but also a work of upcycling art. Its artistic nature opens the gates to aesthetic theory. It raises the question which role art – and freedom of artistic expression – can play in society.

In his aesthetic theory, Theodor Adorno underlines the societal relevance of art. Against the background of the alienation which the individual faces in a fully rationalised, efficiency-driven world, he warns of the affirmative nature of art. An artwork bringing a conciliatory reflection of enchantment into the disenchanted, empirical reality offers comfort in the rationalised world and supports the unbearable status quo.[61] In the light of the inhumanity of the real world, art would make itself an accomplice of present and coming disasters if it sustained positive visions of society and obscured the defects and poorness of reality.[62] With the prospect of a better world which, as an ultimate truth,[63] shimmers through each genuine artwork,[64] art may falsely pretend that existing societal conditions are acceptable. Therefore, art is constantly at risk of becoming guilty of supporting the inhuman status quo and fortifying present ideologies.[65]

On the other hand, art must not be condemned altogether because artworks are capable of unmasking the negativity of present societal conditions. Showing visions of a better, happier life, art can rouse opposition against the existing reality and contribute to necessary societal changes.[66] Artworks can play a decisive role in society because they generate utopian views of a better life that may become drivers of a change for the better. This role of art defines its social character: art is the 'social antithesis' of society.[67] Given this delicate position in the social fabric of modern societies, there is a fine line to be walked: the artist must relentlessly expose the inhumanity of reality without offering any prospect of reconciliation. In doing so, the artist creates genuine works which, by their very nature, offer shining visions of a better life and a better society in spite of the hopelessness reflected in the artworks

[61] T Adorno, *Ästhetische Theorie* (G Adorno and R Tiedemann, eds) (Suhrkamp, 1970)10, 34.
[62] Ibid 28, 503.
[63] Ibid 128, 196–197.
[64] Ibid 199–200.
[65] Ibid 203.
[66] Ibid 25–26, 56.
[67] Ibid 9–10, 19, 53.

themselves.[68] As an antithesis of real-world disasters, art becomes the messenger of an ideal, utopian world.[69]

According to Adorno, there is thus an inescapable dualism in contemporary artistic productions: the sadness of presenting a happier life as a goal that remains unattainable under present societal conditions.[70] To accomplish this task, art must seek to escape tendencies to undermine and neutralise its critical and irrational impetus, such as the efforts of the cultural industry to commercialise and canonise even the most rebellious and resistant works.[71] Reacting to the growing demand for enchantment in the disenchanted, rationalised reality,[72] the cultural industry offers artworks as consumer goods: abstract objects that function as a *tabula rasa* into which the purchaser can project her own feelings and aspirations.[73] As a result, an artwork becomes an echo and confirmation of the viewer's own hopes and attitudes. It becomes an escape from the unbearable real world.

This, however, leads to the 'disartification' of art. Once art is consumed as an object of pleasure that offers comfort in an inhuman world, its critical impetus – the exposure of shortcomings of reality as an impulse for societal changes – is negated.[74] To escape this threat of disqualification, art must insist on its difference and autonomy by refusing claims for rule obedience and resisting the temptation to fulfil societal expectations. It must preserve its opposition and dissonance by producing works of a non-identical and fragmentary nature that negate the unity of traditional productions, fall outside aesthetical categories and bring chaos in the established order.[75] Distancing itself from reality, the world of art must become a counter universe: the last refuge of humanity in an inhuman world that is disfigured by deal and profit maxims.[76] Remaining alien to the world, true art, by definition, is puzzling and gives rise to conflicting interpretations based on internal tension in the work or its connection to conflicts in society.[77]

[68] Ibid 127, 199.
[69] Ibid 55–56.
[70] Ibid 204–205.
[71] Ibid 32.
[72] Ibid 34.
[73] Ibid 33.
[74] Ibid 27–28, 32–33.
[75] Ibid 41.
[76] Ibid 337–338.
[77] Ibid 197–198.

This aesthetic theory makes it possible to develop arguments in favour of freedom of referential use in upcycling cases. In line with Adorno's analysis, the use of third-party trademarks in upcycling projects constitutes a communicative act protected by the freedom of expression with particular value for society: using fabric fragments and embellishments from worn pieces of clothing or parts of unused bags as source materials for new fashion items, upcyclers create important counterpoints to the glamorous, shining world of fashion that causes waste problems. In fact, it has been reported that many luxury brands, including Louis Vuitton, destroy unsold products every year to prevent discount sales and preserve the aura of exclusivity.[78]

Breaking this vicious circle of lavish overproduction and end-of-season destruction, upcycling projects, such as Duran Lantink's activities, create an aura of luxury and exclusivity without using brand-new, polished product components.[79] Instead, source materials can be old and used. It is the inclusion in an art project that lends upcycled fashion products the status of unique masterpieces. Creating this contrast, works of upcycling art mirror current societal conditions and, at the same time, offer a vision of a better society in the sense of Adorno's theory: the use of worn pieces of clothing – instead of new fabrics – reflects the urgent need for a radical change of production and consumption patterns. Upcycling artworks reflect the policy goal of environmental sustainability that has been confirmed in Article 37 CFR. At the same time, they attest to the necessity of limitations of trademark rights that offer breathing space for freedom of expression. For upcycling artists to develop their alternative vision of fashion production and consumption, they must be free to transform worn garment components into new fashion items and offer these new fashion items in the marketplace. Only in this way can they show that there is no need to use – and waste – new raw materials. Creations made from used clothes are equally capable of satisfying the appetite for iconic fashion.

Arguably, this message is particularly clear and strong when fashion upcycling involves the use of trademarked pieces of clothing.

[78] S Kaur, 'Does Louis Vuitton Really Destroy Unsold Bags?', *Luxury Viewer* (December 24, 2020) <https://luxuryviewer.com/does-louis-vuitton-really-destroy-unsold-bags/> (hereafter Kaur, 'LV'). See also Elia, 'Fashion's Destruction', above n 4, 547–548, 557–560, who explains as well that luxury brands cause their own, significant environmental problems by destroying unsold items.

[79] For an analysis of the importance and magnetism of this aura, see Tan, 'Semiotics', above n 58, 225–227.

Trademarked fashion elements allow consumers to recognise and identify the second-hand resources that have served as raw materials for the upcycled fashion product. Strong brands play a central role in this context: the more iconic the source material, the sharper the contrast produced by the upcycling project. An upcycled fashion product with LV leather elements is more surprising and has a deeper impact than the transformation of less prestigious or no-name fashion items. The use of iconic brand insignia indicates clearly that the whole sector must rethink and change its production and marketing strategy. The luxury segment is not exempted from the obligation to contribute to more sustainable modes of production and consumption.[80] Instead of fostering and profiting from wasteful materialism and consumerism, the fashion industry as a whole must find new, more sustainable ways of steering and satisfying consumer demand.

Creating this alternative vision of production and consumption, fashion upcycling with trademarked fashion elements reduces the pressure of consumerism and materialism substantially. This insight can be derived from Peter Bürger's analysis of avant-garde movements of the last century. Bürger refers to the central goal of avant-garde movements to organise a new life practice on the basis of art.[81] The avant-garde artists sought to overcome the isolation of art as a societal institution for the preservation of values that had no place in the modern, rationalised world, such as humanity, happiness, truthfulness and solidarity. Criticising the detachment of art from everyday life, they strove for the integration of art in the societal mainstream to transform the inhuman, rationalised world by providing models for a new, better practice of life.[82]

According to Bürger, these avant-garde movements failed: art has not become a transforming factor changing daily life for the better. Instead, a false integration of art occurred. Due to the efforts of the branding industry, everyday products have become more aesthetical. Consumer goods have become more appealing. This aestheticisation of daily life, however, enhances the pressure of consumerism and materialism.

[80] In fact, the fashion waste problem is not only due to the wasteful use of relatively cheap raw material by fast fashion producers. See Elia, 'Fashion's Destruction', above n 4, 547–548, 557–560; Kaur, 'LV', above n 78.

[81] P Bürger, *Theorie der Avantgarde* (Suhrkamp, 1974)28–29, 67 (hereafter Bürger, *Theorie*).

[82] Ibid 67–68.

It intensifies the subjection of the individual to the dictates of the market. Life does not become more human, truthful, solidary and happier. By contrast, the pressure of the rationalised world is further increased. Instead of helping the individual to emancipate herself from the pressure of consumerism and materialism, aesthetical consumer goods are a driving force and stabilising factor behind the rationalisation of daily life. They encourage mainstream consumption patterns. At the same time, they mask the exertion of pressure in the form of enhanced consumerism and materialism by lending mainstream consumption patterns the air of extravagance.[83]

Bürger's analysis can easily be placed in the context of Adorno's theory about works of art showing visions of a better, happier life that can rouse opposition against the existing reality and contribute to necessary societal changes.[84] Considering the ambition of historical avant-garde movements to change life for the better on the one hand, and the risk of aesthetical consumer goods intensifying and obscuring the inhumanity of the status quo on the other, it becomes possible to draw a distinction between 'true' art capable of fulfilling the societal function of providing a stimulus for societal change, and 'false art' making consumer goods more appealing: art that stabilises the modern, rationalised world and does not provide impulses for societal change.

Applying this matrix to fashion upcycling, it can be said that creations, such as Duran Lantink's works, constitute true artworks that deliver on the promise of historical avant-garde movements to impact daily life and change it for the better. Employing LV leather bags as raw material, fashion upcycling reverses the false integration of art that Bürger denounces. Duran Lantink's work does not enhance the pressure of consumerism and materialism. It refrains from adding a false, aesthetic gloss to daily life and concealing the need for reforms. Instead, it employs the gloss of iconic fashion products – exponents of the false integration of art that only makes consumer goods more appealing and amplifies the trend towards wasteful consumerism – to mirror the false, pressure-enhancing aestheticisation of daily life. In this way, fashion upcycling reveals the risk of harmful production and consumption patterns.[85]

[83] Ibid 72–73. As to the magnetism and importance of brand culture, see Tan, 'Semiotics', above n 58, 225–227.

[84] Ibid 60–63, 81–85.

[85] For a detailed description of these risks and the need for a change of production and consumption patterns, see Teibel, 'Waste Size', above n 2, 601–616.

It does not distract from the environmental crisis. By contrast, it points directly at it.

8.5 Honest Upcycling Practices

Considering these lessons from cultural sciences, it becomes apparent that strong free expression objectives undergird fashion upcycling.[86] In the quest for environmental sustainability, upcycling projects in the fashion sector provide important alternative visions of production and consumption patterns. With the creation and sale of upcycled fashion products bearing third-party trademarks – and even iconic third-party brand insignia that constitute well-known marks[87] – upcyclers make a critical statement on the wasteful use of resources in the fashion industry.

To allow upcyclers to create this counterpoint to the fashion waste machinery, it is necessary to develop robust defences: defence arguments that are capable of immunising the unauthorised use of third-party trademarks in upcycling projects from trademark infringement claims. The referential use defence laid down in Article 14(1)(c) EUTMR and Article 14(1)(c) TMD can fulfil this function. As explained, the use of trademarked fashion elements plays an essential role. It makes the use of second-hand source material visible to consumers and enables them to understand the upcycled fashion product as an exponent of an alternative, different approach: as a harbinger of an indispensable change of course. The message emanating from upcycled fashion products carries particular weight in the current environmental crisis. It reflects the need for strategies to reduce fashion waste and paves the way for a fundamental change of production and consumption patterns. Rightly understood, the use of third-party trademarks in upcycling projects, thus, is a legitimate form of referring to the original branded fashion items as goods stemming from the trademark owner. It is a specific form of referential use that is legitimate and particularly important in the light of the overarching goal of environmental protection (Article 37 CFR) and the

[86] Cf Schenerman, 'Upcycling's Place', above n 1, 772–775.

[87] *Paris Convention for the Protection of Industrial Property*, WIPO TRT/PARIS/001 (September 28, 1979) art 6bis; Marrakesh Agreement Establishing the World Trade Organization, opened for signature April 15, 1994, 1869 UNTS 299, 33 ILM 1197 (signed April 15, 1994) art 16(2), 16(3). Cf Martin Senftleben, 'The Trademark Tower of Babel – Dilution Concepts in International, US and EC Trademark Law' (2009) 40 *International Review of Intellectual Property and Competition Law* 45, 50–77.

need to protect the fundamental right to freedom of artistic expression (Articles 11 and 13 CFR).

Moreover, fashion upcycling projects allow the societal subsystem of artistic production to emancipate itself from the false integration of art in the fashion industry. Instead of developing aesthetic design to lull the public and distract from the need for reforms, upcycling projects use the gloss of iconic fashion to shake up consumers. With the sharp contrast arising from second-hand use of iconic fashion items, upcycling art points directly to the urgent need for profound change in the light of the environmental crisis. Within the upcycling habitat, individual artistic creations, such as the pieces designed by Duran Lantink, can provide important *haute couture* prototypes for broader upcycling projects. Individual masterpieces offer key impetus and central reference points for broader initiatives leading to the productive reuse of second-hand fashion items on a larger scale.

Therefore, both – the overarching societal objective to attain environmental sustainability and the fashion designer's individual freedom of artistic expression – must be factored into the equation when exposing upcycled fashion products to a trademark infringement analysis. The fact that third-party brand insignia remain visible must not automatically tip the scales against the upcycling project. Both constitutional arguments – environmental protection and freedom of artistic expression[88] – strongly support an interpretation of defences that enables upcyclers to rebut infringement arguments. Both constitutional arguments support the transformation of the referential use defence into a robust bulwark against allegations of trademark infringement. Rightly understood, fashion upcycling constitutes a legitimate form of use for the purpose of identifying and referring to reworked fashion products as those of the trademark proprietor. As a socially desirable and particularly important form of referential use, it falls within the scope of Article 14(1)(c) TMD and Article 14(1)(c) EUTMR.

However, the invocation of limitations of exclusive rights in EU trademark law, such as the exemption of referential use, depends on compliance with honest practices in industrial or commercial matters. This additional, open-ended prerequisite follows from Article 14(2) TMD and Article 14(2) EUTMR. Before jumping to the conclusion that EU trademark law offers sufficiently strong defence arguments for fashion upcycling, it is thus necessary to explore the proviso that the referential use defence 'shall only

[88] Charter of Fundamental Rights of the European Union [2000] OLJ 364/1 art 11, 13, 37.

apply where the use made by the third party is in accordance with honest practices in industrial or commercial matters'.[89]

Unfortunately, this overarching requirement of honest practices can pose substantial difficulties. The CJEU tends to determine compliance with honesty in industrial and commercial matters on the basis of the same criteria that inform the analysis of *prima facie* infringement in trademark confusion and dilution cases.[90] This jurisprudence has led to concerns that the inquiry into honest commercial practices may ignore competing societal values, such as the attainment of environmental sustainability and freedom of artistic expression.[91] Instead of shaping the honest practices test in a way that offers room for competing policy objectives, the CJEU may simply focus on the values underlying trademark protection[92] and replicate standard criteria of the trademark infringement analysis. In *The Gillette Company and Gillette Group Finland Oy v LA-Laboratories Ltd Oy*, for instance, the Court held that use would fail to comply with honest practices in industrial and commercial matters if:

- it is done in such a manner as to give the impression that there is a commercial connection between the third party and the trade mark owner;

[89] Regulation (EU) 2017/1001 of the European Parliament and of the Council of June 14, 2017, on the European Union Trade Mark (codification) [2017] OJL 154/1 art 14(2); Directive (EU) 2015/2436 of the European Parliament and of the Council of December 16, 2015, to approximate the laws of the Member States relating to trade marks [2015] OJL 336/1 art 14(2).

[90] *Portakabin Ltd and Portakabin BV v Primakabin BV*, Case C-558/08, ECLI:EU:C:2010:416, at [69] (CJEU, July 8, 2010); *The Gillette Company and Gillette Group Finland Oy v LA-Laboratories Ltd Oy*, Case C-228/03, ECLI:EU:C:2005:177, at [49] (CJEU, March 17, 2005). Cf Kur and Senftleben, *European Trade Mark Law*, above n 11, para 6.73; Martin Senftleben, Lionel Bently and Graeme B Dinwoodie et al, 'The Recommendation on Measures to Safeguard Freedom of Expression and Undistorted Competition: Guiding Principles for the Further Development of EU Trade Mark Law' (2015) 37 *European Intellectual Property Review* 337, 339 (hereafter Senftleben, Bently and Dinwoodie, 'Recommendation'); Martin Senftleben, 'Adapting EU Trademark Law to New Technologies - Back to Basics?' in C Geiger (ed), *Constructing European Intellectual Property* (Edward Elgar, 2013) 168–169 (hereafter Senftleben, 'Back to Basics'); Ilanah Simon Fhima and Robin Jacob, 'Unfair Advantage Law in the European Union' in Daniel Bereskin (ed), *International Trademark Dilution* (Thomson Reuters Westlaw, 2014) 274; Ilanah Simon Fhima, 'The Role of Legitimacy in Trade Mark Law' (2012) 65 *Current Legal Problems* 489, 501–502.

[91] Senftleben, 'Robustness', above n 2, 588–590.

[92] Cf Kur and Senftleben, *European Trade Mark Law*, above n 11, para 1.06–1.15.

- it affects the value of the trade mark by taking unfair advantage of its distinctive character or repute;
- it entails the discrediting or denigration of that mark;
- or where the third party presents its product as an imitation or replica of the product bearing the trade mark of which it is not the owner.[93]

While some of these assessment factors can be traced back to EU legislation in the field of comparative advertising,[94] the prohibition of use that gives the impression of a commercial connection with the trademark owner, and the ban on use that damages or takes unfair advantage of the mark's distinctive character or repute, correspond to infringement criteria in the field of trademark protection against confusion and dilution.[95] The risk of circularity is obvious: by copying almost literally the criteria for establishing *prima facie* infringement, the CJEU subjects defences to additional scrutiny in the light of the same criteria that enabled the trademark owner to bring the infringement claim in the first place. This circular line of reasoning may render defence arguments, such as referential use, moot in practice.[96] In the keyword advertising case *Portakabin Ltd and Portakabin BV v Primakabin BV*, for instance, the Court did not find it contradictory to conclude that:

> the circumstances under which a trade mark proprietor is, pursuant to Article 5(1) of Directive 89/104 [nowadays Article 10(2)(a) TMD], entitled to prevent an advertiser from using a sign identical with, or similar to, that trade mark as a keyword may [. . .] easily correspond to a situation in which the advertiser cannot claim that it is acting in accordance with honest practices in industrial or commercial matters, and cannot therefore validly rely on the exception. . .[97] (comment within brackets added)

[93] *The Gillette Company and Gillette Group Finland Oy v LA-Laboratories Ltd Oy*, Case C-228/03, ECLI:EU:C:2005:177, at [49] (CJEU, March 17, 2005).

[94] Directive 2006/114/EC of the European Parliament and of the Council of December 12, 2006, Concerning Misleading and Comparative Advertising [2006] OJL 376/21 art 4(d), (f), (g), (h). Cf Kur and Senftleben, *European Trade Mark Law*, above n 11, para 6.72.

[95] Regulation (EU) 2017/1001 of the European Parliament and of the Council of June 14, 2017, on the European Union Trade Mark (codification) [2017] OJL 154/1 art 9(2)(b), (c); Directive (EU) 2015/2436 of the European Parliament and of the Council of December 16, 2015, to approximate the laws of the Member States relating to trade marks [2015] OJL 336/1 art 10(2)(b), (c).

[96] Cf Kur and Senftleben, *European Trade Mark Law*, above n 11, para 6.73, and the further references, above n 90.

[97] *Portakabin Ltd and Portakabin BV v Primakabin BV*, Case C-558/08, ECLI:EU:C:2010:416, at [69] (CJEU, July 8, 2010).

The corrosive effect of this circular approach on defence arguments that could support fashion upcycling is evident. Following the current CJEU approach, the same findings that have led to the verdict of *prima facie* infringement, support the denial of compliance with honest practices. In consequence, the requirement of use in accordance with honest practices in industrial or commercial matters degenerates into a torpedo which the trademark proprietor can employ to neutralise referential use arguments that support the activities of fashion upcyclers. The symmetry of criteria for assessing *prima facie* infringement and determining honesty in industrial and commercial matters can easily lead to a situation where a finding of a likelihood of confusion or unfair freeriding already foreshadows a finding of dishonest practices.

Hence, the question arises whether, despite the described CJEU jurisprudence, it is possible to alleviate the problems arising from a circular approach to the test of honest practices. A first signpost for potential solutions came to light during the debate on the amendment of EU trademark law. Seeking to provide guidance for the 2015 law reform, the 'Recommendation on Measures to Safeguard Freedom of Expression and Undistorted Competition in EU Trade Mark Law'[98] proposed to solve the problem of circularity in the honest practices jurisprudence as follows:

> The only way to make sense of the wording would be to clarify that although the basic concepts (likelihood of confusion, abuse of reputation) informing the evaluation of honest business practices are the same as those governing infringement, their application is different in that the leeway for using a basically conflicting mark is much broader where applications or limitations apply, thereby confining the proprietor's right to oppose such use to cases of disproportionate harm.[99]

The argument, thus, runs as follows: even if the assessment of honesty in industrial and commercial matters rests on the same criteria that have previously been used to establish *prima facie* infringement, the outcome can still be different when the criteria are applied in a more flexible way.[100] The required flexibility can be derived from the values underlying

[98] Senftleben, Bently and Dinwoodie, 'Recommendation', above n 90, 341–343. Cf Kur, 'Protection of Color', above n 54, 105; Kur and Senftleben, *European Trade Mark Law*, above n 11, para 6.74.

[99] Senftleben, Bently and Dinwoodie, 'Recommendation', above n 90, 339.

[100] Kur, 'Protection of Color', above n 54, 105. Cf Kur and Senftleben, *European Trade Mark Law*, above n 11, para 6.74; Vincenzo Di Cataldo, 'The Trade Mark with a

the defences in EU trademark law, such as freedom of referring to trademarked fashion elements for the purposes of environmental protection and freedom of artistic expression in cases where fashion upcyclers invoke the referential use defence. Weighing the interests of the trademark owner[101] against the interests of the upcycler and the societal interest in a change of production and consumption patterns in the fashion industry, trademark judges can attach particular importance to the values that support the application of the referential use defence and avoid the verdict of infringement in this way. In the balancing process, the principle of proportionality plays a central role.[102] The scope of the trademark owner's exclusive rights should be confined to cases of disproportionate harm.

Operationalising this approach, one can consider a proposal by Annette Kur in the discussion about the marketing of repaired and refurbished products. She argues for a 'context-sensitive evaluation of infringement'[103] that devotes sufficient attention to the behaviour of the alleged infringer[104] and, in particular, to information surrounding the allegedly infringing product, including labelling that clearly indicates the changed status of the product and the person that has carried out the repair or refurbishment:

> This means that inter alia account must be taken of accompanying information given by the reseller, as well as of overarching aspects such as the societal goal of preserving resources and reducing waste. It is true that by factoring the reseller's motivation as well as his readiness to provide neutral background information into the assessment of trade mark infringement, the evaluation gradually shifts from a pure trade mark law analysis towards an unfair competition-informed approach. However, that phenomenon is neither new nor unusual.[105]

Reputation in EU Law – Some Remarks on the Negative Condition "Without Due Cause"' (2011) 42 *International Review of Intellectual Property and Competition Law* 833, 837 (hereafter Cataldo, 'Negative Condition').

101 Charter of Fundamental Rights of the European Union [2000] OLJ 364/1 art 17(2).

102 Ibid at art 52(1).

103 Kur, 'Sale of Repaired Goods', above n 38, 235–236.

104 For a further plea for a stronger focus on the concrete behaviour of the alleged infringer, see Lotte Anemaet (2021), 'Which Honesty Test for Trademark Law? Why Traders' Efforts to Avoid Trademark Harm Should Matter When Assessing Honest Business Practices' (2021) 70 *Gewerblicher Rechtsschutz und Urheberrecht – International* 1025, 1037–1038 (hereafter Anemaet, 'Honesty').

105 Kur, 'Sale of Repaired Goods', above n 38, 236.

For the development of appropriate labelling rules in upcycling cases, the CJEU decision in *Viking Gas A/S v Kosan Gas A/S* can serve as a reference point.[106] The case concerned composite gas bottles which were intended for reuse a number of times. Against this background, the Court was satisfied that the bottles did not constitute mere packaging, but had an independent economic value which made them goods in themselves. Purchasers would be prevented from fully enjoying this property if the trademark proprietor could restrict their rights even after the first sale with her consent.[107] For this reason, the Court held that the sale of a composite bottle exhausted trademark rights and transferred to the purchaser the right to use that bottle freely, including the right to exchange it, or have it refilled, by an undertaking of his choice, including competitors of the trademark proprietor. As a corollary of this right of purchasers, competitors had the right to refill and exchange empty bottles – as long as they kept their activities within the limits of the honest practices proviso following from Article 14(2) TMD.[108]

Arriving at this conclusion, the CJEU had the opportunity to formulate guidelines for meeting the honest practices test in refill cases. As a general rule, the Court emphasised the obligation to act fairly in the light of the legitimate interests of the trademark proprietor. More concretely, competitors offering refill services had to avoid the erroneous impression of a commercial connection with the trademark proprietor. To assess whether this condition was met, it was necessary to take into account the labelling of the bottles, the circumstances in which they had been exchanged, the practices in the sector concerned, and, in particular, whether consumers were accustomed to empty containers being filled by other dealers.[109] In *Viking Gas*, it had been established that the composite gas bottles at issue bore word and figurative marks made up of the name and logo of the original producer and trademark owner Kosan Gas, and that these marks remained visible when the competitor Viking Gas affixed additional labels indicating that it had refilled the bottles.[110] According to the Court, this additional product labelling

[106] Cf Dorenbosch, 'Upcycling', above n 1, 148–149; Kur, 'Sale of Repaired Goods', above n 38, 235–236.

[107] *Viking Gas A/S v Kosan Gas A/S*, Case C-46/10, ECLI:EU:C:2011:485, at [30]–[33] (CJEU, July 14, 2011).

[108] Ibid at [35].

[109] Ibid at [39]–[40].

[110] Ibid at [11].

constituted a proper means of reducing the risk of an erroneous impression of a commercial connection and escaping the verdict of trademark infringement.[111]

In the more recent decision in *Soda-Club (CO2) SA and SodaStream International BV v MySoda Oy*, the CJEU confirmed these guidelines.[112] In particular, the Court stated again that a finding of non-infringement is possible even if the trademark of the original seller remains visible on the refilled product. As long as additional product labelling ensures clarity about the commercial source of the refilled product in the light of the practices in the sector and consumer awareness, the use can be permitted without prior authorisation of the trademark proprietor.[113]

Applying these guidelines to the fashion upcycling cases, it can be said that the behaviour of the upcycler is decisive. In particular, it is important to assess the effort made to avoid the impression of a commercial connection with the trademark proprietor.[114] Appropriate labelling of upcycled products – clearly indicating the logo of the upcycler – plays a central role. To give fashion upcycling a chance and realise the societal benefits of environmental sustainability and artistic expression based on the reuse of trademarked goods,[115] it can be assumed that upcycling is an accepted and increasingly widespread contemporary practice in the fashion industry.[116] Moreover, it should be assumed that consumers are well aware that second-hand fashion pieces may be reworked and included in upcycled products.[117] Third-party trademarks that remain visible as a result of the productive reuse process may be reminiscent of the original fashion items that served as raw materials. Consumers, however, are unlikely to misinterpret these references to the original products as indications of the commercial source of the upcycled product. They are also unlikely to assume that these upcycled products are in any way

[111] Ibid at [39]–[41].

[112] *Soda-Club (CO2) SA and SodaStream International BV v MySoda Oy*, Case C-197/21, ECLI:EU:C:2022:834, at [54] (CJEU, October 27, 2022). For a discussion of underlying circular economy considerations, see Vrendenbard, 'IE', above n 43, 973–974.

[113] Ibid at [54].

[114] Cf Anemaet, 'Honesty', above n 104, 1037–1038, 1041.

[115] Charter of Fundamental Rights of the European Union [2000] OLJ 364/1 art 11, 13, 37. As to the need for a proper balance that gives room for circular economy initiatives, see Vrendenbard, 'IE', above n 43, 973–974.

[116] For a similar line of argument in the area of repaired goods, see Tischner and Stasiuk, 'Spare Parts', above n 29, 35–36.

[117] Cf Tischner and Stasiuk, 'Spare Parts', above n 29, 41–42.

approved or endorsed by the original brands.[118] Instead, consumers will look for additional labelling, such as the upcycler's logo on clothes, tags showing the logo on the inside, logos displayed on packaging, in shops etc. Indicating the upcycler's logo clearly on the products themselves and offering appropriate information in connection with their sale, the upcycler can thus dispel concerns about (post-sale)[119] confusion, and avoid the impression of blurring, tarnishment or unfair freeriding.[120] In the light of the overarching policy objective to support environmental sustainability and artistic expression, the assessment must be based on the perception of an average consumer who knows about upcycling and looks actively for indications of commercial origin which the upcycler has added to ensure transparency.[121]

Additional support for this approach can be offered by drawing a parallel with the use of trademarks in appropriation art. In the preceding section, fashion upcycling has already been placed in the context of aesthetic theory and artistic expression. Duran Lantink's creations, for instance, show clearly that upcycling projects can have an artistic nature. Considering this connection with the field of art, it is consistent to rely on honest practice guidelines that can be derived from trademark decisions in appropriation art cases. The decision of the Benelux Court of Justice in *Moët Hennessy* is of particular interest. In this case, the Court reached beyond traditional parody rulings[122] and developed a broader *exceptio*

[118] Schenerman, 'Upcycling's Place', above n 1, 765–766. Admittedly, a study of consumer responses to repaired goods bearing the logo of the original manufacturers yielded mixed results and showed that, in this specific case, consumers may be misled. See Tischner and Stasiuk, 'Spare Parts', above n 29, 53. The situation in the field of upcycled products, however, is different because third-party trademarks will appear on reworked, modified products. It is not the purpose of upcycling to restore the original appearance of products. The consumer perception will thus be different.

[119] Schenerman, 'Upcycling's Place', above n 1, 778–780.

[120] Tischner and Stasiuk, 'Spare Parts', above n 29, 33–34; Kur, 'Sale of Repaired Goods', above n 38, 235; Anemaet, 'Honesty', above n 104, 1037–1038 and 1041; Schenerman, 'Upcycling's Place', above n 1, 766–769; Keats, 'Trendy Product', above n 2, 717–718.

[121] As to the inclusion of normative considerations in the consumer concept and the determination of the consumer's level of knowledge, see Senftleben, *The Copyright Trademark Interface*, above n 34, 352–355; Graeme B Dinwoodie and Dev Gangjee, 'The Image of the Consumer in European Trade Mark Law' in Dorota Leczykiewicz and Stephen Weatherill (eds), *The Images of the Consumer in EU Law: Legislation, Free Movement and Competition Law* (Hart, 2016) 367.

[122] *Mercis BV and Hendrik Magdalenus Bruna v Punt.nl BV* (Court of Appeals of Amsterdam, September 13, 2011, ECLI:NL:GHAMS:2011:BS7825) at [4.19]. For a further example of the successful invocation of the due cause defence in an artistic context, see *Lila Postkarte*, Case I ZR 159/02, 585 (German Federal Supreme Court, February 3,

artis that does not require a critical statement in the guise of brand mockery.[123] The case concerned the use of the trademarked Dom Pérignon bottle[124] in stylised form and neon colours in paintings which, according to the artist Cédric Peers, played with pointillism and pop art.[125] To rebut infringement arguments based on blurring, tarnishment and unfair freeriding,[126] Peers invoked the open-ended defence of 'due cause' that is available under Article 2.20(2)(d) of the Benelux Convention on Intellectual Property.[127]

Assessing the unauthorised use of Hennessy's trademark in Peers' artworks, the Benelux Court of Justice stated that artistic freedom – as an aspect of the artist's right to freedom of expression – could constitute a due cause when 'there is an artistic expression that is the original result of a creative shaping process'.[128] The Court added that the artistic expression must not specifically aim at harming the trademark or the proprietor of the trademark.[129] Accordingly, the Court required

2005). Cf Martin Senftleben, 'The Perfect Match – Civil Law Judges and Open-Ended Fair Use Provisions' (2017) 33 *American University International Law Review* 231, 256–265.

[123] *Moët Hennessy Champagne Services v Cedric Art*, Case A2018/1/8, at [9] (Benelux Court of Justice, October 14, 2019). As to the traditional parody requirement of a critical comment, see Geiger, 'Proportionality of Criticism', above n 13, 317.

[124] IR no 323543.

[125] See 'Cedric' (*Cedric Gallery*) <https://www.cedricgallery.com/> for examples.

[126] Regulation (EU) 2017/1001 of the European Parliament and of the Council of June 14, 2017, on the European Union Trade Mark (codification) [2017] OJL 154/1 art 9(2); Directive (EU) 2015/2436 of the European Parliament and of the Council of December 16, 2015, to approximate the laws of the Member States relating to trade marks [2015] OJL 336/1 art 10(2). As to these three anti-dilution actions, see *L'Oréal SA and Others v Bellure NV and Others*, Case C-487/07, ECLI:EU:C:2009:378, at [39]–[41] (CJEU, June 18, 2009). Cf Kur and Senftleben, *European Trade Mark Law*, above n 11, para 5.182–5.192; Senftleben, 'Back to Basics', above n 90, 152.

[127] As to the due cause defence at EU level, see Regulation (EU) 2017/1001 of the European Parliament and of the Council of June 14, 2017, on the European Union Trade Mark (codification) [2017] OJL 154/1 art 9(2); Directive (EU) 2015/2436 of the European Parliament and of the Council of December 16, 2015, to approximate the laws of the Member States relating to trade marks [2015] OJL 336/1 art 10(2). See also *Interflora Inc and Interflora British Unit v Marks & Spencer plc and Flowers Direct Online Ltd*, ECR I-08625, at [91] (CJEU, September 22, 2011); *Leidseplein Beheer BV and Hendrikus de Vries v Red Bull GmbH and Red Bull Nederland BV*, Case C-65/12, ECLI:EU:C:2014:49, at [54]–[58] (CJEU, February 6, 2014). Cf Kur and Senftleben, *European Trade Mark Law*, above n 11, para 5.265–5.268 and 6.59–6.63; Cataldo, 'Negative Condition', above n 100, 833.

[128] *Moët Hennessy Champagne Services v Cedric Art*, Case A2018/1/8, at [9] (Benelux Court of Justice, October 14, 2019).

[129] Ibid.

evidence of an intention by the artist to harm the trademark or the trademark owner.[130]

Similar to the CJEU approach in *Viking Gas* and *Soda-Club*, this decision brings the behaviour of the appropriation artist into focus.[131] To succeed in a trademark infringement action, merely *some* likelihood of confusion, risk of damage, or a likelihood of exploiting the magnetism of an iconic fashion trademark, would not suffice; more is necessary. The trademark owner must demonstrate that the appropriation artist deliberately aims at causing damage or deriving unfair profit.[132] Applying this assessment standard *mutatis mutandis* to the question of honest practices in upcycling cases, it can be said that the threshold for accepting arguments based on blurring, tarnishment or unfair freeriding is particularly high. Unless the circumstances of the upcycling project indicate clearly that the upcycler specifically aimed at causing harm or exploiting the third-party brand in an unfair manner, no dishonesty can be found.[133]

Again, appropriate labelling is decisive. The use of the upcycler's own logo on garments (typically sewn on as the inside tag), on packaging, in shops etc. can serve as evidence that the upcycler has no intention of bringing damage or deriving unfair profit. Instead, the labelling proves that the upcycler seeks to act fairly and inform consumers about the commercial origin of the upcycled goods. The third-party trademark only serves as a reference to the original fashion product that is made to pave the way for circular sustainable modes of fashion production and consumption. Using customary modes of indicating the commercial origin of fashion products, upcyclers can thus ensure compliance with honest practices in industrial or commercial matters, as required by Article 14(2) TMD and Article 14(2) EUTMR. Achieving this result, they can ensure at the same time that their referential use defence prevails over trademark infringement arguments. The referential use defence, thus, allows upcycling initiatives in the fashion industry to survive allegations of trademark infringement. The productive use of trademarked fashion elements as raw materials does not amount to trademark infringement when customary modes of labelling are used to indicate the true commercial origin of upcycled products.

[130] Ibid.

[131] Cf Anemaet, 'Honesty', above n 104, 1037–1038.

[132] Cf Senftleben, *The Copyright Trademark Interface*, above n 34, 468–469.

[133] Cf Senftleben, 'Robustness', above n 2, 598–600.

The facts underlying the US case *Chanel, Inc. v Shiver and Duke LLC, Edith Anne Hunt and John Does* shed light on the limits of this defence argument. Shiver and Duke sold jewellery incorporating recycled Chanel buttons featuring the famous 'CC monogram' consisting of two interlocking back-to-back letter Cs.[134] Seeking to rebut Chanel's trademark infringement claims, Shiver and Duke argued that the inclusion of buttons displaying the CC monogram in its own products constituted a permissible act of reusing Chanel fashion items. According to Shiver and Duke, the button reuse was intended to contribute to the reduction of fashion waste.[135]

However, even in the light of the described relaxed infringement test that requires deliberately misleading use, or use that deliberately aims at causing damage or deriving unfair benefit from the trademark, Shiver and Duke's use of the CC monogram can hardly escape the verdict of infringement. In this specific case, the use of Chanel trademarks is a mere pretext for exploiting the magnetism and selling power of the original brand. Instead of conveying the message that consumption patterns in the fashion industry must change to save the planet, the glorification of CC monogram buttons on Shiver and Duke jewellery only confirms the luxury brand message and its problematic environmental implications. A redefinition of Chanel brand insignia in an upcycling context is sought in vain. The distance from the original brand and the contrast with the original brand message are missing. In consequence, consumers will find it difficult to distinguish Shiver and Duke jewellery from Chanel jewellery once the Shiver and Duke shopping environment is left and clear indications of a different commercial origin no longer prevent confusion. The reuse of Chanel buttons in the Shiver and Duke case, thus, cannot be regarded as a valid form of permissible upcycling. The described referential use argument and the accompanying relaxation of infringement criteria are incapable of shielding Shiver and Duke against trademark infringement claims.[136] The use of the CC monogram is merely an

[134] *Chanel, Inc. v Shiver and Duke LLC, Edith Anne Hunt and John Does*, Case 1:21-cv-01277 (Order of Dismissal) (SDNY, August 30, 2022).

[135] See the disclaimer on the Shiver and Duke website, 'S+D creates unique designs using Authentic buttons and bags to preserve their beauty while reducing waste and its impact on the planet': 'Non-Affiliation' (Shiver + Duke) <https://shiverandduke.com/pages/non-affiliation>.

[136] There is no final word on the infringement issue in the United States because of a settlement. See *Chanel, Inc, v Shiver and Duke LLC, Edith Anne Hunt and John Does*, Case 1:21-cv-01277 (Order of Dismissal) (SDNY, November 14, 2022).

attempt to disguise unfair brand exploitation as a legitimate form of fashion waste reduction.

8.6 Conclusion

Fashion upcycling is a productive form of reworking second-hand garments that has particular societal importance. Considering the environmental crisis – fuelled by the wasteful use of resources in the fashion industry – it is desirable to develop robust defences that enable fashion upcyclers to prevail in trademark infringement cases. In EU law, the referential use defence has the potential to offer solid support. Rightly understood, fashion upcycling constitutes an important, constitutionally protected form of free expression. Upcyclers use second-hand fashion elements to convey the important message that production and consumption patterns in the fashion sector must change. Considering the overarching policy objective to ensure a circular economy, the use of fashion elements that bear third-party trademarks for this purpose can be qualified as a legitimate form of referential use. The reference to products of the original trademark owner is made for the socially valuable purpose of providing a vision of better, more sustainable production and consumption practices in the fashion sector. Using customary modes of labelling to indicate the true origin of upcycled products, the upcycler can ensure compliance with honest practices in industrial or commercial matters. As a result, the referential use defence can be invoked successfully to rebut infringement arguments – regardless of whether these arguments are based on confusion, blurring, tarnishment or unfair freeriding.

9

Shanzhai Fashion and Intellectual Property in China

JYH-AN LEE AND JINGWEN LIU

ABSTRACT

Since the 2000s, Chinese factories have been notorious for imitating and copying luxury fashion designs, a phenomenon known as '*shanzhai*'. Within the fashion industry, two primary categories of *shanzhai* practices exist: the imitation or copying of a brand's name or trademarks, referred to as "counterfeits," and the imitation or copying of a brand's designs, referred to as 'knockoffs'. While band owners can easily enforce their legal rights against the trademark-infringing counterfeits, knockoffs remain a significant concern for international brand owners, since these design features are frequently denied trademark protection. Recent judicial practices suggest that fashion designs and design features in China can be protected under the Anti-Unfair Competition Law. Moreover, Chinese courts are increasingly open to the registration of signature design patterns as non-traditional trademarks, including three-dimensional trademarks and colour trademarks. This chapter provides a comprehensive exploration of China's evolving approach to these issues and provides a detailed comparison of copyright, trademark, design patent and unfair competition protections against fashion copycats.

9.1 Introduction

The first two decades of the twenty-first century witnessed the emergence and expansion of the *shanzhai* phenomenon in China.[1] Originally a term

[1] Barton Beebe, 'Shanzhai, Sumptuary Law, and Intellectual Property Law in Contemporary China' (2014) 47 *UC Davis Law Review* 849, 860–861 (explaining the emergence and conventional history of *shanzhai* in the mid-2000s); Haochen Sun, 'Can Louis Vuitton Dance with Hiphone – Rethinking the Idea of Social Justice in Intellectual Property Law'

used to describe a fortress in a mountainous region, *shanzhai* has gained a metaphorical meaning in the country, denoting local factories' low-cost imitation or copying of a well-known product from an international brand,[2] a phenomenon specific to China's labour-intensive, low-value-added economy and top-down imitation strategy at that time. Despite having been massively covered by Western media and thoroughly investigated in economics studies, there is no precise definition of *shanzhai*, given its dynamic characteristics.[3] In the fashion world, *shanzhai* usually refers to fashion items, including outfits, handbags or accessories, pirated from designer brands, typically with an inferior quality and a lower price. In the fashion industry, there are two perceived types of *shanzhai*: imitation or copying of a brand's name or trademarks (defined as 'counterfeit' items) and imitation or copying of a brand's designs (defined as 'knockoffs'). While international brand owners have successfully claimed trademark infringement against makers of 'Amani'[4] or 'Baneberry' garments,[5] they are often stymied by cheap knockoffs that merely copy their iconic designs, such as Gucci's green-red-green stripes or Burberry's famous check pattern. Although these design elements have a source-identifying function, it is much more challenging for the company to protect them as trademarks due to their lack of distinctiveness.[6]

As one of the largest consumer markets for fashion items, China has also been noted as the major source of fake fashion products in the past

(2012) 15 *University of Pennsylvania Journal of Law & Social Change* 389, 395 ('China has witnessed the rise of the *shanzhai* phenomenon over the past few years').

2 Sky Canaves and Juliet Ye, 'Imitation Is the Sincerest Form of Rebellion in China', *Wall Street Journal* (January 22, 2009) <https://www.wsj.com/articles/SB123257138952903561>.

3 Sun, above n 1, at 396 ('Despite having many references, *shanzhai* has no precise definition that can encapsulate all of its dynamic elements. This is because the phenomenon itself has developed very rapidly over the years with the mushrooming of new products and events, all labeled as *shanzhai*.').

4 *Qiaozhi Amani Youxian Gongsi Su Guangzhou Lideng Biaoye Youxian Gongsi Deng* (乔治·阿玛尼有限公司诉广州利登表业有限公司等) [*Giorgio Armani S.P.A. v Guangzhou Lideng Timepiece Co, Ltd et al*] (Guangzhou Baiyun District Court 2022).

5 *Boboli Youxian Gongsi Su Xinboli Shangmao Youxian Gongsi Deng* (博柏利有限公司诉新帛利商贸有限公司等) [*Burberry Limited v Baneberry Trading Co. Ltd et al*] (Jiangsu Suzhou Interim People's Court November 29, 2020) (hereinafter *Baneberry*).

6 Eg, Van Cleef & Arpels' failure in securing the three-dimensional (3D) trademark registration of its four-leaf clover jewellery in China. See *Fanke Yabao Youxian Gongsi Deng Su Guojia Zhishi Chanquan Ju* (梵克雅宝有限公司等诉国家知识产权局) [*Van Cleef & Arpels et al, v China National Intellectual Property Administration*] (Beijing High People's Court, December 26, 2020) (hereinafter *VCA v CNIPA*).

few decades.[7] However, since late 2010s, China has moved aggressively from an imitation economy to an innovation economy[8] and endeavoured to strengthen its long-criticised lax intellectual property (IP) system. Improving protection for fashion designs is a key aspect of its innovation strategy.[9] In addition to more active legislation and enforcement pertaining to IP,[10] recent judicial developments reveal that Chinese courts are more willing to embrace the registration of signature design patterns as non-traditional trademarks, such as three-dimensional (3D) trademarks or colour trademarks. In 2018, the Supreme People's Court (SPC) of China signalled the possibility of acquiring distinctiveness through use by ordering the Trademark Review and Adjudication Board (TRAB)[11] to reconsider a decision against Dior's 3D trademark application for the J'Adore fragrance bottle.[12] The Beijing High Court similarly ordered the TRAB to re-examine the registrability of Christian Louboutin's signature red-soled shoe as an non-traditional trademark, and the decision was upheld by the SPC.[13] Will these new trends help ameliorate luxury houses' concerns related to *shanzhai* in China? Are there any alternative solutions for fashion houses to guard their iconic designs? This chapter

[7] Angela Terese Timpone, 'The True Price for Your Fake Gucci Bag Is Life: Why Eliminating Unsafe Labor Practices Is the Right Answer to the Fashion Counterfeit Problem' (2017) 15 *Cardozo Public Law Policy & Ethics Journal* 351, 371.

[8] See generally, *Guojia Chuangxin Qudong Fazhan Gangyao* (国家创新驱动发展战略纲要) [Outline of the National Innovation-Driven Development Strategy] (promulgated by the Central Committee of the Communist Party of China and the State Council, May 2016). English translation could be found at <https://cset.georgetown.edu/publication/outline-of-the-national-innovation-driven-development-strategy/>.

[9] See *'Shi Si Wu' Guojia Zhishi Chanquan Baohu He Yunyong Guihua* ('十四五'国家知识产权保护和运用规划) [The 14th 'Five-Year Plan' National Plan on Intellectual Property Protection and Utilization] (promulgated by the State Council, October 2021), Article 3.

[10] All three departmental IP laws had been amended from 2019 to 2020.

[11] Having been absorbed and replaced by the China National Intellectual Property Administration (CNIPA) since 2019.

[12] *Kelisidiang Diaoer Xiangliao Gongsi Su Yuan Guojia Gongshang Xingzheng Guanli Zongju Shangbiao Pingshen Weiyuanhui* (克里斯蒂昂迪奥尔香料公司诉原国家工商行政管理总局商标评审委员会) [*Parfums Christian Dior v The Former Trademark Review and Adjudication Board of the State Administration of Industry and Commerce*] (Supreme People's Court April 26, 2018) (hereinafter *Dior*).

[13] *Kelisiti Lubutuo Su Yuan Guojia Gongshang Xingzheng Guanli Zongju Shangbiao Pingshen Weiyuanhui* (克里斯提鲁布托诉原国家工商行政管理总局商标评审委员会) [*Christian Louboutin v The Former Trademark Review and Adjudication Board of the State Administration of Industry and Commerce*] (Beijing High People's Court, December 24, 2018) (hereinafter *Louboutin v TRAB*).

seeks to answer these questions through a detailed examination of recent court decisions in the country.

This chapter first briefly introduces the piracy ecosystem in fashion, consisting of blatant counterfeits and knockoffs. It then compares brand owners' different approaches under Chinese law to claim copyright, trademark, design patent and unfair competition protection against imitators. Finally, by examining changing judicial practices, this chapter details China's changing attitude towards the registration and enforcement of fashion design and design features, which may be a reflection of the country's policy-level shift to an innovation-driven strategy.[14]

9.2 A Two-Tier Piracy Hierarchy in the Fashion Industry

As has been noted by many indie designers, entrepreneurs and persons immersed in the fashion industry, 'fashion is a lucrative business'.[15] According to the career site Zippa, the global fashion industry was valued at US$1.7 trillion as of 2022.[16] Due to its fast pace, short product life and ever-changing fashion trends,[17] creativity is the heart of the fashion industry.[18] Therefore, many believe that IP plays a critical role in the

[14] See, eg, *Zhonghua Renmin Gongheguo Guomin Jingji He Shehui Fazhan Di Shisi Ge Wunian Guihua He 2035 Nian Yuanjing Mubiao Gangyao* (中华人民共和国国民经济和社会发展第十四个五年规划和2035年远景目标纲要) 'Outline of the 14th Five-Year Plan for National Economic and Social Development of the People's Republic of China and the Long-Term Goals for 2035' (promulgated by the Central Committee of the Communist Party of China and the State Council March 12, 2021) <www.gov.cn/xinwen/2021-03/13/content_5592681.htm> (China).

[15] Africh Royale, 'Interview with Adelaja Temitope Adeola, Fashion Designer and CEO Of Grat Apparel' <https://africhroyale.com/fashion-is-a-lucrative-business-says-the-ceo-of-grat-apparel/>.

[16] Sky Ariella, 'Dazzling Fashion Industry Statistics [2022]: How Much Is the Fashion Industry Worth', Zippa (October 3, 2022) <www.zippia.com/advice/fashion-industry-statistics/>.

[17] Violet Atkinson et al, 'Comparative Study of Fashion and IP: Copyright and Designs in France, Europe and Australia' (2016) 11(7) *Journal of Intellectual Property Law & Practice* 516, 528; Paige Holton, 'Intellectual Property Laws for Fashion Designers Need No Embellishments: They Are Already in Style' (2014) 39 *Journal of Corporation Law* 415, 418; Ronald Urbach and Jennifer Soussa, 'Is the Design Piracy Protection Act a Step Forward for Copyright Law or Is It Destined to Fall Apart at the Seams?' (2008) 16 *Metropolitan Corporate Counsel* 28, 28.

[18] Pammi Sinha, 'Creativity in Fashion' (2002) 2(1V) *Journal of Textile and Apparel, Technology and Management* 1, 2–3 ('Creativity is a form of problem solving and fashion design is a problem.').

fashion industry, which requires intensive creativity.[19] However, the existence of 'piracy paradox', a theory purporting that design copying does not drive out but rather fuels creativity by accelerating fashion cycles, has constrained IP law's intervention in fashion to the minimal.[20] That said, as noted by Kal Raustiala and Christopher Sprigman, it is important to distinguish between the copying of brand names and the copying of designs.[21] While brand names and logos can undisputedly be protected as trademarks, specific design patterns, elements or features cannot be easily protected by IP law.[22]

9.2.1 Counterfeits

Although sometimes used interchangeably, the terms 'counterfeit' and 'knockoff' are conceptually different in IP literature.[23] *Counterfeit*, by definition, refers to a pirated product bearing the trademark of the original brand with the obvious intention to imitate and deceive consumers that this is indeed a genuine product.[24] Therefore, *counterfeits* inevitably involve trademark infringement and passing off.[25] While counterfeit product logos may exhibit similarities to the original trademarks, they are not necessarily exact replicas. These counterfeit items are often indistinguishable from authentic products for Chinese consumers, particularly when the trademarks are in foreign languages. Examples of such counterfeits include 'Amani' T-shirts or 'Baneberry' trench coats with designs slightly different from the originals, which could easily be

19 C Scott Hemphill and Jeannie Suk, 'The Law, Culture, and Economics of Fashion' (2009) 61 *Stanford Law Review* 1147, 1150 ('In the legal realm, this social dynamic of innovation and continuity is most directly engaged by the law of intellectual property.').

20 See generally Kal Raustiala and Christopher Sprigman, 'The Piracy Paradox: Innovation and Intellectual Property in Fashion Design' (2006) 92 *Virginia Law Review* 1687.

21 Ibid, 1692 ('Our focus is the copying of apparel designs, not brand names .... It is also important to distinguish textile designs from apparel designs, though there is sometimes overlap.').

22 Ibid.

23 Marra M Clay, 'Copycat Cosmetics: The Beauty Industry and the Bounds of the American Intellectual Property System' (2021) 106 *Minnesota Law Review* 425, 436; Kenneth L Port, 'A Case against the ACTA' (2012) 33 *Cardozo Law Review* 1131, 1141; Meghan Collins et al, 'Knock-off the Knockoffs: The Fight against Trademark and Copyright Infringement' (2009) 9 *Illinois Business Law Journal* 227, 231.

24 Port, above n 23, 1141–1142; Clay, above n 23, 436–437; Julio O De Castro et al, 'Can Entrepreneurial Firms Benefit from Product Piracy?' (2008) *28 Journal of Business Venturing* 75, 78.

25 Port, above n 23, 1141–1142; Clay, above n 23, 436–437.

mistaken for authentic Armani or Burberry products. Sometimes, the imitators even register trademarks over their counterfeited designs or logos. For example, the defendant in *Burberry Limited v Baneberry Trading Co. Ltd. et al* had managed to register its 'Baneberry' trademark in China in multiple classes.[26] Amusing as it may seem at first glance, there is actually a fair chance of consumer confusion when such counterfeiting techniques are combined with other imitative tactics (e.g., displaying the counterfeits in a physical or online store whose layout is also confusingly similar to that of the original brand).[27] Although consumers are aware that they are buying counterfeits, the court held that actionable initial-interest confusion prior to the sale existed when they were attracted to those products. In these scenarios, infringement still exists due to the substantial similarity between the counterfeited trademark and the original mark, alongside the imitator's intention to free-ride on the original mark's reputation.[28] This type of clumsy imitation accounted for a great proportion of *shanzhai* fashion in China in the 2000s and are still sold today. The following products were found in Manila, Shenzhen and Hong Kong (Figures 9.1–9.4).

Trademark owners' enforcement options against such blatant counterfeits are straightforward. As long as the original brand owner has secured valid trademark registration for its brand name or logo, it will enjoy a fair chance of success in civil proceedings.[29] In the *Baneberry* case mentioned above, Burberry successfully obtained a preliminary injunction enjoining the copyist from selling and marketing the counterfeited garments in a manner that was found to be confusing and deceptive.[30] When the value of the counterfeited goods meets the

[26] *Baneberry*, above n 5.

[27] See, eg, *Baneberry*, above n 5. In that case, the Court reasoned that the alleged infringement was a 'multi-dimensional imitation' of the Burberry brand, which will inevitably degrade, dilute and damage the distinctiveness, recognisability and reputation of Burberry.

[28] *Baneberry*, above n 5.

[29] *Shangbiao Fa* (商标法) [Trademark Law] (promulgated by the Standing Comm National People's Congress, April 23, 2019, effective November 1, 2019) (China) (hereinafter Trademark Law 2019), Article 60 ('Where any party has committed any of such acts to infringe the exclusive right to use a registered trademark . . . where they are reluctant to resolve the matter through consultation or the consultation fails, the trademark registrant or interested party may institute legal proceedings in the People's Court or request the administrative authority for industry and commerce for actions.').

[30] *Baneberry*, above n 5.

Figure 9.1 *Shanzhai* 'GUDID' evocative of 'GUCCI'.
Credit: David Tan

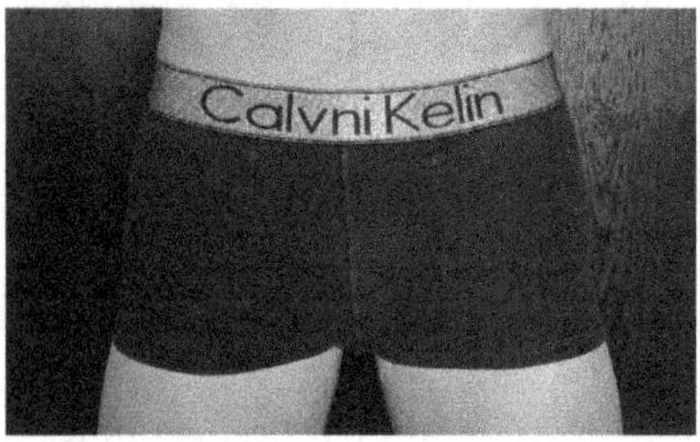

Figure 9.2 *Shanzhai* 'CALVNI KELIN' evocative of 'CALVIN KLEIN'.
Credit: David Tan

criminal threshold, the manufacturer could even be held criminally liable.[31] The brand owner can also resort to administrative remedies,

[31] *Xing Fa* (刑法) [Criminal Law] (promulgated by the Standing Comm National People's Congress, December 26, 2020, effective March 1, 2021) (China) Article 213 ('Whoever, without permission from the owner of a registered trademark, uses a trademark which is identical with the registered trademark on the same kind of commodities shall, if the circumstances are serious, be sentenced to fixed-term imprisonment of not more than three years or criminal detention and shall also, or shall only, be fined; if the circumstances are especially serious, he shall be sentenced to fixed-term imprisonment of not less than three years but not more than seven years and shall also be fined.'). According to the Interpretation of the Supreme People's Court and the Supreme People's Procuratorate on Several Issues Related to the Application of Law in Adjudicating Criminal Cases of Intellectual Property Infringement, a trademark infringement is 'severe' if the infringer is with a turnover of more than RMB 50,000 or with a revenue of more than RMB 30,000. See *Guanyu Banli Qinfan Zhishi Chanquan Xingshi Anjian Juti Yingyong Falv Ruogan Wenti De Jieshi* (关于办理侵犯知识产权刑事案件具体应用法律若干问题的解释)

Figure 9.3 *Shanzhai* 'CHAINE' evocative of 'CHANEL'.
Credit: Jingwen Liu

Figure 9.4 *Shanzhai* 'CHRISTAN DORIO' evocative of 'CHRISTIAN DIOR'.
Credit: Jingwen Liu

such as filing complaints with local administration for market supervision or seeking assistance from customs.[32]

9.2.2 *Knockoffs*

A knockoff is usually labelled with the imitator's own trademark, which is sometimes completely unrelated to the brand of the original mark owner.[33] The product's resemblance to the original comes solely from the imitation of style and design features (Figures 9.5–9.7). There is only a thin line between licit and illicit knockoffs,[34] since it is hard to discern if a subsequent design is plagiarising a prior work or just treats it as a source of inspiration. Popular fast fashion brands such as H&M, Zara and Forever 21 are frequently accused of knocking off designers.[35]

One key feature that distinguishes knockoffs from counterfeits is that knockoffs do not aim to create consumer confusion.[36] An ordinary consumer can easily discern that a bomber jacket she purchases from Forever 21 – although it has similar design features or confusing elements, such as green and red stripes – is not actually a Gucci product, based on its texture, material, price, other design features and, most obviously, the 'Forever 21' label inside. In fact, many consumers consciously and actively seek to purchase more affordable knockoffs because the original products from coveted luxury fashion brands are often

[Interpretation on Several Issues Related to the Application of Law in Adjudicating Criminal Cases of Intellectual Property Infringement] (promulgated by the Supreme People's Court and the Supreme People's Procuratorate, December 8, 2004, effective December 22, 2004) (China).

32 Trademark Law 2019, above n 29, Article 60.

33 Clay, above n 23, 437.

34 Beebe, above n 1, 852 (explaining that *shanzhai* is sometimes licit but usually illicit).

35 See, eg, *Forever 21, Inc v Gucci America, Inc, et al*, No. 2:17-cv-04706 (C.D.Cal), in which case Forever 21 filed a suit against Gucci to seek a declaratory judgment determining its use of the green-red-green stripes on clothing does not infringe Gucci's trademark. The case was settled outside the court before a substantive ruling could be made. See also *Anna Sui Corp v Forever 21, Inc, et al.*, No. 1:07-cv-03235 (SDNY 2008); Irene Tan, 'Knock It Off, Forever 21 – The Fashion Industry's Battle against Design Piracy' (2010) 18 *Journal of Law & Policy* 893, 913–921; 'The Many (Law)suits of Forever 21', *TFR News* (October 2, 2019) <https://tfr.news/articles/2019/10/2/the-many-lawsuits-of-forever-21>; 'Converse Sues Wal-Mart, H&M over Knockoff Sneakers', *CNN Wire* (October 15, 2014) <https://kdvr.com/news/money/converse-sues-wal-mart-hm-over-knockoff-sneakers/>. Most of the disputes above were settled outside the court.

36 Port, above n 23, 1141 ('When no consumer confusion is likely, the appropriate label is *knockoff*.').

Figure 9.5 Handbags – knockoffs of FENDI, LOUIS VUITTON and GUCCI.
Credit: Jingwen Liu

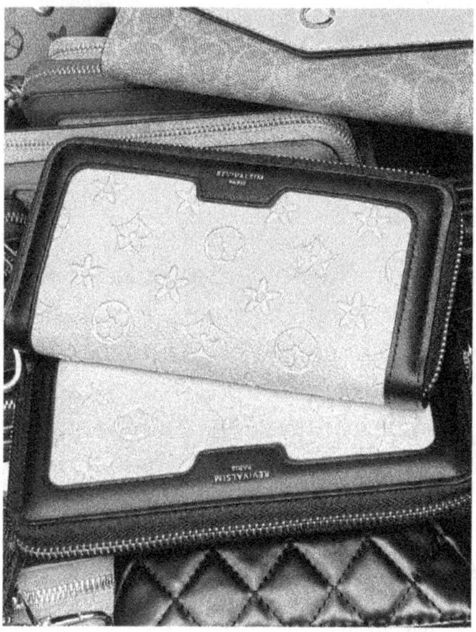

Figure 9.6 Wallets – knockoff of LOUIS VUITTON with own brand name 'REVIVALSM'.
Credit: Jingwen Liu

Figure 9.7 Handbags – knockoff of LOUIS VUITTON 'Damier' but no logo.
Credit: Jingwen Liu

beyond their financial means. If consumer confusion is eliminated, claims based on trademark infringement or passing off are less likely to succeed.[37] Therefore, legal actions against the producers of such knockoffs are generally more limited and more challenging than those against the producers of trademark-infringing counterfeits.[38] Not surprisingly, in recent years, knockoffs have become a major form of *shanzhai* and a

[37] Clay, above n 23, 436 ('Under this definition, knockoffs are not illegal unless a brand can prove that a knockoff is so close to the original product that the consumer is misled into believing they are purchasing the original.').

[38] Notably, such disputes and accusations of design piracy often occur between two high fashion houses or between two fast fashion brands. See, eg, *Christian Louboutin S.A. et al v Yves Saint Laurent American Holding, Inc et al,* 696 F 3d 206 (2nd Cir. 2012) (hereinafter *Louboutin v YSL*); *H&M Hennes & Mauritz AB v Forever 21, Inc,* No. 1:15-cv-05678 (SDNY 2015).

major challenge for fashion companies in China. Section 9.3 focuses on how and to what extent these design elements in fashion products are protected in China.

9.3 Protection of Design Elements under Chinese Law

Design companies have sought to protect their design elements through different categories of IP. This section explains the use of copyright, trademarks, design patents and unfair competition to protect those elements, as well as the limitations of each approach.

9.3.1 Copyright

It is occasionally disputed whether fashion products, such as clothing, shoes and handbags, are subject to copyright protection because their aesthetic value is sometimes built upon their utility function.[39] For instance, in 2022, the Federal Court of Australia refused to recognise the Neoprene tote bag as a work of artistic craftsmanship.[40] The court ruled that the subject design was undoubtedly constrained by functional considerations because the designer intended to design a stylish 'carry all' bag from the beginning, and in that endeavour, the function and utility of the bag to 'carry all' had governed the overall design of it.[41] In contrast, the design of a pair of sandals was protected in Germany under the category of 'applied art' in the same year.[42] The Regional Court of Cologne, applying the framework established by the Court of Justice of

[39] See, eg, *Galiano v Harrah's Operating Co.*, 416 F.3d 411, 422 (5th Cir. 2005); Raustiala and Sprigman, above n 20, 1699. See also *Shanghai Lukun Fushi Youxian Gongsi Su Shanghai Rongmei Pinpai Guanli Youxian Gongsi Deng* (上海陆坤服饰有限公司诉上海戎美品牌管理有限公司等) [*Shanghai Lukun Clothing Co, Ltd v Shanghai Rongmei Brand Management Co, Ltd et al*] (Shanghai Intellectual. Property People's Court, May 10, 2018) (China) (hereinafter *Shanghai Lukun*). An exception in this respect may be France, capital of the fashion world. In addition to recognising garment designs as copyrightable subject matters, the French law, as well as the law of the European Union (EU), also provides a design registration system and allows for cumulative protection from copyright, registered design and unregistered design. See Raustiala and Sprigman, above n 20, 1735–1737 (introducing the EU design registration system and the EU approach for design protection); Atkinson et al, above n 17, 531 ('Australian law does not recognize copyright as existing in a garment itself – whereas French law does.').

[40] *State of Escape Accessories Pty Limited v Schwartz* (2022) FCAFC 63.

[41] Ibid.

[42] Regional Court of Cologne (Landgericht Koln), case no. 14 O 366/21, decision of March 3, 2022 (Germany). For detailed discussion of the two cases, see The Bird &

European Union (CJEU), decided that the sandal design 'went beyond mere functional elements and was not exclusively determined by technical considerations'.[43] Some commentators observed that this case suggested a lower threshold for applied art that blurred the boundaries between copyright and design systems in the European Union (EU).[44]

This divergence of viewpoints also exists in Chinese judicial practices. In *Yunchuang Design v Kashilan Clothing*, the plaintiff registered copyright for a sun dress design, while the defendant offered for sale online dresses with a similar design. The court held that the contour of the sun dress together with the black-and-white dots reflected the designer's personal choice and special arrangement, and thus the garment had the aesthetic value of a 'work of art' required by the Copyright Law.[45] The Chongqing Pilot Free Trade Zone People's Court explained that if the contour or black-and-white dots were revised or removed, the function of the piece of clothing would be unaffected.[46] Therefore, the aesthetic value of the dress could be separated from its utility functions.[47] Notably, the court's perspective on separability mirrors that of the US Supreme Court's decision in *Varsity Brands, Inc. v Star Athletica, LLC.*[48] The Supreme Court held that the design features of a cheerleading uniform, such as stripes, chevrons, zigzags, and colour-blocking, were 'wholly unnecessary' and separable from its ability to cover the body, permit free movement and wick moisture.[49] Nevertheless, at around the same time of the Chongqing court's decision, Yunchuang's action against another knockoff designer in Guangzhou for the same dress was rejected by the

Bird IP Team, 'Round-up of Fashion-related IP Decisions in 2022' (2023) 18(3) *Journal of Intellectual Property Law & Practice* 199.

43 Ibid at 202.

44 Ibid.

45 *Yunchuang Sheji (Shenzhen) Jituan Youxian Gongsi Su Chongqing Kashilan Fushi Youxian Gongsi* (云创设计（深圳）集团有限公司诉重庆卡诗兰服饰有限公司) [*Yunchuang Design (Shenzhen) Group Co, Ltd v Chongqing Kashilan Clothing Co, Ltd*] (Chongqing Pilot Free Trade Zone People's Court, 2021).

46 Ibid.

47 Ibid.

48 *Star Athletica, L.L.C. v Varsity Brands, Inc*, 136 S Ct 1823 (2016).

49 Ibid. However, this decision has been open to wide critiques by scholars. See, eg, Rebecca Tushnet, 'Shoveling a Path after Star Athletica' (2019) 66 *UCLA Law Review* 1216; Christopher Buccafusco and Jeanne C Fromer, 'Fashion's Function in Intellectual Property Law' (2017) 93 *Notre Dame Law Review* 51; Lili Levi, 'The New Separability' (2018) 20 *Vanderbilt Journal of Entertainment & Technology Law* 709; Jane C Ginsburg, '"Courts Have Twisted Themselves into Knots": US Copyright Protection for Applied Art' (2016) 40 *Columbia Journal of Law & the Arts* 1.

Guangzhou Internet Court, which ruled that the design was merely a combination of common design features such as V-neck, short sleeves and invisible zipper, and it fell short of the aesthetic value required by the Copyright Law.[50] The inconsistent application of the law in different Chinese courts indicates that copyright infringement suits against manufacturers of knockoffs face great uncertainty in terms of success and is dependent on the fora or even views of individual judges.

It should be noted, however, that the aesthetics–utility dichotomy only restrains copyright in three-dimensional articles; therefore, fashion sketches, design features and textile patterns printed on a fashion item are not considered 'useful'.[51] In other words, while a bomber jacket itself may be denied copyright, the design patterns (e.g., prints) on it could be eligible for copyright protection. Nevertheless, to be shielded under copyright law, the design pattern needs to demonstrate other requisites of a copyrightable work, such as expression, originality and human authorship.[52] A simple pattern of dots and stripes that falls under the public domain clearly does not possess sufficient originality for copyright protection.[53]

9.3.2 Trademark

If a certain pattern or print has repetitively occurred on almost every product and therefore been perceived as a symbol of a brand, this particular pattern or print may acquire the status of a trademark.[54] For

[50] *Yunchuang Sheji (Shenzhen) Jituan Youxian Gongsi Su Guangzhou Hongboya Trading Co, Ltd.* (云创设计（深圳）集团有限公司诉广州弘薄雅贸易有限公司) [*Yunchuang Design (Shenzhen) Group Co, Ltd v Guangzhou Hongboya Trading Co, Ltd*] (Guangzhou Internet Court, July 21, 2021).

[51] Raustiala and Sprigman, above n 20, 1692.

[52] Zhuozuo Quan Fa (著作权法) [Copyright Law] (promulgated by the Standing Comm National People's Congress, November 11, 2020, effective June 1, 2021) (China) (hereinafter Copyright Law 2020), Articles 3 and 4.

[53] See, eg, *Deyang Kaifa Qu Manwu Xiuhua Fuzhuang Gongzuoshi Su Shaoxing Shi Yuecheng Qu Gongmei Xiupinchang* (德阳开发区满屋绣花服装设计工作室诉绍兴市越城区共美绣品厂) [*Deyang Development Zone Manwu Embroidery Clothing Design Studio v Shaoxing Yuecheng District Gongmei Embroidery Factory*] (Shaoxing Interim Court, February 22, 2022) (reasoning that common geometric patterns including dots, stripes and surfaces belong to the public domain and therefore protection as private right would be an invasion to the public interest)

[54] Article 8 of the Chinese Trademark Law provided that 'any visible sign, including any word, design, letter of the alphabet, numeral, three-dimensional symbol and color combination, or any combination of the above, that can serve to distinguish the goods of a natural person, legal person, or other organization from those of another, may be

example, Louis Vuitton (LV) has successfully trademarked its Toile Monogram, consisting of the entwined 'LV' initials in the United States.[55] The iconic Burberry check and the LV 'Damier' check pattern that appear ubiquitously on many of the brands' products ranging from apparel to accessories have also been trademarked. A trademark, by its statutory definition, is a mark used in trade that identifies the source of goods or services.[56] In the Gucci–Forever 21 dispute, what gives the Forever 21 knockoff a Gucci-vibe is the pattern of the design, especially the green-red-green stripes on the collar and cuffs of the jacket. If the stripes were removed or appeared in other colours, this fashion piece could hardly be considered piracy, because a bomber jacket is a generic apparel design in the fashion market. After being used by Gucci extensively and continuously for decades, the stripes in this particular configuration of colours are associated with the brand by consumers and have become a representative feature of its style and brand image. Therefore, stripes in these colours have, in essence, functioned as a source-identifying trademark, and Gucci has indeed registered the mark in various jurisdictions, including China.[57] In *Gucci Am., Inc. v Guess Inc.*, the District Court for the Southern District of New York recognised Gucci's rights to the green-red-green stripes and imposed a permanent injunction prohibiting Guess from using Gucci's proprietary stripes without authorisation.[58]

The idea of trademarking an iconic design may be attractive. However, the prosecution process is sometimes challenging. Generally speaking, there are three grounds on which a trademark application can be rejected in China: lack of distinctiveness,[59] having adverse connotations[60] and the

made a trademark for application for registration'. See Trademark Law 2019, above n 30, Article 8.

55 Ashley E Hofmeister, 'Louis Vuitton Malletier v Dooney & Bourke, Inc: Resisting Expansion of Trademark Protection in the Fashion Industry' (2008) 3 *Journal of Business & Technology Law* 187, 188–189.

56 Trademark Law 2019, above n 29, Article 8. See also 15 USC § 1127 (United States).

57 See *Yiwu Haiguan Guanyu Yiwu Shilutong Jinchukou Youxian Gongsi Qinfan 'GUCCI (Zhiding Yanse Tuxing Lv-Hong-Lv)' Shangbiao Quan Liankuwa De Xingzheng Chufa Jueding Shu* (义乌市海关关于义乌市诗路通进出口有限公司侵犯 '*GUCCI* (指定颜色图形绿红绿'商标权连裤袜的行政处罚决定书) [Administrative Penalty Decision of the Yiwu Customs on Yiwu Shilutong Import & Export Co, Ltd's Stockings Infringing the Trademark 'GUCCI (Device Designated to Colour Green-Red-Green)'] (Yiwu Customs 2022) (China).

58 *Gucci America, Inc v Guess, Inc*, 843 F Supp 2d 412 (SDNY 2012).

59 Trademark Law 2019, above n 29, Article 11.

60 Trademark Law 2019, above n 29, Article 10.

existence of prior rights, including similar prior marks.[61] The distinctiveness ground has two elements: inherent distinctiveness and acquired distinctiveness.[62] A mark is inherently distinctive when it serves to identify the source of the product or service. An inherently generic mark could acquire a 'secondary meaning' and become distinctive when consumers have developed an association between the mark and the source of the product or service.[63] Some fashion designs fail the distinctiveness test because they are inseparable parts of the underlying products.[64]

In 2014, Van Cleef & Arpels (VCA) applied for registration in China of its signature four-leaf clover–inspired jewellery design as a three-dimensional (3D) trademark, which proceeded to registration in 2016. This line of jewellery is branded under VCA's 'Alhambra' trademark. In 2018, a third party initiated an invalidation proceeding at the TRAB, successfully requesting that the TRAB nullify the registration in 2019. VCA then appealed to the Beijing Intellectual Property Court and then the Beijing High Court. The Beijing High Court, upholding the lower court's decision, denied the distinctiveness of VCA's most iconic design.[65] The court ruled, first, that the four-leaf clover pattern, although originated by VCA, was more likely to be perceived by the relevant public

[61] Trademark Law 2019, above n 29, Article 9. See also Jyh-An Lee and Thomas Mehaffy, 'Prior Rights in the Chinese Trademark Law' (2015) 37 *European Intellectual Property Review* 673.

[62] Trademark Law 2019, above n 29, Article 11.2 (stipulating that an inherently indistinctive mark could acquire distinctiveness through use). See also Haochen Sun, 'Protecting Non-traditional Trademarks in China: New Opportunities and Challenges' in Irene Calboli and Martin Senftleben (eds), *The Protection of Non-Traditional Trademarks* (Oxford University Press, 2018) 185, 187.

[63] See, eg, *Shenzhen Guang Shifu Wenhua Chuanbo Youxian Gongsi Su Pang Suanguang* (深圳广师傅文化传播有限公司诉庞算光) [*Shenzhen Guang Shifu Cultural Communications Co., Ltd v Pang Suanguan*] (Supreme People's Court, July 7, 2022); *Beijing Mingjia Shuhua Yishu Guan Su Guojia Zhishi Chanquan Ju* (北京茗佳书画艺术馆诉国家知识产权局) [*Beijing Mingjia Gallary of Calligraphy and Painting v China National Intellectual Property Administration*] (Beijing High. People's Court, May 18, 2021). See also *Louboutin v YSL*, 696 F 3d 206, 216 (citing *Inwood Labs, Inc v Ives Labs., Inc*, 456 US 844, 851 n 11 (1982)) ('A mark has acquired "secondary meaning" when, "in the minds of the public, the primary significance of a product feature . . . is to identify the source of the product rather than the product itself."').

[64] See, eg, *VCA v CNIPA*, above n 6; *Yidali Aimashi Gongsi Su Guojia Gongshang Xingzheng Guanli Zongju Shangbiao Pingshen Weiyuanhui* (意大利爱马仕公司诉国家工商行政管理总局商标评审委员会) [*Hermes Italia SpA v Trademark Appeal Board of the State Administration of Industry and Commerce*] (Supreme People's Court, December 13, 2012) (hereinafter *Hermès v TRAB*).

[65] *VCA v CNIPA*, above n 6.

as the shape, appearance or ornament of the product when used on the designated goods, rather than a source identifier, and hence was inherently indistinctive.[66] Second, although VCA had adduced evidence to show its extensive use of the applied-for mark, such use was, again, found to be the shape, appearance or ornament of the designated goods, diluting its function as a source-identifier.[67]

VCA was not the first company to lose a case because of inadequate distinctiveness. Hermès encountered a similar setback a few years before the *VCA* decision when attempting to trademark the design of its world-renowned Kelly bag as a 3D symbol. The SPC, in dismissing Hermès' petition for a retrial against a Beijing High Court decision, reasoned that when a 3D symbol cannot be separated from the product, consumers are more likely to view it as a component of the product rather than a trademark, unless the unique features make the symbol distinguishable from those on similar products or there is sufficient evidence to prove that the relevant public associates the symbol with the brand. The SPC ruled against both the inherent and acquired distinctiveness of the design features of the Kelly bag.[68]

It is worth mentioning that the disputed marks in both cases are 3D marks. While Chinese Trademark Law acknowledges 3D marks,[69] two-dimensional (2D) marks, such as words, devices, letters and numbers, constitute the majority of marks in the country. These 2D marks are typically considered as traditional trademarks, whereas marks incorporating other elements such as colour configurations or shapes are generally viewed as less conventional.[70] For instance, the 'BOTTEGA VENETA' logo is what one typically associates with a mark; the intrecciato weave ranging from 8–12 mm in width – registered as a mark in many jurisdictions – would be an unconventional one. Trademark examination and judicial practices have set a higher bar for 3D and other non-traditional trademarks in the determination of distinctiveness. Although VCA's above-mentioned 3D mark was declared invalid by the court, its registration and enforcement of the 2D device trademark over the same

[66] Ibid.

[67] Ibid.

[68] *Hermès v TRAB*, above n 64. See also Sun, above n 62, 189.

[69] Trademark Law 2019, above n 29, Article 8.

[70] Sun, above n 62, 185 ('Non-traditional trademarks ... offer new ways to attract consumers, as they differ from the words, logos, letters, and numbers that are traditionally used as trademarks.').

four-leaf clover design has been successful.[71] In another invalidation case brought against this 2D trademark, both the China National Intellectual Property Administration (CNIPA) and the Beijing Intellectual Property Court recognised the 2D mark's inherent distinctiveness.[72] In reaching that decision, the Beijing Intellectual Property Court explicitly stated that the standards to determine distinctiveness for a 3D trademark and those for a 2D trademark should be differentiated.[73] While the court did not explicitly specify these standards, it is reasonable to assume that the threshold for a 3D trademark to be considered 'distinctive' should be higher than that for a 2D trademark.

9.3.3 *Design Patent*

There are many examples of registering a novel design of apparel, shoes or watch as a design patent in China. For example, Nike has various design patent registrations in China for its footwear designs.[74] In one case, a domestic brand successfully enforced its design patent rights against an online store selling garments with similar designs and obtained damages of RMB 420,000 (US$57,600), in addition to an injunction.[75] However, design patents have their limitations. First and foremost, the Patent Law requires novelty, which means that the design is not known by the public before the application.[76] This requirement contradicts with the promotional nature of the fashion industry, which frequently built consumer excitement by showcasing new designs and

[71] See, eg, PRC Trademark No. 48311547 (China National Intellectual Property Administration) <http://wcjs.sbj.cnipa.gov.cn/txnS02.do?b9La8sqW=i.3owqlqEherz8jODW3xpJHDU6hiRHrkFfWBVpEuLozEDF4gxx8OWmhYHSOoHPjVxFYBF2GCA2OD_R4eCBTzJhkVJzyVtvFIK4HDBIwhgNDsiaaecnC3vG>.

[72] *Feng Wei Su Zhonghua Renmin Gongheguo Guojia Zhishi Chanquan Ju* (冯伟诉中华人民共和国国家知识产权局) [*Feng Wei v China National Intellectual Property Administration*] (Beijing Intellectual Property Court, July 2022).

[73] Ibid.

[74] See, eg, PRC patent publications nos. CN308000051S, CN307950857S, CN307950671S, CN307935731S, and CN307935734S <https://pss-system.cponline.cnipa.gov.cn/conventionalSearch>.

[75] *Nanjing Shengdiao Shizhuang Youxian Gongsi Su Liu Shiqin Deng* (南京圣迪奥时装有限公司诉刘世琴等) [*Nanjing SDeer Clothing Co, Ltd. v Liu Shiqin et al*] (Nanjing Interim People's Court 2016).

[76] *Zhuanli Fa* (专利法) [Patent Law] (promulgated by the Standing Comm National People's Congress, October 17, 2020, effective June 1, 2021) (hereinafter Patent Law 2020), Article 23.

products long before their official launch dates.[77] To illustrate, LV filed a design patent for its Archlight sneaker in China in 2017. In December 2020, upon the application of a third party, the CNIPA invalidated the said patent. The reason is simple and somehow ironic: The design had been disclosed to the public by the photos and videos featuring the Archlight sneaker posted on Chinese social media platforms Tencent and Sohu before the application date as a result of LV's promotional activities.[78]

Second, the filing and examination procedure associated with patent application is incompatible with the fast-paced nature of the fashion industry.[79] In contrast, the EU regime allows an unregistered community design (UCD) to be enforced without prior registration, which entails no acquisition fees.[80] This is why the EU is usually viewed as being more designer friendly.[81] Compared to design patents, copyright is sometimes a more efficient option because it does not require filing and examination. Trademarks also have the advantage of being renewable every 10 years hence conferring a perpetual monopoly,[82] whereas the duration of design patents in China is 15 years.[83]

9.3.4 *Unfair Competition*

The Anti-Unfair Competition Law (AUCL) provides fashion companies with another option to protect their designs. Specifically, Article 6.1 of

77 See generally, Anne Theodore Briggs, 'Hung out to Dry: Clothing Design Protection Pitfalls in United States Law' (2002) 24 *Hastings Communications & Entertainment Law Journal* 169.

78 *Wuxiao Xuangao Qingqiu Shencha Juedingshu Di 47305 Hao* (无效宣告请求审查决定书第47305号) [Decision No. 47305 on the Examination of Invalidation Application] (China National Intellectual Property Administration, December 30, 2020).

79 Atkinson et al, above n 17, at 528; Holton, above n 17, at 418; Urbach and Soussa, above n 17, at 28.

80 Council Regulation (EC) 1891/2006 amending Regulations (EC) No 6/2002 and (EC) No 40/94 to give effect to the accession of the European Community to the Geneva Act of the Hague Agreement concerning the international registration of industrial designs (2006) OJ L386/14.

81 See, eg, Kaitlyn N Pytlak, 'The Devil Wears Fraud-a: An Aristotelian-Randian Approach to Intellectual Property Law in the Fashion Industry' (2016) 15 *Virginia Sports & Entertainment Law Journal* 273, 286–287; Anya Jenkins Ferris, 'Real Art Calls for Real Legislation: An Argument against Adoption of the Design Piracy Prohibition Act' (2008) 26 *Cardozo Arts & Entertainment Law Journal* 559, 573.

82 Trademark Law 2019, above n 29, Article 40.

83 Patent Law 2020, above n 76, Article 42.

the AUCL prohibits business operators from using without authorisation 'product names, packages, decorations and other identical or similar symbols with certain influence' in a way that would mislead the public to associate the product with others.[84] Although VCA was not able to claim a 3D trademark over its above-mentioned four-leaf clover jewellery design, it successfully relied on Article 6.1 to protect the design against a knockoff manufactured by Shanghai Aijing Jewellery Co., Ltd. (SAJC), which brought an invalidation action against VCA's 3D trademark to the CNIPA.[85] After VCA's 3D trademark was declared invalid by the CNIPA, the Beijing Chaoyang District Court nonetheless accepted VCA's claims based on the AUCL and granted VCA damages of RMB 1.5 million (US$215,000).[86]

The Beijing Chaoyang District Court reasoned that, first, although a 'decoration' in the AUCL typically requires the separability of functionality and artistic values, the nature and features of the jewellery meant that the whole piece had no function other than being ornamental.[87] As such, it was fair to recognise the whole piece of jewellery as a decoration.[88] Second, the four-leaf clover pattern was uniquely developed by VCA and was not generic in jewellery design.[89] No other firm had used similar designs before VCA, and any subsequent use could not directly deprive the design of its distinctiveness.[90] Third, VCA had adduced evidence to show that the relevant public would associate the decoration with the brand, establishing itself as a 'decoration with certain influence' as stipulated by the AUCL.[91]

[84] *Fan Buzhengdang Jingzheng Fa* (反不正当竞争法) [Anti-Unfair Competition Law] (promulgated by the Standing Comm National People's Congress, April 23, 2019, effective April 23, 2019) (China) (hereinafter Anti-Unfair Competition Law 2019), Article 6(1). This is similar to the Lanham Act § 43(a) (United States).

[85] *Fanke Yabao Youxian Gongsi Su Shanghai Aijing Zhubao Youxian Gongsi Deng* (梵克雅宝有限公司诉上海瑷晶珠宝有限公司等) [*Van Cleef & Arpels SA v Shanghai Aijing Jewelry Co, Ltd et al*] (Beijing Chaoyang District. People's Court 2021) (China) (hereinafter *VCA v Shanghai Aijing*).

[86] Ibid.

[87] Compare this with the aesthetic functionality doctrine in the United States: *Christian Louboutin SA v Yves Saint Laurent America Hldg*, 696 F 3d 206, 220 (citing *Pagliero v Wallace China Co*, 198 F 2d 339 (9th Cir. 1952); *Qualitex Co v Jacobson Products Co*, 514 US 159, 162 (1995); *Knitwaves, Inc v Lollytogs Ltd*, 71 F 3d 996, 1006 (2nd Cir. 1995)).

[88] *VCA v Shanghai Aijing*, above n 85.

[89] Ibid.

[90] Ibid.

[91] Ibid.

VCA's successful enforcement of the AUCL against the knockoff manufacturer has provided an important precedent for itself, as well as for other fashion design companies. Subsequently, VCA embarked on more anti-piracy enforcement projects in China based on unfair competition claims.[92] Apart from the traditional copyright, trademark and design patent approaches, designs now have the potential to be protected as a 'decoration with certain influence' under the AUCL. Compared to trademark and design patent claims, a claim made under the AUCL does not require *ex ante* prosecution. This protection of design elements resembles trade dress protection in the United States.[93] First, they both entail a lower degree of market recognition than what is required under trademark laws. In *Two Pesos, Inc. v Taco Cabana, Inc.*, the US Supreme Court expressly ruled that a trade dress could be inherently distinctive and therefore acquiring secondary meaning was not necessary.[94] Second, aligned with the US Supreme Court's refusal to extend trade dress protection to a functional design that was the subject of an expired patent,[95] the Beijing court's decision in *VCA v Shanghai Aijing* seems to suggest a similar approach, requiring a finding of an absence of functionality to obtain protection under the AUCL.[96] Since a separate protection for fashion works is currently unavailable, a trade dress protection or its equivalent may be the best alternative.[97] The

[92] See, eg, *Fanke Yabao Youxian Gongsi Su Yiwu Zhuiyi Shipin Youxian Gongsi* (梵克雅宝有限公司诉义乌市缀宜饰品有限公司) [*Van Cleef & Arpels SA v Yiwu Zhuiyi Accessories Co, Ltd*] (Zhejiang Jinhua Interm. People's Court 2021).

[93] 15 USC §1125(a).

[94] *Two Pesos, Inc v Taco Cabana, Inc*, 505 US 763 (1992).

[95] *TrafFix Devices, Inc v Marketing Displays, Inc*, 532 US 23 (2001).

[96] *VCA v Shanghai Aijing*, above n 85. See also *Guanyu Shiyong <Zhonghua Renmin Gongheguo Fan Buzhengdang Jingzheng Fa> Ruogan Wenti De Jieshi* (关于适用〈中华人民共和国反不正当竞争法〉若干问题的解释) [Interpretation on Issues Related to the Application of the <Anti-Unfair Competition Law of the People's Republic of China>] (promulgated by the Supreme. People's Court, March 16, 2022, effective March 20, 2022) (China) (hereinafter 'Interpretation on the Anti-Unfair Competition Law 2022').

[97] Inga Munsinger, 'Trade Dress for Success: Fashion Designs as Distinctive Product Configurations' (2000) 1 *Texas Review of Entertainment & Sports Law* 47, 49 ('Absent a new statutory approach to design infringement, trade dress law is the remaining best approach.'); S Priya Bharathi, 'There Is More Than One Way to Skin a Copycat: The Emergence of Trade Dress to Combat Design Piracy of Fashion Work' (1996) 27 *Texas Technology Law Review* 1667, 1689.

shortcoming, however, lies in the claim's dependence on the owner's market reputation, which is a relatively vague concept.[98]

9.4 Accepting Design Elements as Non-traditional Trademarks

When comparing the prosecution and enforcement histories of VCA's 2D and 3D trademarks, one can observe that while a 3D trademark typically offers broader protection than a 2D trademark for the same design in litigation, obtaining a 3D trademark is also more challenging due to its higher distinctiveness threshold. This is illustrated by the fact that, while the 3D registration for the 'Alhambra' design was invalidated, the attempt to invalidate the 2D registration ultimately failed. The same is true for the pairing of a colour trademark and a regular trademark applied to particular colours. Although colour trademarks are usually harder to acquire, they could have a larger protection scope than a regular trademark designated to particular colours, as they are not confined by the shape of the specimen. For example, should Gucci have registered its green-red-green stripes as a colour trademark instead of a device mark, it would not be confined by the specimen filed in the application, which would allow greater flexibility in enforcement actions.[99] However, recent judicial practices[100] and the revision of trademark examination standards in 2021[101] have sent a positive signal to fashion companies regarding the use of non-traditional trademarks to protect their designs.

9.4.1 3D Trademark

In 2021, a 400-page review and examination guideline was issued by the CNIPA, replacing the previous version and elaborating in great detail

[98] Jyh-An Lee, 'Unfair Competition and Antitrust Law' in Christopher Heath (ed) *Intellectual Property Law in China* 418–19 (Wolters Kluwer, 2nd edn, 2021).

[99] For example, enforcement actions could be brought against similar marks where one of the three stripes, say, the red one in the middle, could narrower or wider than the other two.

[100] See, eg, *Dior*, *above* n 12; *Louboutin v TRAB*, above n 13.

[101] *Shangbiao Shencha Shenli Zhinan* (商标审查审理指南) [Guide on Trademark Review and Examination] (promulgated by the China National Intellectual Property Administration, November 16, 2021, effective January 1, 2022) (China) (hereinafter Guide on Trademark Review and Examination 2021).

examination standards under the 2019 Trademark Law.[102] According to this guideline, a 3D trademark refers to a trademark consisting of a stand-alone 3D symbol or a 3D symbol containing other elements.[103] When determining the distinctiveness of a 3D symbol, the examiner should also look into the way in which it is used before drawing conclusions about its source-identifying role.[104] An inherently indistinctive 3D symbol may acquire distinctiveness through use.[105] However, if a 3D symbol is considered 'functional', it cannot be registered, even with extensive evidence of use.[106] The ability to register 3D marks is important especially for luxury fashion brands whose iconic products in fact comprise widely recognisable features that are then replicated by a *shanzhai* manufacturer such as the Bottega Veneta's intrecciato weave and Hermes' Birkin and Kelly bags.

The section focusing on 3D symbols in the guideline was largely derived from the SPC's 2018 decision in *Christian Dior v China National Intellectual Property Administration* (hereinafter *Dior*).[107] In this case, Dior sought to extend its international 3D trademark registration of the J'Adore fragrance bottle to China through the Madrid Protocol, but the extension application was rejected by the China Trademark Office,[108] and Dior's appeals were denied all the way up to the Beijing High Court.[109]

Dior then petitioned the SPC based on two grounds: (1) the Trademark Office and the TRAB had mistakenly examined the application as a regular device trademark instead of a 3D trademark; and (2) the J'Adore fragrance bottle was uniquely devised and not a generic design for perfume bottles (and therefore possessed inherent distinctiveness); the design had also been extensively used and promoted in China and generated considerable market reputation and public association (and therefore acquired distinctiveness).[110] The SPC acknowledged the procedural error in not properly identifying the application as a 3D trademark and ordered the TRAB to re-examine the

[102] Ibid.
[103] Ibid at Chapter 6, Article 2.
[104] Ibid.
[105] Ibid at Chapter 6, Article 3.2.5.
[106] Ibid at Chapter 6, Article 3.3.
[107] *Dior*, above n 12.
[108] Taken over by the CNIPA since 2019.
[109] *Dior*, above n 12.
[110] Ibid.

registrability of the applied-for mark. Nonetheless, the SPC did not comment on the distinctiveness issue but only named a few factors that the TRAB should take into consideration before reaching a decision, including the time when the applied-for mark entered the Chinese market, the evidence supporting the use and promotion of the concerned trademark, the possibility of acquiring source-identifying function and the consistency of examination standards.[111] The SPC seemed to imply that these are the factors to be considered in the determination of acquired distinctiveness.

Pursuant to the SPC's order, the TRAB reissued a decision in 2019, allowing the registration of the J'Adore fragrance bottle as a 3D trademark designated on 'perfumes' in class 3, while rejecting the application on all other goods applied for.[112] The reason was that, while the TRAB still found the bottle inherently indistinctive, it accepted Dior's evidence of use and made a finding of acquired distinctiveness.[113] However, the evidence of use could only justify public association when used on perfumes; therefore, the application related to all other goods was rejected.[114]

Considering the difficulties in protecting fashion design with 3D trademarks, Dior's victory in China is commendable. Examples in other jurisdictions include the European Intellectual Property Office's (EUIPO) partial refusal in 2022 to grant a 3D trademark to another example of Dior's famous designs – the design of its Saddle Bag – based on a lack of distinctiveness.[115] Hermès also encountered failure in Italy when trying to enforce its EU-registered 3D trademarks on the shape of their Kelly and Birkin bags against a competitor, when both the Court of Florence and the Florence Court of Appeal upheld the defendant's invalidity

[111] Ibid. Just like Van Cleef & Arpels and the four-leaf clover, Dior's registration of the J'Adore fragrance bottle as a 2D device mark was accepted by the TRAB. It is for such reason that the SPC mentioned the consistency issue when correcting the TRAB's decision.

[112] *Guanyu Guoji Zhuce Di 1221382 Hao 'Tuxing (Sanwei Biaozhi, Zhiding Yanse)' Shangbiao Bohui Fushen Juedingshu* (关于国际注册第1221382号 '图形(三维标志、指定颜色)'商标驳回复审决定书) [Review Decision on the Refusal of Trademark International Registration No.1221382 'Device (3D Symbol, Designated Colour)'] (Trademark Review and Adjudication Board, January 14, 2019) (China).

[113] Ibid.

[114] Ibid.

[115] EUIPO Decision of the Second Board of Appeal in *Christian Dior v EUIPO*, Case R 32/2022-2 (EUIPO Board of Appeal, September 7, 2022).

counterclaim.[116] However, following the instruction of the Italian Supreme Court, this case will soon go through a second appeal, and some practitioners have predicted a favourable result for Hermès.[117]

9.4.2 Colour Trademark

China currently does not accept the registration of single-colour trademarks because of the monopoly power this may create,[118] nor does it generally accept registration of a colour-combination mark because a colour-combination mark is presumed to be inherently indistinctive. According to the examination standards,[119] the owner must submit evidence to prove that the colour combination mark has acquired sufficient distinctiveness through use to get it registered.[120] Again here, the fashion brands that use specific colours as emblematic of their products – such as Christian Louboutin's lacquered red sole or Gucci's red-and-green stripes – would desire to secure trademark registration so that they may more easily enforce their rights against *shanzhai* manufacturers as well as knockoffs by fast fashion brands.

In fact, there have been debates within China on the registrability of a single colour. The Draft Amendment of the Trademark Law, published in 2012, included a paragraph stating that 'a single colour used on a product or package of a product, which has acquired distinctiveness and can distinguish the product from others, can be registered as a trademark'.[121] However, this sentence was deleted in the final version.[122] China decided to take a rather conservative approach to recognising and protecting single colours as trademarks.

Nevertheless, there have been some encouraging developments for fashion design companies interested in obtaining 3D trademarks in China. Christian Louboutin has faced defeats in several countries,

116 *Hermès International Scpa (+1) + Buti S.r.l. (+2)*, Decision no. 30455 (Italian Supreme Court, 17 October 2022).

117 The Bird & Bird IP Team, above n 42.

118 Guide on Trademark Review and Examination 2021, above n 101, at Chapter 7, Article 2.

119 Ibid.

120 Ibid.

121 *Shangbiao Fa Xiuzhengan (Caoan)* (商标法修正案（草案）) [Draft Amendment of the Trademark Law] (promulgated by the Standing Comm National People's Congress, December 28, 2012) (China), Article 2(2).

122 Trademark Law 2019, above n 29, at Article 8.

including Japan, France and Switzerland, in trademarking its famous high-end women's high-heeled shoes with a red-lacquered outsole design,[123] but succeeded in the United States. In 2010, Louboutin filed an international registration for its red sole under the Madrid Protocol and sought to extend the registration to several member states, including China.[124] The TRAB rejected registration because the mark lacked distinctiveness. The TRAB first identified the mark as a combination of a high-heeled device and a single colour applied to the sole, which was inherently indistinctive.[125] The TRAB also held that the evidence submitted by Louboutin did not meet the threshold for acquired distinctiveness.[126] The case then went to the Beijing High Court. Eventually, the SPC upheld the Beijing High Court's decision recognising Louboutin's design as 'a single-colour trademark designated to a particular position', although it was not listed in Article 8 of the Trademark Law.[127] This categorisation is consistent with Louboutin's filing strategy in the EU, which was accepted by the CJEU.[128]

Louboutin's trademark application strategy in the United States might have valuable implications for China as well. The Court of Appeals for the Second Circuit instructed the United States Patent and Trademark Office (USPTO) that the registration of the red-sole mark could be approved for 'only those situations in which the red lacquered outsole contrasts in colour with the adjoining "upper" of the shoe'.[129] In other words, Louboutin could only obtain a trademark for the red sole with a contrasting upper colour (i.e., non-red). Since defendant Yves Saint Laurent's (YSL) outsole and the adjoining upper of the shoe were both red, its design did not infringe Louboutin's red-sole mark;[130] it was also worth noting that the YSL range of monochromatic high-heeled shoes all

[123] Cassidy Aranda, 'The Worldwide Trademark Battle over the Iconic Red Bottom Shoe', *Chicago-Kent Journal of Intellectual Property* (January 22, 2023)<https://studentorgs.kentlaw.iit.edu/ckjip/the-worldwide-trademark-battle-over-the-iconic-red-bottom-shoe/>.

[124] See Yong Wan and Hongxuyang Lu, 'Trademark Protection of Single-Colour Trademarks: A Study of the Chinese Louboutin Case' (2020) 10 (2) *Queen Mary Journal of Intellectual Property* 255, 257.

[125] *Louboutin v TRAB*, above n 13.

[126] Ibid.

[127] *Guojia Zhishi Chanquan Ju Su Kelisiti Lubutuo* (国家知识产权局诉克里斯提鲁布托) [*China National Intellectual Property Administration v Christian Louboutin*] (Supreme People's Court, December 24, 2019) (China) (hereinafter *CNIPA v Louboutin*).

[128] *Louboutin v Van Haren Schoenen BV*, Case C-163/16 (CJEU, June 12, 2018).

[129] *Louboutin v YSL*, above n 38.

[130] Ibid.

featured soles in the same colour as the adjoining upper of the shoe (e.g., red-red, blue-blue, green-green). The concept of a red sole with a contrasting upper colour is similar to the colour-combination trademark, but the former provides trademark owners with broader protection because there is no need to identify the exact contrasting upper colour.

9.5 Conclusion

In the fashion world, *shanzhai* has been a concern for both high-end luxury brands and indie designers for many years. While it is easier to report to local authorities or claim trademark infringement in legal proceedings against manufacturers of counterfeits, the most effective action against knockoffs remains ambiguous. Design elements may be protected by laws governing copyright, trademarks, design patents and unfair competition, but each of these laws has some limitations. Just like the originality requirement for copyright and the novelty requirement for design patents, the distinctiveness requirement has prevented numerous fashion designs from being registered as trademarks.

Although the SPC's decision in *Dior* suggests that it is possible for a sign that was not inherently distinctive to acquire distinctiveness through use, and ultimately qualify for registration as a trademark, the standard for achieving that is extremely high and almost equal to that for a 'well-known trademark'. Alternatively, *VCA* has provided the fashion industry with a rather innovative approach based on the protection of 'decoration with certain influence' in the AUCL. It is easier for design companies like VCA to prove that their design elements have 'certain influence' under AUCL than that they have 'acquired distinctiveness' under the Trademark Law. Notably, Louboutin has also successfully enforced its rights against a knockoff designer of similar red-sole heels in China under the AUCL,[131] while the status of its trademark application is still uncertain. Chanel also protected the shape of its signature No.5 fragrance bottle under the AUCL against a perfume brand in China.[132] The series

[131] *Kelisiti Lubutuo Jianyi Gufen Youxian Gongsi Deng Su Guangdong Wanlima Shiye Gufen Youxian Gongsi Deng* (克里斯提·鲁布托简易股份有限公司等诉广东万里马实业股份有限公司等) [*Christian Louboutin Ltd et al v Guangdong Wanlima Industrial Co, Ltd*] (Beijing Intellectual Property Court 2022). The case is pending appeal at Beijing Higher People's Court.

[132] *Xiangnaier Gufen Youxian Gongsi Su Yiwu Shi Aizhiyu Huazhuangpin Youxian Gongsi* (香奈儿股份有限公司诉义乌市爱之语化妆品有限公司) [*Chanel, Inc v Yiwu Story of Love Co, Ltd*] (Shaanxi High People's Court, 2021).

of cases revealed that there is huge potential for fashion companies to use the AUCL to protect their designs in China.

Nevertheless, the legal standards with respect to the application of the AUCL need to be further clarified by the judiciary. The current law does not clearly distinguish between 'certain influence' and 'acquired distinctiveness'. Moreover, while the AUCL stipulates that a symbol possesses 'certain influence' when it exhibits a specific level of market recognition and distinctive attributes that can identify the product's source,[133] the statutory wording is remarkably similar to the definition of distinctiveness in the Trademark Law.[134] This similarity could lead to confusion regarding the legal treatment of a symbol under the AUCL and a mark under the Trademark Law. It is also unclear whether the standard used to determine the separability of aesthetic value and functionality in the AUCL is the same as that used in copyright law. If they are different, a clear explanation regarding how, why and to what extent they differ is desirable. If these issues are resolved, the AUCL is anticipated to become the most potent tool for fashion designers in the fight against knockoffs. This, in turn, would address fashion houses' enduring concerns about investing in creativity and expanding in the Chinese market.

[133] Interpretation on the Anti-Unfair Competition Law 2022, above n 96, at Article 4.1.

[134] See Guide on Trademark Review and Examination 2021, above n 101, at Chapter 4, Article 2 ('The distinctiveness of a trademark requires a mark to have features that enable the relevant public to identify the source of the product of service.').

PART IV

Looking Ahead

10

Threads That Last

Geographical Indications for Textiles

DEV S GANGJEE*

ABSTRACT

For traditional textiles, geographical indication (GI) protection offers improved brand visibility while insulating a hard-earned reputation against misuse. This form of IP has additional synergies with the shift towards more sustainable production and consumption in the global fashion industry. These textiles have conventionally used natural fibres, organic dyes and artisanal methods. They are also meant to be reused, unlike fast fashion. This chapter investigates this 'GI optimism', asking whether there are legal and institutional mechanisms to systematically reinforce sustainability commitments. It unpacks a recent regulatory reform in the EU, whereby the GI product specification can incorporate voluntary 'sustainability undertakings' by producer groups. The chapter concludes by observing that synergies between different aspects of sustainability should not be taken for granted, if GI law is to truly deliver on 'threads that last'.

10.1 Introduction

Harris tweed, Banaras silk saris and Kente cloth enjoy a considerable reputation, as traditional textiles feted for their quality and provenance. Geographical indications (GIs) offer a mode of place-based branding for

* I would like to thank David Tan, for weaving this project together. I would also like to thank Delphine Marie-Vivien and Flavia Guerrieri for substantive feedback. The usual caveat applies. The title for this chapter is inspired by Kenyan poet Beatrice Kariuki: 'We need circular industries where old looks are made new . . .. Less packaging, more reuse. Threads that last.' See UN Environment Programme, 'Wasted: Fast Fashion Is Fueling Our Ecological Crisis #beatpollution', YouTube (November 25, 2022) <https://www.youtube.com/watch?v=0v7f0KeNpv8&t=4s>.

such regional products. This form of intellectual property can help to shape a distinct brand identity and ensure better legal protection for their reputations. Once protected, the price premium derived from this reputation makes GI production potentially sustainable across three registers.[1] In socio-cultural terms, legal recognition as a GI can sustain the demand for heritage textile products, renewing important symbols of cultural identity, traditional production practices and local communities. In economic terms, improving market access can also support producer communities whose livelihood depends on these products, while facilitating closer collaboration within these communities. Where successful, this results in sustainable employment, often in rural or under-developed regions. Moreover, the GI approach, with its emphasis on local resources and artisanal methods, potentially avoids environmental sustainability criticisms targeting the mainstream fashion industry. GI protection may therefore align promisingly with the 'three pillars' model of sustainability: social, economic and environmental.[2]

GIs are an attractive option because the sustainability credentials of the global fashion industry are being scrutinised more closely than ever. Focusing primarily on environmental sustainability, this chapter critically assesses whether this 'GI optimism' is warranted, asking whether there are legal and institutional mechanisms to *systematically reinforce* sustainability commitments, focusing on recent legal reforms in the EU. Following this introduction, Section 10.2 outlines the basics of GI protection and describes how crafts and textiles are increasingly accommodated within this field of IP law. It then sets out why the sustainability crisis of global fashion might be an opportunity for traditional textiles,

[1] For a framework and indicators to assess sustainability in the agricultural products context, see Emilie Vandecandelaere et al, 'The Geographical Indication Pathway to Sustainability: A Framework to Assess and Monitor the Contributions of Geographical Indications to Sustainability through a Participatory Process' (2021) 13(14) *Sustainability* 7535 (hereafter Vandecandelaere et al, 'Geographical Indication'). See also Giovanni Belletti, Andrea Marescotti and Jean-Marc Touzard, 'Geographical Indications, Public Goods, and Sustainable Development: The Roles of Actors' Strategies and Public Policies' (2017) 98 *World Development* 45.

[2] Ben Purvis, Yong Mao and Darren Robinson, 'Three Pillars of Sustainability: In Search of Conceptual Origins' (2019) 14 *Sustainability Science* 681. The 'pillars' are also reconceived as intersecting circles in some of the literature, to suggest that they interact. However, even this set of approaches is premised on sustainable *growth*. The incompatibility of relentless GDP-oriented growth with the health of the biosphere, or with human wellbeing, has led to calls by heterodox economists for prosperity without growth: Giorgos Kallis, *Degrowth* (Agenda, 2018); Tim Jackson, *Prosperity without Growth: Economics for a Finite Planet* (Routledge, 2nd edn, 2016).

which are territorially embedded. Section 10.3 unpacks a recent regulatory experiment in the EU, which will allow the product specification, describing how and where GI products can be made, to accommodate voluntary 'sustainability undertakings' by producer groups. However, sustainability is being emphasised in different ways in EU GI policy. While the agricultural GI regime embraces the social, economic and environmental dimensions of sustainability, the crafts and textiles regime prioritises economic sustainability, given the relatively small-scale nature of production. This is an oversight, since commercial pressures can lead to adaptations that are justified in economic terms but have significantly detrimental environmental consequences. Section 10.4 briefly concludes by observing that synergies between different aspects of sustainability should not be taken for granted in GI law and policy, if it is to truly deliver on 'threads that last'.

10.2 GIS: The Hope

10.2.1 What Are GIs?

Like trademarks, GIs are signs that convey information about products to consumers and can function as valuable brands. Article 22.1 of the TRIPS Agreement[3] describes them as '*indications* which identify a good as originating in the territory of a Member, or a region or locality in that territory, where a given *quality, reputation or other characteristic* of the good is *essentially attributable to its geographical origin*' (emphasis added). Prominent examples include Champagne, Bordeaux and Prosecco for wine, Café de Colombia for coffee, Darjeeling for tea, Roquefort for cheese and Parma for ham. GI protection is therefore concerned with preventing unauthorised uses of such signs, which may either cause harm to their communicative functions – for example, by misleading consumers about provenance – or misappropriate their brand image. Notably, these regimes protect signs but do not protect the underlying production methods. Thus 'GIs are about what things can be called. They are about labelling, packaging and marketing. Nothing in GI rules prevents any producer anywhere from using the techniques specified as being associated with the GI name. But they may not use

[3] Marrakesh Agreement Establishing the World Trade Organization, opened for signature April 15, 1994, 1869 UNTS 299, 33 ILM 1197 (signed April 15, 1994) Annex 1C.

the name to communicate the production techniques they have used'.[4] While Champagne is a protected term in many jurisdictions, the *méthode champenoise* has been widely adopted by sparkling wine producers around the world.

Despite this shared commitment to the protection of signs, four features set GIs apart from trademarks.[5] First, as per the TRIPS definition in Art 22.1, GIs indicate geographical origin (a place) as opposed to trade origin (commercial source) for a product. Second, all producers from within the region of origin who follow the established production methods are invested in their use. This gives rise to co-ordination issues around product definition and a collective interest in any ensuing reputation.[6] Third, in order to qualify as a GI, producers must demonstrate – in a causally verifiable manner – that the product in question owes its qualities or reputation to the region of origin. In this regard, wine is the archetypal subject matter with *terroir* providing the causal explanation for the distinctive quality or typicity (*typicité*) of wine.[7] However, as we will see immediately below, crafts and textiles cannot be linked to a place in the same way that grapes anchor wines to geologically and climatically defined regions. Fourth, there needs to be a consensus around the underlying product that is referenced by the sign. If a GI is promising something about a product to consumers, we need to be clear about the content of this promise. Sui generis protection systems for GIs usually require an application to be made to a public registrar.[8] At the core of this application is the product specification, also referred to as the qualification document or *cahier des charges*. A crucial part of legally defining a GI is therefore a detailed product description, emphasising its distinctive

[4] Hazel Moir, 'Geographical Indications: An Assessment of EU Treaty Demands' in Annmarie Elijah et al (eds) *Australia, the European Union and the New Trade Agenda* (Australian National University Press, 2017) 122.

[5] For an overview of legal features and forms of GI protection, see Michael Blakeney, *The Protection of Geographical Indications: Law and Practice* (Edward Elgar, 2nd edn, 2019).

[6] Xiomara F Quiñones-Ruiz, et al, 'Why Early Collective Action Pays Off: Evidence from Setting Protected Geographical Indications' (2017) 32(2) *Renewable Agriculture and Food Systems* 179.

[7] Alessandro Stanziani, 'Wine Reputation and Quality Controls: The Origin of the AOCs in 19th Century France' (2004) 18 *European Journal of Law and Economics* 149; Percy H Dougherty (ed), *The Geography of Wine: Regions, Terroir and Technique* (Springer, 2012).

[8] Dev S Gangjee, '*Sui Generis* or Independent Geographical Indications Protection' in Irene Calboli and Jane C Ginsburg (eds), *The Cambridge Handbook of International and Comparative Trade Mark Law* (Cambridge University Press, 2020) 256 (hereafter Gangjee, '*Sui Generis*').

qualities that set it apart from similar products – what makes *this particular* handwoven fabric different from others?[9] These differentiating features which characterise the product should then be causally linked back to the region of origin in verifiable ways:

> [The application] should demonstrate in what way the product's characteristics are due to the geographical area and what the natural, human and other elements are which give its specificity to the product . . .. [It] must describe the specificities of the product and of the geographical area which produces or influences these factors, and how these two are linked. This is the 'link' between the geographical area and the quality of the product. The description must also underline in what way the methods of production for the product are superior to others and contribute to its specific and distinctive character.[10]

This link between product and place distinguishes GIs as a form of intellectual property. Formal examination by a public registrar serves to certify this nexus.

One further clarification is helpful at this stage. In the case of a traditional textile, when can its quality, reputation or characteristic features be 'essentially attributable' to its geographical origin? For such products, a combination of natural and human factors usually influences the end result. Natural factors include the sourcing of raw materials from within the defined region. Examples include the conical hats from Hué in Vietnam, prepared from a local variety of leaves,[11] or the fleece of the mountainous goat breed Capra Hiracus for making Kashmiri Pashmina shawls from India.[12] Pashmina is a down fibre or under coat derived from this native breed, which lives at high Himalayan altitudes with

[9] For an overview of the specification and other registration requirements when applying for a GI, see World Intellectual Property Organization (WIPO), *Compilation of the Replies to Questionnaire I on the National and Regional Systems that can Provide a Certain Protection to Geographical Indications*, SCT/40/5 (2019) Annex 104-115 (hereafter WIPO, *Compilation*).

[10] See, in the context of Agricultural GIs, 'Guide to Applicants – How to Compile the Single Document', *European Commission* (July 6, 2023) <https://agriculture.ec.europa.eu/system/files/2023-07/guide-to-applicants-of-single-document_en.pdf>.

[11] Barbara Pick, Delphine Marie-Vivien and Dong Bui Kim, 'The Use of Geographical Indications in Vietnam: A Promising Tool for Socioeconomic Development?' in Irene Calboli and Ng-Loy Wee Loon (eds), *Geographical Indications at the Crossroads of Trade, Development, and Culture: Focus on Asia-Pacific* (Cambridge University Press, 2017) 305.

[12] Yaseer Ahmad Mir and Mushtaq Ahmad Darzi, 'Kashmir Pashmina: A Journey of Standardization through Geographical Indication' (2017) 3(5) *International Journal of Applied Research* 1.

severe winter temperatures. The resulting fabric is renowned for its fineness and warmth. Human factors refer to the practical skills and inter-generational, collectively transmitted know-how crucial to the manufacture of such textiles.[13] Delphine Marie-Viven describes the skill involved in the production of Kancheepuram silk saris, woven in the famous temple town of Kanchipuram in Southern India:

> The method of production is characterized by the use of thick silk yarn which gives it its heavy weight and bright colours as well as by the use of two extra shuttles on each side of the loom, besides the shuttle used for the main body of the sari, to weave the borders in contrasting colors. The reputation of Kancheepuram saris also lies in the use of silver, gold and red silk threads known as 'zari'. It is generally accepted that counterfeit Kancheepuram saris are made of thinner silk yarn and have only one border and do not contain gold. The method of production includes dressing the yarn, sizing, the degumming of the yarn, including the number of times it is rinsed and the time required to do so, as well as a meticulously detailed dyeing process.[14]

However, in many cases it may *only* be human factors that link a product to a specific region, with raw materials being drawn from a wider catchment area. Even in such situations, producers' skills will have evolved through interactions with local environmental features or localised socio-economic circumstances. While artisans can migrate with their skills, the knowhow associated with such famous regional products has usually been shaped by its geographical context (e.g., climatic conditions favouring light, porous fabrics, or textile designs bearing motifs that have local religious or cultural significance).[15] Where these natural and/or human factors are responsible for the product's characteristic features and associated reputation over time, this aligns with the definitional requirements of Art 22.1 TRIPS.[16]

[13] European Commission, Green Paper: Making the Most out of Europe's Traditional Know-How: A Possible Extension of Geographical Indication Protection of the European Union to Non-Agricultural Products, COM 469 (July 15, 2014)4 (hereafter European Commission, Green Paper).

[14] Delphine Marie-Vivien, 'Do Geographical Indications for Handicrafts Deserve a Special Regime? Insights from Worldwide Law and Practice' in William van Caenegem and Jen A Cleary (eds) *The Importance of Place: Geographical Indications as a Tool for Local and Regional Development* (Springer, 2017) 221, 231 (hereafter Marie-Vivien, 'Geographical Indications for Handicrafts').

[15] Ibid 243–244.

[16] Gangjee, '*Sui Generis*', above n 8, 36; Andrea Zappalaglio, Flavia Guerrieri and Suelen Carls, 'Sui Generis Geographical Indications for the Protection of Non-Agricultural

Finally, the applicant group is required to submit inspection or verification criteria (which specific manufacturing processes, or product features, will be tested for compliance with the product specification) and additionally identify who will be responsible for ensuring compliance (frequently an unrelated third party with the necessary certification expertise).[17] Consequently, while the source indication function and brand dimensions of GIs overlap with trademarks, the collective interest in protection, geographical embeddedness and certification of the causal link set them apart.

10.2.2 *GIs Protection for Traditional Textiles*

GI protection seeks to preserve the ability of a sign to communicate the distinctive geographical origin and associated quality of a product. While the initial regimes originated in the context of guaranteeing the regional provenance of wines in France,[18] over time the subject matter categories have expanded. Today, GIs are registered around the world for wines, spirits, foodstuffs, agricultural produce and crafts.[19] Within the broad category of craft GIs one finds several examples of textiles as well as leather and jewellery products, which are of relevance for the fashion sector.[20]

Products in the EU: Can the Quality Schemes Fulfil the Task?' (2020) 51 *International Review of Intellectual Property and Competition Law* 31.

17 European Union Intellectual Property Office, Protection and Control of Geographical Indications for Agricultural Products in the EU Member States, European Commission (December 2017) (hereafter European Union Intellectual Property Office, Protection and Control); Delphine Marie-Vivien and Isabelle Vagneron, 'One Size Fits all or Tailor-Made? Building Appropriate Certification Systems for Geographical Indications in Southeast Asia' (2017) 3(2) *World Food Policy* 105.

18 On the historical evolution of GI protection, see Dev S Gangjee, *Relocating the Law of Geographical Indications* (Cambridge University Press, 2012); Andrea Zappalaglio, *The Transformation of EU Geographical Indications Law: The Present, Past and Future of the Origin Link* (Routledge, 2021).

19 WIPO 'World Intellectual Property Indicators', World Intellectual Property Organisation (2022) 144 ('GIs in force relating to wines and spirits (51%) accounted for just over half of the 2021 global total, while agricultural products and foodstuffs accounted for 43.6% and handicrafts 3.9% of the total.').

20 Case studies of textile GIs include Mohammad Ataul Karim and Mohammad Ershadul Karim, 'Protection of "Handicraft" as Geographical Indications under Municipal Law, TRIPS and BTAs vis-à-vis CETA: "Bangladeshi Jamdani" as Case Study' (2017) 7(1) *Queen Mary Journal of Intellectual Property* 49; Servjaeta Verma and Nandita Mishra, 'Recognition and Marketing Opportunities of a "GI" Tag in Handloom Product: A Study of Banaras Brocades and Sarees' (2018) 23 *Journal of Intellectual Property Rights* 101; Michelle Okyere and Janice Denoncourt, 'Protecting Ghana's Intellectual Property Rights in *Kente*

The Organisation for an International Geographical Indications Network (oriGIn), a non-profit non-governmental organisation (NGO) advocating for better GI protection, maintains a searchable international compilation of GIs. This includes 381 textile-related protected GIs – including for brocades, silks, woollens, saris, cashmere, tweeds, embroidery work, block printed materials, tie-dyed fabrics, kimonos and shawls – from a range of countries.[21] The Lisbon Express database managed by WIPO contains 37 international registrations for textile products registered under the Lisbon System,[22] almost exclusively from the Czech Republic, France and Iran.[23] National GI registers in countries such as India and Thailand contain sizeable numbers of registrations for crafts, including textiles.[24] An in-depth study of Indian handloom GIs identifies 74 registrations as of 2021, since they are an important part of the informal economy, which nevertheless generates significant employment.[25] Several examples of traditional textiles are found across Latin America, including Colombia (Wayuu), Guatemala (Maya), Bolivia (Textileros de Cochabamba), El Salvador (San Sebastián) and Panama (Kuna).[26] In a significant development, the European Union has recently introduced a registration system for non-agricultural products, including extracted products such as marble, crafts and textiles, including lace and embroidered products.[27]

Textiles: The Case for Geographical Indications' (2021) 16(4–5) *Journal of Intellectual Property Law and Practice* 415(hereafter Okyere and Denoncourt, 'Protecting Ghana').

21 'Worldwide GI Compilation', Organization for an International Geographical Indications Network <https://www.origin-gi.com/worldwide-gi-compilation/>.

22 The Lisbon System protects GIs across 72 countries, through international registration. It draws its membership from a combination of the original Lisbon Agreement, 1958, and the more recent Geneva Act of that Agreement, 2015. See 'Lisbon – The International System of Appellations of Origin and Geographical Indications', World Intellectual Property Organization <https://www.wipo.int/lisbon/en/>.

23 'Lisbon Express Structured Search', World Intellectual Property Organization <https://lisbon-express.wipo.int/struct-search> (using the search parameters: (*) AND (CAT/NONFOOD) AND (CAT/TEXTILE) AND (ST/false) AND (LISBON_ACT/Y) (GENEVA_ACT/Y)).

24 Marie-Vivien, 'Geographical Indications for Handicrafts', above n 14, 222–223.

25 Nidhi Buch and Hetvi Trivedi, *Geographical Indications of Indian Handlooms: Between Legal Right and Real Right* (Routledge, 2022) 3 (hereafter Buch and Trivedi, *Indian Handlooms*).

26 Patricia Covarrubia, 'Geographical Indications of Traditional Handicrafts: A Cultural Element in a Predominantly Economic Activity' (2019) 50 *International Review of Intellectual Property and Competition Law* 441.

27 Regulation (EU) 2023/2411 of the European Parliament and of the Council of October 18, 2023, on the protection of geographical indications for craft and industrial products and amending Regulations (EU) 2017/1001 and (EU) 2019/1753 [2023] OJL 1/56.

Once registered, GIs are protected against statutorily defined unauthorised uses. The widely shared intuition that counterfeits or fakes are undesirable can be further unpacked via the information efficiency hypothesis, which relates to the degree of information reflected in the prices of products in efficient markets.[28] Within mainstream neoclassical economics, consumers are characterised as utility maximising agents attempting to make optimal choices.[29] Rational decision-making is premised on the availability of sufficient information in the marketplace. However, GI products can be characterised as either experience goods or credence goods, whose quality cannot be easily verified by consumers prior to purchase ('How can I tell if this is a genuine Bordeaux wine?'). In these situations, sellers possess more information about the products than buyers, whereupon information asymmetry arises.[30] This informational imbalance could lead to familiar forms of market failure such as adverse selection and the ensuing 'market for lemons', driving quality downwards.[31] Reputation signals and the conveying of reliable information relating to product attributes are two methods of restoring informational efficiency. Public authorities intervene by establishing a legal regime that grants exclusive rights, thereby regulating who can legitimately use a sign for traditional

[28] Joseph E Stiglitz, 'Imperfect Information in the Product Market' in Richard Schmalensee and Robert D Willig (eds) *Handbook of Industrial Organization* (Elsevier Science, 1989) vol 1, 769.

[29] There are convincing challenges to this account, once bounded rationality is acknowledged: Peter Diamond and Hannu Vartiainen (eds), *Behavioural Economics and Its Applications* (Princeton University Press, 2012). However, it qualifies but does not entirely reject the core economic assumption that additional information is deemed helpful for decision-making, since it respects an individual's autonomy.

[30] Dwijen Rangnekar, 'The Socio-Economics of Geographical Indications', United Nations Conference on Trade and Development-International Centre for Trade and Sustainable Development Project on IPRs and Sustainable Development, Issue Paper No 8 (May 2004); Cerkia Bramley, Estelle Biénabe and Johann F Kirsten, 'The Economics of Geographical Indications: Towards a Conceptual Framework for Geographical Indication Research in Developing Countries' in *The Economics of Intellectual Property* (World Intellectual Property Organization, 2009) 109; Ramona Teuber, 'Protecting Geographical Indications: Lessons Learned from the Economic Literature', European Association of Agricultural Economists Congress, Zurich, No 116081 (August 30, 2011). Informational efficiency is further supplemented by other economic theories relating to club goods or conventions, which explore the costs and benefits of establishing producer groups, product specifications and the expenses of legal protection (exclusion from the club).

[31] George A Akerlof, 'The Market for "Lemons": Quality Uncertainty and the Market Mechanism' (1970) 84(3) *Quarterly Journal of Economics* 488.

regional products. As a result, protected signs can be trusted. This not only reduces consumer search costs but also prevents undesirable free riding. Additionally, for GIs, credible information is provided – via the examination preceding registration – about provenance, quality attributes and modes of production. Two products bearing the same protected GI should share the same origin-specific qualities. In other words, registration empowers consumers by converting credence or experience attributes into quasi-search ones.

The informational efficiency account justifies one important tier of GI protection rules. Signs or logos for traditional textiles are protected against unauthorised misleading uses relating to origin or quality. Article 22.2 of TRIPS requires members to 'provide the legal means for interested parties to prevent . . . the use of any means in the designation or presentation of a good that indicates or suggests that the good in question originates in a geographical area other than the true place of origin in a manner which misleads the public as to the geographical origin of the good'. Article 40(1)(c) of the recent EU Crafts and Industrial Products [CIP] Regulation (EU) 2023/2411 prohibits any 'false or misleading indication as to the provenance, origin, nature or essential qualities of the product . . . [used in packaging or advertising] liable to convey a false impression as to its origin'. Article 40(1)(d) of the CIP Regulation broadly prohibits 'any other practice liable to mislead the consumer as to the true origin of the product'.

Increasingly, sui generis regimes also prevent unauthorised uses that free ride on a product's reputation, or else harm the brand image of regional products, via dilution or tarnishing associations, even where no consumers are misled.[32] For instance, Article 40(1)(a) of the CIP Regulation prevents the use of a protected craft or textile GI against 'any direct or indirect commercial use of the [GI] in respect of products not covered by the registration . . . where the use of the name exploits, weakens, dilutes, or is detrimental to, the reputation of the protected geographical indication'. Article 40(1)(b) prevents any 'misuse, imitation or evocation of the [protected name], even if the true origin . . . is indicated or if the protected geographical indication is translated or accompanied by an expression such as "style", "type", "method", "as produced in", "imitation" [etc]'. This second, far more generous tier of protection exists to protect the reputation that arises from the collective,

[32] World Intellectual Property Organization, *Compilation*, above n 9, Annex 286–309.

inter-generational investment in the underlying product.[33] GIs therefore appeal as a form of brand-based protection for traditional crafts and textiles, since it has previously proved challenging to accommodate such products within the 'content protection' fields of IP such as copyright and design law.[34]

Premised on these normative foundations, legal protection creates the conditions for legitimate GI producers to obtain a price premium, by ensuring exclusive use of the sign for the purposes of differentiating their products. An EU study calculated the average value premium – the price difference between EU GI products and comparable standard products – as 2.07 in 2017.[35] The premium across different categories of products is further differentiated, with wines at 2.85, spirits at 2.52 and agricultural products and foodstuffs at 1.5. There is an expectation that consumers' willingness to pay a price premium also exists for crafts and textiles GIs as well, once consumers become aware of the certification guarantees performed by GIs.[36] These products often rely on artisanal modes of

[33] *Comité Interprofessionnel du Vin de Champagne v Aldi*, Case C-393/16, ECLI:EU:C:2017:991, at [38] (CJEU, December 20, 2017) ('[GI protection exists to] offer a guarantee of quality due to their geographical provenance, with the aim of enabling agricultural operators to secure higher incomes in return for a genuine effort to improve quality, and of preventing improper use of those designations by third parties seeking to profit from the reputation which those products have acquired by their quality.'); *European Commission v Council of the European Union*, Case C-389/15, ECLI:EU:C:2017:604 at [AG77] (CJEU, July 26, 2017) ('[The] purpose of geographical indications is to preserve traditional knowledge, cultural expressions and specific manufacturing skills, and to ensure that consumers are given reliable information about the quality of the goods in question.').

[34] For an overview, see WIPO, 'The Protection of Traditional Cultural Expressions: Updated Draft Gap Analysis', WIPO/GRTKF/IC/37/7 (2018); J Janewa Osei-Tutu, 'Protecting Culturally Identifiable Fashion: What Role for GIs?' (2021) 14 *Florida International University Law Review* 571, 578–580.

[35] AND-International, 'Study on Economic Value of EU Quality Schemes, Geographical Indications (GIs) and Traditional Specialities Guaranteed (TSGs) – Final Report', European Commission, Directorate-General for Agriculture and Rural Development (February 12, 2021) 100–102. A synthesis of studies measuring the price premium can be found in Áron Török et al, 'Understanding the Real-World Impact of Geographical Indications: A Critical Review of the Empirical Economic Literature' (2020) 12(22) *Sustainability* 12–15.

[36] Mohsin Shafi, 'Geographical Indications and Sustainable Development of Handicraft Communities in Developing Countries' (2022) 25(1) *Journal of World Intellectual Property* 122, 127 (hereafter Shafi, 'Handicraft Communities'); Dyah Permata Budi Asri et al., 'Valuing Local Heritage: Issue and Challenges of Geographical Indication Protection for Local Artisans in Indonesia Kasongan Village Heritage' (2022) 25(1) *Journal of World Intellectual Property* 71.

production, while researchers have noticed a 'handmade effect' which positively shapes consumer purchase preferences. Handcrafted products appear more attractive to consumers, since they perceive them as embodying the artisan's love for their craft in a way that machine-made products cannot replicate.[37] In addition, there is also a perceived prestige value associated with handmade fashion products such as clothing, handbags and shoes. One study identifies (verifiable) craft authenticity, the purchaser's knowledge about the craft and social identity as the key determinants that influence purchases by Indian consumers.[38] Another study from India concludes from survey evidence that GI labels that convey reliable quality information about traditional handlooms do increase trust and positively influence consumer purchase intentions.[39] A review of the EU context suggests that where artisanal crafts or textiles have shorter and less complex value chains, 'it is more likely that the price premium stays with producers'.[40]

However, the same study also notes that there is comparatively less research on willingness to pay a premium for non-agricultural GIs, while distribution effects may vary: 'The question is whether the premium will cover the costs [since GIs are usually more expensive to produce] and who will benefit.'[41] It should be noted that the beneficiaries of this price premium will vary in accordance with the power dynamics specific to each supply chain. For some agricultural GIs, the price premium is captured by local farmers, whereas in others it is captured by traders and distributors.[42] These concerns carry over to craft and textile GIs; for

[37] Christoph Fuchs, Martin Schreier and Stijn MJ Van Osselaer, 'The Handmade Effect: What's Love Got to Do with It?' (2015) 79(2) *Journal of Marketing* 98. See also Francielle Frizzo et al, 'The Genuine Handmade: How the Production Method Influences Consumers' Behavioral Intentions through Naturalness and Authenticity' (2020) 26(4) *Journal of Food Products Marketing* 279.

[38] Ajay Kumar Koli, 'Handmade OK Please: Key Criteria for Purchasing Craft Items by Indian consumers' (2023) 13(1) *Journal of Cultural Heritage Management and Sustainable Development* 43.

[39] Sangeetha K Prathap and Sreelaksmi CC, 'Determinants of Purchase Intention of Traditional Handloom Apparels with Geographical Indication among Indian Consumers'(2022) 4(1) *Journal of Humanities and Applied Social Sciences* 21.

[40] Julia Rzepecka et al, 'Economic Aspects of Geographical Indication Protection at EU Level for Non-Agricultural Products in the EU', European Commission, Directorate-General for Internal Market, Industry, Entrepreneurship and SMEs (2020) 27 (hereafter Rzepecka et al, 'Economic Aspects').

[41] Ibid 30.

[42] Emilie Vandecandelaere et al, *Strengthening Sustainable Food Systems through Geographical Indications: An Analysis of Economic Impacts* (Food and Agriculture

example, a price premium has not resulted in equitable wages for the weavers of the reputed Indian Banaras sari.[43]

While questions therefore remain about who benefits from legal protection, in its absence the harm to traditional craft and textile producers is abundantly clear. Lookalike products enter the market at lower price points, while misleadingly using the GI designation and frustrating consumer expectations:

> Competition comes mostly from competitors located outside of the region, who produce either similar products or imitation products at lower costs then abusing the GI name and deceiving consumers. Besides the fact that consumers might be attracted by the 'lower price' of the other products, they are often not able to perceive the difference between a genuine and a counterfeited or imitation product, as the quality of the counterfeits are becoming increasingly better.[44]

The lower price is often attributed to factors such as less costly labour outside the original region of production, cheaper raw materials or the adoption of industrial-scale, mechanised production processes. To take one example, the city of Varanasi in the state of Uttar Pradesh in India is a historic weaving centre famed for its Banaras saris. The favourable reputation is due to the finely textured silk and intricate weaving techniques, often involving brocade work with *zari* or metallic thread and displaying complex design motifs or *bootis*.[45] In the recent past, concerns have included a flood of far more economical, lower quality imitations from China as well as the other states in India (such as Gujarat); the imitations being made by power looms as opposed to more labour-intensive traditional techniques, the use of synthetic materials or other cheaper varieties of silks in these imitations and the poaching of the best

Organization, 2018) 15 (hereafter Vandecandelaere et al, *Strengthening Sustainable Food Systems*); Leonardo Cei, Edi DeFrancesco and Gianluca Stefani, 'From Geographical Indications to Rural Development: A Review of the Economic Effects of European Union Policy' (2018) 10(10) *Sustainability* 3745 (hereafter Cei, DeFrancesco and Stefani, 'From Geographical Indications').

43 Amit Basole, 'Authenticity, Innovation, and the Geographical Indication in an Artisanal Industry: The Case of the Banarasi Sari' (2015) 18(3–4) *Journal of World Intellectual Property* 127 (hereafter Basole, 'Authenticity, Innovation').

44 InSight Consulting et al, 'Study on Geographical Indications Protection for Non-Agricultural Products in the Internal Market', Final Report for the European Commission (February 2013) 100-101 (hereafter InSight Consulting et al, 'Internal Market').

45 Geographical Indication Application No 99, filed on July 4, 2007 (Registered on September 4, 2009) <https://search.ipindia.gov.in/GIRPublic/Application/Details/99>.

weavers by other sari manufacturing regions.[46] The threat is not just external. Some technological advances prove irresistible to established producers *within* the region of origin, such as the adoption of powerlooms.[47] Based on extensive fieldwork in the Varanasi area, Amit Basole has described this new development as 'home-based and small workshop-based weaving, often (but not necessarily) carried out with second-hand looms obtained from textile mills'.[48] Whilst recognising the political economy dimensions of who does and does not adopt the more capital-intensive powerlooms, Basole questions whether the introduction of the powerloom should be viewed as a threat at all:

> [The Banaras sari] GI has been developed without significant participation of the artisanal community and is 'preservationist', that is, freezes current production methods in the name of craft preservation. In contrast artisans take a dynamic approach to their knowledge and innovate in response to market pressures as well as changing resource bases. A GI that seeks to preserve artisanal traditions, as they exist now, risks punishing artisans for innovating.[49]

We return to the issue of (im)permissible adaptations in Section 10.3.2 of this chapter. Nonetheless, there is a broad consensus that effective intellectual property protection is required to combat fakes or counterfeits.[50] Legal protection, alongside a basket of other support

46 Kasturi Das, 'Prospects and Challenges of Geographical Indications in India' (2010) 13 *Journal of World Intellectual Property* 148; Basole, 'Authenticity, Innovation', above n 43; Meghna Chaudhary, Bhawna Agarwal and Meena Bhatia, 'Geographical Indications in India: A Case of Handicraft Industry in Uttar Pradesh' (2022) 25(3) *Journal of World Intellectual Property* 617; Nikita Doval, 'The Rise and Fall of the Banarasi Handloom Sari', *Mint* (December 1, 2016) <https://www.livemint.com/Politics/BHUXH59k2Z1YANffG64AQO/The-rise-and-fall-of-the-Banarasi-handloom-sari.html>.

47 Shefalee Vasudev, 'Ground Report – The Banaras Bind', *Mint* (November 23, 2013) <https://www.livemint.com/Leisure/5h1lnyORjhtn9Pr0Z4wiXL/Ground-Report–The-Banaras-bind.html> ('Sections of the industry invest in "keeping the Banarasi alive" without worrying about "authenticity" by produrcing imitations that are hard to distinguish from the traditional handcrafted variety.').

48 Amit Basole, 'Informality and Flexible Specialization: Apprenticeships and Knowledge Spillovers in an Indian Silk Weaving Cluster' (2015) 47(1) *Development and Change* 157.

49 Basole, 'Authenticity, Innovation', above n 43, 128.

50 Okyere and Denoncourt, 'Protecting Ghana', above n 20, 419 ('The main danger affecting *kente* today is the economic misappropriation of the cloth by third parties.'). For a representative discussion on EU producers' concerns regarding fakes and counterfeits, see Frithjof Michaelsen et al, 'Study on Control and Enforcement Rules for Geographical Indication (GI) Protection for Non-Agricultural Products in the EU', European Commission, Directorate-General for Internal Market, Industry, Entrepreneurship and

policies, is seen as a crucial bulwark to prevent the eventual dying out of traditional crafts, where producers can no longer make a sustainable living. An EU study in 2020 reveals that from a sample of 834 potential craft and textile GIs identified in 2013, 'many of the products, as of 2019, were simply not produced anymore. Other products had lost their geographical roots, for example by being used as trade mark by multinational companies without maintaining any actual presence in the region of origin'.[51]

10.2.3 Fashion and Sustainability: An Opportunity for Traditional Textiles

The preceding analysis has set out the case for why GI protection has advantages for geographically embedded traditional textiles. However, what do GIs offer the fashion industry, in terms of the provenance guarantee that they represent? Put differently, what are the synergies between GI protection for local, traditional textiles and the priorities of the increasingly globalised fashion industry? One compelling response is the claim that traditional textiles have better sustainability credentials. It is now widely acknowledged that mainstream models of fashion production and retail are both ecologically and socio-economically unsustainable, although the concept of sustainability is understood in different ways across the sector.[52]

This chapter adopts the Brundtland Report's widely accepted, broad definition of sustainability as meeting 'the needs of the present without compromising the ability of future generations to meet their own needs'.[53] In the context of fashion, as opposed to focusing on any given item of clothing being sustainable, the approach should be process-oriented: 'Sustainable describes the processes and behaviours involved

SMEs (2021) 165–166 (hereafter Frithjof Michaelsen et al, 'Study on Control and Enforcement').

[51] Rzepecka et al, 'Economic Aspects', above n 40, 16.

[52] Kedron Thomas 'Cultures of Sustainability in the Fashion Industry' (2020) 24(4) *Fashion Theory* 715.

[53] Gro Harlem Brundtland et al, 'Our Common Future: Report of the World Commission on Environment and Development' World Commission on Environment and Development (1987)[27]. Today, the United Nations' Sustainable Development Goals provide a more comprehensive framework of 17 Sustainable Development Goals and 169 more specific targets; see 'The 17 Goals', United Nations Department of Economic and Social Affairs <https://sdgs.un.org/goals>.

in producing that [fashion] product.'[54] While the focus of this chapter is on environmental considerations, the full range of sustainability concerns spans inequitable labour practices, the health and safety of workers, gender inequality as well as the wasteful production and consumption of fashion goods. A United Nations Environment Programme (UNEP) report highlights the ecological sustainability concerns:

> [Fashion is] a sector struggling to address its impacts, including significant natural resource use and pollution, with 215 trillion litres of water consumed per year, and 9% of annual microplastic losses to oceans. This sector is contributing to the triple planetary crisis of climate change, nature and biodiversity loss, and pollution and waste. A crisis which is exacerbated by the way in which we produce and consume, and the textile sector is significant in driving unsustainable patterns of both, with consumers using items 36% less before discarding compared to 15 years ago, and the equivalent of a garbage truck full of clothes being thrown away every second.[55]

This implicates the entire fashion value chain. On the production side, wet processing (the bleaching/dyeing/finishing stage of textile production) and synthetic fibre production stand out, while the effluents and energy usage from laundering as well as discarding items after only a few wears are prominent consumption-based aspects.[56]

The fast fashion industry is of particular concern, as a significant global polluter. Emerging in the 1990s, this new model emphasised the shortening of lead times for both production as well as distribution, offering new products to the market as fast as possible.[57] While fashion has historically been premised on trends and cycles, it is the pace of change that makes this far more frenetic iteration remarkable. It was initially feted as a retail strategy for democratising couture and bringing trendy, affordable items to the masses. Brands today associated with this trend include Zara, Forever 21, H&M, TopShop, Shein and Primark.

[54] Johanna Gibson, 'The Intellectual Property in Sustainable Fashion: Standards Are up to the Mark' (2023) 13(2) *Queen Mary Journal of Intellectual Property* 141, 142–143.

[55] Laila Petrie, *Sustainability and Circularity in the Textile Value Chain – A Global Roadmap* (United Nations Environment Programme, 2023) 6.

[56] Philippa Notten, *Sustainability and Circularity in the Textile Value Chain – Global Stocktaking* (United Nations Environment Programme, 2020).

[57] Donald N Sull and Stefano Turconi. 'Fast Fashion Lessons' (2008) 19(2) *Business Strategy Review* 4; Nikolay Anguelov, *The Dirty Side of the Garment Industry: Fast Fashion and Its Negative Impact on Environment and Society* (CRC Press, 2015) 1–20.

Although this development can in turn be situated within a broader historical trend of increasingly industrialised, mass-produced and standardised garment manufacture,[58] there is nevertheless a distinctive set of concerns associated with fast fashion. The pressure to sell newer lines at lower prices has undermined working conditions and wages, while the environmental costs of this model are increasingly apparent.[59] One prominent policy response to the latter is the recent EU Strategy for Sustainable and Circular Textiles:

> As clothing comprises the largest share of EU textile consumption (81%), the trends of using garments for ever shorter periods before throwing them away contribute the most to unsustainable patterns of overproduction and overconsumption. Such trends have become known as fast fashion, enticing consumers to keep on buying clothing of inferior quality and lower price, produced rapidly in response to the latest trends … Moreover, the growing demand for textiles is fueling [*sic*] the inefficient use of non-renewable resources, including the production of synthetic fibres from fossil-fuels. These negative impacts have their roots in a linear model that is characterised by low rates of use, reuse, repair and fibre-to-fibre recycling of textiles, and that often does not put quality, durability and recyclability as priorities for the design and manufacturing of apparel. The shedding of microplastics from synthetic textiles and footwear during all stages of their lifecycle further adds to the environmental impacts of the sector.[60]

The EU strategy seeks to address this set of challenges through measures such as clamping down on greenwashing, taking steps to reduce the export of textile waste and setting mandatory minimums for the inclusion of recycled fibres in textiles, making them longer lasting, as well as easier to repair and recycle.[61]

This policy shift towards encouraging more sustainably produced, longer-lasting garments creates an opportunity for traditional textiles, which have conventionally relied on natural fibres and dyes as opposed to synthetic ones, to be valued for artisanal modes of production

58 Sara Idacavage, 'Fashion History Lessons: The Origins of Fast Fashion', *Fashionista* (October 17, 2018) <https://fashionista.com/2016/06/what-is-fast-fashion>.

59 Rachel Bick, Erika Halsey and Christine C Ekenga, 'The Global Environmental Injustice of Fast Fashion' (2018) 17 *Environmental Health* 1.

60 European Commission, 'EU Strategy for Sustainable and Circular Textiles', COM 141 (2022) 1 (internal citations omitted) <https://environment.ec.europa.eu/strategy/textiles-strategy_en>.

61 Ibid.

connected to local communities and are bought to be kept, not discarded.[62] In other words, the titular 'threads that last'. Environmental sustainability has been expressly linked to traditional textile GIs in the draft proposal for the new EU non-agricultural GIs protection regime, which 'also shares specific objectives with the Commission's forthcoming EU strategy on sustainable textiles, which aims to create a better business and regulatory environment for sustainable and circular textiles within the Union'.[63] This potential can be illustrated by Dabu (variously spelled Dhabu or Daboo), from Western India. Dabu means 'to press' and is a form of block printed textile production relying on mud-resistant printing techniques.[64] While natural dyes are used for colouring, local mud is used to make a dye-resistant paste, which is then painstakingly stamped, using carved wooden or metal blocks bearing attractive motifs, onto the fabric. Since the mud prevents the natural dyes from attaching to the fabric, artisans create patterns and designs by intentionally preventing dye penetration in selected areas. The process is labour intensive, involving various stages of washing, stamping and dyeing. Producers rely on natural materials such as clay or mud, lime gum, wheat husk, florals and fruits. It should however be noted that traditional textile production methods evolve in ways that sometimes cut against sustainability objectives. For example, natural dyes require chemical supplements to bind more effectively with fabrics and retain colour over time, with the residual binding chemicals washed away after the final rinsing.[65] In Section 10.3, we therefore examine whether specific binding and meaningful commitments to sustainability could be facilitated by GI legislation.

[62] Miguel Angel Gardetti and Subramaniam Senthilkannan Muthu (eds), *Handloom Sustainability and Culture: Artisanship and Value Addition* (Springer, 2021); Thushari Wanniarachchi, Kanchana Dissanayake and Carolyn Downs, 'Improving Sustainability and Encouraging Innovation in Traditional Craft Sectors: The Case of the Sri Lankan Handloom Industry' (2020) 24(2) *Research Journal of Textile and Apparel* 111.

[63] European Commission, Proposal for a Regulation of the European Parliament and Council on Geographical Indication Protection for Craft and Industrial Products and Amending Regulations (EU) 2017/1001 and (EU) 2019/1753 of the European Parliament and of the Council and Council Decision (EU) 2019/1754, COM 174 (2022) 2.

[64] Janmay Singh Hada and Chet Ram Meena, 'Dabu, The Sustainable Resist Printed Fabric of Rajasthan' in Subramaniam Senthilkannan Muthu (ed), *Sustainable Approaches in Textiles and Fashion: Manufacturing Processes and Chemicals* (Springer, 2022) 69.

[65] Hana Křížová, 'Natural Dyes: Their Past, Present, Future and Sustainability' in Dana Křemenáková (ed), *Recent Developments in Fibrous Material Science* (Kosmas, 2015) 59.

The second reason why GIs seem promising is they ostensibly fit well with contemporary policy approaches to sustainable development. Since these products are, by definition, locally embedded to varying degrees, they have the potential to act as a platform for territorial development strategies.[66] As opposed to a top-down national (or in the EU's case, region-wide) approach to sustainable development, territorial strategies focus on leveraging the unique characteristics, strengths and opportunities present within a particular region. This approach recognises bespoke policy interventions tailored to specific local needs. Key principles include prioritising local context, that is, natural resources (and their constraints), cultural heritage, economic arrangements and social dynamics and inclusive or participatory governance whereby local stakeholders are involved in decision-making. This emphasis on place or local geography complements a growing consumer awareness of where and how garments are made. The COVID-19 'pandemic contributed to [drawing] attention to nearness and quality, enhanced cultural connections with the territory, and, to a certain extent, triggered a centripetal as opposed to a centrifugal movement, which is at the heart of the concept of localism'.[67]

The territorial approach to development, which values local context, has been informed by social science research that ranges widely beyond the formal legal act of GIs registration. A recent review of the lessons learned from agricultural, wines and spirits GIs concludes that legal recognition is 'not a magical tool and that the local conditions which can influence their establishment and management are crucial to the efficiency and local sustainability of the GI'.[68] The review goes on to identify the following operational conditions:[69]

i. respecting, as a matter of operational practice, the casual link between quality and origin that is clearly defined in the product specification (both in order to satisfy the conditions for granting a legal (IP) right and to ensure meaningful product differentiation in markets);

[66] Sarah Bowen, 'Embedding Local Places in Global Spaces: Geographical Indications as a Territorial Development Strategy' (2010) 75(2) *Rural Sociology* 209; Riccardo Crescenzi et al, 'Geographical Indications and Local Development: The Strength of Territorial Embeddedness' (2022) 56(3) *Regional Studies* 381.

[67] Sara Cavagnero and Simona Giordano, 'Sui Generis Geographical Indications Fostering Localized Sustainable Fashion: A Cross-Industry Assessment' (2022) 14(9) *Sustainability* 5251 (hereafter Cavagnero and Giordano, 'Cross-Industry Assessment').

[68] Vandecandelaere et al, 'Geographical Indication', above n 1, 2.

[69] Ibid.

ii. creating the conditions for successful collective action, described as 'the ensemble of individual and collective choices and initiatives made by producers as a group for a common objective'[70] and ensuing territorial governance strategies, on an ongoing basis;
iii. effective marketing, which incorporates the GI term and accompanying official logos;[71] and
iv. an efficient legal framework and the role of the public sector, as it pertains to effective protection of GIs against misuse.

With sustainability in mind, the product specification remains an important legal site, since it defines acceptable production techniques, influences value chain efficiency and delimits the production region.[72] However, one needs to step back and review the full 'biography' of the GI product – its existence both prior to and past the initial product specification, as influenced by the decisions of supply chain actors amidst changing circumstances – when evaluating the potential for sustainability.

10.3 Legally Reinforcing Sustainable Production for Textiles

The preceding analysis has outlined how the fashion industry is increasingly being held to account for its sustainability record, with a particular emphasis on environmental sustainability. Here we ask whether there are legal and institutional mechanisms within GI law that *systematically* guarantee the environmental sustainability of traditional textile production? Alternatively, instead of a mandatory legal obligation, might GI rules incrementally nudge textile producers to either maintain or proactively adopt environmentally sustainable practices? While the

[70] Flavia Guerrieri, 'Governing Governance: Collective Action and Rulemaking in EU Agricultural and Non-Agricultural Geographical Indications' University of Amsterdam, PhD Thesis (2023)xxi.

[71] Effective marketing, alongside support in accessing markets, is recognised as being crucially important for success. For crafts and textiles in particular, see Ruppal W Sharma and Shraddha Kulhari, *Marketing of GI Products: Unlocking their Commercial Potential* (Centre for WTO Studies and Indian Institute of Foreign Trade, 2015)(hereafter Sharma and Kulhari, *Marketing of GI Products*); Buch and Trivedi, *Indian Handlooms*, above n 25, 79–114.

[72] Marianna Guareschi, Maria Cecilia Mancini and Filippo Arfini, 'Geographical Indications, Public Goods and Sustainable Development Goals: A Methodological Proposal' (2023) 103 *Journal of Rural Studies* 103122.

territorial or *terroir* anchor generates theoretical expectations that GIs align with sustainability objectives, there has been far less analysis of the role that legal architecture plays in supporting these objectives. Drawing on recent regulatory experimentation in the EU as a case study, this Section (i) outlines newly adopted legal mechanisms for encouraging sustainable production while arguing that there is slippage between the different senses of sustainability – in particular, economic and environmental – in EU GI policy and (ii) subsequently analyses why this slippage matters, because commercial pressures can lead to the adoption of less environmentally sustainable production methods.

10.3.1 Making Binding Sustainability Commitments?

In recent years, EU policymakers have actively engaged with ways to reinforce sustainability commitments via the legal framework regulating GIs. However, the difference in emphasis between the environmental and economic dimensions of sustainability has gone largely unnoticed. The following analysis foregrounds how *both dimensions* are prominent in the agricultural products context (used broadly here, to include wines and spirits), while the focus seems to be mainly on *economic sustainability* for crafts and textiles. This difference matters and Section 10.3.2 explores the potential tension between commercial pressures and more environmentally friendly production techniques.

To begin with, this policy interest in sustainability hinges on the centrality of the link, shared by all GIs, between distinctive products and specified regions.

> Even if environmental protection or animal welfare are not the main objectives of GIs . . . these kind of products can have a direct or indirect impact on both domains because they are strongly associated with specific territories and local resources . . . and because [product specifications] often contain rules about traditional production practices linked to their geographical origin as well as traditional know-how, or the choice of specific varieties, that might have an impact on the environment and animal welfare even indirectly.[73]

[73] AND International, ECORYS and COGEA, 'Evaluation Support Study on Geographical Indications and Traditional Specialities Guaranteed Protected in the EU', Final Report, European Commission, Directorate-General for Agriculture and Rural Development (December 2020), 236 (hereafter AND International, ECORYS and COGEA, 'Evaluation Support Study').

This link or territorial association is elaborated in the product specification, where the product – including its distinctive characteristics – is described along with the (often traditional) methods of production that give the product those characteristics. Specifications also delimit the production region, identify permitted raw materials and their sourcing while sometimes additionally prescribing modes of packaging.[74]

Turning first to environmental sustainability, surveys of producer groups in the agricultural context reveal that the following measures have been found, to varying degrees, in product specifications:

> The mitigation of the impacts on landscape [such as preventing soil erosion] . . ., fostering the use of old breeds or plant varieties . . . mitigating of the impact on water quality . . . and limiting the use of water . . . fostering extensive production practices [producing a lower yield per unit of land, such that many more units of land are required in order to be profitable], mitigating of the impact on biodiversity and fostering organic production . . .. The least cited relates to the limitation of [greenhouse gas] emission and impact on air quality and of the use of energy.[75]

Whereas mandatory environmental standards must be complied with, certain producer groups have taken the initiative to adopt stricter standards that are more environmentally friendly, such as a commitment to using animal manure instead of chemical fertilisers, mechanically controlling weeds or using certain insect species to combat pests.[76] A recent proposal to consolidate the three distinct EU GI regimes for agricultural products, wines and spirits recognises sustainability in the 'three pillars' sense: 'GI agricultural/food products incorporate some sustainability characteristics in one or more of the three dimensions of the term: environmental, stemming from GI products intrinsic link to a specific area with its specific natural factors and resulting from production methods adapted to that area; [social . . .] and economic: as the value added in a GI product is secured for the local producers and cannot be delocalised.'[77]

[74] The product specification requirements are outlined in Dev S Gangjee, 'Proving Provenance? Geographical Indications Certification and its Ambiguities' (2017) 98 *World Development* 12.

[75] AND International, ECORYS and COGEA, 'Evaluation Support Study', above n 73, 239–240.

[76] Ibid 244–246.

[77] European Commission, 'Commission Staff Working Document: Impact Assessment Report Accompanying the document Proposal for a Regulation of the European Parliament and of the Council on European Union geographical indications for wine,

Environmental sustainability is an increasingly visible priority because agricultural GI law is situated within the EU food quality policy framework. Given the environmental impacts of food production, distribution and consumption, this policy framework is being reshaped by the European Green Deal, aiming to make Europe the first climate-neutral continent and its subsidiary Farm to Fork strategy, seeking to establish a fair, healthy and environmentally friendly food system.[78]

The case for economic sustainability is premised upon GI status resulting in higher margins for producers, via the price premium that consumers are willing to pay for distinctive products.[79] This ensures the survival of production-related local know-how, thereby preserving viable employment in the region and possibly even growing employment where demand increases, as a result of enhanced visibility and access to new markets. The formation of a GI producer group allows for better co-ordination and the ability to collectively confront external pressures (such as contractual negotiations with large retailers or other intermediaries). GI status can also be a bargaining chip when negotiating more flexible solutions, when it comes to regulatory compliance for a certain product sector (e.g., demonstrating that products made with unpasteurised milk are nevertheless suitable for consumption, or where smoking or salting a product can effectively preserve it). Finally, there are the positive spillovers: potential benefits for local food processing industries that use local GI ingredients – the hotels, restaurants and catering sectors and tourism more generally.[80]

The final text of this Consolidating Regulation 2024/1143 explicitly references all three dimensions of sustainability in its opening recitals.[81]

spirit drinks and agricultural products, and quality schemes for agricultural products, amending Regulations (EU) No 1308/2013 (EU) 2017/1001 and (EU) 2019/787 and repealing Regulation (EU) No 1151/2012', SWD 135 (2022) 11 (hereafter European Commission, 'Impact Assessment Report').

[78] Flavia Guerrieri, 'The Farm to Fork Strategy as an External Driver for Change: Possible Impacts on Nested GI Rule Systems' (2021) 16 *Journal of Intellectual Property Law and Practice* 331.

[79] Ibid Annex 7, 68–77.

[80] Ibid. See also Vandecandelaere et al, *Strengthening Sustainable Food Systems*, above n 42; Cei, DeFrancesco and Stefani, 'From Geographical Indications', above n 42.

[81] Regulation (EU) 2024/1143 of the European Parliament and of the Council of April 11, 2024, on geographical indications for wine, spirit drinks and agricultural products, as well as traditional specialities guaranteed and optional quality terms for agricultural products, amending Regulations (EU) No 1308/2013 (EU) 2019/787 and (EU) 2019/1753 and repealing Regulation (EU) No 1151/2012 [2024] OJ L 1143 (hereafter Consolidating Regulation 2024/1143)Recital 2 (The European Green deal included the design of a 'fair,

One of the stated purposes of instituting an EU-wide system of GI protection is to ensure 'that producers acting collectively have the necessary powers and responsibilities to manage the [GI] concerned, including to respond to societal demands . . . for products resulting from sustainable production in its three dimensions of economic, environmental and social value' and – by preventing unfair competition or misuse – 'ensure a fair return for producers and a capacity to invest in the quality, reputation and sustainability of their products'.[82] The commitment to sustainability takes the form of an optional *sustainability undertaking* in the final text. Producer groups 'may agree on sustainable practices to be adhered to in the production . . . [or other requirements associated with the product] in the product specification . . .. Such practices shall aim to apply sustainability standards higher than those laid down by Union or national law in terms of social, environmental or economic sustainability or animal welfare'.[83] The specific environmental sustainability objectives mentioned include 'climate change mitigation and adaptation, the sustainable use and protection of landscapes, water and soil, the transition to a circular economy, including the reduction of food waste, pollution prevention and control, and the protection and restoration of biodiversity' alongside the reduction in usage of pesticides.[84]

The key move is thus to provide an option to embed these enhanced sustainability undertakings – if mandatory for all producers – within the product specification, via the initial GI registration or subsequent amendment procedure.[85] The ability of producer groups to agree such sustainable practices is further recognised when describing their role and

sustainable . . . and more environmentally-friendly food system'); Recital 3 (GIs 'can play an important role in terms of sustainability, including in the circular economy'); Recital 19 ('Producers acting collectively have more powers than individual producers and take collective responsibilities to manage their geographical indications, including responding to societal demands for products resulting from sustainable production', going on to mention a fair income for producers and benefits to remote, rural regions); Recitals 23 (GI producers 'should be encouraged to adhere to sustainable practices that go beyond mandatory standards encompassing environmental, social and economic objectives'), etc.

82 Ibid art 4(1)(a).

83 Ibid art 7(1).

84 Ibid art 7(2).

85 Ibid art 7(3); . On the modest extent to which new amendments reflect environmental sustainability initiatives, see Andrea Marescotti et al, 'Are Protected Geographical Indications Evolving Due to Environmentally Related Justifications? An Analysis of Amendments in the Fruit and Vegetable Sector in the European Union' (2020) 12(9) *Sustainability* 3571.

functions.[86] Where producer groups have chosen to make such a commitment, it becomes visible to the public in two complementary ways: (i) by forming part of the product specification, accessed via a publicly available electronic database[87] and also potentially a legally binding commitment, if incorporated into the certification compliance criteria (when verifying that a GI producer satisfies the commitments in the product specification); and (ii) a periodically updated, publicly available sustainability report by the producers, 'comprising a description of existing sustainable practices implemented in the production of the product, a description of how the method of obtaining the product impacts on sustainability, in terms of social, environmental, economic or animal welfare commitments, and information necessary to understand how sustainability affects the development, performance and position of the product'.[88] The underlying rationale seems to be that producers are more likely to be rewarded by consumers who are made aware of their commitment to enhanced sustainability.[89] It also underscores the seriousness of the commitment, while implicitly raising the sanction of reputational damage if this turns out to be merely greenwashing.

It is therefore evident that a more comprehensive concept of sustainability informs recent developments in the agricultural GIs context. By contrast, since craft and textiles GIs tend to be produced by micro, small and medium enterprises (MSMEs) in the EU,[90] the policy emphasis has been on legal protection as a means of achieving *economic sustainability* for producers. The Green Paper in 2014, introducing the possibility of legally recognising craft GIs at the EU level, highlights positive spillover effects such as 'encouraging tourism, trade fairs and cultural activities and, consequently, creating more job opportunities'.[91] A European Parliament Resolution supporting such a regime, which protects traditional, high-quality knowhow, would ensure 'a more

[86] Consolidating Regulation 2024/1143, above n 81, art 34(1)(c).

[87] 'eAmbrosia: The EU Geographical Indications Register', European Commission <https://ec.europa.eu/agriculture/eambrosia/geographical-indications-register/>.

[88] Consolidating Regulation 2024/1143, above n 81, art 8.

[89] Studies indicate that the COVID-19 accelerated the demand for products derived from nature-friendly production systems. See, eg, Etleva Muça, Iwona Pomianek and Mariya Peneva, 'The Role of GI Products or Local Products in the Environment—Consumer Awareness and Preferences in Albania, Bulgaria and Poland' (2021) 14(1) *Sustainability* 4.

[90] Rzepecka et al, 'Economic Aspects', above n 40, 68–69.

[91] European Commission, Green Paper, above n 13, 9 and FN16.

socially, economically and environmentally sustainable approach to *economic development*'.[92] Detailed preparatory studies analysing the economic potential for craft GI protection emphasise regional and sustainable development in the senses of increased productivity, employment, improved marketing efforts and greater producer co-operation.[93] This emphasis continues in the text of the CIP Regulation, where Recital 8 declares that protection will 'contribute to the creation of valuable and sustainable jobs, including in rural and less-developed regions, which would help counter depopulation trends', especially where a substantial proportion of the value added is generated within the defined region. Article 45(2) of this Regulation, which identifies the tasks undertaken by GI producer groups, recognises that such a group 'may [ie, optionally] ... agree to undertake commitments with regard to sustainability, whether or not included in the product specification or as a separate initiative'.[94] While the draft Consolidating Regulation clearly envisions sustainability in the 'three pillars' sense, by contrast the CIP framework references sustainability as a general concept, with more detailed references pertaining only to economic sustainability. It is also apparent that the crafts version of the sustainability undertaking – 'whether ... in the product specification *or as a separate initiative*' (emphasis added) and with no provision for an updated sustainability report or other visibility enhancing mechanisms – is relatively diluted.

It is unclear why this differential treatment exists for two EU legislative processes that have unfolded in parallel. One part of the answer may have to do with their origins. Their legislative incubators and associated institutional priorities differ: 'It is noteworthy that [the Consolidating Regulation] originates within [the policy department, Directorate-General or] DG Agriculture and [the CIP Regulation] originates within DG Grow – Internal Market, Industry, Entrepreneurship and SMEs.'[95]

92 European Parliament resolution of 6 October 2015 on the possible extension of geographical indication protection of the European Union to non-agricultural products [2017] OJC 349/2 (emphasis added).

93 Rzepecka et al, 'Economic Aspects', above n 40, 29–30; InSight Consulting et al, 'Internal Market', above n 44, 112–149.

94 See also Council of the European Union, Proposal, above n 81, art 2(a) (Recognising that the Regulation will facilitate producers in carrying out the tasks necessary to manage GIs, 'including in response to societal demands for sustainable products').

95 Devanshi Saxena, 'The Compromise Text of the New Regulation on Crafts and Industrial Geographical Indications: A Compromise on Sustainability?', *The IPKat* (September 20, 2023)<https://ipkitten.blogspot.com/2023/09/guest-post-compromise-text-of-new.html>.

Another, more substantive driver of differential treatment may be the reluctance to impose additional regulatory compliance burdens on CIP producers, in the form of enhanced environmental sustainability standards. This 'compliance costs' concern has emerged as a consistent theme during the drafting of the CIP Regulation, given the small-scale nature of craft and textile production across the EU. A study of the cost effectiveness of formal certification, verification and enforcement concludes that costs 'tend to be higher for certification marks (with verification procedures) and GIs (verification procedures and detailed scrutiny of the application) compared to the other schemes'.[96] It was therefore proposed that as opposed to more expensive (and rigorous) external verification compliance checks – testing whether the producer being inspected makes crafts in accordance with the specification – 'self-certification and random controls should lower the application and verification costs'.[97]

As a result of this sensitivity to regulatory compliance burdens, the CIP Regulation has introduced two alternative pathways for verification compliance. One, contained in Article 52, mirrors the conventional approach found in the agricultural GI domain, where verification is carried out by designated competent authorities in each Member State, or else this responsibility is delegated to independent bodies (or individuals) with the relevant certification expertise. Competent bodies in the agricultural GI context are usually 'the intermediaries between the applicants and the EU Commission'[98] and often a public body under the relevant Ministry of Agriculture or Rural affairs.[99] The second, alternative, pathway in Article 51 relies on a self-declaration by a producer, periodically updated every three years and submitted to the national authority. This declaration is scrutinised at the level of formal compliance: is the prescribed form complete and providing consistent information? An external verification layer by a product certification body can be *optionally* added to this self-declaration mechanism, if the GI applicant group so chooses. A surprisingly light-touch verification process,

[96] Frithjof Michaelsen et al, 'Study on Control and Enforcement', above n 50, 71; see also 125.

[97] European Commission, 'Impact Assessment Report', above n 77, 58.

[98] Andrea Zappalagio et al, 'Study on the Functioning of the EU GI System' (2022) 1 *Max Planck Institute for Innovation and Competition* 56.

[99] European Union Intellectual Property Office, Protection and Control, above n 17, 14.

resting on self-certification, is therefore envisaged to ensure that craft and textile producers comply with product specifications.

What consequently emerges from the EU experiment is that for the CIP Regulation, the priority given to economic sustainability clearly overshadows environmental sustainability. It also showcases voluntary sustainability undertakings being incorporated into the product specification, as an operational mechanism. These undertakings can potentially be made (i) binding, via the verification process and (ii) more visible, within the GI register. However, unlike agricultural GIs, there is no mention of an accompanying sustainability report for craft GIs. Furthermore, the verification process for crafts has itself been diluted, by opting for producer self-certification in order to reduce operational costs. Sustainability is being deployed to achieve seemingly different ends in the agricultural and crafts GI contexts.

10.3.2 Pressures to Adapt

Section 10.3.1 analysed the potential for *enhanced* sustainability objectives to be formally recognised within the GI registration and subsequent operationalisation processes. However, the very real risks of *backsliding* should also be acknowledged. Where textiles have conventionally used more sustainable traditional methods of production, how do commercial pressures to adopt less environmentally friendly measures manifest? There is an assumption in some of the GI literature that crafts and textile GIs can harmoniously accommodate the social, economic and environmental dimensions of sustainability.[100] Milano and Cazella characterise this as a more general assumption, based on theories of territorial development and the production of public goods by agriculture: 'The hypothesis that GIs simultaneously generate positive environmental, social and economic results is widely accepted in the literature.'[101] However, we have seen immediately above that the recently enacted

[100] See illustratively, Shafi, 'Handicraft Communities', above n 36, 123 (Emphasising the 'the cultural and environmental benefits (aside from economic and social) of GI legislation in the context of the handicraft industry'); Cavagnero and Giordano, 'Cross-Industry Assessment', above n 67.

[101] Marja Zattoni Milano and Ademir Antonio Cazella, 'Environmental Effects of Geographical Indications and Their Influential Factors: A Review of the Empirical Evidence' (2021) 3 *Current Research in Environmental Sustainability* 100096 (arguing that the empirical literature paints a more nuanced and varied picture, depending on local institutional arrangements).

EU CIP Regulation prioritises the economic dimensions of sustainability, with environmental sustainability being relatively invisible. The 'three pillars' paradigm is also used in fields such as environmental or administrative law as a principled approach for reconciling interests, which in turn recognises that these interests *can and do* conflict, depending on how they are framed.[102]

> Goals of environmental and social sustainability may be conflicting rather than compatible. For example, efforts to overcome social inequalities and develop human capabilities could easily mean increasing the use of natural resources to the detriment of the conservation or resilience of the biophysical environment.[103]

There are examples from the agricultural GIs literature that point to the unintended consequences of economic success, in the form of an increased demand for a GI product. A pioneering study by Bowen and Zapata analysed spirit drink production in the Amatitán-Tequila Valley in Mexico.[104] This was conducted against the backdrop of a 15-year-long expansion of the Tequila market, 'driven by a shift in control and ownership of the major Tequila companies to transnational liquor companies, and . . . accompanied by the concentration, industrialization, and standardization of Tequila production'.[105] While ostensibly introduced to remedy persistent cycles of surplus and shortage in the agave cactus supply chain, these changes led to detrimental revisions of the Tequila product specification, such as the increased use of chemical inputs at the expense of more labour-intensive production practices. The revised production rules, which favoured standardisation, did 'little to preserve traditional Tequila production methods or the environmental specificity of Tequila. Thus, Tequila is evolving into a generic, mass-produced liquor; and the farmer knowledge, artisanal production practices, and environmental resources that are associated with the specificity and

[102] Volker Mauerhofer, '3-D Sustainability and Its Contribution to Governance Assessment in Legal Terms: Examples and Perspectives' in Volker Mauerhofer (ed) *Legal Aspects of Sustainable Development* (Springer, 2016) 35.

[103] Magnus Boström, 'A Missing Pillar? Challenges in Theorizing and Practicing Social Sustainability: Introduction to the Special Issue' (2012) 8(1) *Sustainability: Science, Practice and Policy* 3, 8.

[104] Sarah Bowen and Ana Valenzuela Zapata, 'Geographical Indications, Terroir, and Socioeconomic and Ecological Sustainability: The Case of Tequila' (2009) 25 *Journal of Rural Studies* 108.

[105] Ibid 112 [NB: Tequila has been capitalised in the text cited, to reflect its status as a protected designation].

heritage of tequila are being degraded'.[106] In the case of the Spanish almond-based desserts, Turrón de Jijona and Turrón de Alicante, manufacturers seeking to scale up production removed the requirement to source the primary ingredient (almonds) from the region's low-input farms and opted for intensively produced ingredients imported from abroad (primarily California).[107] A study of hairy mitten crabs from the Yangcheng Lake region in Suzhou, China concludes that their increasing economic value incentivised farmers to expand crab breeding zones. This expansion, accompanied by the increased adoption of crab feed pellets, contributed to water pollution.[108]

Similar stresses arise in the context of traditional textile production, as the following example from India illustrates. Fabrics produced in the Bagru hand block-printing cluster in the state of Rajasthan are protected under Indian GI law.[109] While the neighbouring cluster in Sanganer, also famous for block-printing, has gradually shifted to screen and machine printing, Bagru is still acknowledged for its hand block-printing technique that is over three centuries old.[110] It is also reputed for using natural dyes, which rely on mixtures of flowers, tree barks, roots and clay. Key features from the GI specification include a cream or off-white base colour with block prints being dominated by red or black, traditional methods being used to prepare vegetable dyes and create prints, five main groups of small motifs (leaves and buds, geometrical designs, etc), the use of Dabu (resist) soil from local black clay and its association with the community of Chippas based in that region.[111] In the Indian context, the impact of COVID-19 restrictions and disruptions on supply chains for traditional artisanal production clusters has been widely

[106] Ibid.

[107] Emily Reisman, 'Protecting Provenance, Abandoning Agriculture? Heritage Products, Industrial Ideals and the Uprooting of a Spanish Turrón' (2022) 89 *Journal of Rural Studies* 45 (Californian almond farmers 'rely on extensive water imports, heavy synthetic fertilizer loads and an expanding array of pest control measures to compensate for their high density plantation scale').

[108] Denian Cheng, 'Sustainability for Stakeholders and the Environment? Understanding the Role of Geographical Indications in Sustaining Agri-Food Production' (2023) 34 *International Journal of Gastronomy and Food Science* 100839.

[109] Geographical Indication Application No 183, filed on August 10, 2009 (Registered on January 4, 2011) <https://search.ipindia.gov.in/GIRPublic/Application/Details/183>.

[110] Oinam Bedajit Meitei and Tanveer Ahemad, 'Communication and Challenges of Capacity Development: A Case Study of Bagru Hand Block Printing' (2021) 20(3) *Textile* 311 (hereafter Meitei and Ahemad, 'Communication and Challenges').

[111] 'Bagru Hand Block Print' (2011) 37 *Indian Geographical Indications Journal* 12, 13–14.

acknowledged.[112] The effects of the pandemic in Bagru have exacerbated longer term challenges that undermine many of the key features of this traditional fabric. The traditional method of production has made the cluster vulnerable to fabrics that are screen-printed mechanically in larger volumes (as opposed to block-printing by hand) and relying on chemical dyes (as opposed to natural ones).[113] These are often sold as if genuinely handmade.

> Many manufacturers today continue to sell screen printed textiles under the name of hand block-printed [ones] due to the lack of certificates and [effective] authentic labelling in this industry. This practice has discouraged many firms to continue with traditional practices. Manufacturers respond to market dynamics very quickly in order to maintain steady profits.[114]

These commercial pressures have serious consequences for the production cluster as a whole: 'Natural vegetable mixtures are being replaced by synthetic materials as they are cheaper to produce, take less time to prepare as compared to the lengthy natural dyeing process [which] has increased the artisan's exposure to potential hazards. A study . . . revealed that 95% of printers and chemical mixers suffer from asthmatic tendencies or chronic bronchitis and other respiratory issues [while] 61% of workers have below normal hand grip strength.'[115] To the extent that registered GI status increases the visibility of traditional textiles and facilitates access to new markets, this often generates associated pressures to scale up production volumes while reducing production times. From an environmental sustainability perspective, economic success can be a double-edged sword.

A counter-example can be found in the Harris Tweed industry, which is recovering from a period of decline by prioritising design-led innovation in recent years. 'The environmental impact of a small pedal powered industry, such as the Harris Tweed® industry is comparably

112 Kanupriya, 'COVID-19 and the Indian Textiles Sector: Issues, Challenges and Prospects' (2021) 25(1) *Vision* 7; Meghavatu Krishnaprasanna Naik, Prabhas Bhardwaj and Vinaytosh Mishra, 'Post-COVID Assessment of Small Business Weavers in an Indian Handloom Industry: Identifying and Prioritizing Key Challenges' (2023) *Research Journal of Textile and Apparel* 40.

113 Sakshi Tokas et al, 'Tracing the Journey of a Craft from "Embeddedness" to "Commercialisation": A Case of Hand Block Printing from the Jaipur Region' (2023) 24 *Asian Ethnicity* 301.

114 Ibid 314.

115 Meitei and Ahemad, 'Communication and Challenges', above n 110, 319.

low to those of a greater scale, or which require a greater amount of automated machinery.'[116] It also showcases a single country of origin supply chain, with the wool being sourced from the United Kingdom.[117] Significantly, the artisanal element is a core legal requirement that is respected in practice. Harris Tweed is defined as 'tweed which ... has been handwoven by the islanders at their homes in the Outer Hebrides, finished in the Outer Hebrides, and made from pure virgin wool dyed and spun in the Outer Hebrides'.[118]

The preceding analysis therefore does not imply that any innovations in the traditional textile space are impermissible.[119] In legal terms, environmentally harmful backsliding could be framed as inadequate GI enforcement against third parties outside the GI club who misuse the protected term without complying with the specification requirements. Where producers within the GI club also begin to adopt such undesirable methods, it points to inadequate verification mechanisms.[120] Robust enforcement needs to be accompanied by a supportive web of interlinked policies, to assist those producers who do follow sustainable methods of production. These include loans to provide working capital for investing in raw materials, tools or (recognised) technology; assistance with certification compliance; financial support with marketing, attending

[116] Josie Steed, Karen Cross and Beth Wilson, 'Collaborating with a Scottish Heritage Brand towards Enhancing and Preserving Sustainable Artisan Hand-Weaving Practices through a Knowledge Transfer Partnership' (2023) 11(1–2) *Journal of Textile Design Research and Practice* 127.

[117] See: 'Low Impact', Harris Tweed Hebrides <https://www.harristweedhebrides.com/pages/low-impact>.

[118] Harris Tweed Act 1993, s 7 (UK).

[119] See Basole, 'Authenticity, Innovation', above n 43, 129–130 (arguing against a 'preservationist' paradigm); Camilla Roman, 'Technological Change and Innovation in Middle India: The Case of Arni's Silk Cluster' in Barbara Harriss-White (ed), *Middle India and Urban-Rural Development. Exploring Urban Change in South Asia* (Springer, 2016) 177; W N Jazmina and W Ariffin et al, 'Handicraft Innovations: A Strategic Approach to Preserving Intangible Cultural Heritage of Malaysia' (2023) 10(7) *International Society for the Study of Vernacular Settlements* 137.

[120] In the Indian context, both (internal) verification and (external) enforcement are significantly underdeveloped. See Yogesh Pai and Tania Singla, 'Vanity GIs: India's Legislation on Geographical Indications and the Missing Regulatory Framework' in Irene Calboli and Ng-Loy Wee Loon (eds), *Geographical Indications at the Crossroads of Trade, Development, and Culture: Focus on Asia-Pacific* (Cambridge University Press, 2017) 333; Niharika Sahoo Bhattacharya and Kuhu Tiwari, 'A Study on the Quality Control and Enforcement of Registered Geographical Indication Goods in India' in Niharika Sahoo Bhattacharya (ed), *Geographical Indication Protection in India: The Evolving Paradigm* (Springer Nature, 2022) 27.

international exhibitions, distribution and accessing export markets; the introduction of innovative new designs; and establishing e-commerce channels.[121]

10.4 Conclusion

For traditional textiles, GI protection offers the potential for both increased visibility and more effective legal protection for a hard-earned reputation. Supporting traditional textiles through this form of IP has additional synergies with the shift towards more sustainable production and consumption in the global fashion industry. By utilising natural fibres, organic dyes, artisanal modes of production and fabrics intended to be worn multiple times, GIs are positioned as the polar opposite of fast fashion; as 'threads that last'. This chapter has investigated whether there are legal and institutional mechanisms to *systematically reinforce* sustainability commitments, focusing on recent legal reforms in the EU that accommodate sustainability undertakings within a GI product specification, as a case study.

However, sustainability is understood in different senses. While the agricultural GI regime embraces the social, economic and environmental dimensions of sustainability, the crafts and textiles regime prioritises economic sustainability, given the relatively small-scale nature of production. This is an oversight, since commercial pressures can lead to adaptations being introduced that are justified in economic terms but have significantly detrimental environmental consequences. The EU experiment therefore offers practical methods to lock in sustainability commitments for traditional textiles while also reminding policymakers that synergies between different aspects of sustainability should not be taken for granted.

121 Craft and textile specific support in India is described in T C James, 'Successful vs. Unsuccessful Stories of Indian GIs', IPC-EUI Training Workshop on GIs for Producers, Attorneys and Advisors (2017) <https://ipc-eui.com/ipc-eui/sites/default/files/events/files/T.C.J_Indian%20Geographical%20Indications%20successful%20vs%20unsuccessful.pdf>; Buch and Trivedi, *Indian Handlooms*, above n 25, 115–145; Sharma and Kulhari, *Marketing of GI Products*, above n 71, 52–70 (describing the range of support mechanisms for Chanderi sari producers). For a more comprehensive, comparative review of GI support policies, see Barbara Pick, *Intellectual Property and Development: Geographical Indications in Practice* (Routledge, 2022).

11

Culture Appropriation and the Global Fashion Industry

KAL RAUSTIALA AND CHRISTOPHER JON SPRIGMAN*

ABSTRACT

The global fashion industry is increasingly subject to accusations of cultural appropriation. We analyse why the fashion industry's practices – in particular, its mashup-magpie mode of creativity and its rapid innovation cycle – make it a frequent target of these claims. We explain the challenges to legal protection for cultural designs; explore and critique the normative case for property claims in traditional cultural designs; and offer a qualified defence of the industry's practice of re-interpreting those designs. Throughout, we suggest that many designs seen as originating in a particular culture have roots that extend outward to other cultures; this network of cultural interchange often undermines any particular ownership claim. And while appropriation can signal disrespect for source cultures and be objectionable for that reason, appropriation is not disrespectful per se. Indeed, there are strong normative arguments supporting many instances of appropriation.

11.1 Introduction

In 2018, French luxury fashion house Christian Dior featured, as part of its 'cruise' collection,[1] a number of dress designs inspired by Mexican *escaramuza*. A women-only event within Mexico's otherwise all-male sport of *charrería* (Mexican-style rodeo), *escaramuza* features teams of women on horseback, dressed in traditional costumes inspired by the

* The authors thank participants in the Fashion & Intellectual Property Scholars' Roundtable at National University of Singapore for comments on an earlier draft.

1 A 'cruise' or 'resort' collection is an inter-season line of clothing produced to be worn by people going on warm-weather winter vacations.

Adelitas – female soldiers who fought in the Mexican Revolution.[2] *Escaramuza* teams perform intricate and graceful choreographed equestrian manoeuvres at rushing speed. It's an impressive spectacle entwining strength and femininity in a way that obviously appealed to the designers at Dior.

Dior launched its *escaramuza*-inspired collection at the Domaine de Chantilly, a museum near Paris dedicated to the relationship between human and horse. The lavish night-time show, billed as 'Diorodeo' and held outside in a huge equestrian ring, featured an eight-woman Mexican *escaramuza* team flown in for the occasion. Dressed in custom Dior finery, the riders wheeled their mounts around the brightly lit ring with a wood-planked catwalk circling its outer edge, down which models paraded while the riders performed. It began to rain during the show; the downpour, the lights piercing through the rain, the closely confined horses and people and the motion and color all combined, according to attendees, to produce a beautiful effect.[3]

And yet right from the start there was some disquiet about the Chantilly event, with one journalist later writing that 'at a time when the fashion industry is confronting its less-than-politically-correct tendencies, this slightly missed the mark . . . as people were clearly a little uneasy with the display'.[4] But the real trouble came months after the opening event, when Dior released its collection, along with an ad campaign featuring actor Jennifer Lawrence. The campaign provoked sharp criticism – *Teen Vogue* wrote that Dior was now 'under fire' – along with much negative commentary online accusing Dior of 'appropriating' Mexican culture.[5]

The Dior episode is not unusual for fashion firms, which regularly find themselves embroiled in controversies over alleged cultural appropriation. Indeed, the *escaramuza* controversy is not even the most

[2] See 'Charrería, equestrian tradition in Mexico' UNESCO <https://ich.unesco.org/en/RL/charreria-equestrian-tradition-in-mexico-01108>; Lauren Cocking, 'A Guide To Charrería, Mexico's National Sport', Culture Trip (December 30, 2016) <https://theculturetrip.com/north-america/mexico/articles/a-guide-to-charreria-mexicos-national-sport/>.

[3] See 'DIOR holy escaramuzas!', EQLuxe (May 30, 2018) <http://eqluxe.com/dior-holy-escaramuzas/>.

[4] Ibid.

[5] Mekita Rivas, 'Jennifer Lawrence's New Dior Ad Is Being Accused of Cultural Appropriation', *Teen Vogue* (November 16, 2018) <https://www.teenvogue.com/story/jennifer-lawrence-dior-ad-accused-of-cultural-appropriation>.

recent such imbroglio for Dior.[6] In this chapter, we link these controversies to the fashion industry's creative practices, in particular, the industry's practice of 'referencing' and remixing existing designs, including traditional designs from cultures across the globe. The contemporary fashion industry features a global reach, rapid fashion cycles and a creative practice based in mimicry and re-contextualisation. This combination is a formula that will undoubtedly produce continued accusations of cultural appropriation, especially given the widening global influence of a viewpoint that treats cultural artifacts such as traditional designs as property, owned by an originating culture and off-limits to use by outsiders. .

In what follows we take a close look at this debate. We analyse why the fashion industry has been a frequent target of appropriation claims, explore the legal and normative considerations at play and offer a qualified defence of the fashion industry's practice of re-interpreting traditional designs. Specifically, we argue four main points:

First, the fashion industry, due to its global reach, its rapid innovation cycle and its magpie, mashup creative practices, is particularly prone to adapting pre-existing designs in ways that provoke claims of appropriation.

Second, there is little basis in existing intellectual property law to address these charges, and substantial barriers to changing the law to do so.

Third, the normative case against many forms of cultural appropriation in the fashion industry is weaker than the often reflexively critical media and social reactions imply. As an empirical matter, many cultural practices and traditions that critics seek to protect from appropriation in fact are themselves the product of a sort of appropriation, in that they represent the melding of older, diverse traditions. This view of culture is 'one of far-flung influences, brought together through contact; of innovation driven by broken traditions patched together from recovered shards'.[7] The 'authentic', in short, is often little more than a label we put on something that is both after-the-fact and in spite of the

[6] Dior's 'Sauvage' campaign in 2019, featuring Johnny Depp and extensive Native American iconography, was pulled after an outcry deriding Dior's cultural insensitivity. Interestingly, Dior's 2023 cruise collection, first shown in June 2022 and in ads in late fall 2022, is full of flamenco-inspired designs (flamenco is at least partially of Romani origin) set against a backdrop of Moorish architecture and décor. It wouldn't be too surprising if Dior's use of Romani and Moorish sources led to complaints, but so far there have been none.

[7] Martin Puchner, *Culture: The Story of Us, From Cave Art to K-Pop* (W. W. Norton, 2023) 7. (hereafter *Culture*)

facts; many designs, recipes and art forms that are promoted as originating in a particular culture have roots that extend outward to other cultures. In many cases, this network of cultural interchanges and influences undermines any particular ownership claim.

Fourth, although there are instances of appropriation that signal disrespect for source cultures and are normatively objectionable for that reason, appropriation is not disrespectful per se. Indeed, there is a strong normative argument supporting many instances of fashion appropriation. That argument is based in a set of ideas that travel together under the label 'cultural cosmopolitanism', which, for now, can be shorthanded as the view that the mixing of cultural elements is more important to human flourishing than any one group's ability to seal off its culture to outsiders, that identities are fluid and that the use of art and design originating in another culture can be an opportunity for connection and empathy and not merely depredation.

11.2 Cultural Appropriation in Fashion Design

Let's refer back to the Dior *escaramuza* controversy. Is it objectionable that Dior, a global fashion firm based in France, and its Italian-born creative director Maria Grazia Chiuri, used elements of Mexican *escaramuza* designs in their collection? To answer that question, it is important first to understand precisely what use Dior made of *escaramuza*.

Dior did not design items purporting to be authentic *escaramuza* outfits. Rather, Dior designed apparel and accessories *inspired*, at least in part, by *escaramuza*. By 'inspired', we mean that the outfits were not direct copies or knockoffs of typical *escaramuza* designs, nor did they claim to be true *escaramuza* wear. Dior's collection was rather a kind of fantasia that mixed *escaramuza* design elements with other elements of both traditional and modern European fashion design. Chiuri and her team directly spoke of the *hybridity* of their designs. For example, Stephen Jones, the milliner for the collection, described how he designed a hat that referred to *escaramuza*, but which re-contextualised those elements within a more modern and posh aesthetic:

> This hat was the very early prototype that I made for Maria Grazia. She liked the shape, but the straw was too rough. And she wanted something that was more Avenue Montaigne [the 8th arrondissement street that is Paris's epicentre of high-fashion showrooms], and less Zocalo in Mexico City.[8]

[8] 'The Escaramuzas', Dior News <https://www.dior.com/diormag/en_gb/article/the-escaramuzas>.

Dior's re-working of *escaramuza*-associated design was also linked to a feminist narrative – Dior promoted the *escaramuza* riders as a cultural archetype of strong but feminine women. One might be tempted to chalk this up to mere marketing: fashion houses love to tell a story about their collections, in part to give fashion journalists something to say beyond mere visual description. But in this case, Dior's decision was a continuation of Chiuri's self-described practice of exploring feminist themes.[9] As Chiuri explained:

> Usually, the female role in rodeo culture is to be there to support their husbands and sons, but these women have decided they want to do it all themselves. But they do it in traditional dress because they don't want to give up their femininity. Women are always being made to feel they have to change who they are to fit in. This collection speaks about that.[10]

Chiuri also explained how the dresses' design vocabulary drew on a variety of sources:

> Among our reference ideas are the images of *escaramuzas*; women on the front line in rodeo .... And the collection obviously refers to these elements, but not in a didactic way. After all, Dior's archives contained riding jackets and outfits to which we have referred, but clearly interpreted them in a contemporary way, in cotton to communicate another kind of attitude. We are in Chantilly. Chantilly is famous not only for horses but also famous for its lace. This is as much a part of the French tradition of the south of France as it is of southern Italy – but also of South America.[11]

In an interview with *Women's Wear Daily*, a leading trade paper, Chiuri expanded on her last point about how common artifacts and techniques, such as embroidery, connect different cultures:

[9] In the first year of her tenure at Dior, *Vogue France* had already noted the strong feminist themes underlying Chiuri's work: 'Under Chiuri, the catwalk has become a platform for an ongoing conversation about feminism and the arts. This season, she paid tribute to two powerful women, constructing a showspace in the style of artist and former Dior model Niki de Saint Phalle's Tarot Garden in Tuscany, and sending Breton-striped shirts stamped with the title of art historian Linda Nochlin's 1971 essay, "Why have there been no great women artists?" down the catwalk.' Lauren Indvik, 'Maria Grazia Chiuri: 'Dior Has to Be about Female Empowerment', *Vogue France* (November 3, 2017) <https://www.vogue.fr/fashion/fashion-inspiration/diaporama/maria-grazia-chiuri-dior-collection-fashion-week-feminism/46923>.

[10] Redacción El Universal, 'Dior Pays Homage to Mexican Escaramuzas', El Universal (May 14, 2019) <https://www.eluniversal.com.mx/english/dior-pays-homage-mexican-escaramuzas>.

[11] Ibid.

> This kind of tradition of embroidery is part of my culture, which comes from southern Italy where my father was born, but also in the south of France, as in South America . . .. In some way, I think that all the South has the same language. When we speak about lace, when we speak about embroidery, it's such a part of different countries that it's very difficult to understand where they come from.[12]

Chiuri here is speaking the language of cultural connection; in particular, the way that embroidery is, in her view, part of a shared design language that pervades 'the South'. Many may disagree with Chiuri's suggestion that the particular contemporary social construct of 'the South' should include southern France and Italy. But set that aside: Chiuri's principal argument – that many of the design elements associated with *escaramuza* clothes are common to a number of cultures and traditions – is correct. While the name and the exact combination used in *escaramuza* is unlikely to be found anywhere else, the constituent elements – riding jackets and boots, embroidered skirts, ruffled petticoats – are not unique to *escaramuza*, or even to Mexico.

Still, to some observers, Dior was simply stealing traditional Mexican designs and profiting off them. Such claims, as we've already noted, are not unique to Dior. In fact, Dior isn't even the only fashion house recently accused of appropriating designs alleged to be Mexican cultural property. In 2020, the *New York Times* reported that the Mexican Minister of Culture had written a letter to Venezuelan-born designer Carolina Herrera alleging that she had appropriated traditional Mexican *Istmo de Tehuantepec* floral and *Saltiillo* serape patterns in 2020. On social media, many echoed the charge, calling the Herrera designs stealing.[13]

The Herrera brand replied respectfully (albeit also a bit pompously), stating that 'the emblematic fashion house recognizes the wonderful and diverse craft and textile work of Mexican artisans, its collection inspired by the culture's rich colours and artisanal techniques'. That acknowledgement was not enough for the *New York Times*' fashion critic, who decreed that fashion appropriation 'is clearly a hangover of an old colonial mentality' and that Herrera's use of Mexican designs

[12] Jenni Avins, 'Mexico's Female Rodeo Stars Inspired Dior's Latest Collection', *Quartz* (May 26, 2018) <https://qz.com/quartzy/1290086/mexicos-female-rodeo-stars-inspired-diors-latest-collection/>.

[13] See Vanessa Friedman, 'Homage or Theft? Carolina Herrera Called Out by Mexican Minister', *New York Times* (June 13, 2019) <https://www.nytimes.com/2019/06/13/fashion/carolina-herrera-mexico-appropriation.html> (describing social media reaction).

'underscores the way that traditional fashion practices are increasingly problematic and out of date'.[14]

The word 'stealing', though often appearing in these disputes, is almost never meant literally, at least not in the legal sense of the term. So why do people use the term to describe what's objectionable about fashion appropriation? Of course, claims of appropriation (and related claims of inauthenticity) are often found in other creative domains, including food, film and music. But the controversies appear to occur more often in fashion – and to burn hotter. The frequency of appropriation disputes in fashion may relate to high fashion's huge budget for advertising. But it is also almost certainly linked to the industry's particular creative practices, in particular the very fast and frequent fashion cycles that characterise apparel. Fashion designers occasionally present something that is largely if not totally new. But far more common is to see older designs (sometimes much older) renewed and recombined to create something that, if not quite new, is at least fresh. This synthetic, recursive mode of creating is central to the fashion industry's success. But this creative culture, combined with the industry's global reach, does appear to lead ineluctably to accusations of cultural appropriation. And because luxury fashion houses in particular cater to a wealthy and largely white clientele, charges of appropriation gather energy from the racial and social class conflicts that underlie them.

Are these indictments of cultural appropriation in the fashion industry compelling? Responding to that question requires us to consider both the legality and the morality of the practice. We'll consider the legality question first, although, to be clear, we acknowledge that many critiques of cultural appropriation in the fashion industry are not grounded in legal claims and use the language of stealing and property loosely. That said, the question of legality is, in our view, always relevant. To the degree the term 'cultural appropriation' is used to claim that design elements are owned, or, at minimum, that someone or some group has control over the use of those elements, it is generally a misreading of the law. Cultural appropriation is only very lightly regulated by intellectual property law, which does not recognise ownership of most intangible cultural artifacts or design elements.

The primary reasons for that are easy to state. First, traditional designs are often quite old – too old to be protected by copyright law or the

[14] Ibid.

various sorts of design protection laws. In addition, these designs are rarely associated with a particular *producer* in the way that trademark law typically understands that term, and so trademark, for the most part, does not provide protection. Other laws, such as those defining and protecting so-called geographical indications, may provide some peripheral protections, but these are too narrow to impact most re-use of traditional designs by the global fashion industry.

In short, the vast majority of designs, dances, musical styles, culinary preparations and other cultural materials and practices that have been associated with claims of cultural appropriation are unprotected by contemporary IP law. Below we detail the intersection of IP and cultural appropriation. In particular, we discuss the lack of fit between IP's utilitarian and rights-based justifications and property rights in traditional cultural expressions like apparel designs.

11.3 Cultural Property and Cultural Appropriation

The term 'cultural property' refers to a wide range of things, only some of which are germane to the debates we address here. The 1970 UNESCO Convention on the Illicit Trafficking of Cultural Property, for example, offers an expansive definition, but one largely rooted in tangible artifacts that relate to specific cultures or traditions, such as musical instruments or sculptures. That said, the term 'cultural property' is often used with regard to intangible as well as tangible works. For example, legal scholarship related to indigenous peoples often refers to 'cultural property' and 'cultural heritage' interchangeably and uses cultural property as a covering term for a wide range of artistic, literary and religious works and practices. And indeed, contemporary debates over cultural appropriation often focus on *intangible* creative works – that is, the types of works typically addressed by intellectual property law.

11.3.1 Utilitarian Arguments for Protection

A dominant justification for IP rights, at least in the US, is utilitarian – we grant these rights as an incentive for the creation of new works.[15]

[15] This is widely held to be true of US intellectual property law (United States Constitution, art I, § 8, cl 8 gives Congress the power to create copyright and patent laws 'to promote the progress of science and useful arts') but also of IP laws globally, as, for example, noted in the preamble to the World Trade Organization's TRIPs Accord ('recognizing the

Framed in that way, it's easy to see that traditional cultural works are a poor fit with the justification for IP rights. These works have already been created, typically long ago, and so incentives to create are definitionally irrelevant. One might argue that while traditional cultural creations may be old, they are constantly updated by the relevant community, and therefore the community should enjoy some protection for that new, revised creative work. (We will return below to the very difficult question of who is comprised by the term 'community' in this context.) Yet the protection afforded would only apply to the new innovations added to the old creative form and not the traditional elements of that form. The more the new elements contribute to a work's appeal, the less traditional the underlying creation is. Protection and tradition, in short, are fundamentally in tension.[16]

There is another problem, related to the incentives problem yet independent of it: traditional works are usually far too old to be protected by the limited-term rights that are granted under copyright and design rights (design patent in the United States), which are the most relevant forms of legal regulation. While in principle copyright or design rights could be extended for hundreds of years, the underlying notion of time limitation is critical. The incentive to create that the law provides is meant to be balanced against the harms that result from restrictions on reproduction and use that limit competition and raise prices paid by consumers.

Indefinite IP rights do exist, such as trademark (including trade dress) and trade secret. Yet these rest on a different utilitarian rationale altogether. Trade secret law protects commercially valuable information against disclosure if reasonable steps are taken to keep it secret. The classic example is the formula for Coca-Cola. In the vast majority of cultural appropriation controversies, trade secret law is not relevant

underlying public policy objectives of national systems for the protection of intellectual property, including developmental and technological objectives'). For an assessment of copyright's utilitarian justification, see generally Christopher Jon Sprigman, 'Copyright and Creative Incentives: What We Know (and Don't)' (2017) 55 *Houston Law Review* 451.

[16] A tension that European policymakers largely ignore. See 'Why Do Geographical Indications Matter to Us?', European Commission (July 30, 2003) <https://ec.europa.eu/commission/presscorner/detail/en/MEMO_03_160> ('GIs are key to EU and developing countries' cultural heritage, traditional methods of production and natural resources'). See also Dev S Gangee, 'Geographical Indications and Cultural Heritage' (2012) 4 *World Intellectual Property Organization Journal* 92 (noting the growth of cultural heritage justifications for GI protections).

because the material that is appropriated has not been kept secret and was never meant to be.

That leaves us to consider the application of trademark law. There is no insuperable barrier to adapting trademark to protect cultural creations – indeed, as we shall explain below, the related category of geographical indications provides at least a partial analogy to protections for some forms of traditional culture. However, the nature of trademark law makes it of limited use here. Unlike patents, copyrights and trade secrets, trademarks and trade dress protections are not centrally designed or intended to spur investment in socially valuable creativity. Rather, they are justified primarily to protect consumers. Certain words, symbols and designs are protected from copying because they function for consumers as indicators of the source of products or services. In short, trademark law seeks to ensure that consumers do not become confused about the source of the good.[17]

But there are factors that limit trademark law's relevance to most instances of cultural appropriation in the fashion industry. First, protection normally requires that the words, symbols or designs be used in commerce in association with products or services and that these marks become well known enough, or are simply distinctive enough, that they are clearly associated in the mind of the relevant public with the *source* of the good – that is, the producer – rather than the good itself. Trademark law thinks of that single source typically as a firm, but it's imaginable that the law could be re-purposed to understand the concept of 'source' to refer to a particular culture, rather than a particular firm.

Yet there are two fundamental problems with this approach. First, there are already ways other than trademark law to protect legitimate consumer interests regarding the source of a traditional design or product. If consumers care whether a dress with a *Saltillo* fabric pattern originates in Mexico, that information can be provided by marking the garment with a tag stating that it's made in Mexico, or, at least, that it originates with a Mexico-based producer, and using truth-in-labeling/selling laws to regulate these indicators. (This, in essence, is the approach of the US Indian Arts and Crafts Act,[18] which bans the sales of goods that are falsely represented as being Indian-made, or sold in a way that falsely makes it seem like they are Indian-made.) And if people

[17] See, eg, Mark McKenna, 'A Consumer Decision-Making Theory of Trademark Law' (2012) 98 *Virginia Law Review* 67, 73.

[18] Indian Arts and Crafts Act 1990, 25 USC § 305–305(e) (US).

care that the product comes from a particular cultural group within Mexico, truth-in-labeling laws can be tailored to serve that interest. Consumer protection does not require limiting the use of *Saltillo* patterns only to Mexican producers.

Second, and more pervasively, given that the origins of many traditional names or designs are unknown to consumers, and given the frequency with which bits and pieces originating with one culture are incorporated into creative works produced outside the originating culture, liability under a trademark law re-fashioned to protect traditional cultural materials would likely be narrow. Consider Dior's *escaramuza* collection. Few consumers of these products would perceive these designs – or in fact the traditional designs worn by *adelitas* from which they draw – as coming from any single source. From the perspective of many Dior customers – who might live in Shanghai, Dubai or London – the overall look and feel of the clothing is vaguely Mexican and equestrian, or perhaps, even more broadly, vaguely Latin American. In short, these designs lack distinctiveness for most Dior buyers – a globally dispersed group – even if the concept is stretched to embrace a nation or ethnic group (rather than a firm) as a source.[19]

Moreover, even if a traditional name or design used on a product is capable of indicating source, protection would be limited to uses that confuse consumers into believing (incorrectly) that the product originates with the source community or that it is affiliated with or licensed or endorsed by that community. In the cases where the cultural origin of the name or design is widely known – as it would have to be to achieve distinctiveness – consumers are unlikely to believe, in many if not most instances, that products marked with names or designs famously identified with a particular culture originate with or are otherwise endorsed by that culture. (Or, perhaps more precisely, were endorsed by some official with the power to speak on behalf of the originating culture.) For example, consider the case of Kim Kardashian's (brief) use of the term 'kimono' for underwear. It seems virtually impossible to believe that consumers seeing the term used on Kardashian's products would think

[19] The trademark dilution cause of action is no more promising as a means of enforcing rights in traditional cultural elements. The most relevant form of dilution would be dilution by blurring, which, if trademark law were adapted to protect a particular culture, rather than a particular firm, as a source, would fit quite awkwardly, since the national or regional source of most garments is not visible from the outside. And as far as the labels go, any dilution of the could again be addressed by truth-in-labelling laws.

they had any actual relationship to Japan – not least because the term was used in association with trademarks that powerfully identify the products as Kardashian's. Indeed, the Kardashian brand in some sense actually *is* the product.

Those are all doctrinal problems, but the practical difficulties are perhaps even greater. The first one is, once we've decided to establish property rights, who is the owner? Rights in traditional designs would be *collective* rights, and defining the relevant community that would hold and exercise ownership rights is vexingly difficult. There are two interrelated and thorny problems here. One is that different groups may lay claim to the same (or very similar) traditional creations. Who invented riding boots, or short cloth jackets or embroidery? The other is that even within a clearly delineated group with a valid claim to creation, individuals may differ on whether and how to share the creation or collaborate with others. Communities may, or may not, have rules for the use of their traditional expressions. When such rules exist, they may or may not meet widely shared standards of representativeness or consent. But whatever the governance regime internal to a particular community, there are no agreed-upon ways for IP law to choose among different would-be users within the community.

One might imagine IP protection for traditional cultural materials that relies on temporal priority to choose among rival claimants – that is, who did it first? But this is unlikely to work in most cases. Often it is impossible to determine which group created a particular element of traditional culture first. The problem deepens when the question involves in-group ownership among rival claimants: in these cases, a rule of priority is usually of no help at all. And in some cases, traditional cultural practices are not actually all that traditional. Certainly, *escaramuza* has unique Mexican embellishments. Yet much of the costume developed out of Spanish and other European influences – most centrally, the horse itself. This sort of hybrid cultural expression is common and often it is not even recognised as 'appropriation' – at least until the person or firm doing the taking is identified as belonging to a dominant culture and the culture taken from is identified, in some sense, as subordinated.

Overarching all of these difficulties is a pervasive line drawing problem: how to determine which cultural materials will be protected and which have passed into the public domain. The answer cannot be that all traditional culture belongs to the source community; such a rule would be both profoundly destructive and unadministrable. As a thought experiment, consider what would happen if the US government sent a letter to the mayor of Mexico City complaining about the many jazz clubs that exist there, on the grounds that they were stealing and profiting from a cultural product that belongs to an American marginalised group. Jazz is incontrovertibly an American art form produced originally by a marginalised community. In that sense it is not dissimilar to the indigenous designs the Mexican culture minister complained about in the Herrera incident, the only notable difference being that jazz has been immeasurably more influential on global culture and thus more heavily appropriated across the globe.

One immediate problem, from a practical point of view, is who gets to decide whether jazz in Mexico is or is not objectionable; that is, who speaks on this topic for Americans, or jazz musicians or African-American jazz musicians. Even within source communities, often there is little agreement on what constitutes an objectionable use of culture and what does not. This is illustrated by numerous incidents in the art world, such as the controversy around Catholic painter Chris Ofili's *Holy Virgin Mary*, a portrait of the Virgin covered in elephant dung. (Ofili's painting, when first displayed in the Brooklyn Museum, led then-Mayor and Catholic Rudy Giuliani to denounce the painting as 'sick' and try to cut off city support for the museum.) Is Ofili due extra latitude as a Catholic himself to test the boundaries of acceptable use of a Catholic cultural icon? Does it matter that Giuliani is Catholic?[20] These difficult internal questions of who gets to use what cultural material, how and when, are fundamentally unpoliceable by our legal system.

A second problem is defining what counts as a given cultural product for this purpose. There is no official arbiter of musical styles, for instance. Do jazz hybrids count as jazz? When, in 1970, Miles Davis recorded *Bitches Brew* with electric guitars and multiple drummers, irritating purists and essentially creating jazz fusion, was that working within the genre or creating something new? Would our hypothetical American jazz

[20] From the perspective of one important institution in the Catholic community, the Catholic Church itself, Ofili may have *less* latitude, as a Catholic, to demean the Virgin. That is the message conveyed by the Vatican's 2006 statement recommending Madonna's excommunication in response to the singer's staging of a mock-crucifixion as part of her concert in Rome. In that episode, Cardinal Ersilio Tonino, speaking with the approval of Pope Benedict, characterised Madonna's performance as 'a blasphemous challenge to the faith and a profanation of the Cross. She should be excommunicated. To crucify herself . . . in the city of popes and martyrs is an act of open hostility'. Frances Romero, 'Madonna, Over and Over', *Time* (October 20, 2010) <https://content.time.com/time/specials/packages/article/0,28804,2026525_2026524_2026526,00.html>.

policeman care about the appropriation, in Mexico, of jazz fusion, or just 'traditional' jazz?

Still a third problem is what happens if an American jazz musician is invited to invest in a jazz club in Mexico. Is the connection with an American member of the jazz 'source community' sufficient to immunise the Mexican club against charges of cultural appropriation? Or consider again the Carolina Herrera example. What if Herrera, for instance, had hired as part of their design team a single individual from among the local indigenous people associated with the traditional serape designs they modified? What if they simply hired someone who is from the same ethnic group as the source community but who lives in New York City (where Herrera's fashion house is based)? What if the head designer was herself Mexican? What if the prime minister or monarch of a nation that contains the source community gave his or her imprimatur to the cultural borrowing? Would any of these facts matter for purposes of claims of appropriation?

As these hypotheticals and examples show, it is often very difficult to know who should be in a position to authorise any given act of 'appropriation'. This is just one of a multitude of thorny practical problems that must be addressed as part of an argument justifying legal protections for traditional cultural materials, at least if one wants to move beyond casual social media shaming or tsk-tsking by fashion journalists. Unless the property right is untransferable and unlicenseable, someone has to have the capacity to authorise.

11.3.2 Rights-Based Arguments for Protection

There are, in addition to the incentives-based rationales for IP, two well-established rights-based justifications. The first grows out of the theory of property famously set out in John Locke's *Two Treatises of Government.* Locke identified the individual's contribution of labour as the mechanism by which objects are reduced to property and focused on the harm – in terms of fairness rather than wealth maximisation – when another deprives the owner of the fruits of that labour. A person owns her own labour, and that person adds that labour whenever she appropriates a thing from the commons. If another takes the object the first person has appropriated, that person also takes the labour that the first person has added. That taking of labour is a harm.

Some commentators have questioned whether the Lockean framework readily carries over to the realm of intangible creative expression. There is a critical difference between the two. Reading a book and accessing its intellectual content is *non-rivalrous*; any number of people can do it without 'exhausting' or degrading the work. Consuming the work is not the same as taking the book itself (the physical item), which only one person can possess. This has led some philosophers to argue against Lockean justifications for IP rights.[21]

But there is a deeper problem here, one that goes to the heart of what it means to 'labour' within the Lockean framework. For most traditional cultural expressions, current members of the in-group have not laboured to create them – they are labouring to *reproduce* or to *perform or display* them. That sort of labour is present in any act of copying, and it cannot be the sort of labour that gives rise to ownership within the Lockean framework, else every copyist would also be an owner. To justify collective rights within the Lockean framework, one must sustain an argument that the labour of someone in the group (usually an unknown person or persons and usually much earlier in time) justifies labour-based rights for the rest of the group, thereby making copies made by a group member different than those made by someone outside the group. No such argument has been made, to our knowledge, from within the Lockean framework. But if such an argument *were* made, it would run directly into the problem of determining who belongs to the group and how decisions must be made about use of the property right, if we were to establish one.

Of course, to the extent that individuals are currently creating works that, while recognisably falling within the boundaries of a form of traditional cultural expression, add new creativity to that form, then, as we have already noted, current IP law will grant rights in that new creative portion only.

A second rights-based justification for copyright protection is found in the idea that because original expression reflects and embodies an author's personality, respect for creators' autonomy requires the recognition of property rights in creative works. This justification grows out of theories set out by Hegel, Kant and, much more recently, Margaret Radin.[22]

Personality theory is based in the autonomy interests associated with property. The theory posits that property provides an especially powerful mechanism for self-definition, for personal expression and for society's

[21] See, eg, Seana Valentine Shiffrin, 'Lockean Arguments for Private Intellectual Property' in Stephen R Munzer (ed), *New Essays in the Legal and Political Theory of Property* (Cambridge University Press, 2001) 138.

[22] Margaret J Radin, 'Property and Personhood' (1982) 34 *Stanford Law Review* 957.

recognition of the dignity of an individual. Personality theory is appealing in part because it aligns with modern understandings of the importance of property: in a consumer society, we are (in part) what we own. And given popular adherence to a Romantic conception of authorship in the West, where most major fashion houses are based, the fashion industry is apt to find a particularly strong link between an individual creator's personality and his or her creative expression.

The question, again, is whether the justification extends to a *community's* claim of ownership over traditional designs. Personality theory at its root is about affording *individuals* the capacity for self-realisation through the ownership of property. Adapting this argument to provide a justification for community ownership of traditional culture requires more. First, that the ability of a community to express itself is implicated in human flourishing. This basic communitarian argument is, we believe, fairly straightforwardly sustained. And of course, if a community is *barred* from using traditional cultural expressions – a policy that at various times has been imposed by majorities on marginalised groups across the globe – that seems very likely to harm the community's ability to sustain its identity.

The more difficult part is specifying when and how a community's ability to sustain itself is likely to be harmed when traditional culture is used by individuals *outside* the community. It is possible that the source community could lose some, or all, of its capacity to identify itself to others as a community if outsiders are free to make use of their traditional arts or designs. On the other hand, it may be that use by outsiders (especially if that use is coupled with some form of attribution to the source community) increases public recognition of that community and the cultural materials associated with it. The outcomes will almost inevitably differ case by case, and the effects of any particular case likely will be difficult to understand in advance.

Moreover, even if harm to the source community seems likely, that community's group interest is not the only interest at stake. The appropriator has an interest in his or her individual creative freedom that cannot be dismissed solely on the grounds that he or she used 'someone else's' source materials unless there is a compelling reason to believe that the community's interest should always override the individual's (and that the source material at issue is, in fact, someone else's). This is especially true in cases of cultural appropriation, such as in the Dior and Herrera examples, that involve creative re-contextualisation as opposed to mere copying. Each of us has an interest in being able to use the culture that we're exposed to, whether it originates from the national or local community to which we happen to belong or elsewhere. Cultural artifacts and forms – whether *Istmo de Tehuantepec* floral designs, or American jazz – impress themselves upon the consciousness of an ever-wider diversity of people as they travel. This isn't a process we can control. Nor do people choose what bits and pieces of culture they connect with. And that's why a Japanese musician living in Osaka who loves jazz has an interest in 'appropriating' the form and creating new jazz that is difficult to distinguish from the interest of an American musician living in New York.

In short, if one wants to seriously propose a method of protection for traditional creations, it is very hard to fit that protection into well-accepted IP concepts, whether approached from a utilitarian or rights-based perspective. As a matter of IP theory and doctrine, traditional culture is a very poor fit – deliberately. And as a matter of practicality and politics, the obstacles are daunting. All that said, there are some more peripheral forms of IP that may provide some measure of protection to some types of traditional cultural expression.

Perhaps the most potentially useful is the geographical indication, or GI. Akin to a collective trademark, these designate a given geographic location as the sole source of the good. Well-known examples include Bordeaux, Barolo and Roquefort. The notion, roughly, is that only certain places can 'authentically' produce certain products, which are made singular by some combination of the natural and physical characteristics of a region (*terroir*) plus local knowledge. Use of the name with products from another location, this line of reasoning goes, is misleading to consumers.

There are many conceptual and practical problems with the protection of GIs. But doctrinally, they are recognised in many national legal systems, including that of the United States, and also under international law, such as in the WTO Trade-Related Intellectual Property agreement. GIs are not limited to agricultural products. There are various textiles and clothing products currently protected via GIs, and so there is no reason that the Mexican styles at stake in the Dior and Herrera cases could not, in theory, be given a GI designation.

However, all GIs do is bar the use of certain descriptive words or place-names. They do not bar the mimicking of style, taste or appearance. In other words, wine called Chablis, but not made in Chablis, runs afoul of the GI rule. But nothing stops a winemaker in Australia from making a wine that tastes just like Chablis – they just can't call it Chablis. Similarly, nothing would stop a designer such as Carolina Herrera from making a dress in the style, or spirit, of the Mexican traditional patterns, as long as the GI-designated name for those patterns was not employed. In short, GIs would not address the underlying phenomenon of appropriation that critics are concerned with.[23]

In short, the law governing IP is of very limited use with regard to nearly all claims of cultural appropriation. None of this is to gainsay the fact that traditional designs or practices sometimes are copied and used by outsiders in ways that are troubling. But given the deep structure and articulated categories of IP law, the protections available under any justifiable IP regime are very limited. The vast majority of extant cultural appropriation claims are simply not addressable without a wholesale shift in our understanding of what IP law is supposed to be about. There is currently no meaningful legal path forward to the 'problem' of cultural appropriation.

11.4 Moral Objections to Cultural Appropriation

Of course, even if cultural appropriation is legal, that doesn't mean that it's right. The very label 'cultural appropriation' suggests a moral transgression, as opposed to a more positive term, like 'cultural interchange' or 'cultural borrowing'. The strong negative charge of the label suggests that the practice presents a clear case for moral condemnation. Yet, at least with respect to the practice overall, as opposed to specific examples, the case for moral condemnation is often unclear and only rarely as straightforward as some of the critics of appropriation make it out to be.

In part this is because, as we noted above, creations or designs claimed to have originated in a particular tradition often are in fact the product of *multiple* traditions. It is often said, for example, that bucatini amatriciana is one of the four traditional pastas of Rome. And it is. But the dish isn't really *from* Rome. It originated in the village of Grisciano, approximately

[23] As was mentioned earlier, in the United States, in addition to GI protection for things like Napa Valley wine, the Indian Arts and Crafts Act protects against claims of Indian manufacture by non-Indians. As the Department of Interior states, the law is a truth-in-advertising law that prohibits misrepresentation in the marketing of Indian arts and crafts products within the United States. It is illegal to offer or display for sale, or sell any art or craft product in a manner that falsely suggests it is Indian produced, an Indian product or the product of a particular Indian or Indian tribe or Indian arts and crafts organisation, resident within the United States. While useful and important, the statute does not stop the copying of Indian designs – just the misrepresentation of the identity of the designer as coming from the Indian source community. Obviously, a general statute modelled on the Indian Arts and Crafts Act would, like geographical indications, not touch most instances of alleged cultural appropriation.

150 km northeast. The shepherds in this hilly rural area took to mixing their pasta with cured pork jowl (guanciale) and the local pecorino cheese. They called this simple dish *griscia*. Griscia transformed as it spread to the nearby village of Amatrice, where it was remixed by adding tomato sauce. Rechristened as 'amatriciana', the dish eventually migrated to Rome. Rome is where the recipe was *popularised*, not where it was invented. It is also where the dish became associated with the hollow bucatini pasta; in Amatrice it was more typically made with spaghetti.

The hybridity of the dish, of course, runs deeper. It is impossible at this point to reconstruct the origin and early spread of pasta, but it is clear that different types of pasta have long existed not only in Italy but also in the Mediterranean as a whole and in China (and elsewhere).[24] The tomato, of course, was unknown in Italy before 1548, when it was introduced from the New World, and wasn't widely adopted in Italian cuisine until the early eighteenth century. So, in a dish which is considered the quintessence of Roman cuisine, we see origins that lie both outside of Rome and outside of Italy, or indeed, Europe. There are many similar examples in which foods, styles or designs from varied places or peoples are combined to create something now considered authentic to a single place or people. This complexity not only calls into question the authenticity of a particular design or feature as a conceptual matter; it complicates any putative ownership claim as well.

Returning to Dior and *escaramuza*, neither Mexican culture in general nor *escaramuza* in particular are hermetic – like many traditions that are said to belong to a particular nation or people, *escaramuza* has long and tangled roots and combines elements that can, in many cases, be found elsewhere as well. The designs associated with *escaramuza* are themselves a blend of traditional European equestrian designs and practices and indigenous Mesoamerican ones. Indeed, the central, signature feature of *escaramuza* – the horse – is a European import.

And the point runs in the other direction as well: traditions associated with a particular place travel with the people from that place – or, as is the case with Mexico and the United States, as national borders move but people (and often their cultural practices) remain. California, where the Dior ad campaign was shot, was widely criticised online as a location choice for a Mexican-inspired collection. Yet California was part of Mexico until the mid-nineteenth century. Mexico the nation cannot

[24] For a deeply learned account of pasta's murky origins, see Silvano Serventi and Francoise Sabban, *Pasta: The Story of a Universal Food* (Columbia University Press, 2002).

claim the *only* moral interest in the designs associated with *escaramuza* – at minimum, Mexicans and Mexican-Americans in the United States also have an interest in the development of these cultural practices. But the interest runs beyond Mexicans, wherever they may live. As a particular cultural practice spreads, it often impresses itself on members of out-groups who have not encountered it before. Those out-group members might develop an affinity for it; they may even adopt it as a core aspect of their identity. This is inevitable in any world in which people move around or communicate across borders, and those who are exposed to a culture have an interest in being free to respond to it that cannot just be waved away by invoking the word 'appropriation'.

The upshot is that as cultural practices travel, they interact, are received, adopted and transformed. This sort of transmission of cultural content is precisely what Maria Grazia Chiuri, Dior's creative director, intended. Chiuri stated that she admired the way in which the *escaramuza* reconcile tradition and modernity, femininity and strength. The *escaramuza* designs, if you take Chiuri at her word, are not just meant to be pretty. They are part of a narrative in which she invokes *cultural values* in the form of particular visual elements. Chiuri incorporates those already hybrid visual elements into new designs that mix Mexican and European traditions to make a case that the sort of muscular femininity that *escaramuza* embodies is in fact a disposition shared by women across cultures.

A common response is that Mexicans should be empowered to control the use of *escaramuza* and its traditional attire because they are part of a subordinated culture and people. Dior represents the wealthy, powerful North; Mexico the poor, colonised South. (Recall Chiuri's perhaps unintentional attempt to assimilate Southern Europe to the 'South'.) This argument is important, but it raises a host of issues. One of them is that the hierarchy is not always clear. We see this in a recent cultural appropriation spat that doesn't involve fashion but rather the motion picture industry.[25] In 2023, Netflix premiered a docudrama series, titled 'African Queens', which focuses on female African rulers. One of the queens was Cleopatra, portrayed in the series by a Black actress from the United Kingdom, Adele James. 'We don't often get to see or hear stories about Black queens, and that was really important for me, as well as for

[25] See Vivian Yee, 'Whose Queen? Netflix and Cleopatra Spar Over an African Cleopatra', *New York Times* (May 10, 2018) <https://www.nytimes.com/2023/05/10/world/middleeast/cleopatra-netflix-race-egypt.html.>.

my daughter, and just for my community to be able to know those stories because there are tons of them', Jada Pinkett Smith, who produced 'African Queens', said in a Netflix-sponsored article about the show.[26]

The most famous Hollywood actress to play Cleopatra was, of course, Elizabeth Taylor, who starred in the movie of that name in 1963. It's almost unimaginable that an actress who looks like Elizabeth Taylor would be chosen to play the part today. But now the choice of a Black woman to portray Cleopatra in 'Africa Queens' has sparked a lot of pushback from Egyptians, who note that Cleopatra wasn't a Black African but rather the last of a dynasty that originated in Macedonian Greece. Even the Egyptian government complained. 'Statues of Queen Cleopatra confirm that she had Hellenistic (Greek) features, distinguished by light skin, a drawn-out nose and thin lips', Egypt's government said on Twitter in 2023.[27]

Whether Roman statues, which are often executed in a standard Hellenistic portrait style that idealises more than portrays, actually confirm anything about Cleopatra's appearance is an open question. But it's noteworthy that the Black Americans behind 'African Queens' want to see Cleopatra as African, while many Egyptians prefer to see her as specifically *Egyptian*, and, more generally, prefer to see Egypt not as simply African but as a racial mélange with long-standing and continuing ties to Europe and the Middle East. Whose vision ought to prevail?

There is another problem, one that has to do with what it means for a culture to be 'subordinated'. One of the ways cultures may be subordinated is when perspectives and practices from that culture are ignored in debates within dominant cultures. Referring again to Dior, we might question whether that is happening, or, rather, the reverse. One way of seeing Chiuri's use of *escaramuza* designs is as a bid to make the cultural views and practices associated with *escaramuza* known and salient to a wider world. Simply deriding what Chiuri has done as 'appropriation' misses how use of designs from subordinated cultures, at least if done with reasonable acknowledgement of the source (as Chiuri and Dior have generally done) can both introduce and honour a source culture for a

[26] Tudum Staff, '"Queen Cleopatra" Shows a Side of the Infamous Royal You Haven't Seen Before', *Tudum By Netflix* (May 12, 2023) <https://www.netflix.com/tudum/articles/african-queens-release-date-cast-news>.

[27] Ministry of Tourism and Antiquities, 'Statues of Cleopatra Confirm That She Had Hellnistic (Greek) features', *X* (May 1, 2023) <https://twitter.com/TourismandAntiq/status/1652744796509814784>.

new, and wider, audience. And in doing so, the 'appropriation' both creates something new and can, as in this case, transmit some of the values of the source culture. Of course, firms like Dior make money in the process, which is a source of much of the objection we catalogue.

These processes are not static, and precisely what happens to culture when it travels is case-specific. Often, as a cultural practice takes root in a new place, it changes; no cultural practice remains pure when transmitted. Interaction among cultures has never produced purity. This reworking of transmitted culture is ubiquitous and, we believe, is a significant driver of cultural innovation.[28]

None of this means that some instances of appropriation aren't objectionable. When Gucci put turbans on white models, as it did in Milan Fashion Week in 2018, or when Marc Jacobs featured white models wearing multi-coloured dreadlocks, as he did at New York Fashion Week in 2016, people might reasonably react by asking whether a white designer is disparaging minority cultures or at least treating them with disrespect. But those who label as 'cultural appropriation' every use by a rich-world actor of a cultural artifact from another community are taking the argument too far. This view that cultural appropriation involves power disparities – that it is not cultural mixing in itself that is wrong but rather only the instances in which actors from the rich world use source material from the Global South – is understandably attractive to some. But it is often overly simplistic in its analysis of the evolution of culture and, as we have suggested, difficult to apply with any consistency in practice.

11.5 Why Do Cultural Appropriation Debates Capture So Much Attention Today?

Finally, we turn to an underlying question that we think vital: What is driving the seeming growth in concern over cultural appropriation, whether in the fashion industry or elsewhere? In the fashion world, as we argued earlier, such charges are easy to level because it is a global industry in which the dominant creative approach of fashion designers is to mix and match ideas from different eras and places. But the forces pushing cultural appropriation claims into the conversation are more complex and pervasive than that. At bottom, we think that the expanding

[28] For a fascinating inquiry extolling the virtues of hybrid styles, see Gustavo Arrellano, *Taco USA: How Mexican Food Conquered America* (Simon & Schuster, 2013).

boundaries of the behaviour labelled with that term reflect a recent and curious convergence of right and left ideas about culture. The most media-saturated objections to cultural appropriation come almost entirely from the left. These claims are typically rooted in a dynamic of the powerful versus the powerless. At the same time, a troubling parallel critique of cultural mixing has emerged on the political right. As populist and nationalist movements have taken hold in many states, we see concerns with cultural property and cultural purity taking root that are, at a very broad level of generality, akin to the left-wing concerns that formerly have driven the debate.

The increased salience of right-wing objections to cultural hybridity is grounded in (often racist) concerns over cultural and demographic transformation and 'pollution'. They have not been connected to left-wing objections to cultural appropriation. But while the underlying claims and rationales on the left and right are very different, the shared belief system is clear: only certain people have the right to engage with certain cultural practices. Cultural purity is good; cultural mixing, dilution and exchange are suspect.

The view that particular peoples should be able to control the development of their cultures and that the freedom of outsiders to adopt, interpret or dilute that culture should be restricted is at the core of this ascendent trans-partisan ideology of cultural purity. The left-wing variant focuses on the right of minority cultures or marginalised communities to control the development of their own cultures and ensure that 'outsiders' do not misuse, profit from or even simply employ their cultural expressions. The right-wing variant inverts this focus: it is the majority culture's right to self-definition that is under threat from invasion and involuntary cultural hybridity.

Consider a recent opinion survey of the British public:

> More than half of British people feel hostile not just to refugees, but to ethnic minorities – many of them British people themselves – already living here. This can be put down to various perceived economic and social threats – a quarter think immigrants take away jobs, and a third that they remove more from society than they contribute. But more sinister is its generality. *More than half of the British people surveyed felt that people from ethnic minorities threatened their 'culture'.*[29]

[29] Afua Hirsch, 'Brexit is Entrenching Some Dangerous Myths about 'British' Culture', *The Guardian* May 25, 2017) <https://www.theguardian.com/commentisfree/2017/may/25/brexit-myths-british-culture-history-ethnic-minorities>.

Examples of the concern on the right with cultural purity are unfortunately not limited to the United Kingdom. Illiberalism is on the rise and fear of foreigners and their cultural practices and traditions growing in many places. In Hungary, for example, Viktor Orban has solidified his rule by vilifying foreign cultures. His regime has hung posters throughout the country that read 'If you come to Hungary, you must respect Hungarian culture!' And of course, the real goal is less fostering respect for Hungarian culture than keeping foreigners and their cultures out in the first place. The goal is not respect but cultural purity. In this vein, right-wing Italian Prime Minister Giorgia Meloni, in her autobiography, 'I am Giorgia', published in 2021, 'compared mass immigration to Italy to the forced transfers of populations in the old Soviet Union, aimed at diluting local customs and religions.' 'The right wants to preserve these same deep-rooted identities that the left wants to cancel', she wrote, warning of the dangers of 'ethnic substitution' and the dilution of Europe's Christian culture.[30]

Of course, one need not go to Europe to see this tendency. Donald Trump's political strategy was built on fomenting racial and cultural anxiety among white voters, and much of his strategy for stoking white racial and cultural grievance focused on migrants and their cultural influence. The argument often focuses quite explicitly on the threat of cultural invasion: as the co-founder of Latinos for Trump famously declared during the 2016 election, there will be 'taco trucks on every corner' if Mexican immigration is not stanched. English-only laws, common throughout the nation, instantiate this same idea: foreign cultural practices are dangerous and their importation must be resisted.

These efforts on the right are, of course, very different than those on the left. We are not equating them. Yet the commonalities are striking. In the left-wing version of this argument, minority cultures are the victims. In the right-wing version, minority cultures are the perpetrators. But in each version, the crime is the same.

The antithesis of this view, and a normatively much more attractive vision, is so-called cultural cosmopolitanism, which, as Salman Rushdie has put it, celebrates 'hybridity, impurity, intermingling, the transformation that comes of new and unexpected combinations of human beings, cultures, ideas, politics, movies, songs'. Cultural cosmopolitanism 'rejoices in mongrelization and fears the absolutism of the Pure.

[30] Angelo Amante, 'Italian First! Meloni's Nationalists Defend Cultural Identity at Risk of Irking EU', Reuters (April 12, 2023).

Melange, hotchpotch, a bit of this and a bit of that is *how newness enters the world*'.[31]

Persuasive defences of cosmopolitanism have already been mounted by Rushdie, Anthony Appiah,[32] Jeremy Waldron[33] and others. We have little to add to their broad claim that cultural mixing is, generally, a force for good in the world. But it is important to underscore that from the perspective of intellectual property theory, and the underlying goals animating the protection of intellectual property, efforts to hive off of cultures and prevent mixing (and remixing) of cultural expressions are disfavoured. IP law exists not only to stop copying; it is also intended to preserve the public domain and foster creative work. Creativity often, if not always, rests on prior expressions, genres and conventions. The ability to rework and pay homage to past creations is integral to the development and evolution of culture, broadly understood as human creation. It is perhaps Martin Puchner who has best capsualised this point:

> In our debates over originality and integrity, appropriation and mixture, we sometimes forget that culture is not a possession, but something we hand down so that others may use it in their own way; culture is a vast recycling project in which small fragments from the past are retrieved to generate new and surprising ways of meaning-making.[34]

Of course, what Puchner says here is, at least to a lawyer, somewhat overstated. We do recognise property rights over some bits and pieces of our shared culture. That's the point of copyrights and patents – although it is important to remember that these expire and so apply only to relatively recent elements of culture. We also grant trademark rights to certain commercial signs and symbols, and trademark rights can last (at least theoretically) forever. This is why it's important that trademark law develop robust rules to allow people to make expressive uses of culturally significant source indicators. But Puchner's general point stands. Culture is not, at its core, about property rights, whether held by individuals or particular communities or nations. It is a resource common to us all, as humans.

[31] Salman Rushdie, *In Good Faith* (Penguin, 1990).

[32] Kwame Anthony Appiah, *Cosmopolitanism: Ethics in a World of Strangers* (W. W. Norton, 2007).

[33] Jeremy Waldron, 'Minority Cultures and the Cosmopolitan Alternative' (1992) 25 *Michigan Journal of Law Reform* 751.

[34] Puchner, *Culture*, above n 7, 13.

To be sure, we recognise that there are uses of cultural materials that are in poor taste, or which profit off of cultural practices in ways that ought to be morally condemned even if they cannot be legally barred. But we think that neither categorical condemnation of appropriation, nor legal prohibition, is warranted or workable. Even control through social norms (via social condemnation and shaming) is an enterprise that should be undertaken with caution, as difficult issues of definition, line-drawing and expressive freedom attend virtually all conduct that some might be tempted to condemn as 'cultural appropriation'.

It is important also to stress that we do not believe that, like Goldilocks' third serving of porridge, existing IP law is 'just right' in its balance struck between property rights and access by others. Indeed, we are critics of many aspects of existing intellectual property doctrine and have long argued that IP is overused and overbroad.[35] We also have, along with many scholars, demonstrated that IP protection is not in fact necessary for creative fields to thrive.[36] For much the same reasons, we are sceptical of assertions that seek to expand these rights into new domains today, whether grounded in a politics of majority rule or minority rights.

At bottom, we share Salman Rushdie's belief that the mixing of cultures is 'how newness enters the world'. That capacity for creating newness, perhaps the most precious possession of humankind, should not be surrendered lightly to claims that some bit of our human cultural patrimony is being appropriated rather than shared.

[35] See, eg, K Raustiala and C Sprigman, *The Knockoff Economy: How Imitation Spurs Innovation* (Oxford University Press, 2012).

[36] Ibid; K Raustiala and C Sprigman, 'The Piracy Paradox' (2006) 92 *Virginia Law Review* 1687.

INDEX

Printed by Integrated Books International,
United States of America